About this book

Seven million Filipinos live or work abroad. One in five wants to emigrate. So, what has gone wrong in the 20 years since the popular ousting of President Marcos? In this – the first – comprehensive analysis of the politics and economics of the Philippines today, the country's pre-eminent political economist, Walden Bello, and his coauthors analyse the roots of failure.

They show how the political system is still dominated by factional competition within the elite while maintaining a united front against any significant changes that might lead to a programme of economic growth which would address the country's huge social inequalities.

They pinpoint:

- The unravelling of land reform under Cory Aquino;
- Fidel Ramos's incorrect identification of the country's main problem as state intervention, instead of the overwhelming power of private interests;
- The priority, under foreign pressure, given to servicing the foreign debt;
- The huge pressures from the WTO to bend the country to the ideological and inappropriate dictates of free market economics;
- The manner in which sustainable development that would protect the environment was consistently undermined by the neoliberal framework of structural adjustment.

But there is a way out, Bello and his coauthors argue. It must start with the wholesale overhaul of the system of governance, possibly as a result of mass mobilization. Only then can a new development strategy be put in place that revolves around not less but more state intervention; prioritization of the domestic market as the driver of growth; and the Filipino government working with other countries in the South to transform the system of global economic governance so that space is created in the global economy for developing countries to put together unique strategies that respond to the particular values and rhythms of their societies.

THE
ANTI-DEVELOPMENT STATE:

The Political Economy of
Permanent Crisis in the Philippines

Walden Bello

Co-authors

Marissa de Guzman
Mary Lou Malig
Herbert Docena

Zed Books

LONDON | NEW YORK

The Anti-Development State was originally published in the Philippines by Focus on the Global South and the University of the Philippines Sociology Department in 2004.

International edition published in 2005 by Zed Books Ltd, 7 Cynthia Street, London, N1 9JF UK and Room 400, 175 Fifth Avenue, New York, NY 10010.

www.zedbooks.co.uk

ISBN 1 84277 630 4 hb
ISBN 1 84277 631 2 pb

Editorial and Production Supervision Laura L Samson
Copyediting and technical support Jocelyn de Jesus, Nestor De Guzman and Armando Venerando Ilowa II
Book Design Cecille P. Mantes
Cover Design Nadya Melina David

Printed in Malta by Gutenberg Press Ltd

Distributed in the USA exclusively by Palgrave, a division of St Martin's Press LLC, 175 Fifth Avenue, New York, NY 10010.

A catalogue record for this book is available from the British Library.
Library of Congress cataloging-in-publication data is available from the Library of Congress.

CONTENTS

Acknowledgments

That this book has seen the light of day is due to many colleagues and friends.

Marco Garrido and Maryann Manahan contributed substantially to this book, and for this we are very grateful.

Our thanks go as well to the members of the faculty and the staff of the Sociology Department of the University of the Philippines (UP Diliman). We are especially indebted to Sociology Department Chairperson Prof. Laura Samson, without whose pressure, advice, and management of the editorial and production process this book would still be an abstract idea in the minds of the authors.

For their warm encouragement, collegial support, and critical commentary, our gratitude goes to many UP Diliman colleagues, among them Prof. Randy David, UP President Francisco Nemenzo, Chancellor Emerlinda Roman, Dean Cynthia Bautista of the College of Social Sciences and Philosophy (CSSP), UP Vice President for Academic Affairs Maris Diokno, Prof. Esther de la Cruz, Prof. Nanette Dungo, Prof. Leonor Briones, Dean Maricon Alfiler of the National College of Public Administration, Dean Rene Ofreneo of the School of Labor and Industrial Relations, and Prof. Gareth Richards.

We also thank the Sociology Department staff—Antonio Oliva, Imelda Reyes, Melanie Baluyot, and Roberto de los Santos for indispensable logistical support at various points in the writing and editing process.

A big thanks too to Joy Chavez-Malaluan, Julie de los Reyes, Joseph Purugganan, Lou Torres, Shalmali Guttal, Nicola Bullard, Aileen R. Kwa, Anoop Sukurmaran, Marco Mezzera, Praphai Jundee, and the rest of the "Focus family" in Manila, Bangkok, Mumbai, Singapore, and Rome for advice, encouragement, and—not to be underestimated—financial support.

We also note, fondly and with gratitude, the moral and emotional support provided by the following individuals: Sue Ann Malig-Nolida, Reggie Nolido, Pat and Sandra de Guzman, Capt. Romy and Diana Malig, RA Rivera, Angie Driskell, Raz de la Torre, Miggy Basconcillo, Forsyth Cordero, Suzanne Lavetoria, Norman Baguisa, Richelle Pancho, Marie Ronquillo, Camina Flores, Baby Manahan, Tess Manahan, Marilen Abesamis, Ami Ferrer, Annette Ferrer, Evelyn Soriano, Zon Moraleda, Lucille and Oscar Dypiangco, Mil and Marlene Sabio, Bianca Chavez Malaluan, Jesse Broad Cavanagh, and Gilda Figueroa.

We would like to extend our gratitude to all our informants, but especially to Vic Ramos, Lidy Nacpil, Nepo Malaluan, Jude Esguerra, Jimmy Tadeo, Von Hernandez, Red Constantino, Jun Borras, Jennie Franco, Ernie Lim, Bert Baniqued, and Omi Royandoyan. Advice and insights provided by Benedict Ng, Edgardo Rodriguez, Freddie de Leon, Boy Ramos, and Vic Lim are also greatly appreciated.

We would also like to thank those who provided us with intellectual inspiration owing to their outstanding work on the politics and political economy of the Philippines: Joel Rocamora, Temi Rivera, Paul Hutchcroft, Men Sta. Ana, Sheila Coronel, the late Renato Constantino, Letizia Constantino, Butch Montes, Noel de Dios, Maitet Diokno, Joseph Lim, Robin Broad, John Cavanagh, Alejandro Lichauco, Conrad de Quiros, and Jim Boyce.

This book was produced in the midst of engagement in campaigns; the authors' understanding of the issues was deepened by discussions with activist friends such as Congresswoman Etta Rosales of Akbayan (Citizens' Action Party), Ronald Llamas, Freedom from Debt Coalition President Princess Nemenzo, Joshua Mata, Cenon Nolasco, Pancho Lara, Au Regalado, Josie Cajiuat, Raffy Albert, Danny Edralin, Ric Reyes, Jimmy Regalario, Isagani Serrano, Lisa Dacanay, Louie Corral, Bobet Corral, Tina Ebro, Jun Carlos, Jean Enriquez, Gigi Francisco, and Hanneke van Eldrik-Thieme.

Parts of this book were initially published as commentaries or news stories in *Business World* and the Internet version of *Philippine Daily* Inquirer, and for this we thank the late Raul Locsin, Letty Locsin, Marvin Tort, JV Rufino, and Iris Gonzalez.

We are grateful as well to members of the editorial and production team: Jocelyn de Jesus, Cecille Mantes, Nestor De Guzman, Armando Venerando Ilowa II, and Nadya Melina David.

Funding for this research project was provided by the Commission on Higher Education of the Republic of the Philippines (CHED), the Canadian agency Inter Pares, and the Land Reform Action Network (LRAN).

Last but not least, we give thanks to the undergraduate and graduate students of UP that we had the privilege to teach—and learn from—over the years. Nothing sharpens one's arguments better than debating the students of UP Diliman.

The strengths of this book stem in great part from the support of all these colleagues and friends. Its flaws and shortcomings are our responsibility and ours alone.

Walden Bello
Herbert Docena
Marissa de Guzman
Mary Lou Malig

Quezon City
March 10, 2004

List of Acronyms

ACP – African, Caribbean, and Pacific

ADB – Asian Development Bank

ADR – appropriate discount rate

AFMA – Agriculture and Fisheries Modernization Act

AFTA – ASEAN Free Trade Area

AGILE – Accelerating Growth, Investment, and Liberalization with Equity

AMC – asset-management corporation

AO – Administrative Order

AOA – Agreement on Agriculture

APEC – Asia-Pacific Economic Cooperation

APT – Asset Privatization Trust

AR – agrarian reform

ARC – agrarian reform community

ASEAN – Association of Southeast Asian Nations

ATO – Air Transportation Office

BAIDA – Bukidnon Agro-industrial Development Area

BIR – Bureau of Internal Revenue

BOT – build-operate-transfer

BSP – (Fil.) Bangko Sentral ng Pilipinas

CAB – Civil Aeronoautics Board

CALABARZON – Cavite, Laguna, Batangas, Rizal, and Quezon

CAP – Common Agricultural Policy

CARL – Comprehensive Agrarian Reform Law

CARP – Comprehensive Agrarian Reform Program

CEPT – Common Effective Preferential Tariff

CLOA – certificate of land ownership award

CLT – certificate of land transfer

CMARP – Community-Managed Agrarian Reform Project

COP – Committee on Privatization

CPAR – Congress for a People's Agrarian Reform

CPP – Communist Party of the Philippines

CSG – Compliance and Surveillance Group

DA – Department of Agriculture

DAR – Department of Agrarian Reform

DARAB – Department of Agrarian Reform Adjudication Board

DENR – Department of Environment and Natural Resources

DKMP – Demokratikong Kilusang Magbubukid ng Pilipinas

DMG – Deutsche Morgan Grenfell

DOJ – Department of Justice

DTI – Department of Trade and Industry

ECA – Energy Conversion Agreement

EDSA – Epifanio de los Santos Avenue

ELAC – Environmental Legal Assistance Center

EMFM – emerging market fund manager

EO – Executive Order

EP – emancipation patent

EPA – extraordinary price adjustment

EPIRA – Electric Power Industry Reform Act

EU – European Union

FAO – Food and Agricultural Organization

FCDU – foreign currency deposit unit

FDC – Freedom from Debt Coalition

FPJ – Fernando Poe Jr.

FTA – Fair Trade Alliance

FTAA – Financial and Technical Assistance Agreement

G-20 – Group of 20

GATS – General Agreement on Trade in Services

GATT – General Agreement on Tariffs and Trade

GDP – gross domestic product

GENCO – generating company

GNP – gross national product

GO – government organization

GSIS – Government Service Insurance System

HB – House Bill

HVA – high-value-added

ICC – Investments Coordination Committee

IFC – International Finance Corporation

IFI – international financial institution

IMF – International Monetary Fund

IPP – independent power producer

IPR – intellectual property right

IPRA – Indigenous People's Rights Act

JVA – joint venture agreement

KMP – Kilusang Magbubukid ng Pilipinas

LAD – land acquisition and distribution

LGU – local government unit

LTI – land tenure agreement

MALR – market-assisted land reform

MAPALAD – Mapadayonong Panaghiusa sa Lumad alang sa Damlag

MAV – minimum access volume

MFA – multifiber agreement

MODE – Management and Organizational Development for Empowerment

MTPDP – Medium-Term Philippine Development Plan

MWSS – Metropolitan Waterworks and Sewerage System

NCIP – National Commission on Indigenous Peoples

ND – National Democrat

NEDA – National Economic Development Authority

NGO – nongovernment organization

NIC – newly industrializing country

NPA (1) – New People's Army

NPA (2) – nonperforming asset

NPC or Napocor – National Power Corporation

NPL – nonperforming loan

NQSRMDC – Norberto Quisumbing Sr. Management and Development Corporation

NSC – National Steel Corporation

NTAE – non-traditional agricultural export

ODA – Official Development Assistance

OECD – Organization for Economic Cooperation and Development

OFW – overseas Filipino worker

OSG – Office of the Solicitor General

PA 21 – Philippine Agenda 21

PAGCOR – Philippine Amusement and Gaming Corporation

PAL (1) – Philippine Airlines

PAL (2) – private agricultural land

PAMALAKAYA – Pambansang Lakas ng Kilusang Mamalakaya ng Pilipinas

PARAD – provincial agrarian reform adjudicator

PARCODE – People's Agrarian Reform Code

PARRDS – Partnership for Agrarian Reform and Rural Development Services, Inc.

PCA – Philippine Coconut Administration

PCGG – Presidential Commission on Good Government

PCI Bank – Philippine Commercial International Bank
PCIJ – Philippine Center for Investigative Journalism
PCSD – Philippine Commission on Sustainable Development
PD – Presidential Decree
PL – Public Law
PLDT – Philippine Long Distance Telephone Co.
PNB – Philippine National Bank
PNBRFI – PNB Retirement Fund Inc.
PO – people's organization
Posco – Pohang Iron and Steel Company
PPA – Power Purchase Agreement
PSE – Philippine Stock Exchange
PVP – Plant Variety Protection
RA – Republic Act
RCBC – Rizal Commercial Banking Corporation
ROPOA – "real and other properties owned and acquired"
RP – Republic of the Philippines
SAL – structural adjustment loan
SAP – structural adjustment program
SD – Social Democrat
SDO – stock distribution option
SEC – Securities and Exchange Commission
SMC – San Miguel Corporation
SNR!C – Stop the New Round! Coalition
SONA – state of the nation address
SP – special agricultural product
SPAV – special purpose asset vehicle
SPV – special purpose vehicle
SSM – special safeguard mechanism
SSS – Social Security System
TGA – Tribal Gagao Association
TLA – timber licensing agreement
TNC – transnational corporation
TRIMs – Trade-Related Investment Measures

TRIPS – Trade-Related Aspects of Intellectual Property Rights
TRO – temporary restraining order
TRQ – tariff rate quota
UCPB – United Coconut Planters Bank
UK – United Kingdom
UN – United Nations
UNCTAD – United Nations Conference on Trade and Development
UNDP – United Nations Development Programme
UNESCAP – United Nations Economic and Social Commission for Asia and the Pacific
UP – University of the Philippines
UPOV – (Fr.) Union for the Protection of New Plant Varieties
US – United States
USAID – US Agency for International Development
USTR – United States Trade Representative
VLT – voluntary land transfer
WTO – World Trade Organization

Requiem for the EDSA System?

The history of the last eighteen years has been a dreary one for most Filipinos. The promise of political liberation and economic and social progress that accompanied the overthrow of the Marcos dictatorship in February 1986 has remained just that: a promise.

The current political regime in the Philippines stems from the historic uprising that began when tens of thousands of Filipinos congregated in late February 1986 along Epifanio de los Santos Avenue (EDSA) in front of Camp Aguinaldo to stop troops loyal to then-President Ferdinand Marcos from storming the barracks, where anti-Marcos rebel soldiers were holed up. Now remembered as the "EDSA Revolution," the rebellion triggered a chain of events that ended with Marcos's ouster and the inauguration of a new, election-based political system.

This is the regime that we call the "EDSA system" in this book. This is the system of governance that many feel is now in terminal condition, following the elections of May 2004. The administration and opposition slates were made up of candidates pirated from one another's ranks; yesterday's enemies are today's comrades. There was an overwhelming need for a program of economic growth that would address the country's gaping social inequalities, and yet it was a subject studiously avoided by the leading candidates—the administration because it led the country to its worst fiscal crisis ever, the opposition because its presidential candidate would otherwise have been exposed for his lack of grasp of basic economies.

A carbon copy of the electoral democracy that was the country's system of governance before it was destroyed by Ferdinand Marcos in September 1972, the EDSA system has reproduced most of the flaws of the former: it has encouraged maximum factional competition among the elite while allowing them to maintain a united front against any change in the system of social and economic inequality.

Two Sides of the EDSA System

The staying power of the EDSA system stems from the fact that, in contrast to the Marcos regime, it is democratic. Yet it is democratic in the narrow sense of making elections the arbiter of political succession. In the principle of "one man/woman, one vote," there is formal equality. Yet this formal equality cannot but be subverted by its being embedded in a social and economic system marked by great disparities of wealth and income. Like the American political system after which it is modeled, the genius of the EDSA system, from the perspective of the Philippine elite, is the way it harnesses elections to socially conservative ends.[1] Running for office at any level of government is prohibitively expensive, so that only the wealthy or those backed by wealth can usually think about standing for elections. Thus the masses do choose their representatives, but they choose from a limited pool of people of means that may belong to different factions—those "in" and those "out" of power—but are not ideologically different. The beauty of the system is that by periodically engaging the people in an exercise to choose among different members of the elite, elections make voters active participants in legitimizing the social and economic status quo. Thus has emerged the great Philippine paradox: an extremely lively play of electoral politics unfolding above an immobile class structure that is one of the worst in Asia.

Throughout the EDSA years, the Filipino masses were largely a force that was manipulated electorally to achieve the political ends of competing elite alliances. But alongside the electoral tradition of the EDSA system is an insurrectionary dimension that derives its legitimacy from the manner in which Marcos was ousted from power. In the last eighteen years, it was through an appeal to this insurrectionary tradition that the masses occasionally erupted on the national scene, bursting the electoral parameters to which the elite usually wanted to confine them. In January 2001, the middle class, driven by anti-corruption sentiments, served as the base for the extra-constitutional removal of Joseph Estrada from the presidency in what is now known as EDSA 2. Then three months later, in what is now known as EDSA 3, the lower classes, particularly the urban poor, came together in a mass uprising that was only dispersed by the military at the gates of Malacañang.

Especially in the case of EDSA 3, elite personalities were only nominally at the head of an angry class-based urban insurgency that took the form of a movement to restore to power a defrocked leader who, despite a record of corruption, was seen as a man of the masses. After each insurgency, however, politics settled down to a normal electoral competition managed by elite politicians.

The Anti-Development State

While entrenched corruption is the feature of the EDSA system that has elicited loud protest from the middle class, it has been the utter failure of the system to deliver economic prosperity and reduce inequality that is the greatest source of mass alienation. Close to 10 percent of the Filipino population, or more than seven million Filipinos, now work or live abroad and, according to recent surveys, one out of five Filipinos wants to migrate. The sense of frustration is deepened by the widespread perception that our neighbors in Southeast Asia were achieving "economic miracles" while we remain paralyzed by factional politics and mistaken policies. However much we decry its authoritarian policies, it is hard to deny that Singapore, with its controlled competition, prosperity, and security, has become to many Filipinos the ideal polity, the antithesis of an EDSA system that has become deeply dysfunctional.

Economic stagnation, according to some analysts, may be related to the political system's focus on elite representation and its accompanying parliamentary mechanisms rather than on the development of a strong central bureaucracy that is relatively autonomous from the private sector.[2] The influence of the pre-1930s American model of governance that guided the formation of the colonial and postcolonial state in the Philippines is again evident here. With the rationale of discouraging tyranny, the American pattern of a weak central authority coexisting with a powerful upper-class social organization ("civil society" in today's parlance) was reproduced in the Philippines, creating a weak state that was constantly captured by upper-class interests and preventing the emergence of the activist "developmental" state that disciplined the private sector in other societies in postwar Asia.

In his influential book on contemporary politics in the United States, Daniel Lazare says, "Government in America doesn't work because it's not supposed to work."[3] For much the same reason—the subversion of the democratic potential of the masses by the realities of concentrated wealth and power—one can say the same thing of the Philippines.

Let us briefly review the history of promise and disillusionment of the last eighteen years in order to grasp the depths of disenchantment.

Some say that the promise of the EDSA system was killed early on when President Corazon Aquino made two historic compromises. First, in protecting the family estate Hacienda Luisita, she failed to put her moral authority behind land reform, resulting in an agrarian reform law with a thousand and one loopholes. Second, she chose to make repayment of the foreign debt the national economic priority, thus starving the country of the investment necessary for development. The combination of the lack of structural reform and capital starvation doomed the country to stagnation in the period 1986 to 2003.

President Fidel Ramos tried to take another path, that of triggering growth by liberalizing trade, deregulating the domestic economy, and privatizing state or state-run enterprises and services in line with neoliberal, free-market doctrine. The Ramos saga ended instead with the recession of 1998, which was brought about by the panicky exit of the speculative capital that Ramos's technocrats had courted, precisely by eliminating many controls on their volatile movements and liberalizing the financial sector.

Lower-class disaffection with conservative social and economic policies resulted in the election of Joseph Estrada. Estrada's populism, however, transmogrified into a mafia capitalism in which the president became the apex of an engine of capital accumulation that linked the underworld and the state. The more established section of the elite allied itself with the middle class to overthrow Estrada and displace the nouveau riche faction during EDSA 2. The disaffected nouveau riche tried to get back by riding the spontaneous lower-class anger at Estrada's arrest during the aborted EDSA 3.

Under Gloria Macapagal Arroyo, all social-reform initiatives, including land reform, were placed on the backburner, and development policy was reduced to a strategy of getting US aid and investment by allying the Philippines with Washington in the so-called

War against Terror. The administration's overriding preoccupation became that of getting Arroyo reelected.

How long such a state of affairs can persist is anybody's guess. But the really deep sense of frustration, bitter electoral competition, and EDSA's insurrectionary tradition can interact in volatile ways. EDSA 3 showed how this mix could produce a lower-class insurgency, something that could be set off by a concatenation of events. To many observers, the question is not if EDSA 3 could happen again but when.

Plan of the Book

This book seeks to understand how and why every attempt at economic and social change failed during the EDSA period.

The first chapter, "The Political Economy of Permanent Crisis," explores the interaction of several factors to provide an explanation: the failure to address the underlying structural problems of the country with a program of agrarian reform, the Aquino and succeeding administrations' prioritizing foreign-debt service, and the hegemony of the neoliberal, free-market perspective among policy makers that was institutionalized in the program of unilateral liberalization and membership in the World Trade Organization (WTO).

The second chapter, "Agrarian Reform: Promise and Reality," is a close look at the unraveling of land reform from being what the Aquino administration labeled a "centerpiece program" into its present "orphan" status under President Arroyo. A basic contention of this chapter is that a failure of leadership of great proportions must be attributed to President Aquino herself. Her spectacular inability to lead by example in refusing to allow her family estate to be subjected to land reform eased the passage and implementation of a land reform law designed to make redistribution of private lands difficult and unworkable.

The third chapter, "The Neoliberal Revolution and the Asian Financial Crisis," takes the reader from the rise of neoliberal ideology in the technocracy to the Asian financial crisis and its aftermath. When Ramos came to power, economic reform was high on his agenda, but reform was to be pursued by diluting the power of the state, by emasculating its ability to lead the process of change. Wrongly identifying state intervention—instead of the overwhelming power of private interests—as the main problem, President Ramos pursued a program of liberalization, deregulation, and privatization along the lines of Adam Smith's dictum that "that government is best that governs least." The result was a series of free-market reforms, including capital account liberalization, which left the economy extremely vulnerable when the Asian financial crisis hit in 1997, with the government standing on the side as speculative capital fled the country and brought down the economy.

The fourth chapter, "Multilateral Punishment: The Philippines in the WTO, 1995-2003" details the wrenching process by which the political economy of the Philippines was made "consistent" with membership in the WTO, the most potent multilateral body ever created. Paying special attention to the wide-ranging deleterious impacts of the Agreement on Agriculture, the chapter places the Philippine experience in the context of international trade negotiations that climaxed with the failure of the Fifth Ministerial of the WTO in Cancun, Mexico, in September 2003.

The fifth chapter, "The Panacea of Privatization," analyzes the travails of the privatization program, with the focus on the unraveling of the scandal-ridden privatization of the Metropolitan Waterworks and Sewerage System, one of the biggest privatization programs ever attempted globally.

Environmental degradation, a hallmark of the two decades of the Marcos dictatorship, continued throughout the EDSA period. The sixth chapter, "Unsustainable Development," shows how the goal of environmentally sensitive development, also known as "sustainable development," to which every administration has paid lip service, was consistently undermined by the prevailing neoliberal framework of structural adjustment.

The seventh chapter, "Corruption and Poverty: Barking Up the Wrong Tree?" brings together case studies of crony capitalism, a phenomenon that was especially evident during the Estrada presidency. Surely crony capitalism, in varying degrees, was a characteristic of other administrations. However, more important, the chapter asserts that given the fact that politics in neighboring countries which have enjoyed rapid growth have been marked by corruption and crony capitalism as bad or worse than that of the Philippines, the country's economic stagnation cannot be attributed to these factors. The chapter strongly suggests that a "strong state" that promotes development and disciplines the elite and the private sector is what is missing in the Philippines.

The conclusion, aptly titled "Is There a Way out of the National Impasse?" brings together the various strands of analysis to a synthesis and offers some suggestions for the future direction of Philippine political and economic development.

This book is the product of a truly collective process. However, specific individuals take principal responsibility for the different chapters: Walden Bello for the introduction, chapters 1, 3, and 4, and the conclusion; Marissa de Guzman for chapter 2; Marylou Malig for chapters 5 and 6; and Herbert Docena for chapter 7. Marco Garrido and Maryann Manahan contributed to chapter 2.

Notes

1. A comparison between elite democracy in the United States and the Philippines is undertaken by Walden Bello in "Parallel Crises: Dysfunctional Democracy in Washington and Manila," in *Back to the Future*, ed. Corazon Villareal (Manila: American Studies Association of the Philippines, 2003), 80-91.

2. See Paul Hutchcroft, "Oligarchs and Cronies in the Philippine State: The Politics of Patrimonial Plunder," *World Politics* 43, no. 3 (April 1991): 414-50; also, Temario Rivera, *Landlords and Capitalists* (Quezon City: UP-CIDS, 1994).

3. Daniel Lazare, *The Frozen Republic: How the Constitution Is Paralyzing Democracy* (New York: Harcourt Brace and Co., 1996), 5.

CHAPTER 1

The Political Economy of
Permanent Crisis

The late 1980s and 1990s are not an appetizing subject for a student of Philippine economy. These were, for the most part, dismal years without the drama of the '70s and early '80s.

The overall reality was that of an economy trapped by its accumulated structural weaknesses. It became fashionable in line with the reigning neoliberal ideology to speak about the state suffocating the creativity of the market, but the fundamental reality that linked the Marcos period, the Cory Aquino period, and the post-Cory Aquino period was the existence of an unchanging class structure, in which asset and income distribution was one of the worst in the developing world.

Structural Change and Economic Change

For Filipinos familiar with the experience of the newly industrializing countries (NICs) of Northeast Asia, the importance of profound structural change could not be understated. Massive land reform was a necessary condition of the so-called economic miracle in these societies. Driven by counterrevolutionary motives, land reform in Taiwan and Korea was extensive and swift. Land reform created relatively egalitarian income structures that became the source of domestic demand which drove early industrialization in the 1950s and 1960s.[1]

This type of industrialization based on income redistribution was hardly noticed in the 1950s and early 1960s, when the dazzling import-substitution industrialization of the Philippines, which registered 6 percent to 10 percent annual growth rates in industry, was the envy of Southeast Asia. But the process ran aground, manifested by significantly lower growth rates, in the late '60s. The fundamental structural problem had reasserted itself: the narrowness of the market owing to massive income inequality.

However one thinks about the 1970s and early 1980s, one must acknowledge the fact that the dominant solutions offered to address the problem of underdevelopment did face the structural problem head-on. For the Communist Party of the Philippines-led National Democratic Front, the dominant force on the Left, revolutionary social change was the key, one that while addressing the inequity from a social justice perspective would also provide the solution to the development question. Revolutionary land reform and nationalist industrialization were the twin pillars of a thoroughgoing social structural transformation, one byproduct of which was economic development.

The Marcos regime's response was equally ambitious. At bottom it was Keynesian, that is, informed by a demand-led growth model. Advised by the World Bank to avoid the limited markets of the import substitution strategy, Marcos chose to hitch industrial growth in the country to export markets, which the World Bank pictured as unlimited. The export market thrust became even more critical after the failure of Marcos's land reform program, which was conceived not from a development but from a counterinsurgency standpoint.[2]

Export orientation was, however, more rhetorical than real, and the program eventually amounted to setting up a few export enclaves within a predominantly domestic market-oriented industrial and manufacturing structure. As one analyst noted:

> In fact, trade reform efforts revealed the limits on the power of the liberal technocrats and their multilateral supporters…The incentives to [import substitution] were hardly dismantled and the government's commitment to [export promotion] was limited. Export enclaves remained just that: enclaves within an inward-oriented economy.[3]

The Labor Export Policy

With land reform failing to take off and export-oriented growth lacking dynamism, a third Marcos program that was initiated in the mid-'70s became critical in addressing the problems of employment and generating income for a rapidly expanding population: the labor-export policy. Marcos bluntly stated the aims of the policy:

> For us, overseas employment addresses two major problems: unemployment and the balance-of-payments position. If these problems are met or at least partially resolved by contract migration, we also expect an increase in national savings and investment levels.[4]

What was initially conceived as a temporary palliative, however, became a permanent institution that was upheld by the administrations that succeeded the dictatorship. This was because it had become so central to the survival of millions of Filipinos amidst generalized economic stagnation. Almost 6.3 million Filipinos have been deployed for overseas jobs from 1984 to 1995.[5] Currently, according to labor-export specialist Jorge Tigno, "the total number of Filipinos overseas is estimated at roughly 6.5 million, a figure that comprises almost 10 percent of the country's total population. It is said that Filipino overseas migrant workers are approximately equivalent to as much as 15 percent of the Philippines' 26 million labor force. In Metro Manila, one out of every three households has a member who was abroad."[6]

In economic terms, the impact of labor export was massive. Recorded remittances of overseas workers rose from $103,000 in 1975 to $4.88 billion in 1995. By 2002, workers' remittances reached $6.9 billion, an increase attributable to the rise in the number of higher-paid workers such as caregivers, engineers, and performing artists in an area formerly dominated by lower-skilled workers such as domestics and seamen.[7] An International Labor Organization study, in fact, claimed that remittances could come to more than 20 percent of export earnings, and as much as 4 percent of gross domestic product (GDP).[8]

What overseas employment amounted to then was, politically, an absorber of energies that might otherwise have gone into radical or revolutionary solution and, in economic terms, an external employment mechanism in the absence of development. In fact, the economic function of labor export went beyond employment: remittances from overseas workers became a key factor in propping up the peso after the Asian financial crisis.[9]

Structural explanations and structural solutions to Philippine underdevelopment disappeared during the Aquino administration as liberal democracy was restored and the revolutionary movement ran out of steam. Under the Aquino administration, democracy was restored, but the priority of economic policy became that of repaying the country's massive external debt of $26 billion that had been contracted by the Marcos regime during the easy petrodollar era in the 1970s. One cannot, however, understand the full consequences of the debt problem without taking into consideration the imposition of structural adjustment in the Philippines.

Structural Adjustment and Debt Repayment

"Structural adjustment" did not refer to an effort to transform the fundamental socioeconomic structures of the country to consciously bring about development, but to one designed to alter the balance between the market and the state in the Philippine economy in order to promote economic efficiency. Structural adjustment in the Philippines, which was initiated in 1980, sought—at least at the rhetorical level—to achieve greater efficiency through thoroughgoing liberalization, deregulation, and privatization. Growth and development were to be byproducts of efficiency in the narrow sense of reducing the unit cost of the output of productive activity. Adjustment was not, however, divorced from conjunctural needs: among the immediate problems it was meant to address was to gain the foreign exchange to service the Philippines' burgeoning foreign debt via greater export orientation.

Adjustment unfolded in roughly three phases: the first from 1980 to 1983, when the emphasis was placed on trade liberalization; the second, from 1983 all the way to 1992, when the focus shifted to debt repayment; and the third, from 1992 until the end of the decade, when all-sided free-market transformation marked by rapid deregulation, privatization, and trade and investment liberalization was the order of the day.

During the first phase, a process of trade liberalization was pushed on a hesitant government in which close associates of the Marcos regime were waging a rearguard war to protect their privileged positions, and local firms were seeking to preserve their preferential access to the domestic market. Despite this resistance, structural adjustment, which was implemented with two laws from the World Bank, forged ahead. Between 1981 and 1985, quantitative restrictions were removed on more than 900 items, while the nominal average tariff protection was brought down from 43 percent in 1981 to 28 percent in 1985.[10]

But liberalization slowed down significantly in 1983, when international recessionary trends combined with the structural adjustment program's liberalization component and its tight fiscal and monetary policies to create a vicious cycle that plunged the Philippine economy downward. "Whatever the merits of the SAL [structural adjustment loan]," noted one analyst, "its timing was deplorable."[11] The program failed to adjust to the onset of a world recession, so that instead of rising, exports fell, while imports, taking advantage of a liberalized regime, severely eroded the home industries. Instead of allowing the government to promote countercyclical mechanisms to arrest the decline in private sector activity, the structural adjustment framework intensified it with its policy of high interest rates and tight government budgets. Not surprisingly, the gross national product (GNP) shrank precipitously two years in a row, contributing to the deepening of the political crisis that resulted in the ousting of Ferdinand Marcos in February 1986.

By that time, the Philippines' foreign debt had risen to over $26 billion from $21 billion in 1981, when the process of adjustment began. This led the World Bank and the International Monetary Fund (IMF), under strong pressure from the big commercial creditors, to put the emphasis on debt repayment on their agenda for the new administration of President Corazon Aquino. Fairly quickly, international finance faced the fledgling democratic administration with an unpalatable choice: either limit debt service payments or fully comply with debt obligations in order to preserve creditworthiness even at the risk of throttling growth.

The first position was espoused by Professor Solita Monsod, then the director of the National Economic Development Authority (NEDA) and some of her colleagues at the University of the Philippines School of Economics, who wrote: "The search for a recovery program that is consistent with a debt repayment schedule determined by our creditors is a futile one and should therefore be abandoned."[12] Central Bank Governor Jose "Jobo" Fernandez, a Marcos holdover, "warned of the risk of 'economic retaliation against the country' should it take unilateral actions in defiance of its creditors. Trade credit lines could be withheld 'paralyzing foreign trade,' and foreign assistance could be terminated."[13] Citibank President John Reed visited the Philippines and warned that debt repudiation "would produce immense suffering and difficulty for the people."[14]

The so-called model debtor strategy won, partly because proponents of the opposite position did not put up more than token opposition. This was a mistake, notes one analyst, in light of concurrent developments:

> The credibility of these threats is...open to serious doubt. Brazil defied its commercial creditors for 18 months, beginning with the unilateral suspension of debt service announced in February 1987. Its defiance provoked much posturing by the banks, but little genuine retaliation. The holders of paper assets proved to be paper tigers. Similarly, the well-publicized but less drastic debt service ceiling imposed by Peruvian President Alan Garcia did not bring grievous penalties; the Garcia government's heterodox economic program ultimately failed despite the debt policy, not because of it. More quietly, Bolivia halted most debt service payments in 1984, and three years later won [a] very favorable debt buy-back deal.[15]

The model debtor strategy was inaugurated by President Aquino's Proclamation 50, which committed the government to honoring all of the Philippines' debt, including odious ones like those contracted to build the Bataan Nuclear Power Plant as well as the so-called behest loans made by cronies of the Marcos dictatorship. The strategy was institutionalized by Executive Order 292, which affirmed the "automatic appropriation" of the full amount needed to service the debt from the budget of the national government that was originally mandated by Marcos's Presidential Decree 1177.[16]

A financial hemorrhage marked the succeeding years, with the net transfer of financial resources to external creditors coming to a negative $1.3 billion a year on average between 1986 and 1991.[17] In the late '80s, foreign-debt servicing came to $3.5 billion a year, or about 10 percent of the country's gross domestic product.[18] A decade later, in 1999, the level of outflow of financial resources continued to be massive. The fundamental irrationality of the process was underlined by the fact that as overseas workers were remitting hard-earned dollars into the country, an equal if not greater amount was leaving it.

The Neoliberal Perspective

To the neoliberal economists who came to dominate the technocracy and the academe in the late '80s and early '90s, however, structural adjustment was seen as a precondition for growth and debt repayment as an unpleasant but temporary condition. For these economists, many with newly minted Ph.D.'s from US universities, others with resumés boasting stints at the World Bank, the problem was too little market and too much state. They were deeply envious of the performance of our East Asian neighbors and were resolved to "catch up." The key to the success of the NICs, Filipinos were told, were their free-market policies. Structural adjustment was a policy in the right direction but its impact had been uneven. Freeing trade was the answer, even if this process was a unilateral one.

In 1991, while free-marketeer Jesus Estanislao was finance secretary, the Aquino administration came out with Executive Order 413, which sought to "simplify" the Philippine tariff structure into four rates: 30 percent for finished products, 20 percent for intermediate inputs, 10 percent for raw materials, and 3 percent for capital equipment.[19] Among the architects of the 1991 tariff reforms was Cielito Habito, who went on to become the head of NEDA under President Fidel Ramos (1992-1998). In that capacity he spearheaded the tariff liberalization effort that resulted in the famous Executive Order 264, which committed the Philippines to unilaterally bringing down tariffs on all but a few sensitive products to 1 percent to 5 percent by 2004.

The model for Habito and other neoliberal technocrats was the Chilean tariff reform under the dictator Augusto Pinochet, which had brought all tariffs to 11 percent or under. If the Chileans could manage to bring down their tariffs to 11 percent, surely the Filipinos could manage to bring them to 5 percent and below! In their eagerness to catch up with our neighbors, what the Filipino technocrats saw was only Chile's growth rate, not the enormous social crises that had been induced by its free-market policies.[20]

In a recent retrospective article on trade liberalization, Habito claims that a program of unilateral trade liberalization was necessary because, prior to the tariff reforms of 1991, "our average tariff rate... was well over 40 percent, which put us at a disadvantage with our neighbors who had pulled ahead of us in economic performance in the 1980s" because they "had begun simplifying and lowering their trade barriers much earlier than we did...."[21]

Habito's remarks go a long way toward revealing why the program of tariff and trade reform went so badly awry—why instead of bringing about prosperity, unilateral trade liberalization has resulted in the rapid erosion of this country's industrial and agricultural base. It is important to dwell on his analysis since it provides the rationale for fateful decisions on tariff reform made twelve years ago, which had such a devastating impact on agriculture and industry in the coming years. His comments provide a case study of how doctrinaire economics can produce analytical errors that lead to tragic policies.

Habito makes three key points: 1) that the average tariff rate stood at over 40 percent prior to the 1991 reforms, 2) that our tariff liberalization was well behind that of our neighbors, and 3) that it was their allegedly swifter and more thorough tariff liberalization that accounted for the superior performance of our ASEAN (Association of Southeast Asian Nations) competitors.

On the first point, he is simply wrong. Way before Executive Order 413 in 1991 initiated the unilateral liberalization program, the Philippine tariff structure had already been radically altered. Under the structural adjustment program of the IMF and the World Bank, the average tariff rate was brought down from 43 percent in 1980 to 28 percent in 1986 while quantitative restrictions were removed on more than 900 items between 1981 and 1985.[22]

The second point Habito makes—that our neighbors outstripped us in trade liberalization in the 1980s—does not survive critical scrutiny. The average tariff rates in Indonesia and the Philippines were just about equal in 1989, at 28 percent and 27 percent, respectively. However, the removal of quantitative restrictions in the Philippines proceeded at a faster pace than in Indonesia. In the Philippines, the percentage of goods under import restriction fell from around 34 percent in 1985 to 17 percent in

1986 and further to 8 percent at the end of 1989.[23] In Indonesia, the share of imports subject to non-tariff barriers declined from 43 percent in mid-1986 to 21 percent in 1988 to 13 percent in 1991.[24]

The average tariff rate of 28 percent in the Philippines in 1986, after the IMF-World Bank structural adjustment reform, was actually lower than that in Thailand. And, in fact, in the mid-'80s, the effective rate of protection for manufacturing in Thailand was 52 percent, compared to 23 percent for the Philippines.[25]

Misinterpreting ASEAN Industrialization

Habito's third claim—that it was trade liberalization which accounted for the high growth rates in our neighbors—is highly questionable. This assumption formed part of a broader perspective that many Filipino technocrats had when viewing our neighbors' performance prior to the Asian financial crisis: that these economies were significantly more market-friendly and experienced much less state intervention than the Philippine economy. Typical in this regard are the comments of Estanislao: "Government takes very good care of macroeconomic balances, takes care of a number of activities like, for example, infrastructure building, and leaves everything else to the private sector. And that is exactly what Singapore, Malaysia, Indonesia, and Thailand have done, and that is what the Philippines should be doing, and we are beginning to do it."[26]

This picture did not correspond to reality. True, in Indonesia, Malaysia, and Thailand, the state may have played a less aggressive role than in Korea and Taiwan, but an activist state posture—manifested in industrial policy, protectionism, mercantilism, and intrusive regulation—was central in the drive to industrialize.

For instance, Thailand began to register the 8 percent to 10 percent growth rates that dazzled the world, when it was moving to a "second stage of import substitution"—the use of trade policy to create the space for the emergence of an intermediate goods sector—during the second half of the 1980s.[27]

In the case of Malaysia, while it is true that some privatization and deregulation favoring private interests took place in the late 1980s, it would be a mistake to overestimate the impact of these policies. Two examples suffice to underline the central—and positive—role of state intervention. Petronas, the state oil company, was consistently rated as one of East Asia's best-run firms. And certainly one of the most innovative—and successful—enterprises in the whole region was a state-directed joint venture between a state-owned firm and a foreign automobile transnational corporation, Mitsubishi, which produced the so-called Malaysian car, the Proton Saga. The Proton Saga now controls two-thirds of the domestic market and turns a profit for its producers. Yet its development exemplified all the so-called sins of industrial policy that neoclassical economists such as Habito and Estanislao have warned against: discriminatory tax treatment of competitors, strategic industrial targeting or a systematic plan to manipulate market incentives to create a local car industry, and forced local sourcing of components to encourage the growth of local supplier industries.[28]

As for Indonesia, some change along market-oriented lines did take place in the 1980s and 1990s, but up to the end of the Suharto period in May 1998, the state continued to be the most important actor in the economy. Hardly any of the big state enterprises passed to the private sector. State enterprises contributed about 30 percent of total GDP and close to 40 percent of non-agricultural GDP. Government production accounted for 50 percent of the mining sector, 24 percent of manufacturing GDP, 65 percent of banking and finance, and 50 percent of transport and communications.[29] Indeed, in the last decade of the Suharto regime, there was a resurgence of statist policy in the form of trade policy, subsidies, and other mechanisms directed at the creation of a heavy-industry nucleus around which to center the economy, including the development of an automobile industry, an integrated steel complex, a shipbuilding complex, and an aircraft industry.

In sum, some liberalization was going on in our neighbors' economies, but it was selective liberalization pursued in the context of strategic protectionism driven by the state, the objective of which was to deepen the industrial structure.

To recapitulate, contrary to Habito's contention, the pace of trade liberalization in the Philippines in the 1980s did not differ from that of its neighbors, so that it is difficult to attribute the difference in economic performance to this factor. Nor is it possible to argue, as does Estanislao, that it was the presence of a non-interventionist state that accounted for our neighbors' superior economic performance, for, if anything, government was more intrusively interventionist among our neighbors than in the Philippines.

Japanese Capital: The Missing Factor

So what spelled the difference between the Philippines and its neighbors? The short answer is Japanese capital. In the period 1985-93, some $51 billion worth of Japanese investment swirled through the Asia Pacific in one of the most rapid and massive outflows of foreign capital toward the developing world in recent history. The cause of the massive outflow was the Plaza Accord of 1985. By sharply raising the value of the yen relative to the dollar and other major hard currencies, this agreement made production in Japan prohibitive in terms of labor costs, forcing the Japanese to move the more labor-intensive processes of their manufacturing operations to low-wage areas, in particular to China and Southeast Asia.

Some $15 billion worth of Japanese direct investment flowed into Southeast Asia between 1985 and 1990, with Indonesia receiving $3.1 billion, Thailand $3.7 billion, and Malaysia $2.2 billion.[30] The inflow of Japanese capital allowed these countries to have access to foreign capital at a time when US and international banks were tightening up on lending owing to the Third World debt crisis. Even more important, Japanese investment allowed the Philippines' neighbors to surmount recession and move on to a path of high-speed growth as they not only received Japanese capital but were tranformed into essential parts of regional industrial economy that was being forged around a Japanese center. As one Japanese diplomat candidly put it, "Japan is creating an exclusive Japanese market in which Asia-Pacific nations are incorporated in the so-called *keiretsu* [financial/industrial bloc] system."[31]

Thai technocrats, for instance, had no doubts about the source of their country's dynamism. As one of them wrote, "The current explanation of Thailand's accelerated growth was the 1985 appreciation of the value of the yen, rendering Japanese production more costly. Japanese multinational companies were forced to look for new lower-cost production locations. In 1987, Japanese investment approvals by Thailand's Board of Investments exceeded the cumulative Japanese investment for the preceding 20 years."[32] The truth is that whatever might have been the Thai government's policy preference—protectionist, mercantilist, or market-oriented—the vast amounts of Japanese capital coming into Thailand could not but trigger rapid growth. The same was true in the two other favored recipients of Japanese investment, Malaysia and Indonesia.

The Philippines was bypassed by this massive flow of Japanese investment. Relying on various sources, Japanese expert Kunio Yoshihara estimates that between 1987 and 1991, a paltry $797 million entered the Philippines, while Thailand received $12 billion.[33] Including investment from Taiwan and Hong Kong that followed in the Japanese wake, the difference was even more marked: Thailand received $24 billion in investment during the same period, or 15 times the amount invested in the Philippines, which came to $1.6 billion. "This difference in the flow of foreign investment from the three countries," Yoshihara rightly noted, "produced a significant disparity in growth performance of the two countries [Philippines and Thailand] during the period."[34] Moreover, in contrast to Thailand, the Philippines was barely integrated into the dynamic regional industrial economy being constructed around the Japanese center.

A Depressed Market

This brings up a more fundamental issue: Why did the Japanese avoid the Philippines? Some say it had to do with political instability—these were, after all, the years when the Philippines was wracked by six attempts at a military coup. But Japanese investors have not been known to shun conflict situations where there is a prospect of making a profit, so this was probably not decisive.

Was it because of foreign investment legislation? Again, this is unlikely since Thailand, for instance, had the same discriminatory provisions against foreign investors as the Philippines: foreigners were not allowed to own land; they were prevented from entering certain industries by Alien Business Law; they were not allowed to own majority of equity in retail trade enterprises; and there were restrictions on the number of foreign technicians allowed to work in Thailand.[35]

Were the Japanese put off by corruption? But corruption was endemic to all the Philippines' tiger neighbors that Japanese capital migrated to, from South Korea to Indonesia. Politics in South Korea, for instance, was, at least, just as corrupt as in the Philippines.[36] Indonesia was widely known in the '80s and '90s as being more corrupt than the Philippines, with Vice President Adam Malik admitting that it reached epidemic proportions in the bureaucracy and business.[37] As for another favored site, Thailand, part and parcel of the boom of the late '80s and '90s was an inflation of corruption.[38] A favorite theme of establishment writings on the tiger economies prior to the Asian financial crisis, the "neutral technocracy" theory to explain NIC success was, in fact, buried after the collapse by the same people, who began to attribute it to Philippine-style "crony capitalism" in these societies.[39]

Perhaps far more important in explaining the relative absence of Japanese capital were simple profit calculations. Japanese investors are strategic investors—that is, they invest if there is the prospect of a growing market. They are not just interested in cheap labor or using a country as an export-production platform; they are keen to exploit local markets. In the late 1980s, the Philippines was simply not attractive since development, expansion of the market, reducing poverty to create more purchasing power were all being sacrificed to the national priority of repaying the foreign debt—a goal forced on the country by the IMF and the World Bank acting on behalf of the country's foreign lenders.

The GDP registered average growth of below 1.5 percent between 1983 and 1993, and the reason is not hard to find. Government is by far the biggest investor in the Philippines, and during the Aquino administration debt repayment ate up funds that would otherwise have gone into capital expenditures. Very little could be spared for improving the country's physical, technical, and educational infrastructure. As one analyst noted toward the end of the 1980s, servicing the debt "required what are euphemistically termed 'adjustments': domestic consumption and investment had to be curtailed to free resources for debt service."[40] Moreover, the "negative net transfer can be expected to continue indefinitely, unless temporary relief arrives in the form of a massive infusion of new lending (implying in turn still larger debt service obligations in the future) or a more permanent solution is achieved by means of an alternative debt management strategy."[41]

The Aquino administration chose the path of least resistance: go into more debt. New debt was piled on to past debt, partly to pay for past debt coming due. From Php 625.6 billion in 1986, public debt rose to Php 945.2 billion in 1991.[42] Obliged to cover the payments coming due by the automatic appropriations law, the government allocated 50 percent of the national budget to debt service in 1987, with the figure not going below 40 percent in the next four years.[43]

The resulting social impact sent the wrong signal to prospective Japanese investors interested in profitably exploiting the domestic market: Filipino families living below the poverty line in 1991 came to 46.5 percent—a marginal reduction from the 1985 figure of 49.3 percent.[44] Income distribution actually worsened with the share of income going to the lowest 20 percent of families falling from 5.2 percent to 4.7 percent, while that going to the top 10 percent rose from 36.4 percent to 38.6 percent.[45] True, income inequality was also growing in our neighbors, but, unlike in the Philippines, rapid growth was pushing down poverty levels and bringing more people into the market.

From the perspective of Japanese investors, the Philippines appeared to be a strategically depressed market—one not worth sinking a lot of investment in. And so they bypassed the country and deprived it of the same externally induced boom experienced by our neighbors.

The Tragic Consequences of Doctrinaire Economics

It is amazing how these realities could elude our neoliberal technocrats. Yet it is not unusual. In the history of the natural sciences, as Thomas Kuhn claimed in his pathbreaking *The Structure of Scientific Revolutions*, paradigms harden into doctrines that filter out realities inconsistent with the premises of the paradigm.[46] The tragedy of the Philippines is that instead of being guided by realities on the ground, the neoliberals allowed doctrine—the dictum that the unfettered market would bring about the best of all possible worlds—to guide their analysis and subsequent policies. Not only did they err in discerning the causes of economic stagnation in the Philippines, but they misinterpreted the factors that led to rapid growth among our neighbors. And it was this doctrinal distortion of our neighbors' experience that served as the justification for the policy of unilateral liberalization.

Instead of carefully calibrating trade policy and industrial policy, as our neighbors did, they brought about an indiscriminate liberalization of trade that has destroyed many local industries, destabilized agriculture, and thrown hundreds of thousands of people out of work.

Instead of taking steps to stop the hemorrhaging of financial resources, that was the main drag on development and repelled investors seeking healthy investment prospects, they allowed the bleeding to go on and on, until by 2002, the public debt was Php 870 billion more than the Philippine GNP.[47]

The hemorrhaging was not, however, only financial. Servicing the debt meant intensifying the export of natural resources to earn dollars. Natural-resource exports accounted for a staggering $23 billion of the $50 billion worth of products exported by the country between 1981 and 1989.[48] But the environmental impact of the decade-long stagnation and crisis that stemmed from the "debt repayment first" strategy was much more comprehensive. As one study pointed out, it

> created so much unemployment that migration patterns changed drastically. The large migration flows to Manila declined, and most migrants could turn only to open access forests, watersheds, and artisanal fisheries. Thus the major environmental effect of the economic crisis was overexploitation of these vulnerable resources.[49]

Instead of channeling resources generated from local production to domestic investment, instead of debt service, they chose the route of capital account liberalization to invite foreign speculative capital to play that role—a policy that led, tragically, to the financial crisis of 1997-98.

Instead of confronting head-on the roots of Philippine underdevelopment in the complex interplay of internal and external forces, structural and conjunctural factors, these academics and consultants came to power armed with a very uncomplicated approach to policy making: radically reduce the role of the state, radically expand the play of market forces.

It was a seductive doctrine that avoided having to learn from the complicated interaction of market and state that had produced the so-called Asian economic miracles. Important policy differences, such as those between selective liberalization and indiscriminate liberalization, and between opportunistic protectionism and strategic protectionism, were conveniently ignored. As a consequence, driven by technocrats who were locked into a paradigm that misinterpreted and distorted the experience of our neighbors, the Philippines passed from a regime of opportunistic protectionism to a free-trade regime that was strategically directionless, one that was simply guided by the faith that the invisible hand of the market would somehow bring about growth. After the interlude that was the Asian financial crisis, the clear superiority of the strategic protectionist model followed by Malaysia and Thailand is once more asserting itself over the indiscriminate liberalization model followed by the Philippines.

Instead of strengthening the state to push the elite and the private sector in development-friendly policy directions, as was the case in Taiwan, Korea, Singapore, and Malaysia, in the name of "market efficiency" and "weeding out corruption," they set about dismantling the state's role in planning, production, trade, and finance. Not surprisingly, under their watch, an already weak Philippine government bureaucracy was even more thoroughly colonized by private interests.

For a time, neoliberalism seduced some sectors of the population, for with its simple formula that doing nothing was government's best contribution to growth, it seemed to offer a relatively costless path to growth. No longer.

A Doctrine Discredited

In 2003 three events symbolized the discrediting of a doctrine.

The first was the admission of the outgoing finance secretary, Isidro Camacho, that owing to massive debt obligations, the country was in a very deep fiscal crisis. "[We] could not deny the numbers," he said in a speech before the Philippine Economic Society. "We have a very high debt that is not sustainable unless we do something."[50] The public sector by the end of 2003 was Php 5.1 trillion in debt. Debt servicing was costing the country around Php 357 billion, or 46 percent of the total budget. Long ignored by government technocrats as a central cause of the Philippines' inability to move into sustained growth, the debt crisis had again exploded with a vengeance.[51]

The second was increasing criticism in government circles of the World Trade Organization (WTO), which had emerged as the principal engine of global trade liberalization in the 1990s. Both the principal representatives of the government to the Fifth Ministerial of the WTO in Cancun, Mexico, then Trade Secretary Manuel Roxas II and Agriculture Secretary Luis Lorenzo Jr., opposed additional tariff reductions on agricultural and industrial commodities demanded by the trade superpowers and hailed the collapse of the meeting as beneficial for the country and the developing world as a whole. Both also proclaimed with pride the adhesion of the Philippines to the Group of 20, a new grouping of developing countries that challenged US and European Union dominance of the trade body.[52]

The third event was the issuing on October 2, 2003, of Executive Order 241, which reversed the twelve-year-old program of unilateral liberalization, much to the dismay of Habito and other architects of the unilateral liberalization program. Several executive orders also increased tariffs or froze tariff reductions on commodities such as vegetables, sugar, and fishery products.

Over two decades of trade liberalization, beginning with the World Bank-IMF structural adjustment, had reduced the effective rate of protection for manufacturing from 44 percent to 20 percent. That had been achieved at the cost of multiple bankruptcies and massive job losses. The list of industrial casualties included paper products, textiles, ceramics, rubber products, furniture and fixtures, petrochemicals, beverage, wood, shoes, petroleum oils, clothing accessories, and leather goods. An indication of the comprehensive negative impact of unilateral liberalization was the decision of a government review committee constituted under Executive Order 241 to raise tariffs on 627 of 1,371 locally produced goods to provide relief to industries suffering from unfair competition from imports.[53] One of the industries most severely affected by the tariff cuts, as well as the abuse of duty-free privileges, was the textile industry, which shrank from 200 firms in the 1970s to less than 10.[54] Camacho's words were unambiguous: "There's an uneven implementation of trade liberalization, which was to our disadvantage."[55]

While consumers may have benefited from tariff cuts, "it has killed so many local industries…"[56]

According to Rene Ofreneo, former dean of the University of the Philippines School of Labor and Industrial Relations, it is worth noting that while most of our tariffs are only a third of those in China and Thailand, it is protectionist China and Thailand rather than neoliberal Philippines that have succeeded in the international market. This outcome is contrary to the prediction of the theory of unilateral liberalization. Citing the observation of economist Josef Yap of the Philippine Institute of Development Studies, Ofreneo continues:

> [T]hree decades after [being] enthroned as the guiding economic framework, the neoliberal economic paradigm has failed to achieve the so-called structural transformation of the economy. The share of manufacturing in total employment, recorded at 10-12 percent in the 1960s, has remained stagnant at 9-11 percent and is even threatening to go down, no thanks to the absence of an active or forward-looking industrial policy that our more successful Asian neighbors have adopted. The neoliberal economic paradigm constitutes a policy of false hopes—hopes that once we open up the economy, the investors would come in and hopefully, they would create new export industries, while domestic industries, hopefully, would invest on modernization and would become globally competitive. By imposing their narrow liberalization program on society, the neoliberal economic technocrats have managed to destroy many of our domestic industries such as textile, rubber, ceramic, and so on, while succeeding only in establishing a very modest level of export orientation based on two industries (garments and electronic assembly) with a shaky and uncertain future.[57]

But deindustrialization was not the only result of trade liberalization. Camacho linked unilateral trade liberalization to the massive fiscal and debt crises bedeviling development, saying, "The severe deterioration of fiscal performance from mid-'90s to last year could be attributed to aggressive tariff reduction." Had the government not implemented its tariff reduction program, Camacho estimated that the government could have earned more than enough taxes to cover its Php 210-billion budget deficit in 2002.[58] Instead, customs collections declined from 5.6 percent of GDP in the mid-1990s to 2.8 percent,[59] forcing government to resort to even greater borrowing from foreign and local sources.

Perhaps a fitting epitaph to the policy of unilateral trade liberalization was provided by Justice Florentino Feliciano, a former presiding judge of the WTO Appellate Body on Dispute Settlement, who called it a policy of "unilateral total disarmament."[60] Neoliberalism had been tried, and it had been found not only wanting but disastrous.

The pragmatic retreat from neoliberalism was not, however, accompanied by an ideological one, for government technocrats still articulated their goals in terms of achieving market efficiency. Nor was there an effort to supplant the discredited strategy with a new, coherent policy of development. Insofar as the Arroyo administration had a development strategy, it was the economics of military alliance with the US in the wake of September 11. Massive economic aid and investment from US business was at the top of President Arroyo's concerns when she reversed ten years of an increasingly independent foreign policy followed by the country since the expulsion of the US bases in 1992. "It's $4.2 billion, and counting," she gushed during her state visit to Washington in October 2001, calculating the sums of aid and capital promised by President George W. Bush. Most of that money failed to materialize, however, leading to a sense of malaise and drift throughout 2002 and 2003, as the fiscal crisis deepened and Arroyo increasingly devoted herself to getting herself reelected.

Economic-policy thinking in the establishment was at a dead end by the beginning of the electoral campaign of 2004—a sad state of affairs proclaimed by the fact that although economic issues were the central concerns of the population, neither the administration nor the opposition dared to talk about an economic agenda—the administration because it had brought the country to a massive fiscal crisis, and the opposition because it had no alternative to offer and because its candidate, Fernando Poe Jr., had little grasp of economic policy.

Notes

1. For an extended treatment on the importance of agrarian reform in Taiwan and Korea's development, see Walden Bello, "Agrarian Reform in Taiwan and South Korea: Positive and Negative Lessons for the Philippines,"

in *International Conference on Land Reform: Positive and Negative Lessons for the Philippines* (Manila: ICAR, 1993).

2. See Walden Bello, David Kinley, and Elaine Elinson, *Development Debacle: The World Bank in the Philippines* (San Francisco: Institute for Food and Development Policy, 1982), 67-99.

3. Stephan Haggard, "The Political Economy of the Philippine Debt Crisis," in *Economic Crisis and Policy Choice: The Politics of Adjustment in Developing Countries,* ed. Joan Nelson (Princeton, NJ: Princeton University Press, 1990).

4. Jorge Villamor Tigno, "Managing the Public Policy Process in the Philippines: RA 8042 and Deregulating the Overseas Employment Sector," (dissertation, National College of Public Administration, University of the Philippines Diliman, Quezon City, April 2003), 65.

5. Ibid., 66.

6. Ibid., 66-67

7. See "Workers Abroad Sent Less Dolars to Kin Last June," *Business World,* August 28, 2003, 1, 7.

8. Tigno, "Managing the Public Policy Process," 69.

9. Ruby Anne Rubio, "Ex-Finance Chief's Comment on Economy Pulls Down Peso," *Business World,* December 12-13, 13.

10. Mario Lamberte, quoted in Joy Chavez-Malaluan, "Shaping Philippine Economic Policy: The Role of Neoclassical Activists" (unpublished study, MODE, Manila, 1996).

11. Charles Lindsay, "The Political Economy of Economic Policy Reform in the Philippines: Continuity and Restoration," in *The Dynamics of Economic Policy Reform in the Philippines,* eds. Andrew MacIntyre and Kanishka Jayasuriya (Singapore: Oxford University Press, 1992).

12. Florian Alburo et al., "Towards Recovery and Sustainable Growth," School of Economics, University of the Philippines, September 1985.

13. James Boyce, *The Political Economy of Growth and Impoverishment in the Marcos Era* (Quezon City: Ateneo de Manila University Press, 1993), 332.

14. Ibid.

15. Ibid.

16. Freedom from Debt Coalition, "The Call for a Congressional Inquiry and Audit of All Public Sector Debt," Quezon City, October 23, 2003.

17. Freedom from Debt Coalition, "Revisiting Philippine Debt," (paper presented at National Debt Conference, Innotech, Commonwealth Avenue, Quezon City, October 9-10, 1997).

18. Boyce, 245.

19. Cielito Habito, "Tariff Reversals," *Philippine Daily Inquirer,* November 24, 2003, B5.

20. In Chile, the proportion of families living below the "line of destitution" rose from 12 percent to 15 percent between 1980 and 1990, and the percentage living below the poverty line (but above the line of destitution) rose from 24 percent to 26 percent. This meant that at the end of the Pinochet period some 40 percent, or 5.2 million, of a population of 13 million people were defined as poor in a country that once boasted of having a large middle class. Poverty translated into hunger and malnutrition; for 40 percent of the population the daily calorie intake dropped to 1,629 in 1990, from 2,019 in 1970 and 1,751 in 1980. See Alvaro Diaz, *El capitalismo chileno en los 90: Crecimiento economico y desigualdad social* (Santiago: PAS, 1991), 58; also, "Chile Advances in a War on Poverty and One Million Mouths Say 'Amen'," *New York Times,* April 4, 1993.

21. Cielito Habito, "Tariff Reversals," *Philippine Daily Inquirer,* November 24, 2003, B5.

22. Mario Lamberte, quoted in Joy Chavez-Malaluan, "Shaping Philippine Economic Policy: The Role of Neoclassical Activists" (unpublished study, MODE, Manila, 1996).

23. Kunio Yoshihara, *The Nation and Economic Growth* (Kuala Lumpur: Oxford University Press, 1994), 108.

24. Amar Bhattacharya and Mari Pangestu, "Indonesia: Development Transformation and the Role of Public Policy," in *Lessons from East Asia,* ed. Danny Leipziger (Ann Arbor, Michigan: University of Michigan, 1995), 408.

25. Scott Christensen et al., "Thailand: The Institutional and Political Underpinnings of Growth," in Danny Leipziger, ed., 354.

26. Jesus Estanislao, interview by Marco Mezzera, November 13, 1996.

27. See Chaipath Sakasakul, *Lessons from the World Bank's Experience of Structural Adjustment Loans (SALs): A Case Study of Thailand* (Bangkok: Thailand Development Research Institute, 1992), 19; and Narongchai Akrasanee, David Dapice, Frank Flatters, *Thailand's Export-led Growth: Retrospect and Prospects* (Bangkok: Thailand Development Research Institute, 1991), 17.

28. See, among other references, Richard Doner, "Domestic Coalitions and Japanese Auto Firms in Southeast Asia" (dissertation, Univesity of California at Berkeley, Berkeley, California, 1987), 511-96.

29. See Hal Hill, "Ownership in Indonesia: Who Owns What and Does It Matter?" in *Indonesia Assessment 1990,* ed. Hal Hill and Terry Hull (Canberra: Research School of Pacific Studies, Australian National University, 1990), 54 55.

30. Figures from Japan Ministry of Finance.

31. Hisahiko Okasaki, "New Strategies toward Super-Asian Bloc," *This*

Is (Tokyo), August 1992, 42-90. Reproduced in *Foreign Broadcast Information Service Daily Report: East Asia Supplement*, October 7, 1992, 18.

32. Thailand Development Research Institute (TDRI), *Thailand's Economic Structure: Summary Report* (Bangkok: TDRI, 1992), 2, 26.

33. Yoshihara, 49.

34. Ibid., 52.

35. Christensen, 363; Yoshihara, 43.

36. See David Kang, *Crony Capitalism: Corruption and Development in South Korea and the Philippines* (Cambridge, UK: Cambridge University Press, 2002).

37. Richard Robison, *Indonesia: The Rise of Capital* (Sydney: Allen and Unwin, 1986), 393.

38. See, among others, Walden Bello, Shea Cunningham, and Li Kheng Poh, *A Siamese Tragedy: Development and Disintegration in Modern Thailand* (Oakland: Food First, 1998), 23-42.

39. See Larry Summers, "The Global Economic Situation and What It Means for the United States" (remarks to the National Governors' Association, Milwaukee, Wisconsin, August 4, 1998). Then-US Undersecretary of the Treasury Larry Summers had been chief economist of the World Bank when the agency was undertaking its famous study that claimed that in the Asian NICs, "a technocratic elite insulated to a degree from excessive political pressure supervised macroeconomic management." World Bank, *The East Asian Miracle* (New York: Oxford University Press, 1998), 348-49.

40. Boyce, 338.

41. Ibid.

42. Ibid., "Government Debt Piling Up," *Business World*, September 29, 2003, 1.

43. "Government Debt Piling Up," *Business World*, September 29, 2003; Freedom from Debt Coalition, *Primer on Philippine Debt* (Quezon City: Freedom from Debt Coalition, 1997).

44. Leonor Briones and Jenina Joy Chavez-Malaluan, "New Social and Political Challenges within the Framework of the Structural Adjustment Process in Southeast Asia (with Focus on the Philippines): Effects on New Population Trends and Quality of Life" (paper prepared for the Population and Quality of Life Independent Commission, Manila, May 1994).

45. Ibid.

46. Thomas Kuhn, *The Structure of Scientific Revolutions* (Chicago: University of Chicago Press, 1971).

47. "Government Debt Piling Up," *Business World*, September 29, 2003.

48. Freedom from Debt Coalition, *Debt and Environment in the Philippines* (Quezon City: Freedom Debt Coalition, 1991), 14.

49. Wilfredo Cruz and Robert Repetto, *The Environmental Effects of Stabilization and Structural Adjustment* (Washington, DC: World Resources Institute, 1992), 48.

50. Eric Boras, "RP Is Suffering from Fiscal Crisis,"*Business World*, December 11, 2003.

51. According to former National Treasuer Leonor Briones, "When 30 percent of the budget goes to interest expense [arising from borrowings], you're in trouble." Romulo Luib, "Public Finance and Politics," *Business World*, November 28-29, 2003, 29.

52. See Iris Cecilia Gonzales, "Roxas: Firms Need to Improve," *Business World*, September 18, 2003; also"Calls for Limits on Tariff Cuts Gain Ground with Collapse of WTO Talks,"*Business World*, September 17, 2003.

53. Iris Gonzales, "Tariff Review Ends," *Business World*, December 8, 2003; also, "Government to Increase Tariffs on Industrial Products," *Business World*, September 2, 2003, 3.

54. Fair Trade Alliance, *Stop De-industrialization: Re-calibrate Philippine Tariffs Now* (Manila: Fair Trade Alliance, 2003), 16.

55. Eric Boras, "Government Loses P120 billion to Tariff Cuts," *Business World*, October 20, 2003.

56. Ibid.

57. Rene Ofreneo, "How to Make the Economy Work for the People," *Business World*, December 1, 2003.

58. Ibid.

59. Ibid.

60. Quoted in Rene Ofreneo, "How to Make the Economy Work for the People," *Business World*, December 1, 2003, 21.

CHAPTER 2

Agrarian Reform:
The Promise and the Reality

Fifteen years following the implementation of the Comprehensive Agrarian Reform Program (CARP), government figures claim that 5.8 million hectares have been distributed to 2.7 million agrarian reform (AR) beneficiaries, or an accomplishment rate of 72 percent. On the surface the figures may seem remarkable, but on closer look, the number represents a terrible performance, especially since the program should have been completed five years ago.

If indeed the accomplishment rate is 72 percent, how come agrarian reform advocates and potential beneficiaries readily write off CARP as a failure? Perhaps, Ric Reyes, executive director of Partnership for Agrarian Reform and Rural Development Services Inc. (PARRDS), was right when he said: "You may see the 72 percent but you certainly don't feel it."

CARP is the compromised result of congressional haggling between lawmaker-landowners and the advocates of reform. The legislation passed, though riddled with loopholes, making it a dubious vehicle for genuine reform. Four presidents, a coterie of agrarian reform secretaries, and one missed completion deadline, CARP remains more than ever an orphan program, lacking state support, adequate resources, and plain good faith.

CARP's performance has varied with administration. Under President Corazon Aquino, its promise was shortly undercut by shady deals, dubious accomplishment reports and, most especially, by the exemption of the Aquino family's 6,000-hectare estate, Hacienda Luisita, from distribution. In a word, Aquino was an accomplice in CARP's emasculation. The pace of CARP appeared to pick up during the presidency of Fidel Ramos. Some observers noted that Department of Agrarian Reform (DAR) Secretary Ernesto Garilao proved a capable helmsman, managing to distribute 57 percent of the total hectarage, or 4.6 of the target 8.1

million hectares. While these numbers comprised mostly non-contentious lands, Garilao's defenders insisted that under his watch CARP's viability was demonstrated, setting a standard for collaboration among government agencies, nongovernment organizations (NGOs), and peasants organizations in expediting CARP implementation.

Under President Joseph Estrada, CARP's promise remained unfulfilled despite the high hopes pinned on DAR Secretary Horacio Morales because of his background in rural development. The Morales-led DAR would instead be remembered for numerous land conversions and cancellations of certificates of land acquisition, the closing of DAR central's door to farmers, and missed targets.

The administration of Gloria Macapagal Arroyo has not demonstrated its commitment to agrarian reform. Despite claims that her administration considers land reform top priority, in deed, Arroyo has shown otherwise. Under her administration DAR performance has been dismal and not too far from coming to a virtual standstill. DAR Secretary Hernani Braganza failed to inspire confidence. Contrary to Arroyo's claim that her land distribution rate is "the biggest in CARP's history," her administration's targets for distribution are the lowest in the program's history—100,000 of private agricultural lands annually until 2004. Roberto Pagdanganan replaced Braganza early in 2003, but one year into his term, Pagdanganan had yet to formulate a clear and coherent policy on land distribution and the management and extension of support services. In fact, CARP under the stewardship of Arroyo and Pagdanganan had been in danger of death.

CARP today finds itself in inhospitable political climes, land reform having lost its legitimate place in the national agenda. The urgency of agrarian reform had issued from the threat of peasant insurgency; the Huk Rebellion of the 1950s is now a distant memory, and the New People's Army (NPA), despite periodic claims of resurgence issued by the military, is not perceived as an immediate threat.

However, some ground has been gained, and "pockets of improvement" achieved. This chapter will follow the history and prospects of CARP, from its inception through its several reinventions. It will focus on problems plaguing CARP implementation—from landowners to land registration, from legislative efforts to water it down to bureaucratic incapacity, from high-level schemes to kill agrarian reform to a state unwilling to firmly back the program.

CARP's handicap has to do with the tremendous powers ranged against it. Efforts to implement CARP precipitate an alignment of forces for and against it. Landlords and local government array themselves against farmer beneficiaries, the DAR, and nongovernment organizations (NGOs). In the ensuing contest for state capital, pro-CARP forces are easily neutralized, especially in the legal arena, where certificates of land acquisition suffer interminable delay. Because legal measures prove insufficient, reform forces often resort to extralegal means, like demonstrations and land occupations, in order to push CARP. Moreover, in itself, the DAR is not enough. When CARP does work, it is because NGOs, people's organizations (POs), and peasants organizations, often take the initiatives to make it work.

This chapter argues that agrarian reform deserves renewed state commitment in the pursuit of genuine national development. Neglecting CARP is forgetting history; it is discounting peasant unrest simmering in the countryside. If CARP's promise is delayed too long, the incremental efforts of NGOs, POs, and peasant movements will not be enough to stem the tide of violence that could well erupt in the countryside.

History

Land reform has almost always been referred to as the cornerstone of every administration. Every Philippine administration—from President Quezon to President Arroyo—has paid some attention to the need for land reform in one way or another: from issues of tenancy, sharecropping, and leasebacks, to Marcos's rice-and-corn land program (Presidential Decree 27), and ultimately, to the Aquino government's historic CARP. Surprisingly, while the Comprehensive Agrarian Reform Law (CARL) was heralded as the single most important piece of government legislation, it has never enjoyed the full support it deserves as an integral part of the national development agenda. Though often dubbed as a centerpiece program, land reform "has never been the overarching framework used by government for its development efforts."[1]

As such, CARP has clearly been a mix of deep-seated contradictions since its inception. These contradictions pervade its philosophy, its mandate, its provisions, as well as its administration.

Lost Opportunities, Lost Advantages

Time and again the Philippine government has tried to use land reform to address problems of national interest like social justice and equity, political instability, and agrarian unrest. Progressives and liberals have always assumed that the road to development requires an equitable redistribution of the nation's resources, foremost of which is land.

With a fresh start following the dark years under martial law, the "People Power Revolt" (EDSA 1) opened opportunities for a self-reliant course of economic, political, social, and cultural development. An open political environment offered a credible promise of democratic reform—one that unleashed various social forces and popular movements seeking to restructure Philippine society in the direction of greater sovereignty, social justice, and equity. It was also an opportune time to diffuse the ownership of the principal means of production—land—and distribute income equitably to alleviate poverty and ensure the rational utilization of resources, primarily through land reform. With the political fluidity in the wake of EDSA 1, the opportunity for social reform never seemed better.

President Aquino restored democratic rights. Repressive labor laws were repealed. The country saw the birth of the current Constitution. In effect, democratic processes, spaces, and institutions were restored, allowing peasants organizations and movements to articulate their demand for a genuine, comprehensive, and effective agrarian reform law. The presence of liberal democratic figures in the government also encouraged reform advocates to push their agenda.

President Aquino initially recognized the importance of agrarian reform as a development strategy for the country's rehabilitation.[2] She heralded her land reform program as revolutionary and a breakthrough in resolving agrarian injustice. Her ascendancy into power created great expectations; large numbers of peasants in Negros even regarded her as the "last hope" for a peaceful agrarian reform. Before the drafting of the 1987 Constitution, Aquino had a rare opportunity to reform the feudal system in the countryside: she enjoyed massive popular support, especially among the middle class; the opposition, particularly the landed bloc, was not yet consolidated; and she possessed "law-making" powers as head of a "revolutionary government." These conditions could have empowered her to act quickly to implement a radical agrarian reform program. But Aquino copped out and left it to Congress to decide on the program's final fate—a decision that would deal a lethal blow to CARP's prospects as the landlord-dominated Congress succeeded in emasculating it. Aquino, a member of a landed elite family, conceded to the interests of her very own class. CARP greatly disappointed reformist hopes. It was a disabled and conservative version of what stakeholders and civil-society actors had clamored for.

"Compromised Agrarian Reform Program"

The great debate in Congress produced nothing but witty sound bytes from supposedly pro-poor, pro-development, pro-Filipino statesmen. Save for a handful of pro-reform congressmen who surprisingly took an uncompromising stand on the swift and meaningful delivery of agrarian-reform benefits, the overwhelming majority of Congress remained allied to the landowning class.

With sustained and growing pressure from the Congress for a People's Agrarian Reform (CPAR), legislators were put to an early test as to how to deal with agrarian reform. Debate accompanied every proposed provision—from landowner retention limits, the speed of implementation, and landowner compensation, to the scope and "comprehensiveness" of CARP.

At the House Committee on Agrarian Reform hearings, landowning representatives put up a fight to deprive CARP of its bite. But in an effort to stall attempts of landowning congressmen to draft a weak agrarian reform law, two members of the House of Representatives hastily came up with a draft bill that substantially mirrored what the CPAR was batting for. Key features of this draft included a quick implementation schedule of five years and a landowner retention limit of no more than the two hectares of land already being cultivated by the landowner. This outraged landowners in Congress who then worked double time on their own draft proposal. They called for a retention limit of twenty hectares and the exemption of crops like sugar, coconuts, pineapples, and bananas. In effect, their proposal called for exempting their own major landholdings.

Representative Bonifacio Gillego's House Committee on Agrarian Reform took on the role of consolidating all these proposals into a single House Bill (HB). While the Gillego HB made a few concessions to the landowners, including raising the retention limit to seven hectares, it retained the provision for a quick five-year implementation. Moreover, it did not allow exemptions or deferments. It also called for the involvement of peasants in the reform process. Later, as the debates heated up, another concession was made: to allow another seven hectares to be awarded to one legitimate heir of the landowner. According to one account:

> The debate on the floor of the House during this period saw a head-on confrontation between the liberal and conservative approaches to reform, encompassing diametrically opposed views on the definition of reform, the nature of property rights, the role of productivity improvement and assumptions about peasant unrest and rebellion.[3]

The new provisions inserted in HB 400 prompted the original sponsors to withdraw their sponsorship of the bill. They said these were "morally unacceptable and incompatible with the democratic and libertarian ideals" of land reform.[4]

With congressmen appealing to natural law—that only God could take away a gift that He had bestowed—and going as far as to liken the loss of land to that of a child, in the end the landowners won the debate. In effect, this produced a watered-down version of what had been touted as a revolutionary program. Said Gillego: "[This] only confirmed the worst fears of our people, that we are a bastion of conservatism at a time when radical reforms are needed."[5]

The bill was passed on April 21, 1988, amidst immediate and open condemnation from the stakeholders it proposed to benefit. It then moved on to its next stage, the Senate, where it was swiftly approved and finally passed as Republic Act (RA) 6657 at the bicameral committee hearing. This gave us the CARP we know—with a five-hectare retention limit plus three hectares for legitimate heirs who are at least fifteen years old, a mandate to cover all agricultural lands regardless of tenure and crops, a provision for the delivery of support services, and the creation of an adjudication body that would have sole responsibility over all agrarian disputes. Its passage clearly expressed the conciliatory nature of Philippine elites—an affirmation that they had indeed reestablished their class power and had utilized state resources to their own advantage.

Table 2.1 Original Scope of CARP (1987)

Phase/Land Type	Hectares
Phase 1	1,454,800
Tenanted Rice and Corn (PD 27)	727,800
Idle and Abandoned*	250,000
Voluntary Offer to Sell	400,000
Sequestered Marcos Crony (PCGG) Lands	2,500
Government-Owned Lands	74,500
Phase 2	7,487,900
Public Alienable and Disposable	4,495,000
Integrated Social Forestry	1,880,000
Settlements	578,500
Private Lands above 50 Hectares	534,400
Phase 3	1,352,900
Private Lands 24-50 Hectares	303,100
Private Lands 5-24 Hectares	1,049,800
TOTAL	10,295,600

Source: Presidential Agrarian Reform Council, *Comprehensive Agrarian Reform Program of the Philippines*, vols. 1 and 2 (Manila, 1988), cited in Jeffrey Riedinger, *Agrarian Reform of the Philippines: Democratic Transitions and Redistributive Reform* (Stanford: Stanford University Press, 1995). (*private estates)

James Putzel, in his many works on agrarian reform, states that an effective agrarian reform program requires technical expertise, planning, mapping, administration, taxation, extension services, and a range of other functions. Before land could be distributed, the government must have a reliable account of what is to be distributed in the first place. This is the basic flaw of CARP: It lacks a reliable and durable system of landownership registration.[6] Not even the 1987 Listasaka project could produce an accurate figure of agricultural lands to be parceled for distribution. It is widely acknowledged that successful agrarian reform programs in the world have been made possible by reliable land-registration data.[7] The absence of such registration documents also makes it impossible for the government to demand appropriate taxes from landowners who, if they declare their possessions at all, tend to undervalue them.

Thus, without accurate records of land registration, it was not clear to the public and stakeholders where the CARP-eligible figure of ten million hectares came from. Nonetheless, the distribution of the original 10.3 million hectares within the scope of CARP was to be implemented by DAR and DENR (Department of Environment and Natural Resources). Expectably, public lands would be targeted first, leaving behind more contentious private lands and corporate farms for distribution toward the end of the program.

The concept of CARP was also open to question. Different sectors understood the program's mandate differently. No one even knew exactly what the comprehensive component meant, what it entailed, and what it would cost. Commonly understood to adhere to the land-to-the-tiller principle, CARP's divergent arrangements, including stock transfer schemes, violated this very principle. The concession regarding retention limits also led to dissatisfaction among potential beneficiaries and pro-reform state actors. For one thing, the limit was too landowner-friendly. The program also contained auxiliary components that gave landowners the right to choose which lands to retain, and granted fifteen-year-old heirs eligibility for three hectares.

Putzel notes that speed is one of the basic dimensions of a successful redistributive reform program.[8] However, with a ten-year implementation schedule landowners could easily find legal loopholes and use them to evade CARP. Numerous provisions inherent in CARP legislation allow landowners to contest DAR rulings including land valuation, the manner of acquisition, target beneficiaries, and actual distribution. Landowners are able to legally question CARP implementation every step of the way, thereby rendering the redistribution process painfully slow. With court cases taking up too much time and effort, landowners have succeeded in stalling CARP while potential beneficiaries languish with meager incomes as tenants, sharecroppers, or seasonal workers. Their loss of livelihood is a consequence of CARP's delay.

CARP Stalls under Cory

The Aquino administration was fraught with scandals, dubious accomplishment reports, conflicting development strategies, and marked by a sweeping disenchantment with a program that had been drummed up as the country's response to agrarian injustice. CARP could not take off because of the turnover in DAR management. Before new leaders could get under way, they would be replaced.

From an acceptance rating of 53 percent in 1987 before it was duly in place, CARP would lose its popularity and support, settling for a 16 percent approval rating by April 1992, the end of Aquino's term. Going mainly by the published numbers, CARP accomplishment during Aquino's term included moving nearly two million hectares of land, raising about 23 percent of the intended budget for CARP implementation or roughly Php 52.7 billion for five years, building 3,000 kilometers of rural roads, irrigating 15,600 hectares of land, and lending about Php 13 billion in rural credit.[9]

But these numbers do not add up with reports from other sources, including the official DAR report. NGOs closely monitoring DAR also provide conflicting figures as to CARP's accomplishment rate. The Aquino administration is widely credited with a 60 percent accomplishment

Table 2.2   DAR'S Land Redistribution Accomplishment
1972-2002 (Area in Hectares)

Mode of Acquisition	Grand Total (1972-1999) 27 years	Marcos (1972-1985) 13 years	Aquino (1986-1992) 6 years	Ramos (July 1992-June 1998) 6 years	Estrada (July 1998-Dec 2000) 2.5 years	Arroyo (Jan 2001-Dec 2002) 2 years
Philippines	3,369,096	70,175	848,519	1,900,034	333,385	215,983
NON-PAL	1,681,336	55,116	399,833	1,050,171	113,353	61,863
GOL	930,429	0	166,348	655,171	77,105	31,805
Settlements	675,560	44,075	208,795	356,646	35,277	29,767
Landed Estates	75,347	11,041	24,690	38,354	971	291
PAL	1,687,760	15,059	448,686	849,863	220,032	154,120
VOS	447,533	0	55,332	256,032	76,893	59,276
VLT	469,875	0	20,734	330,092	73,344	45,705
CA	214,416	0	13,713	120,888	47,771	32,044
OLT	516,282	15,059	358,907	142,851	18,664	10,801
GFI	9,654	0	0	0	3,360	6,294

(PAL = Private Agricultural Lands; GOL = Government-Owned Lands; VOS = Voluntary Offer-to-Sell; VLT = Voluntary Land Transfer; CA = Compulsory Acquisition; OLT = Operation Land Transfer under Marcos' PD 27 [rice and corn lands]; GFI = Government Financial Institutions)

rate.[10] It is unclear, however, what comprises the figure. The closest estimate corresponding to this claim would be the initial three-year target of 761,792 hectares. Going by this number, 60 percent was indeed accomplished, but in the context of the ten-year target, the figure drops to 12 percent.[11]

Table 2.2 shows that Aquino's accomplishment is nowhere near the two million-hectare figure Garilao claims. Throwing in Marcos's total distributed lands to Aquino's column would still not hike the figure up to even a million. This exaggerated estimate strengthens Eduardo Tadem's claim that the Aquino administration had a penchant for padding statistics. Judging from the 1990 DAR report, in which then-DAR Secretary Benjamin Leong initially reported a 310,000-hectare accomplishment in distributed lands, only to keep slashing that figure later on, it has become evident that measuring CARP's performance by the numbers could be misleading. To think that the 1990 report boldly claimed that for a period of ten months—from January to November—DAR distributed 120,909 hectares, but then in the last month of the fiscal year DAR distributed an astounding 172,436 hectares.[12]

Shady Deals, Anomalies, and the Hideous Hacienda Luisita Arrangement

Aquino's DAR had also been marred by a number of land-related anomalies. Land scams were a frequent occurrence partly because then-Secretary Philip Juico used voluntary offer-to-sell instead of compulsory acquisition as his mode of land transfer. This enabled local DAR officials to connive with landowners in overvaluing land. For example, the Garchitorena case involved 1,888 hectares of marginal land voluntarily offered for distribution but passed off as prime agricultural land. With a purchase price of merely Php 3.2 million, it was pegged at Php 62.7 million a month later.[13] This was not an isolated case. The atmosphere at the time was conducive to shady deals. DAR officials excused their actions by rationalizing that farmer beneficiaries would not have to pay this price anyway.

Ironically, the biggest land transaction of the Aquino DAR involved the 6,000-hectare Hacienda Luisita, owned and managed by the family of President Aquino. Arguably the country's most controversial landholding, it was the object of harsh criticism when the agrarian reform law was expanded to accommodate the landowners' desire for a stock distribution option (SDO) to supplant actual land transfer. The sprawling Aquino property was promptly placed under SDO. The move convinced stakeholders and the public that the administration was not serious about implementing CARP. Aquino's own ideological predisposition as a member of one of the country's landed families exemplified a classic conflict of interests. Clearly, the SDO provision was a concession to a few powerful families. The SDO enabled them to retain substantive continued control and management over their land. Many considered the Hacienda Luisita case as the Aquino government's biggest blunder.[14] In a paper presented by the University of the Philippines' Law Center, this case was found to have not only violated social justice provisions but also specific agrarian reform provisions in the Constitution. Ideally, CARP would correct centuries-old injustices by giving land to the landless. In the Hacienda Luisita case, however, land remained in the hands of the landowner—in this case, in the hands of the President's family. This prompted Sixto K. Roxas to remark, "[A]grarian reform is the centerpiece of the [government] program. But Hacienda Luisita is the centerpiece of agrarian reform."[15]

At the time, it was claimed that Aquino's greatest achievement was having given birth to CARP. Although the DAR under Aquino was not an outright failure, having managed to distribute limited amount of land to a few farmer beneficiaries, these gains seem insignificant when matched with proposed targets and grandiose promises.

The Debt Trap

It was not all that surprising, therefore, that the Aquino government's key economic policies reflected not the peasants' interests but the outlook of the powerful business community, multilateral lenders and commercial banks. Key positions in the cabinet were given to private business figures known as the "Makati Mafia." Led by the finance secretary, this clique encouraged free enterprise through privatization to improve the climate for foreign investment. The Economic Stabilization Program had a strong commitment to free market, foreign capital and, above all, debt servicing. It was not easy to reconcile this with Aquino's rhetoric of expanding the base for income, wealth, and resources.

Though Aquino recognized the importance of land reform in correcting social inequalities, her economic and social policies told a different story. She honored all debts and rejected repudiation as a strategy for speedy economic recovery and growth. This was despite earlier recommendations of the National Economic Development Authority (NEDA) led by economist Solita Monsod to reduce the resource outflows associated with the country's external debt through a two-year moratorium on debt servicing and the selective repudiation of international debt that was shown to be fraudulent or corrupt.[16] Since about half of the government budget was automatically earmarked for debt servicing, this left extremely limited funds to invest in development and agrarian reform.

The government also relied heavily on foreign support, caving in to the pressures of the World Bank and the International Monetary Fund (IMF). In fact, the external policies contained in the Philippines' Letter of Intent to the IMF include: continue floating the exchange rate subject to Central Bank intervention, continue trade policy reform, improve access to financing by small- and medium-scale exporters, encourage foreign investment in preferred areas, revise the external-debt conversion scheme, and generally remove distortions and controls that impede private-sector activity.[17] These were reminiscent of the stalled liberalization process under the Marcos dictatorship, which Aquino in fact restarted. Subsequent laws remained faithful to foreign capital. The Foreign Investment Act of 1991 further liberalized the entry of foreign investors and the Common Privatization Act allowed the reform of sectors of Philippine society, especially public utilities. But her economic policies took their toll, with the country experiencing severe economic recession in 1991. Emmanuel de Dios notes that this was related to the government's debt strategy. The Oil Price Stabilization Fund, which maintained high prices of oil, boosted the inflation rate, triggered a supply shock, and lowered the aggregate demands. The severe cutbacks in government expenditures on social services and infrastructure caused a 22 percent fall in real investment for the first semester of 1991. Compliance with the IMF-nominal target deficit proved lethal.

It would seem that land reform was enacted not to stimulate asset reforms but to address peasant unrest in the countryside, and once that was no longer perceived as an immediate threat, the political will to push it vanished. More important, Aquino failed the people by putting the interests of commercial banks and creditors over and above their needs.

Ramos's CARP: "Amidst Neoliberal Winds"

As heir to a sizeable balance of "CARPable" land and tasked to finish the program by his term's end, Ramos was pressured to salvage CARP's promise. Upon assuming office in July 1992, the Ramos administration targeted a number of key areas in which DAR needed strengthening and focus. Foremost of these was stakeholder support. Ramos knew it was vital that he regain the trust and support of farmers who had grown disenchanted with the way CARP was managed under the Aquino administration. Farmers were unhappy with the slow distribution of land and the even slower resolution of land-related legal cases. To win back its stakeholders, DAR had to convince farmers that it was serious about the redistribution of land to the landless and that the new administration's priority was to include the farmers in the redistribution process. The new thinking held that reform worked best when demand-driven. Farmers had to take active part in the CARP process in order to ensure the speedy and efficient delivery of lands and services.

In dealing with its stakeholders, DAR under Ramos ensured regular consultations and dialogues with farmer beneficiaries. The DAR also built stronger ties with NGOs and POs. It acknowledged the benefits this tripartite (NGO-PO-GO [government organization]) synergy could generate. This was perhaps one of the most popular moves of the Ramos administration in terms of CARP: bringing together various agrarian-reform actors to pursue land distribution. This effort has been popularly termed "the *bibingka* strategy."[18] At its best, it attempted to unite the forces of government, stakeholders, and NGOs. Building on the principle of demand-driven reform, it encouraged partnerships among NGOs and POs in pressuring the government to deliver on its promises of land distribution, support services, and infrastructure development. NGOs were generally receptive to this move. Many enjoyed a good working relationship with the Garilao-led DAR. Channels were opened for communication on issues of partnership, strategy, and capacity building; disputes were resolved in a more orderly fashion. NGOs appreciated the space within which DAR allowed them to make the most of CARP.

The Manager and His Report Card

That Ramos was lucky with Garilao is an oft-repeated sentiment of many agrarian-reform actors. At the very least, Ramos must be credited with the decision to stick with Garilao throughout his six-year term. That meant a continuous and stable leadership for DAR, which allowed the DAR bureaucracy to administer CARP. Garilao proved to be an able manager in dealing not only with DAR personnel, stakeholders, NGOs, and POs, but with landowners as well. Garilao's "bibingka" strategy delivered limited but significant gains; he also cleaned up the DAR bureaucracy. By investing in human resources and development, Garilao reeducated DAR personnel on the basics of CARP, and in the process heightened their commitment to its administration.

One of the earliest projects of DAR under Garilao was to undertake the CARP Scope Validation in 1993. Its objective was to verify the actual area under CARP coverage. It further limited CARP scope from 10.3 million hectares to 8.1 million hectares. However, the process happened without the benefit of any public hearing to clarify the issue.

True to its promise of transparency, DAR admitted that all reported accomplishments had been measured solely through land titles. By December 1997, through the administration of both DAR and DENR, land-title distribution through CARP had reached 4.6 million hectares. This represented 57 percent of the total 8.1 million to be distributed. Many agrarian reform advocates, on the other hand, believe that it is a padded figure.

Aurita Carlos of the Presidential Agrarian Reform Council, a monitoring body under the Office of the President, revealed that there had been several instances of double or multiple titling of landholdings during Garilao's term.[19] This meant that both DAR and DENR issued generated CLTs (certificates of land transfer)/CLOAs (certificates of land ownership awards) to the same farmer beneficiary. The irregularity reflects one of the basic problems of land reform in the country—lack of a reliable database and a land-registration system. Moreover, land titles reported as already distributed were still pending either at the provincial or regional DAR offices. Actual installations never occurred. These problems could be blamed partly on the reward or incentive system of Garilao for DAR officials. What was originally intended as a mechanism to fast-track land acquisition and distribution had become the very cause of misleading reports and padded statistics.

Table 2.3 Adjusted Scope of CARP by Agency and Land Type

Land Type	Scope in Hectares
Department of Agrarian Reform	4,293,453
A. Private Agricultural Lands	
Deferred Farms	35,635
Operation Land Transfer	579,520
Voluntary Offer-to-Sell	396,684
Government Financing Institution-Owned	229,796
Voluntary Land Transfer	287,742
Compulsory Acquisition:	
Over 50 Hectares	420,963
24-50 Hectares	312,355
Below 24 Hectares	736,420
SUBTOTAL (Private)	2,999,115
B. Non-Privately-Owned Agricultural Lands	
Settlements	566,332
KKK Lands	657,843
Land Estates	70,173
SUBTOTAL (Public under DAR)	1,294,348
Department of Environment and Natural Resources	3,771,411
Public Alienable and Disposable (A&D) Lands	2,502,000
Integrated Social Forestry Areas	1,269,411
DAR + DENR, or CARP scope GRAND TOTAL	8,064,874

Source: Department of Agrarian Reform.

DAR's own report cites the delivery of agrarian justice as one of its major accomplishments under Garilao. Through management interventions, Garilao saw to it that dramatic improvements in case resolution characterized his administration. His intention to resolve cases swiftly meant slashing the waiting time of litigants to under a year. About 94 percent to 95 percent of land disputes had been successfully resolved during Garilao's term (from 53 percent during the Aquino administration). This was a marked improvement, especially in light of the fact that the overall number of cases had more than doubled during this period while the number the members of the Department of Agrarian Reform Adjudication Board (DARAB) stayed the same.[20] What these figures fail to specify, however, was, in whose favor the majority of these cases had been resolved—the landowners' or the stakeholders'? No figures are available to verify this important detail.

Under Garilao, DAR also secured the trust and confidence of foreign donors that shied away from CARP after a string of anomalies during the Aquino administration. Garilao attracted Official Development Assistance (ODA) funds of up to Php 22.5 billion to finance his development project: agrarian reform communities (ARCs).

Agrarian Reform Communities

To enhance beneficiary development, DAR under Garilao launched the agrarian reform communities project in 1993. The program concentrated the delivery of support services to a cluster of areas benefiting a threshold number of farmer beneficiaries as well as non-farmer beneficiaries. Agrarian reform communities bolstered farm productivity by providing basic services such as irrigation, farm-to-market roads, bridges, infrastructure, and technical assistance. At the end of its term, the Garilao-led DAR had launched 921 agrarian reform communities nationwide covering over 350,000 farmer beneficiaries.

Agrarian reform communities are a people-centered, area-focused rural development strategy involving the employment of support services (credit and technical assistance) and infrastructure (rural roads, potable water, and communal irrigation) to maximize farmers' productivity.[21] The project stemmed from recognition of the fact that the government lacks the funds and resources needed to deliver support services to farmer beneficiaries. For this reason, agrarian reform communities are often funded by donor governments or agencies committed to rural development. The World Bank, for instance, funds the Agrarian Reform Communities Development Project, which sponsors 102 agrarian reform communities spread over fourteen provinces. ARC support services include agriculture and enterprise development, strengthening rural infrastructure, and providing technical assistance to communities. A survey commissioned by DAR in 1995 found that three out of every four farmer beneficiaries perceived a marked improvement in their lives after they had been identified as farmer beneficiaries.[22] They identified significant improvements in income and productivity.[23] Similarly, a more recent DAR-commissioned study[24] showed that agrarian reform has had a positive impact on farmer beneficiaries—higher real per capita income and reduced poverty incidence. Moreover, being in agrarian reform communities tended to improve the quality of life of farmer beneficiaries.

The Ramos-Garilao Legacy

Garilao is proud that he left DAR in a much better shape than when he inherited it in 1992. By his own account, he passed on to his successor a more capable bureaucracy, stronger public and intergovernmental support, and around Php 15.5 billion in ODA in DAR coffers. A ten-year extension for CARP had also been approved, assuring program operation until 2008. Of course this was no assurance that things would be easy for the next secretary, especially since the more highly contentious lands were up for distribution. But a strengthened DAR was ready to take on the tasks at hand with a boost in personnel morale, stakeholder confidence, donor support, and a better relationship with NGOs and POs. By 1998 CARP was a program that appeared to have taken off. While there was much else to improve, 57 percent was not an insignificant accomplishment. Garilao had bought time and space for the new administration to address whatever challenges remained.

It must be remembered, however, that various cases of land conversion and land speculation took place under Ramos's watch. His "Philippines 2000" opened a large section of the countryside to real estate as well as conversion of "CARPable" lands into "technoparks," golf courses, commercial centers, and malls in Southern Tagalog, Central Luzon, and Iloilo.

Estrada's Brief Stint

In February 1998 President Ramos signed Republic Act 8532,[25] which extended CARP implementation to 2008 and provided the program an additional budget of Php 50 billion. When Joseph "Erap" Estrada assumed the presidency in July that year, he was confident his administration would finish CARP in four years, by 2002. He promised to make agriculture the centerpiece of his government's development agenda.[26] Estrada's impassioned promises were matched by his theatrical flair. Before being sworn into office, Estrada visited the MAPALAD (Mapadayonong Panaghiusa sa Lumad alang sa Damlag) farmers on hunger strike in front of the DAR building. He broke bread with the farmers and captured media attention. With a promise to look into conversions—both legal and illegal, past and present—he earned the striking farmers' temporary approval. A few days later, he would deliver on that promise by issuing a temporary moratorium on land conversions.

Farmer beneficiaries expected Estrada to perform according to the script he had helped write in the first place. Everyone knew finishing CARP in four years—with highly contentious landholdings up for distribution—would call for a miracle. Estrada's confident and ambitious pronouncements warranted decisive action for his administration to distribute the 3.46-million hectare CARP balance. He vowed to expedite CARP implementation and promised to improve the lives of poor peasants. He appointed a staunch supporter of small farmers as the DAR secretary, Horacio "Boy" Morales, who seemed highly qualified. Morales had worked on rural development for most of his career and had been directly involved with farmer advocacy.

The First Hundred Days: Dismal Performance, Bleak Prospects

Morales set out to double DAR's annual distribution target from 200,000 to 400,000 hectares. With 1.6 million hectares of private agricultural lands to be distributed, it was highly improbable that DAR would meet the target it had set, especially since Congress had cut the agrarian reform fund and expectations of fierce resistance from landlords. Thus after Estrada's early pronouncements, the end of his administration's first hundred days saw him backtrack on his promise and settle instead for a more doable task—finishing CARP by 2004.

Some three months later, or after the first hundred days, the MAPALAD farmers remained camped outside the DAR building. Estrada's executive secretary, Ronaldo Zamora, had approved at least two controversial land conversions despite Estrada's moratorium. Estrada's promises were obviously lacking in substance. Farmers were no longer optimistic; Morales's target would prove elusive. He succeeded in accomplishing only 50 percent of his target in his first hundred days in office.

Early into his term it was quite apparent that Morales would have to be a Superman in order to accomplish what he had set out to do in six years.[27] Even with the former target of 200,000 hectares annually, he would still fall short of that figure in 1998 as well as in 1999. His first six months in office in 1998 produced a mere 90,842-hectare distribution record, while in 1999 DAR moved a total of 132,069 hectares benefiting 89,511 farmers.[28] The DAR 2000 figures were not impressive either. Total land distributed was lower than the 1999 total. The DAR annual report, however, highlighted a 70 percent accomplishment rate for 2000. This meant having covered 110,478 hectares of the targeted 158,406 hectares for that year. A 70 percent accomplishment might seem laudable but once matched with Morales's initial annual projection of about 270,000 hectares, or even to the conservative DAR base figure of 200,000 hectares, the percentage shrinks considerably. Moreover, at this rate of accomplishment, CARP would require another twenty-two years for completion.

Morales's lackluster performance has been attributed to, among other things, the budget cut that further limited the program's capacity to acquire land from landowners. Morales cited the absence of a good management information system as the reason for the snail-paced distribution of land.[29] Apparently, CARP at that point still lacked land ownership and registration documents required for accurate and efficient land distribution. Jeremias Montemayor[30] also pointed to a "lack of understanding of the philosophy of agrarian reform and commitment among its personnel" as the factor that stymied CARP implementation.

What Went Wrong

Late in 2000 Estrada's presidency was interrupted by his impeachment trial. Government programs ground to a halt. Failure of the state and stakeholders to match landlord resistance, bureaucratic corruption, massive legal and illegal land conversions, reduced congressional funding—all these problems came to a head during the Estrada administration.

But while landlord resistance was not unique to the Estrada administration, new forms of resistance emerged during this phase of CARP distribution. If landlord resistance had once meant harassment by "blue guards," it now included legalistic shenanigans within the space of CARP legislation. Landlords exploited loopholes in CARP legislation to successfully evade implementation. Congressional connections were also exploited to handicap CARP with budget cuts. Without a budget of at least Php 52.85 billion for land acquisition and distribution (LAD), CARP would be unable to acquire more expensive private agricultural lands and commercial farms.

Land conversion is one of the biggest problems facing DAR. So-called development projects like housing units, golf courses, and resorts encroach on farmlands. Between 1987 and 1998, 67,466 hectares of agricultural lands had been legally approved for conversion[31] or a conversion average of 6,133.242 hectares annually. Around 52 percent of the total number of cases had been approved under the Department of Justice Opinion 44, which allowed for the exemption (and legal conversion) of reclassified lands from CARP. Moreover, these figures do not reflect illegal land conversion rates. Several illegal land conversion cases had been brought to the attention of DAR. Even more alarming was Morales's own admission that some DAR officials actually facilitated these conversions.[32] Zamora, Estrada's executive secretary, had ruled in favor of converting agricultural lands—and at the height of Estrada's moratorium on land conversions. Zamora approved the conversion of 53 hectares of prime agricultural land in Rizal into a golf course. He also turned the 108-hectare Hacienda Sapang Palay in Bulacan into an industrial estate despite reports that the land was well irrigated and highly productive. The issuance of an administrative order in 1999 (AO 1) only made matters worse. A provision in AO 1 allowed the departments of agriculture, trade and industry, and tourism, as well as local government units (LGUs) to identify certain sites as priority development areas for commercial and industrial use. It was a pretext for land conversions.

Under Morales, DAR bureaucratic corruption escalated to a point where even DAR personnel would process and expedite conversion cases. A number of large landowners successfully evaded DAR monitoring by coddling DAR insiders. A Malacañang report accused some officials of accepting bribes of as much as Php 50 per square meter, or half a million pesos for every converted hectare.[33]

Rampant Reversals and a Pattern of Reconsolidation

Assessing CARP performance, Dinky Soliman,[34] Arroyo's social welfare secretary, cites the numerous reversals of the last three years as one of the biggest problems of the Morales-led DAR. Soliman accepted that the figures reflect distributed lands but, more significantly, she contended that the figures did not reveal how much of this land actually remained with the farmer beneficiaries. The Morales-led DAR particularly was plagued by rampant land reversals, which, together with land conversions and CLOA cancellations, enabled the craftiest landowners to reconsolidate their lands by allowing farmer beneficiaries to artificially "own" land while the former remained in virtual control.

"*Bigay-Bawi*"[35] had become such a common practice that while paper titles to the land would often be awarded to farmers, no physical installation would take place. Actual installation would have to await the resolution of pending legal cases that had been filed by landowners. Such cases would often be resolved in the landowner's favor and DAR would have to confiscate the titles it had distributed. In 1998 the DAR confiscation figure had reached 20,000 CLTs, 2,500 emancipation patents (EPs), and 320 CLOAs lost, covering 70,000 hectares and affecting 25,000 farmers.[36] Annual accomplishment reports do not reflect the actual situation. The number of distributed "paper titles" are reported but not how many of these have been cancelled.

The Godfather of Agrarian Reform

Perhaps heralding Danding Cojuangco as the "godfather of agrarian reform" was Estrada's attempt at humor. But its irony was lost on both Estrada and DAR under Morales.

For many years Cojuangco has been an untouchable landlord, no administration having ever succeeded in sequestering his haciendas. It was thus a surprise when Cojuangco volunteered his own agrarian reform model to DAR, claiming that he was ready to distribute his land to his longtime farmers.

The "Danding model" takes the form of a joint-venture agreement (JVA). It was further outlined in AO 2 of 1999. On paper, this stressed an initial phase in which land is distributed to farmer beneficiaries. This does not mean, however, that farmers now have control of the land. The JVA scheme compels them to surrender the use and control of land to the former landowner or developer. In effect, farmers would "own" the land but the landowner would retain control and be able to dictate how land is used. Furthermore, a potential beneficiary could not refuse the deal; failure to agree to the terms of the JVA automatically cancelled the farmer's eligibility to "own" the land. The Danding-JVA model violated the very spirit of CARP, which aimed to make farm workers owner-cultivators, with a preferential bias toward small-scale farming. CARP was not only meant to redistribute land but to liberate the tiller as well. This model stripped the farmer beneficiaries of the very control CARP was intended to give them.

The JVA scheme, also known as the "corporative" scheme, was highly questionable in other ways. For one, Cojuangco's ownership of the land had not been clearly established. As a Marcos crony, much of Cojuangco's property was believed to be ill gotten and therefore up for government sequestration. Assuming he was able to prove legal ownership of the land, he would still be hard-pressed to explain how he amassed 4,361 hectares when there was a private ownership limit of 16 hectares and a corporate limit of 1,200 hectares. The JVA terms were patently anti-farmer: ownership was limited to paper titles, the established "corporation" would be in effect for fifteen to twenty years, and the landowner would retain virtual control of the land. There would also be absolutely no government intervention in the whole scheme, which meant DAR would not be empowered to monitor what was happening and thus unable to ensure fair play.

Market-Assisted Land Reform

The Morales-led DAR also championed a variation on an approach to land reform conceptualized by the World Bank: market-assisted land reform (MALR). The MALR is characterized by a "willing seller-willing buyer" framework. In other words, land transfer is accomplished by priming the rural land market. On the supply side, incentives to land retention are reduced or removed as disincentives are created (like higher land taxes); on the demand side, the capacity of poor farmers to acquire land is enhanced (for example, by providing subsidies or easy credit). The idea is to get the market to do what the government would otherwise have to do. MALR is a model of negotiated land reform—in contrast to CARP, which is vested with powers of expropriation. Unlike CARP, MALR, as it was originally conceptualized, lacks a coercive mechanism. Land transfer occurs strictly within the market context; the government cannot force it and can do little to manage it. This appears to present at least one clear advantage over the expropriatory, government-managed model: a much-diminished bureaucracy. The decentralization MALR calls for greatly reduces the need for a bloated bureaucracy and, therefore, the argument runs, administrative costs will be lower, implementing land transfers will be faster, and farms will be worked more efficiently because farmer beneficiaries will be endowed with a greater sense of ownership. But because of the protests against MALR mainly from the NGO community, Morales rejected the scheme. Instead, he initiated the community-managed agrarian reform project (CMARP), which was basically a homegrown variation of MALR, even down to its funding source since the World Bank was approached to fund the project.

The main critique against MALR has to do with the fact that it considers agrarian reform a matter of economics; not only is agrarian reform implementation left to the market, but its rationale is reduced to how productive the land can be rendered. Critics charge that the social justice and political imperatives of agrarian reform, ideally its constitutive rationale, are overlooked. They argue that MARL calls for a land reform program without a guiding social principle, and is thus toothless in precisely those areas where teeth are needed, especially since it lacks expropriatory powers. A study by the United Nations Research Institute for Social Development corroborates these fears, finding that "the market approach is insufficient to reduce poverty and inequality and increase food production."[37]

CMARP also assumes a condition of land surplus, which does not reflect the reality of land scarcity in the Philippines. For negotiated land reform to work, land must be in surplus: generally, the amount of land available must be at least 2.5 times more than the demand for it. Otherwise, land prices would remain high or bloat even further. Since the Philippines is land-poor, however, one of the main selling points of CMARP—that it would bring down land prices—is highly questionable. A draft feasibility study predicted that under CMARP the price of land would rise higher than its Land Bank valuation.[38] It is also arguable whether negotiated land reform would mean a faster and more efficient implementation of CLOAs. That the transfer is negotiable may only provide landowners an opening to delay negotiations or force farmer beneficiaries into compliance.

The Morales-led DAR would ultimately be remembered for missed targets, alarming rates of land reversals and conversions, continued owner resistance in private agricultural lands, a corporative scheme, and a market-assisted land reform scheme. There would also be the unforgettable DAR-sponsored TV commercial showing Morales strolling through wheatfields, as if to say that the remaining CARP task were nothing but a walk in the park. But Estrada's anointment of Cojuangco as the godfather of agrarian reform finally stripped the farmers of whatever illusions they might have had about the Estrada-Morales DAR.

CARP Today: In Limbo under Arroyo

However you look at it, CARP is now in deep crisis.[39] Well into the last phase of its implementation, CARP is at the mercy of a government that lacks the funds to see the program through. Or, more precisely, Congress refuses to deliver the required budget. Furthermore, the global economic and political context does not offer bright prospects for a land reform program. Also, the patently political appointment of

Hernani Braganza and Roberto Pagdanganan as DAR secretaries did not bode well for CARP, particularly because Braganza was a political light-weight with practically no agrarian reform experience. Pagdanganan, on the other hand, has real-estate ties and no background on agrarian reform.[40]

Aiming Low, Achieving Little

In an advertisement commemorating CARP's anniversary in June 2001 and in her first State of the Nation Address (SONA), Arroyo targeted 200,000 hectares to be distributed annually, the lowest in the history of CARP. With a little over five years left in CARP's extension period, a 200,000-hectare annual target—100,000 hectares of private agricultural lands and another 100,000 hectares of public lands—even if it is achieved, would fall short of the aggregate goal of 1.2 million hectares by 2008. Was this a subtle hint that the Arroyo administration had no intention of even trying to accomplish a 100 percent distribution by the legally mandated 2008 deadline?

CARP has entered a highly contentious phase—many commercial farm plantations and prime private agricultural lands are up for distribution. Monitoring the government's accomplishment in land acquisition and distribution then requires a more focused attention on the distribution of these landholdings. Most plantations and haciendas are located in Negros and Bicol. Not coincidentally, these two regions have had the lowest accomplishment ratios—only half of the targeted lands have been distributed from 1988 to date. The government has to distribute 334,970 hectares and 602,951 in Bicol and Western Visayas (Negros and Iloilo), respectively, for the next five years. In all likelihood, it would be very difficult to distribute these landholdings; Bicol and Negros are notorious for their political and economic warlords. Both regions report the highest poverty incidence in the country, making them two of the three hotbeds of agrarian unrest and communist insurgency in the Philippines.

Arroyo commended the performance of DAR for exceeding its 2001 quota of 101,318 hectares. The Braganza-led DAR claimed to have distributed 104,261 hectares to 72,188 farmer beneficiaries, most of whom were awarded in Central Mindanao, Eastern and Western

Visayas, and Southern Mindanao. But agrarian reform actors assessed the initial performance of Arroyo-Braganza partnership as disappointing. The reported figures failed to disclose the fact that of the 104,261 hectares, only 78 percent or 77,849 hectares were private agricultural lands—way below the measly 100,000 target. The remaining are government or public agricultural lands. This belied Arroyo's pronouncement that her administration had the "biggest distribution in just a year" and "the biggest in history."[41]

In fact, Arroyo has had the lowest distribution record in CARP history. Originally, the record belonged to Aquino, with 111,665 hectares of land distributed in 1989. Even the much-maligned Estrada administration did better by distributing an average of 133,355 hectares annually. Ramos, on the other hand, has the highest record of 433,768 hectares in 1994. Even for distributing private agricultural lands, Arroyo scores among the lowest.

DAR leadership is crucial to the effective implementation of CARP. Braganza alienated himself from the peasant sector; he abandoned the "open-door" policy that he adopted at the beginning of his term. Braganza's relationship with farmer groups was conflict-ridden. With his habit of not showing up for meetings and dialogues with farmers groups and his failure to act decisively on urgent policy issues and land tenure cases, it was apparent that his commitments lay elsewhere. In his two-year stint at DAR, no major policies or accomplishments were produced and DAR's accomplishment was at its lowest.

Crusader for Rural Productivity or Devil's Advocate?

After Braganza resigned, Arroyo appointed former Bulacan governor Roberto Pagdanganan as DAR secretary. One year into his term Pagdanganan remained unclear about how he intended to proceed with CARP. With no substantial experience on agrarian reform, Pagdanganan had yet to learn the ropes, and although he was said to have studied the issues he ended up doing nothing.[42] Observers pointed out that Pagdanganan spent more time shaking hands and kissing babies in his numerous out-of-town trips.

An article in *BizNews Asia*, however, hailed his "revolutionized" agrarian reform program. Pagdanganan would focus not on accelerating

the distribution of the remaining 2.26 million hectares but on empow-
ering the farmers who have already received their lands. He intended to
give new meaning and impetus to CARP through cooperatives. Cooperatives, according to him, would free farmers from the stranglehold of
loan sharks. The co-op could then buy the produce of farmers, enabling
the farmers to get better prices and processing facilities for their output.[43] But cooperatives need funding and there was no allocation for
that, and Pagdanganan was not clear on how he intended to implement
this strategy. Agrarian reform advocates also believed that there was
nothing revolutionary about Pagdanganan's approach. It was the same
old style, only recycled and repackaged.

Table 2.4 Average Private Agricultural Lands (PAL) Distribution

	Average PAL Distribution (in hectares)
Aquino (1986 -1992)	74,781
Ramos (July 1992 - June 1998)	141,644
Estrada (July 1998 - December 2000)	87,995
Arroyo (January 2001- December 2002)	77,060

Pagdanganan's policy pronouncements also betrayed his confusion
with regard to who his primary constituencies were and whose interests
he was mandated to promote and protect.[44] In one of his dialogues
with civil-society groups and the media, he declared his commitment
both to improving the quality of life of farmers and guaranteeing proper
and just compensation for landowners. Eventually Pagdanganan yielded
to landlords' pressures. He turned his back on forty-one agrarian reform
beneficiaries of the controversial Hacienda Villanueva in La Castellana,
Negros Occidental. During the hunger protest staged by the agrarian
reform beneficiaries in DAR's premises in June 2003, Pagdanganan helplessly admitted that he could not install the farmers because of stiff
landlord resistance from Gov. Joseph Marañon and the sugar planters. As
he faltered, farmers were at constant risk of being harassed, driven away
or killed in their own lands.

Pagdanganan had also called for more and faster conversions of
agricultural lands. But perhaps the most formidable hindrance to the

implementation of CARP was his blanket support for the passage of the "Farmland as Collateral" bill (Senate Bill [SB] 2553). The rationale behind its provisions are provided by the findings of the study of Cristina David of the Philippine Institute for Development Studies, a discussion paper by Dean Raul Fabella of the University of the Philippines School of Economics, and the assertions of Peruvian Honrado de Soto on asset reforms and property rights. The proposed bill, authored by Sen. Sergio Osmeña, had been touted as the answer to the small farmers' problem of access to rural credit. It intends to improve the flow of credit access by amending a major provision in the CARL: Section 27, which prohibits the beneficiaries from transferring, selling, mortgaging, or conveying the land awarded to them for ten years. Pagdanganan believed that through increased access to credit, farm productivity would rise to record heights, which could then boost the rural economy. Considered a major flaw in the law, this provision has constrained beneficiaries from using their land as collateral, except to the Land Bank, to access credit. However, while it imposes limits on the newly acquired property rights of agrarian reform beneficiaries, the ten-year restriction anticipates and forestalls land reconsolidation and the reemergence of feudal relations.

Pagdanganan was not the only one keen on pushing for the immediate enactment of a law making farmland acceptable as loan collateral; Arroyo herself passionately backed the passage of this law. In her last two SONAs she said that it was included in her 18-Month Reform Agenda and list of priority bills. The apparent objective is not only to improve the flow of credit access for production activities but to stimulate private investment in agriculture, which could then help the ailing economy.

While it is true that there is a rural credit market that could be developed, the proposed bill is not nearly enough to solve poverty in the countryside in its entirety. There are more risks involved than gains that could be reaped. Farmers and agrarian reform advocate groups have expressed their fear that the bill would re-ignite landlessness and bankruptcy in the countryside and, ultimately, the reversal and negation of agrarian reform as it allows the sale and mortgage of CLOAs and EPs to any person, and asks for the lifting of retention limits on lands that have previously been subjected under the agrarian reform law. This fear is not without basis. Various studies have shown that farmers are highly in-debted and are therefore financially unviable, which could make it im-possible for them to repurchase their lands. Ernie Lim remarks that only 50 percent of small farmers take out loans while 30 percent do not because they are not sure they could repay the amount.[45] If farmers ever borrowed at all, it would be for domestic and consumption purposes and not for investment in their farm activities.

Economist Solita Monsod considers SB 2553 a "Trojan Horse"— a great gift from the state to the farmers with the expressed intent of releasing them from the bondage of poverty but one that could well bind them to poverty all the more.[46] Monsod argues that the poison pill that could kill agrarian reform would be the removal of the five-hectare retention limit on land. It would open the floodgates for land reconsolidation in the hands of the landlords. There would be no stop-ping big landowners in getting back their original landholdings by fore-closing on loans to farmer beneficiaries. It could sweep away the hard-earned fruits of agrarian reform in a snap. Though David and Fabella admitted the possibility of land reconsolidation, they prodded the gov-ernment to implement progressive land taxation in order to prevent this. Both still want CARL to succeed.

The bill also ignores the reality of illegal and extralegal transac-tions happening in the countryside. The selling and pawning of land are arrangements loaded in favor of "5-6" moneylenders. The bill's passage could actually legitimize this practice and, when that happens, the farmers can kiss their lands good-bye. The bill misses the point that the real reason for non-investment in agriculture by the private sector is the unprofitability and "high risk" state of Philippine agriculture. There is no guarantee that banks and other formal lending institutions would extend credit to farmers once the bill becomes a law. These banks would rather invest in commercial ventures and pay the penalty as mandated by the Agri-Agra Law than risk their money. The agriculture sector is in such a sorry state not because of the non-collaterability of the land but because of the declining public investment in rural infrastructure. In other words, allowing agrarian reform beneficiaries to use land as collateral without a major commitment in complementary public investments in the rural areas will only result in the loss of lands in favor of lenders. Besides, rural credit is but one crucial support-service component that could enhance agricultural activity and rural incomes.[47] The bill only addresses this particular aspect of the problem of lack of support services for farmers. It does not ensure the productivity, profitability, and viability of the farming enterprise; moreover, it fails to address the needs of farmers.

Perennial Budget Crunches

While Arroyo proudly refers to land reform as among her administration's priorities, she has actually demonstrated otherwise. She allowed a 34 percent cut in the general appropriations fund for agrarian reform, slashing the budget for LAD from Php 4.82 billion to Php 2.95 billion in 2001. This means the LAD budget was only enough to cover around 73,000-80,000 hectares of the already much reduced annual target of 100,000 hectares. Arroyo has not mustered enough political will to arrest the decrease in LAD funding under CARP. In 2002 the funding for LAD was Php 2.8 billion, way below the Php 5.6 billion needed to fund the acquisition and distribution for the year. This year, only Php 516 million was allotted for CARP, not even a fifteenth of the Php 3.8 billion needed to fund land acquisition. This means DAR could only acquire about 20,000 hectares of the planned 120,000 hectares up for distribution.

There is always a large gap between the estimated budgetary requirement needed to complete the program and what is actually allocated by the government.[48] Based on the projected budgetary requirements from 2003 to 2008, CARP requires some Php 151 billion to fund its completion. Even with the authorized appropriation of Php 100 million as mandated by RA 6657 and RA 8532 and a fund balance of Php 86 billion, the fund still falls short of Php 137 billion. The insufficient budget allocated for CARP and the failure to stop the legislative branch from slashing CARP's budget is a great disservice to the peasants.[49]

Lack of funds was the government's justification for using voluntary land transfer (VLT) as the main mode of distribution. Under the VLT scheme, government does not incur any cost as valuation and payment for the land are directly negotiated between the landowner and the beneficiaries.[50] But while this arrangement is less confrontational, it overlooks the reality of the uneven bargaining power between landlords and farmer beneficiaries. Budget deficiencies can only explain part of the problem, for the fact remains that DAR has failed time and again to distribute land via compulsory acquisition, an expropriatory power mandated by CARL.

But there could yet be a sliver of hope for the farmers. The Supreme Court recently declared the Php 38 billion Marcos Swiss deposit as ill-gotten wealth. Another development is the July 11, 2003, Sandiganbayan decision affirming that the coconut levy belongs to the government, which means that the 72 percent equity in the United Coconut Planters Bank (UCPB) rightfully belongs to small coconut farmers. The coco levy is estimated at about Php 100 billion. It has been used by Cojuangco, a former Marcos crony, to set up UCPB and acquire control of San Miguel Corporation (SMC).

Table 2.5 Proposed and Approved CARP Budgetary Allocations
2000-2004 (in PhP)*

Year	Proposed Budget	Approved Budget	Budget Cut
2000	11,861,673,000	11,254,647,000	616,026,000
2001**	11,245,647,000	8,514,538,000	2,731,109,000
2002	10,688,217,000	9,488,217,000	1,200,000,000
2003	11,438,456,000	7,431,750,000	4,006,706,000

Source: Department of Agrarian Reform. (*The components of the CARP Budgetary allocations include Land Acquisition and Distribution [LAD], program beneficiary development [PBD], operational support, and foreign-assisted projects [FAPs]. It comprises the budget for CARP Implementing Agencies [CIAs]: DAR, LBP, DENR, LRA, NIA, DPWH, DTI, and DOLE.

**The 2001 budget is a reenacted budget because of the untimely change of leadership brought about by EDSA 2. Prior to this, Sec. Horacio Morales requested from Congress Php 15 billion for the agrarian reform implementation.)

Instantly, you have Php 138 billion—more than enough to finance and parcel out the remaining CARP balance to farmer beneficiaries. Arroyo has authorized to give Php 8 billion of the escrow account to human-rights victims and the remaining Php 30 billion to agrarian reform. The allocation for agrarian reform is but a recognition of the sacrifice made by the peasantry who were at the forefront of the struggle against Marcos.

DAR, however, intends to use the Php 8 billion for land acquisition and distribution and Php 22 billion for support services. This pronouncement has outraged agrarian reform advocates, who argue that the allocation scheme goes against the very spirit and intent of CARL, i.e., to carry out land distribution to promote social justice.[51] Support services like credit, irrigation, farm-to-market roads, access to input, which complement land distribution, could be financed through other fund sources (particularly ODA money), which are always accessible but never maximized and used wisely.

Congress, on the other hand, refuses to cooperate and allot the money to DAR's budget, even after Arroyo already announced that she would apportion an initial Php 200 million (from the coco levy fund) as investment for the livelihood programs of small coconut farmers. Some legislators arrogantly said that Arroyo could not unilaterally decide on the matter since it is Congress that has the mandate to appropriate the budget. Cojuangco has also refused to let his guard down, cautioning the government against giving false hopes to small coconut farmers that they would finally acquire the fund. He warned that he would "exhaust all his means to keep his shares."[52] The Kilusang Magbubukid ng Pilipinas (KMP) and the Pambansang Lakas ng Kilusang Mamalakaya ng Pilipinas (PAMALAKAYA) have accused Arroyo of having "made a pact with the devil" when she declared support for SMC's 150,000-hectare Cassava Plantation Project in Isabela and Quirino provinces last year.[53] The project allegedly displaced thousands of families, including those who had received their EPs and CLOAs. With Cojuangco considered a potential "ally of the government,"[54] farmers and agrarian reform advocate groups are in for a rough time.

Critical Homestretch

Uncertainties in the change of leadership and diffused public attention do not augur well for the future for CARP. On its fifteenth year CARP has entered its darkest and most difficult phase. CARP's key players realize the need for DAR to be led by a strong and efficient manager at its most difficult phase.

CARP's promise has been diluted by discordant policies and bills. Now more than ever there is great doubt that wealth redistribution could be possible under a framework of a government that pretends to be liberal. Now more than ever CARP has been relegated to a low priority by the government. The state's bias for free enterprise, liberalization, privatization, and debt-driven growth shows that it has chosen to focus the nation's resources toward the international market. Instead of dealing with the centuries-old problem of land, the government has placed itself in the service of powerful international financial institutions like the World Bank.

"CARP is an orphan program"[55]

"CARP is not a priority."[56] But perhaps CARP had been intended more as an ornament than a centerpiece, aimed at political legitimization—which, as Ed Quitoriano observes, "can be gained by posturing but not necessarily consummating the reform agenda."[57] Similarly, Alan de Janvry, in his many works on agrarian reform, states that land reform for non-Communist Third World countries in the postwar period was "an institutional innovation promoted by the ruling order in an attempt to overcome economic and political contradictions without changing the dominant social relations."[58] But CARP has proponents both inside and outside DAR whose efforts in its implementation have moved the program toward being more than a mere posture. CARP in fact continues to be the most "progressive"[59] agrarian reform program in the country's history, but it could be more.

CARP is out of sync with the national agricultural policy, particularly trade and food security, which have become increasingly liberalized, as well as disengaged from development strategy as a whole. As the core of an incoherent and unsupported reform strategy, it is not given the priority it deserves. In contrast, other approaches to "development," specifically neoliberalism, enjoy support.[60]

However, CARP can compete with other development approaches for support. Achieving this largely depends on mustering the social capital to compel the state to honor its reformist vows. Its supporters—primarily DAR, agrarian reform NGOs, and beneficiary POs—must be strategic; their claim must carry enough urgency to overcome imperatives for strict private capital accumulation. Veteran agrarian reform advocates are clear: "If you don't push, you don't get anything!"[61] Quitoriano aptly describes CARP's dilemma:

> CARP is but one modality dangled by the state, but the greater tendency is to go for aggregate growth hitting poverty through spillover effects; I would say that the state is going through the motions of agrarian reform but its real agenda is something else. The ball is really in the hands of social forces—to exert more pressure and demand that the state fulfill its reform promise.[62]

Further Derailing CARP

The massive legal apparatus accompanying CARP—inevitable, given that it redefines property rights—ensnares countless CLOAs and land transfers; it is the landowner's first and last resort and where CARP is most often and effectively stymied. In opposing CARP landowners reflexively resort to what one DAR official has coined "Lobregat Law"; a landlord staunchly opposed to CARP had confronted this official and said, "My problem is how to delay you."[63] Delay is the courts' specialty, and with enough resources to exploit the loopholes inherent in CARL, CLOAs can be kept pending into oblivion. Cases can take a year for DARAB to process, and if a case is appealed to DAR central, a judgment might be forthcoming in six to seven years. Meanwhile, the would-be farmer beneficiaries remain displaced while the landowner could use the time to remake the facts on the ground. With DAR's own courts a great mire for land tenure improvement (LTI), the same DAR official remarked: "Sometimes I wonder if CARP is just a scheme to keep lawyers in business."[64]

Landlords have a great many means to stifle CARP, land conversions being the most rampant and insidious, and sheer force being the most direct and dangerous. By DAR's own account, as of December

31, 2000, DAR approved 34,160 or 87.5 percent out of 39,062 hectares up for conversion. Just over two-thirds of the approved hectarage for conversion was in Luzon, particularly in the CALABARZON provinces (Cavite, Laguna, Batangas, Rizal, and Quezon). Even these figures could only be interpreted as indicative of the actual numbers, which, assuming the high incidence of illegal conversions, are sure to be much higher.

Force is another reliable resort of especially the most powerful landlords. The degree of force varies, but the idea is to keep land in the hands of the landowner and guarantee that potential farmer beneficiaries never win tenure security. Landlords often hire "blue guards" to harass the farmers. They destroy longer-term crops like palay and deliberately damage fences and shelters to ensure that farmers are easily removed. These guards, on orders from their bosses, can be more confrontational. Early in Braganza's term, he and a contingent of Philippine National Police attempted to install a number of farmer beneficiaries on 200 hectares of the Espino estate in Negros. He was met by four guards who successfully refused them entry.[65] Sometimes landlords put up a fight even before their land is deemed "CARPable"— or precisely to prevent its being considered "CARPable." Gov. Carlos Fortich reportedly once threatened DAR surveyors that the only way they would be able to enter his property was if he made fertilizer out of them.[66]

"DAR is not enough"[67]

If CARP's reformist potential is undercut by competing modes of development and often uncooperative if not downright hostile institutions, what it has accomplished is due to more than just DAR alone. DAR by itself is often insufficient to implement CARP: "It lacks manpower in the field and money for support services."[68] Moreover, DAR, being a state agent, is easily neutralized by anti-CARP forces. Farmers and NGOs recognize the pervasive corruption within DAR. Other difficulties are the entrenched "syndicates" in this agency.

Managing land reform is a strategic business. Success depends on the capacity to mobilize allies, within or outside the state, able to overcome not just landlord resistance but DAR's own bureaucratic incapacity.

LTI requires the participation of NGOs and POs, without whose pressure DAR would fall prey to its own bureaucracy.

According to one study,[69] the chief impediment faced by small farmers in becoming farmer beneficiaries is DAR-related (31.5 percent)—mostly because DAR focuses exclusively on land tenants (8.3 percent), it neglects them (5.3 percent), or is slow to implement CARP (5.2 percent). Interestingly, only 5 percent of these potential farmer beneficiaries list landowner resistance as the reason they have not become farmer beneficiaries, while 20 percent say they had never even heard of CARP (this was in 1996 when the program had existed for eight years). Of the problems faced by farmer beneficiaries, the majority is, once again, DAR-related. They cite delayed processing (of claims) by DAR and other government agencies like the Land Bank and the DENR (31.8 percent), yet-to-be individualized CLOAs (16.2 percent), and the lack of capital support services (10.1 percent) as some of their most pressing problems.

Making CARP Work

Given all these weaknesses and vulnerabilities, how does CARP work when it does? It often does so without the state. When potential farmer beneficiaries find little recourse within the state apparatus, they often go outside it—usually with DAR's blessing if not outright cooperation. As one successful farmer beneficiary noted, "extralegal efforts must supplement enforcement of the law."[70]

Extralegal measures are usually undertaken by POs with NGO support reacting to an issue that is either unresolved (such as delays in farmer beneficiary installation) or resolved unfavorably (i.e., for the landowner's benefit). These measures tend to take one or both of two forms—demonstrations or land occupations. Farmer beneficiaries demonstrate to win public sympathy and support; with public backing they hope to be able to force DAR's or the landowner's hand. In April 2001, for example, the farmer beneficiaries that Braganza had failed to install trooped to DAR central and demanded to be installed (and less than a month later they were).[71] Land occupations, on the other hand, are often primarily intended to establish facts on the ground. This has increasingly become an alternative strategy for farmer beneficiaries. However, these could be incredibly hard to sustain without some degree of concession from the state or local government unit, because even with NGO support, landlords, especially if they are within their legal rights, could usually apply greater force against the occupants (e.g., MAPALAD farmers). Landlords also tend to use land occupation as a tactic in creating conflict between two competing groups of farmer beneficiaries. While demonstrations are used to call the state into account for its reformist promise, land occupations, which are more than extralegal but illegal, aim for justice despite the state. These are ways to overcome institutional incapacity or biases, particularly in terms of property rights. With both, however, success depends on strategy; these measures are best used as tactics rather than as ends in themselves.

The dynamic of this dilemma is perhaps best illustrated in the case of the MAPALAD farmers.[72] The plight of these farmers caught the public and presidential eye in 1996-97. Mass demonstrations in support of the farmers specifically and agrarian reform generally, hunger strikes by the farmers themselves, a presidential compromise, and a controversial Supreme Court ruling, had made the MAPALAD farmers a media favorite. Some three years since their defeat at the high court, however, the farmers had been all but forgotten. The 144 hectares DAR intended for 137 farmer beneficiaries lay fallow, and have been so for five years, since the landowner declared his intention to convert the land. While the land awaits use, the MAPALAD farmers languish (an ironic twist, given that the acronym means "fortunate" in English). Also, their living conditions are worse than before they had tried to avail themselves of CARP. The average farmer scrapes by on less than Php 1,000 a month as a farm laborer; the tedious manufacture of brooms adds Php 50 to his income. Dreams of improving their condition lie in hectarage that, despite its tantalizing proximity, they have no legal right over. What is to become of the land? "Who knows?" Peter Tuminhay, former president of the MAPALAD cooperative, muses, "A golf course? A hotel? They say maybe a racetrack."[73]

From the start the lines were drawn. When DAR placed the 144-hectare area in San Vicente, Sumilao, Bukidnon, under CARP in 1990 it encountered resistance from its related entity, the provincial agrarian reform adjudicator (PARAD). It turned out that the area, owned by the

Norberto Quisumbing Sr. Management and Development Corporation (NQSRMDC) and, at the time, leased to Del Monte Philippines (then the Philippine Packing Corporation), was a chief source of provincial revenue as well as a staple of the national export sector. The landowner petitioned and won PARAD support on the basis of its lease agreement with Del Monte, and DAR was ordered to desist. Four months before its lease expired, however, NQSRMDC applied to convert its land from agricultural to agro-industrial use. (If successful, the NQSRMDC hectarage would thereby be exempt from CARP.) The local government unit supported the application and classified the Quisumbing property as an agro-industrial-institutional area, as well as approved the establishment of the Bukidnon Agro-industrial Development Area (BAIDA) project.

LGU collaboration was far from coincidental. The historical nexus between land ownership and political power is exemplified in this case, in which land is the basis of authority and landlordism coincides with local government. The enmity then between agrarian reform and local government is ingrained; the chairman of the agriculture committee of the Sangguniang Panlalawigan argued that "CARP threatens the territorial scope of the LGU and undermines the latter's capacity for sustainable growth through agriculture and land markets."[74] The conflict, in short, is over property rights. By virtue of its redistributive mandate and expropriatory powers, CARP endangers the landed elite's source of political and economic power.

Perhaps aware that DAR had the final say over whether to approve the NQSRMDC application, the Bukidnon LGU cast its battle with pro-CARP forces as "conceptual," parrying suspicion that the case was entirely one out of pure self-interest and effectively stealing some of CARP's reformist thunder.

> The Bukidnon LGU zeroed in on major areas of revenue or potential areas of investment. It contrasted its own model of growth with equity using the agro-industrial development zone framework. The LGU argued that this was essential for global competitiveness and for generating maximum impact on poverty through the employment generated.[75]

A contest had thus been declared between two modes of development, one prioritizing productivity and the other social equity; the prize, state priority. The ensuing alignment of forces made clear the state's bias and CARP's relative isolation. MAPALAD is a clear example of the reluctance of landowners to part with their lands and the collusion of local government units with the landed class.

The provincial director of the Department of Trade and Industry (DTI) threw his weight behind the BAIDA project, adopting it as one of DTI-Bukidnon's flagship projects. Two other CARP-implementing agencies, the Department of Agriculture (DA) and the DENR, did the same. The local DAR, hoping to deflect the tremendous pressure it was receiving from the landlord and provincial governor, did not oppose BAIDA on the understanding that DAR central would deny the petition. Garilao did just that. His ruling was supported by the National Irrigation Authority, which certified the subject property as agriculturally productive (therefore excludable from conversion). NQSRMDC reapplied to the DAR secretary and was, with finality, denied. Unfazed, NQSRMDC and Governor Fortich appealed separately to the Office of the President. Tactics shifted; NQSRMDC filed for an injunction against DAR with the Court of Appeals citing a legal conflict between the local government code (RA 7160) and CARL (RA 6657)—the issue in this case being whether DAR had authority over lands reclassified by the LGU. Meanwhile DAR issued CLOAs for 137 farmer beneficiaries; it did not, however, distribute them, perhaps because the institutional support NQSRMDC had by this time assembled was formidable,[76] and without support from its headquarters, DAR got cold feet. This scenario undoubtedly played into the presidential decision. By 1996, with the political market favoring the landowner-LGU bloc, and with the media eyeing events, Ramos approved the NQSRMDC application for conversion.

In the flurry of ensuing legal motions, about ninety MAPALAD farmers, in defiance of an injunction prohibiting them from entering the contested property, occupied and began cultivating the land. NQSRMDC retaliated by having armed guards harass the farmers and releasing 134 carabaos in the property, trammeling the farmer-built shelters. Cleverly, NQSRMDC also let out portions of its estate to Higaonons of the Tribal Gagao Association (TGA). The Higaonons of the TGA claimed that, unlike the MAPALAD leadership, they were nobly descended. Gifts of land use and weapons won NQSRMDC the TGA's support against MAPALAD. The farmers were forced to vacate. This clearly demonstrates the landlords' penchant for creating and highlighting conflicts over competing claims of access to land by different alienated groups of beneficiaries and communities.

The occupation was short-lived because it was unsupported and insupportable. It lacked the backing of the local population or the participation of MAPALAD's NGO allies and, other than physically occupying the land, the farmers had no strategy as to how to sustain their occupation. Their defeat was a simple matter of might (which the landowner had plenty of) backed by right (the court injunction). Throw intertribal conflict into the mix and it became clear that the farmers were tactically outmaneuvered.

In the following months, however, the farmers became more creative in presenting their case before the last court of appeal—the public. Who better to strike that chord, particularly in the Philippines, than an outraged public? The farmers staged hunger strikes in Cagayan de Oro City and in front of DAR central in Quezon City. Their campaign, dubbed "MAPALAD plus," was led by a team of NGOs and accompanied by a legal strategy.[77] Thanks to a mostly sympathetic media, public support for the MAPALAD farmers grew. The inclusion of other peasants' land claims sparked support from spontaneous coalitions as well as expanded the scope of the "MAPALAD plus" campaign. The issue had become the necessity of implementing agrarian reform and the government's failure to do so.

NQSRMDC, in an attempt to sway public opinion, reacted by discrediting the farmers and alleging that some of them were frauds.[78] Further, to win support from the Department of the Interior and Local Government, the landowner cited its previous contributions to CARP.

The timing of the "MAPALAD plus" campaign was propitious. Ramos, attempting to mitigate the bad publicity surrounding his previous ruling, ruled again, this time striking a compromise between the claims of the two parties. However, his "win-win" formula—offering 100 hectares to the MAPALAD farmers and 44 to the NQSRMDC estate—was summarily rejected by the landowner. Fortich himself petitioned the Supreme Court. The LGU-NQSRMDC bloc argued that Ramos's win-win resolution arrogated the LGU's prerogative to reclassify land. On April

24, 1998, the court upheld the LGUs right to reclassify land and reinstated Ramos's earlier ruling in favor of the landowner.

It cannot be said that the court acted surprisingly despite the presidential ruling. Ramos's first ruling was more in keeping with his presidency; he sided unequivocally with the interests of private capital growth. His second ruling, however, was a direct response to the public clamor for reform. There was enough urgency to compel the government to defend the reformist promises upon which it derives its legitimacy. The second ruling was intended to appease this clamor, with a pittance thrown in for the landowner to make it appear that this new decision was not a complete about-face but actually a compromise. Though the ruling was presidential, it had absolutely no legal basis. Thus the Supreme Court could really come to no other verdict. CARP law simply lacked enough authority to overrule the venerable body of property law. Without sufficient state priority, it was defenseless in all but the court of public appeal. As one DAR administrator mused, "AR is not just DAR."[79] AR is the DENR, DA, the LGU; it is NGOs and POs and, in the final count, it has to be a public that believes in it enough to fight for it.

The Struggle for Land Reform

The country's history reveals that land-reform initiatives such as CARP can work primarily because of the incremental efforts of peasant movements, NGOs, POs, grassroots groups, and civil society in general. They had been in the forefront of land reform struggle since the early '50s. A strong peasant movement demanded for land redistribution under Marcos's long period of harsh repression. With the mushrooming of peasants organizations after the EDSA uprising and with the formidable task of pushing for a genuine agrarian reform program under the new democratic government, the initial response of the peasant sector was to consolidate all genuine peasants organizations. Thus, on May 29, 1987, with the recognition of the opportunity provided by the new Constitution and aware of the urgency to consolidate elements of society supportive of basic reforms, specifically agrarian reform, peasants united under the broadest coalition in the history of the peasant movement—the Congress for a Peoples' Agrarian Reform. CPAR brought together twelve national federations[80] of peasants, rural women

and small fisherfolk united by the belief that a comprehensive and effective agrarian reform was the answer to the country's problem of poverty and underdevelopment, environmental degradation, and social disintegration. Reyes identified the two main currents in the agrarian movement since the passage of the reform law that unified to form CPAR
namely, the Communist Party of the Philippines-led National Democrat (ND) and the more moderate and gradualist groups (left of center,
social democratic or social-reform-oriented groups).[81]

CPAR employed a multipronged strategy in mounting its major
policy campaign. It engaged both the House of Representatives and
the Senate where it presented position papers and worked closely with
sympathetic members of Congress. CPAR members also understood
the important role of the media in their advocacy. Outside the halls
of Congress, the coalition held workshops and conferences with various sectors to generate interest in and support for their proposals,
organized rallies and demonstrations to press for the acceleration of
congressional hearings and debates, and launched a public awareness
campaign—the Agrarian Reform Express—that was capped by a huge
public rally in Manila.[82] CPAR's initiatives bore fruit when their proposal was adopted, though with modifications, as the working document of the House Committee on Agrarian Reform. However, CPAR's
gains were quickly overturned when RA 6657, a disabled version of
their proposal, was signed into law by President Aquino. CPAR unequivocally rejected this law, denouncing it as a sham. Undaunted, CPAR
convened its own Peoples' Congress and passed its own Peoples' Agrarian Reform Code (PARCODE).[83] The coalition mounted a three mil-
lion-signature campaign to recall RA 6657 and replace it with
PARCODE. But the campaign failed miserably because of limited lo-
gistics, weak organization, and inadequate planning.

At the outset, CPAR was already plagued by numerous problems:
ideological differences, resource allocations, power sharing, and the role
of the secretariat, among others. The peasant sector was mainly divided
according to their stance with regard to government and its programs
(e.g., CARP) and the ideological/political backgrounds they represented
(e.g., NDs, Social Democrats [SDs], Democratic Socialists, independents,
government-organized, etc.). These strands in CPAR represented differ-

ent frameworks and approaches to achieve land reform in light of CARP. The ND tradition maintained an agrarian revolution mode, which has an armed struggle component. The militant Left maintained an "expose and oppose" position. On the other hand, the SD orientation took an incremental and non-violent tack. These groups place a high premium on constructive engagement with government to the extent of forging partnerships with government while harnessing mass pressure to implement land reform.[84] There are also some independent groups, which have taken a more collaborative attitude in dealing with government. However, after six years, the strain of coalition work finally took its toll and the coalition decided to "fold up."

Crisis struck the CPP-led movement at the beginning of the '90s, which resulted in major splits among its ranks, foremost of which were its rural constituencies. Some agrarian reform actors considered the situation a positive development—it opened up innovations and creative strategies to push for agrarian reform. Yet the split in the Left contributed to the division in the peasantry, which resulted in the break-up of the KMP into the "reaffirmist" Rafael Mariano-led KMP and the "rejectionist" Jimmy Tadeo-led Demokratikong Kilusang Magbubukid ng Pilipinas (DKMP).[85] Later on, some elements of the faction in the Left's peasant movement that broke away from the Communist Party closely worked with the Estrada administration and were even accused of participating in "smear campaigns" against other peasants groups.

Amidst the deep divisions in the peasant movement and the Left, perhaps it would be less depressing to cite strengths and advantages CPAR gained for the peasant movement. The CPAR experience enhanced the institutionalization of peasants' participation in agrarian reform. Its media projection increased the government's awareness and knowledge of the largest Filipino peasant networks and the reforms for which they struggle.[86] Simply put, CPAR set the tone for the peasants' participation in policy making and governance. However, the main lesson from the CPAR experience was that it was very difficult to maintain unity among "different-minded" groups under a formal coalition since energies tend to be spent on organizational matters, internal squabbling, and "agenda positioning." More successful were issue-based coalitions, as in the case of the Kasarinlan sa Pagkain (KSP), which addressed the rice crisis issue on 1995, and MORE-AR, which acted on the proposed amendment to CARP to exempt commercial farms, fishponds, and prawn farms. Once the issue at hand has been addressed or resolved, the coalition then dissolved. KSP was composed of DKMP, PAKISAMA (Pambansang Kilusan ng mga Samahang Magsasaka), Ugnayan, Kalipunan ng mga Maliliit na Magniniyog sa Pilipinas (KAMMPIL), Citizens Alliance for Consumer Protection and other concerned POs and NGOs.

The same has been the case for KILOS-SAKA and ARISE Now! Coalitions of "like-minded" organizations have also persisted (i.e., AR Now! and PARRDS) but have retained a loser formation or structure. The division within the peasant sector that highly characterized the early '90s (as manifested in the dissolution of CPAR, NACFAR, and other coalitions, and the split of KMP and other peasants groups) is now apparently being reversed through "reaching out" efforts from major peasants groups.

Responding to the call for the ouster of Estrada, peasants groups reconsolidated into loose coalitions, namely KILOS-SAKA and ARISE Now!

The KMP/RA-led ARISE Now! mainly comprises peasants groups allied with the Communist Party and the PAKISAMA bloc. Specifically, its members are: KMP, PAKISAMA, PAMALAKAYA, MAMAMAYAN (Malayang Mangingisdang Magpapaunlad ng Yaman ng Nayon), AMIHAN (Pederasyon ng Kababaihang Magbubukid), LAKAMBINI (Lakas ng Kababaihang Magbubukid), KAMP (Kalipunan ng mga Katutubong Mamamayan ng Pilipinas), NFSW (National Federation of Sugar Workers), STOP-EX (Solidarity of Tobacco Peasants Against Exploitation Ilocos), People's Campaign for Agrarian Reform Network (AR Now!), Task Force MAPALAD-Negros Occidental, NNARA (National Network of Agrarian Reform Advocates), RMP (Rural Missionaries of the Philippines), and SENTRA (Sentro para sa Tunay na Repormang Agraryo).

On the other hand, KILOS-SAKA is composed of independent, Bisig, some peasants groups linked with the breakaway "reject" stream of the Communist Party and also the PAKISAMA bloc.[87] Specifically, these are: PKSK (Pambansang Katipunan ng mga Samahan sa Kanayunan),

PAKISAMA, BUKLOD (Buklod ng Malalayang Magbubukid), PKSMMN (Pambansang Koalisyon ng mga Samahang Magsasaka at Manggagawa sa Niyugan), FFF (Federation of Free Farmers), Samahang 53 Ektarya, BMMBK-Laguna, SARILAYA, ALAB-KATIPUNAN, PASALEY (Peasant Alliance of Samar and Leyte), SANDUGUAN, KABAYANI, CARET (Center for Agrarian Reform and Education Transformation), KAISAHAN (Kaisahan tungo sa Kaunlaran sa Kanayunan at Repormang Pansakahan), COIR (Coconut Industry for Reform), SALIGAN (Sentro ng Alternatibang Lingap Panligal), Tambuyog, AR Now!, MAKABAYAN (Makabayang Alyansa ng mga Magsasaka sa Pilipinas), PPI (Philippine Peasant Institute), and PhilDHRRA (Philippine Partnership for the Development of Human Resources in Rural Areas).

Complex relationships among the Communist Party-linked peasants groups and some "reject" groups have prevented the two major groups from consolidating as one.

The closest that the groups have come to consolidating was the conduct of the "Peasant Voices" conference. The conference was based on the groups' unity against the implementation of the "corporative" scheme and the World Bank's MALR, and the call for Estrada's ouster. It was also attended by almost all of the groups in KILOS-SAKA and ARISE Now!

A third bloc, mostly composed of "reject" peasants groups that have closely worked with Morales, have been antagonistic to the majority of the peasants groups mainly due the perception that this bloc engaged in a smear campaign to isolate the other peasants groups.

Other coalitions that formed around the issue of agrarian reform were SANDUGUAN, composed of thirteen peasants organizations, on February 14, 1987; the Visayas Congress for Agrarian Reform (VICAR), a broad alliance of peasants organizations in the region, which is participated in by thirteen regional alliances and federations, on October 10, 1988; the National Peasant Council (NPC), which was to serve as the consultative body of the DA for the implementation of its Medium-Term Agricultural Development Plan for 1990-1995; the Bukluran ng mga Tagapaglikha ng Butil (BUTIL), a national alliance of corn and rice farmers from twenty-seven provinces, in October 1991; and the Philippine National Peasant Caucus (PNPC), a broad coalition of peasants organizations that vowed to focus on the issues of food security, agrarian reform, and protection of farmers against the ill effects of rapid trade liberalization, in October 1996.

Tremendous Sacrifices, Uncertain Gains

The peasant movement now faces an uphill battle. First, agrarian reform has degenerated into mere posturing on the part of the elites. Problems of reaching out to other sectors continue to hound the struggle for agrarian reform. The program has entered its most difficult phase of distributing contentious and problematic landholdings, foremost of which are the haciendas and plantations of the sacred cows. High-level schemes to kill agrarian reform, such as the farmland-as-collateral bill, and land conversions in the guise of low-cost housing are backed by the state.

Second, local and national movements are vulnerable to the divide-and-rule machinations of the state. They find it hard to match the strength of the landed bloc, much more consolidate their forces. As

Table 2.6 A Brief Matrix of the ARRD Groups vis-à-vis CARP

Outright Opposition	Critical Engagement	Critical Collaboration	Outright Support
Bayan	AR Now!	PARRDS	Peace foundation
KPD	PHILDHRRA	PhilNET	PRRM
KMP	CODE-NGO	AKO	PAG-PRIDI
	PhilCOS		PDI
	Akbayan		UNORKA
	FFF		
	PPI		
	Kaisahan		
	BMFI		
	SALIGAN		
	BALAOD		
	BARRIOS,PADC		
	HEED DG (Negros Occidental)		
	PKSK, KAISA-MO		
	ARADO		
	KAMS		
	MAPISAN/ PENASAHI		
	PAKISAMA		

veteran farmer-leader Jaime Tadeo said, the "[The] movement [has been] in crisis for a long time."[88] Third, international pressures continue to threaten land reform. Access to and tenure of land has come under severe stress from the widespread commercialization of agriculture. With the World Bank pushing for its MALR with the complicity of the Philippine state, the state-led model is in danger of being shelved.

The few token gains from CARP might soon be lost. The peasantry, it seems, has only itself to rely on. Without allies, they would find the challenge of successful reform extremely difficult to attain. There is a need to once more bring the various sections of the rural peoples' movements under one roof.[89] For KMP hope lies in the militant peasant struggle for land. For PARRDS, UNORKA, and other SD groups, unity can be achieved if founded on "pluralism, democracy and respect for the autonomous integrity of local rural organizations." Strategies, tactics, and approaches will differ but all organized forces must realize that they have to find some way of working together or face the reality of failure.

Can and Should CARP Be Saved?

Agrarian reform is the expression of a constitutional directive to provide restitution for the Filipinos whose families have lived and labored for generations under feudalism.[90] It is not just a poverty-alleviation program; it aims to abolish feudalism by creating a class of independent smallholders. Despite the long history of land conflicts in the country and the enactment of CARP, the national government and modern democratic institutions have as yet been unable (and, in most cases, unwilling) to resolve the fundamental issues of equitable and sustained access to land. CARP has failed to change the feudal landscape, much more address the historical roots of land concentration in the hands of a few rural and urban elites. The national policies of the government have always favored economic and political elites, thereby entrenching poverty, and social and economic inequality.

To properly evaluate CARP one must first assess its accomplishment. This is easier said than done. For one thing, there is a marked lack of reliable data. Available data such as DAR-furnished figures could be questionable and misleading. Moreover, these figures can be either meaningless in themselves or freely interpretable depending on who they are from and how one chooses to understand them. For example, by DAR's account, at end-2003 both DAR and DENR redistributed 5.8 million hectares, or 72 percent of its 8.1 million hectare target—that is 58 percent of the country's total farmland, benefiting 2.7 million rural poor households or 44 percent of the country's total peasant population. How do we make sense of this figure? On the one hand, after fifteen years (1988-2003), 72 percent is an insignificant figure, especially if one considers that 72 percent or 5.8 million hectares consists of public lands, which are easier to move. On the other, considering that CARP emerged out of a compromise piece of legislation, it still managed to achieve something. As Jun Borras exclaimed, "What? CARP was able to accomplish 72 percent? I thought it was useless and couldn't achieve anything substantial!"[91] This perspective stresses that despite the fact that CARP was handicapped from the beginning, it has surprisingly not been totally killed off. Defenders of this view say that CARP's accomplishment ranks among the world's major nonsocialist land reforms; that 72 percent is a significant feat considering that the Philippines is neither revolutionary nor dictatorial and thus lacks the kind of sweeping mandate that can truly implement radical reforms.

Be that as it may, 72 percent is still a questionable figure. It accounts for hectarage that has been awarded but not necessarily distributed. The distinction is subtle but significant; it means the difference between whether the farmer beneficiary has tenure security or not—whether the certificate of land ownership award is really in his or her hands. There are several cases of mother certificates of land ownership award having been awarded but not individualized, which means their number can be reported and used to pad DAR's overall LTI accomplishment while in reality changes nothing for the farmer beneficiary.

CARP's LTI accomplishment is perhaps only the most basic measure of its performance. There are more precise measures, particularly the following: 1) the extent of CARP's reach in the countryside, 2) its specific impact on farmer beneficiaries, and 3) whether it does result in greater productivity. There is one general measure: whether it does amount as intended to social equity.

Figures from a study conducted by the Management and Organizational Development for Empowerment, first, show that CARP's effect on landless farmers is limited. Only 8.2 percent of owner-cultivators acquired their land through agrarian reform (and this figure includes Marcos's rice-and-corn lands program), while most inherited it (54.7 percent) or bought it themselves (32.1 percent). More precisely, however, among those entitled to benefit from CARP, only 35.4 percent are actual farmer beneficiaries.

Second, in terms of CARP's impact on farmer beneficiaries, owning land does increase a farmer's income and productivity. The World Bank corroborates this finding that land reform in general (not specifically CARP) "significantly" improves the well-being of its beneficiaries. Farmer beneficiaries accumulate capital and assets at a faster rate than non-farmer beneficiaries, their farms are more productive and their children attend school longer.[92] However, according to DAR's own ARC Level of Development Assessment (2000), over 80 percent of agrarian reform communities have average household incomes below the poverty line, and for rice, corn, and coconut, over 80 percent have productivity levels below the national average.[93] Clearly, despite the finding that CARP does benefit farmers, it does not raise the majority of them above the poverty line. The fact is, Quitoriano writes, "CARP beneficiaries cannot show proof that they are better than the majority of poor in this country."[94]

The third measure—whether CARP leads to overall productivity—has to do with whether CARP breaks up economies of scale by parceling large farms. The assumption is that large farms are generally more productive because they enjoy economies of scale. Reidinger and Kang, however, dispute this. Accordingly, "diseconomies" of scale occur on very large farms as well as very small ones. There is, it turns out, an optimal farm size in terms of maximizing productivity: between three and four hectares. Increased planting on farms larger than approximately four hectares encounters diminishing returns. Moreover, Reidinger and Kang find that improved land-tenure security associates with increased productivity: "Changing tenure status from share tenant to leaseholder, to amortizing farmer beneficiaries and to owner-cultivator result in increases in rice yields of approximately 20 percent, 32 percent, and 19

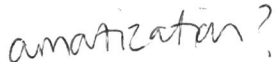
amortization?

percent, respectively," with the greatest yields enhancement associated with the shift from share tenancy to amortizing farmer beneficiaries.[95] As the researchers note, these findings "offer empirical support for the agronomic rationale" behind CARP.

The question of whether CARP leads to social equity is even harder to assess. The answer would depend on how one constitutes social equity. If the question is, for example, has there been a diminution of agrarian unrest? Then one could say, arguably, yes, and cite CARP as one, if not entirely convincing, reason: "On the surface, one can say that two million beneficiaries of land is equivalent to two million families relatively distancing themselves from the fold of the CPP-NPA."[96] Such criterion is clearly inadequate, however, and is a poor indication of any degree of social equity.

In fact, it could be argued to some degree that CARP has exacerbated social inequity. Distorted land markets, land rental restrictions, and decreased landowner ability and willingness to rent out land—all due to CARP—may have reduced access to land for the majority of landless farmers. According to the World Bank year 2000 report, the probability of a landless person being able to access land may have decreased by 60 percent between 1985 and 1998—undoubtedly partly due to CARP. Moreover, as noted in the 1998 Annual Poverty Indicator Survey, 68 percent of households with at least one member involved in agriculture have no access to land other than their residence, and only 3 percent received their land through CARP. In other words, welfare losses to the very poorest due to reduced land access may outweigh CARP's benefit to select farmer beneficiaries. And these welfare losses are significant: the World Bank estimates that landless persons can lose up to 30 percent of their total household income by their lack of access land. These findings paint a very grim picture. But the answer is not to junk CARP but to develop the political will to implement it more effectively.

Another way to qualify CARP's accomplishment is by looking at the degree to which beneficiaries have become self-reliant. The data speak clearly: for the most part, farmer beneficiaries remain beholden to many masters—to traders for example, who set prices and provide credit, to NGOs and to the billions of pesos that filter in as ODA. This is not to say that farmer beneficiaries have largely weaned themselves away from their dependency on landlords. CARP has significantly dented the economic and political might of landlords. At some point, in some way, farmer beneficiaries will have to reckon with them, and the landlords will invariably enjoy the better bargaining position.

Still, owning one's land is better than working someone else's for 30 percent of the produce. With tenure security, productivity will certainly increase, and the quality of the farmers' life—from income to schooling opportunities for his children—will likely improve. Moreover, apart from the land itself, the process of attaining and maintaining the land is educational. Experience has shown that farmers who avail themselves of CARP need to be organized; otherwise farmer beneficiaries would be unable to access the capital, technology, and services. This struggle is, as Quitoriano observes, "a reflection of political maturity." "One measure of civility in civil society is for individuals to own property and have access to education; in this sense, farmer beneficiaries have attained the basic minimum—of owning property and being educated."[97] In this light, the true legacy of CARP remains to be seen.

Notes

1. Jocelyn Hermoso, "One Step Forward, Two Steps Back: Agrarian Reform Policy Today," *CyberDyaryo*, July 3, 1998.

2. The Aquino government's agrarian reform program traces its origin to the early days of the snap presidential campaign. She promised that, if elected, she would implement land reform starting in her own backyard—distributing 6,000-hectare Hacienda Luisita to landless farmers. However, succeeding events would reveal that Aquino was forced by circumstances to implement agrarian reform. No agrarian reform initiatives were taken until the tragic massacre of thirteen peasants during a peaceful rally at Mendiola bridge on January 22, 1987.

3. James Putzel, *A Captive Land: The Politics of Agrarian Reform in the Philippines* (London: Catholic Institute for International Relations; New York: Monthly Press Review, 1992), chapter 8, 265.

4. Catherine V. Valenzuela, "The Aquino Agrarian Reform Program: A Two-Year Assessment," *Philippine Peasant Institute Papers* (July 1990): 4.

5. Congressman Bonifacio Gillego, during CARP debates in Congress, 1988.

6. James Putzel, "Land Reform in Asia: Lessons from the Past for the 21st Century" (a paper presented for the *Asia Back to Basics* conference in Bangkok, July 29-30, 1999).

7. Japan, for example, completed its land reform program within three years because 90 percent of its lands had been legally and properly registered years before the land reform program was put in place.

8. Putzel, op. cit.

9. Ernesto Garilao, "The Ramos Legacy in Agrarian Reform: A Transition Report," Manila, part 3, 6.

10. Romeo Royandoyan, interview, August 29, 2000, Quezon City.

9 Eduardo Tadem, "Disabling a Centerpiece Program"; Tadem is a board member of the Center for Agrarian Reform and Education Transformation (CARET).

12. Ibid.

13. William A. de Lange Jr., "Garchitorena Land Deal Quietly Resolved," *Business World*, August 20, 1988, front page.

14. Arsenio Acuña, lawyer and planter representative, actually said that, "Land reform is the biggest menopausal blunder of this President" (referring to Corazon Aquino). In Putzel's *A Captive Land*, 270.

15. *Philippine Daily Inquirer*, March 3, 1990.

16. Charles Lindsey, "The Political Economy of International Economic Policy Reform in the Philippines: Continuity and Restoration," in *The Dynamics of Economic Policy Reform in the Philippines*, ed. Andrew MacIntyre and Kanishka Jayasuriya (Singapore: Oxford University Press, 1992), 87.

17. Ibid., 89.

18. The term was coined by Jun Borras in his book, "*Bibingka Strategy in Land Reform Implementation: Autonomous Peasant Movements and State Reformists in the Philippines* (Quezon City: Institute for Popular Democracy, 1998)." Simply put, it means mass pressure from below and critical engagements from above. It is one of the many strategies used by social movements, NGOs and POs in pushing for a genuine agrarian reform program.

19. Ironically, it was Garilao himself who instituted the CARP audit as a mechanism to verify the accomplishment reports. The objectives of the PARC audit are twofold: (1) to evaluate and examine the efficacy of the implementation of the program, and (2) to assess and validate the fund utilization and the corresponding physical accomplishment of CARP implementing agencies in relation with their respective approved work and financial plans. For the past five years that PARC conducted its audit, the same set of problems continues to beleaguer CARP's implementation—double titling, installation problems, CLOA/CLT cancellations, and land reversals.

These perennial problems mirror the ineffective strategies that the government and implementing agencies, particularly DAR, use.

20. Jun Borras and Jenny Franco, "A Critical Review of CARP and Its Accomplishments," *Manila Times*, June 11, 1998, 7.

21. Antonio Lopez, "Pagdanganan's Revolutionized Agrarian Reform Program, *BizNews Asia*, July 7-21, 2003, 24-25.

22. Ernesto Garilao, "The Ramos Legacy in Agrarian Reform: A Transition Report," Part 7, 26.

23. ARCDP Director Adelberto Baniqued, in an interview on May 2, 2001, explained how important it is to work on rural development in order to improve farmers' standards of living. Agrarian reform communities endeavor to make farmer beneficiaries more productive, to generate increased income, and to eventually turn them into entrepreneurs. Through limited but meaningful gains, the ARC experience hopes to foster and sustain development in farmer beneficiaries' newly acquired land.

24. Celia Reyes, "Impact of Agrarian Reform on Poverty," CARP Impact Assessment Study, September 2001, executive summary.

25. An Act Strengthening Further the CARP, by Providing Augmentation Fund Therefore, Amending for the Purpose Section 63 of RA 6657.

26. "CARP under Erap: Off to a Slow Start," in *Farm News and Views* 12, no. 3 (May-June 1999). A bi-monthly publication of the Philippine Peasant Institute (PPI).

27. Interview with Romeo Royandoyan of PPI on August 29, 2000. Royandoyan predicted that it would take the Morales DAR twenty-two years to distribute the CARP balance at its current accomplishment rate. His projection prompted him to concede, however, that the task may still be doable in six years—if Morales was superman.

28. Figures as documented in the 1999 DAR Performance Report.

29. Maria Mendoza, "CARP's Rebirth under a New Administration," *Farm News and Views* 12, no. 3 (May-June 1999).

30. Presidential Agrarian Reform Council member

31. Mendoza, op cit.

32. Ibid.

33. Ibid.

34. Interview on February 7, 2001. Dinky Soliman has been an active advocate of agrarian reform. She was a leading force in the Congress for a People's Agrarian Reform during the CARP debates in Congress.

35. Literally it means, "to give then to take back." The concept appears in Annie Ruth Sabangan's article, "Land Reform Lost under Estrada," *Manila Times*, October 12, 1998, A-5. But it was originally conceptualized by a

farmer leader in Rizal, Ka Elvie Baladad, who coined the term in her position paper against CLOA cancellations.

36. Ibid.

37. R. El-Ghomeny in "A Discussion Paper on Market-Assisted Land Reform," prepared by Ernesto G. Lim Jr. for the conference "Peasants' Continuing Struggle for Genuine Agrarian Reform."

38. Ibid.

39. Quoted from "CARP in Crisis," PARRDS statement on the 14th Year Anniversary of CARP.

40. Carmina Flores of Philippine Peasant Institute claims that PPI was the first to criticize Arroyo's decision for appointing Roberto Pagdanganan because of his real estate background. And apart from sponsoring Real Estate Developers' Forum, renewed land conversion drives are blatant under the low-cost housing program scheme of the Arroyo administration. Interview, October 1, 2003.

41. This was part of her speech during CARP's 14th anniversary in 2002. Further claiming that asset reform is a priority focus of her administration.

42. Quoted by Jose Rodito Angeles, spokesperson for Task Force Mapalad in a press statement by the group last April 30, 2003.

43. Tony Lopez, "Obet's Big Bet on CARP and Coops," *BizNews Asia* 1, no. 35 (July 7-21, 2003): 16.

44. "100 days of Limbo Is Enough: The Time for Action Is Now!" AR Now! press statement, June 1, 2003.

45. Alternatives to Collateralizing CLOAs, Anihan online resource center for research and advocacy on agrarian reform and rural development (ARRD), June 1, 2003.

46. Solita Monsod, "Trojan Horse," *Philippine Daily Inquirer*, July 12, 2003, opinion section, A6.

47. Eugene Tecson, "Farmland as Collateral Bills: Re-igniting Landlessness and Bankruptcy," *Farm News and Views* (1st quarter 2003): 4.

48. Carmina Flores, "Agrarian Reform Implementation: Second Generation Problems," *Farm News and Views* (2nd and 3rd quarter, 2002): 27.

49. Gerald G. Lacuarta, "Land Distribution Report: Macapagal Got It Wrong, says Farmers," *Inquirer News Service*, June 12, 2002.

50. See "CARP in Crisis," PARRDS statement on the 14th Anniversary of CARP, June 10, 2002, and Ernie Lim, "What to expect for CARP in 2002," *AR Now! Papers*, 2001.

51. "Php 30 Billion Recovered Marcos Loot: Budget for CARP or Campaign Kitty for 2004?" *PARRDS Brief* 2, no.6 (August 2003).

52. Quoted from an article in *Today*, July 15, 2003.

53. Lacuarta, op. cit.

54. Historically, Danding Cojuangco has been the most sought-after political and economic ally—he was a Marcos crony, Estrada named him as the Godfather of Agrarian Reform, and now Arroyo is doing everything she can within her powers to woo him and win his loyalty for the May elections. There is reason to believe that she already did when Cojuangco finally decided not to run for the presidency.

55. Interview with Bukidnon Provincial Agrarian Reform Officer (PARO), Dylan Recina, May 19, 2001.

56. Interview with Bukidnon ARDA, Nick Peralta, May 16, 2001.

57. Email interview, Ed Quitoriano, May 13, 2001.

58. Cited in Yujiro Hayami, Ma. Agnes Quisumbing and Lourdes Adriano, *Toward an Alternative Land Reform Paradigm: A Philippine Perspective* (Quezon City: Ateneo de Manila University Press, 1990), 264.

59. While this is highly contentious and debatable, looking at the pieces of legislation from the 1950s—Land Reform Code of the Philippines to Presidential Decree 27—CARP can be considered to be (at least) the most progressive land reform program ever implemented in the country's history. Yet the fact remains that it has failed to change the social and political relations in the countryside.

60. This of course is purely a matter of who benefits. Not coincidentally, those who stand to benefit most from neoliberal measures rule the state.

61. Interview with Gerry Bulatao, May 9, 2001.

62. Email Interview, May 13, 2001.

63. Peralta, op. cit. (Pablo) Lobregat is a large and notoriously anti-CARP landlord in Mindanao. The phrase "Lobregat's Law" is doubly interesting because it implies, first, that resorting to courts is a customary CARP-stifling tactic of landowners, and also, that the law itself is the property of the landlord.

64. Ibid.

65. Interview with farmers demonstrating in front of DAR Central from the Espino, Manalo, Cojuangco, and Cuenca estates in Negros, April 26, 2001.

66. Interview with Bukidnon Provincial Agrarian Reform Officer (PARO), Dylan Recina, May 19 2001.

67. Ibid.

68. Ibid.

69. The figures come from a 1996 MODE-sponsored restudy of a nationwide UP Los Baños survey of rural households in 1989-90. The MODE

study had a sample size of 1500 rural households from 300 barangays spread over three ecological zones (upland, lowland, and coastal). The findings are compiled in the booklet: *The Impact of Agrarian Reform and Changing Markets on Rural Households* (MODE 2000), tables 9 and 10.

70. Interview with SALFABO representatives, May 18, 2001.

71. Though not after the DAR Secretary, in a heated exchange, reportedly challenged one of farmers to a fistfight.

72. My own account of the MAPALAD case, as well as much of the analysis that follows it, is deeply indebted to Ed Quitoriano's account of events in the MODE booklet, *Agrarian Struggles and Institutional Change: The MAPALAD Struggle for Land* (2000). The basis for choosing such a case study over others lies in the fact that it received a great deal of national attention and the strategies derived from this particular land struggle.

73. Interview, May 19, 2001.

74. Quitoriano, 15.

75. Ibid., 17.

76. It included the LGU, DTI, DA, DENR, HLURB (Housing and Land Use Regulatory Board), DILG (Department of Interior and Local Government), and OPAMIN (Office of the Presidential Assistant for Mindanao).

77. NGO allies included the Balay Mindanao Foundation, as well as KAANIB (a philDHRRA affiliate), PAKISAMA, KAISAHAN, AR NOW , and SALIGAN formulating the legal strategy.

78. NQSRMDC alleged that there were "fake beneficiaries" among the hunger strikers, or supposed farmer beneficiaries who actually owned various hectares of land but campaigned nonetheless for more.

79. Peralta, op. cit.

80. The twelve national peasant federations include five tendencies and traditions: (1) the national democrat orientation: AMIHAN (Pambansang Pederasyon ng Kababaihang Magbubukid), KMP (Kilusang Magbubukid ng Pilipinas, NFSW-FGT (National Federation of Sugar Workers-Food and General Traders), PAMALAKAYA (Pambansang Lakas ng Kilusang Mamalakaya ng Pilipinas); (2) aligned with the old Partido Komunista ng Pilipinas: AMA (Aniban ng mga Manggagawa sa Agrikultura), KABAPA (Kalipunan ng Bagong Pilipina); (3) democratic socialist tradition: KAMMMPI (Kapatiran ng Malalayang Maliliit na Mangingisda ng Pilipinas, LAKAS or LMMP (Lakas ng Magsasaka, Manggagawa at Mangingisda ng Pilipinas, LMP (Lakas ng Magsasakang Pilipino), PAKISAMA (Pambansang Kilusan ng mga Samahang Magsasaka); (4) independent: KASAMA (Kalipunan ng Samahang

Mamamayan); and (5) associated with the Marcos government: FFF (Federation of Free Workers).

81. "Towards a New Social Movement Strategy for Agrarian Reform" (a paper presented before the ICCO consultation on ARRD, May 15-16, 2003).

82. Vallerie Miller, "NGO and Grassroots Policy Influence," *IDR Reports* 11, no. 5 (1994).

83. Ibid.

84. Reyes, op. cit.

85. The essay, "Reaffrim Our Basic Principles and Rectify Our Errors" written by Armando Liwanag (believed to be the pseudonym of Jose Maria Sison who is the founder and first chairman of the Communist Party of the Philippines) provoked numerous debates within the movement, which eventually led to its fragmentation. The basic text was released on December 26, 1991, which coincided with the 23rd anniversary of the founding of the CPP (Marxist-Leninist-Mao Thought). It urged the comrades to reaffrim the basic revolutionary principles of the Party—the guiding light in taking stock of and celebrating its accomplishments as well as confronting certain long-running problems and unprecedented setbacks. Those who agreed with the basic tenets and principles of the Party were called the reaffirmists while those who rejected its basic revolutionary principles were called the rejectionists. Thus, the "RA-RJ" divide of the national democratic movement was born.

86. Cielito Goño, *Peasant Movement-State Relations in New Democracies: CPAR in Post-Marcos Philippines, Institute on Church and Social Issues,* Pulso Monograph 19, 1997, 123.

87. The Philippine Peasant Institute initiated the first few meetings of KILOS-SAKA. It was also the de facto secretariat of the coalition. But being a loose formation, every one was on equal footing, and consensus building was a practice.

88. Interview with Jaime Tadeo, October 29, 2003, Quezon City.

89. Ric Reyes, "Towards a New Social Movement Strategy for Agrarian reform" (a paper presented before the ICCO consultation on ARRD, May 15-16, 2003).

90. Alternatives to Collateralizing CLOAs, *Anihan online resource center for research and advocacy on agrarian reform and rural development (ARRD),* June 1, 2003.

91. Email interview, May 22, 2000.

92. Klaus Deininger, in *Philippines, Growth with Equity: The Remaining Agenda* (World Bank, 2000).

93. Email interview with Ed Quitoriano.

94. Ibid.

95. Jeffrey Reidinger and Seonjou Kang, "Back to the Land: Revisiting the Rationale for Agrarian Reform," in *The Impact of Agrarian Reform and the Changing Market on Rural Households* (Manila: MODE, 2000).

96. Email interview with Ed Quitoriano.

97. Ibid.

CHAPTER 3

The Neoliberal Revolution
and the Asian Financial Crisis

In the midst of the seemingly endless crisis of the Philippine economy since the Asian financial collapse of 1997, nostalgia for the presidency of Fidel Ramos from 1992 to 1998 is common in some quarters. Typical of this sentiment was this comment by one columnist: "An unadorned accolade for his administration may be found in a simple entry in an online encyclopedia: 'During his presidency the country experienced economic growth'."[1] Less restrained was one executive's testament to the former president:

> Fortunately at the time, we had a president who was willing to roll up his sleeves (also literally!) and work himself almost to exhaustion. By the end of the second year of the Ramos administration, the power crisis was being held at bay and by the third year, it was just a bad memory. A workable accommodation was made quietly with both rightist and leftist groups, including noisy Muslim secessionists. Generally, the stage was set by 1993 for a go-go investment atmosphere.[2]

What is interesting is how the Ramos presidency is detached by such commentators from the Asian financial crisis. The executive, for instance, goes on to say that it was "unfortunate" that "this idyllic situation was rudely awakened by the Asian financial crisis," and blames Ramos's successor, Joseph Estrada, for the collapse of the Philippine economy: "What was doubly unfortunate was that the policies and follow-up to the remedies to the crisis was [sic] being implemented by a laid-back chief executive whose hedonistic proclivities and less-than-sterling integrity will now be the subject of court proceedings."[3]

The truth of the matter, however, is that the same policies that triggered the surface activity of the Ramos years also led to the Asian financial crisis.

Doctrinal Liberalization from Aquino to Ramos

The Aquino period, it must be noted, was marked by stop-and-go liberalization, which testified not only to the administration's preoccupation with repaying the foreign debt but also to the continuing strength of particularistic economic interests. In contrast, consistency was the hallmark of the Ramos administration. Indeed, under Ramos, a program of liberalization, deregulation, and privatization was pursued with almost messianic zeal.

The ideological character of economic policy making during the Ramos period was partly a reaction toward the Marcos regime, which many in the urban middle and upper-middle classes had identified not only with dictatorship and the loss of human rights but also with cronyism, protectionism, and rent-seeking. Equally important in explaining it was the zeitgeist of the Reagan-Thatcher era. Academics and political figures with advanced academic training were key in this process, and many of them had done their graduate work in the late 1970s and 1980s, when state-oriented Keynesianism lost its luster and neoliberalism came into vogue not only in the economics departments of US universities but also in key local institutions such as the School of Economics of the University of the Philippines and the Center for Research and Communications (now University of Asia and the Pacific).

The "neoclassification" of the Philippine technocracy reached its apogee under Ramos not as a result of an intellectual coup but of a gradual takeover of the strategic heights of the technocracy by these free market-oriented policy makers coming from the academe, government, and business. As one pivotal figure pointed out, she and her colleagues who played prominent roles in the country's free-market turn acted not only out of external pressure from the World Bank and the International Monetary Fund (IMF) but also out of belief: "Imposed, maybe in one way, but on the other hand, the mainstream decision makers—[the] technocracy and policy makers—also internally believe in that. So there's a confluence of policy direction."[4] Another figure stressed the emergence of a broader "consensus" among the elite and the middle class around free-market reform: "[No] policy reform becomes credible, workable policies unless the people accepted. Yes, there were re-

searchers and economists pushing for that, yes there were donor communities pushing for that... but ultimately it is a question of whether the
public accepts that policy."[5]

In any event, the "neoclassical revolution" had achieved a critical
mass by the time Ramos came to power, and its hegemony was consolidated during his administration. "It's the dominant sector," one player
put it. "It's the president, it's his chief economic advisers, both formal
and informal; the House of Representatives; the Senate—the mainstream.
The mainstream is pushing for liberalization."[6] This player, Gloria
Macapagal Arroyo, would herself become president in 2001.

Ramos and his allies in government, business, and the academe were
all impatient with getting the Philippines out of the rut and joining the
ranks of the vaunted "Asian tigers." As noted in the introduction, however, their view of how their neighbors achieved success was filtered
through their neoclassical ideological prism. Against much evidence, they
saw the high growth rates of the East Asian and Southeast Asian economies as products of free-market policies instead of strategic state interventions in the market. Typical of this selective interpretation of the
Asian miracle was the comment of Jesus Estanislao, Aquino's finance secretary and a Ramos supporter, who told an interviewer that except for
macroeconomic policy and activities like infrastructure development, the
state left "everything else" to the private sector in Indonesia, Thailand,
Singapore, and Malaysia.[7]

Ideology thus accounts for the speed with which initiatives aimed
at deregulating, liberalizing, and further privatizing the economy unfolded. Liberalization was seen to be an essential component of globalization, a process of global integration of production and markets that,
according to economic pundits—local and foreign—could only lead to
more all-around prosperity. With the state socialist regimes of Eastern
Europe and the Soviet Union having collapsed and the social-demo-
cratic, state-interventionist economy of Sweden in disarray, the ideology of liberalization seemed irrefutable. The prosperous state-assisted
capitalist regimes of East Asia were, of course, a living contradiction to
the neoliberal credo, but even there, technocrats paid profuse lip service
to free markets as a smokescreen intended to defuse US pressures on
them to open up their markets.

Two appointments exemplified the new ideological regime in the Philippines. University of the Philippines at Los Baños Professor Cielito Habito, a straight-arrow neoclassical economist, was appointed head of the National Economic Development Authority, where he promptly discouraged any semblance of planning in what was supposed to be the government's key planning agency. Habito was and continues to be a firm believer not just in trade liberalization but in unilateral trade liberalization, arguing "that Thailand and Indonesia continue to have higher average tariffs for certain products is irrelevant to our policy stance."[8] He also had distinctly elitist views when it came to understanding the economy, maintaining that "we can expect every serious candidate [for political office] to obtain economic advice from largely the same small pool of highly trained economists in the country. [Unlike lawyers, there really aren't all that many of us, believe it or not!]."[9]

Former World Bank staff member Roberto De Ocampo ended up with the position of secretary of finance, from which he declaimed on the virtues of foreign capital, trade liberalization, and capital account liberalization, to the applause of the World Bank-IMF, international business publications like *Euromoney*, which named him Finance Minister of the Year in 1996, and influential local lobbyists for transnational firms like Peter Wallace of the Economist Intelligence Unit.

Profitable government enterprises like the oil-refining and marketing firm Petron, considered the crown jewel of the state sector, were handed over to the private sector, though government continued as a minority shareholder.

The management of public services was privatized under "build, operate, and transfer" schemes in which projects were contracted out to the private sector with payment in the form of rights to manage the finished facility and to part of a stream of the expected future income it would generate.

In February 1997, what was until then the biggest water privatization project in the world took place when the Philippine government parcelled out the Metropolitan Waterworks and Sewerage System (MWSS) to two foreign-linked Filipino concessionaires, the Lopez group and the Ayala group.

The notorious power outages of the Aquino years became a thing of the past when the government brought in independent power producers (IPPs) to generate electricity. Little known then was the fact that to attract the IPPs at a time that the Philippines was seen as a high-risk area for investors, the market necessitated cost guarantees to the power producers that would later bankrupt the state-owned National Power Corporation and rebound against consumers in the form of skyrocketing electricity prices.[10]

Nationality restrictions on foreign investment were loosened considerably, with 100 percent foreign equity allowed in all but a few sectors on a short "negative list" and the government determined to open up even the retail trade sector—long a sacred cow—to foreign firms. A significant amendment to the foreign investment law occurred when Congress, prodded by the administration, passed Republic Act 8179, which deleted the so-called negative list C in the current foreign investment law, which had stipulated that foreign firms could not enter areas that were deemed "adequately served by domestic firms." This was a far more liberal foreign investment code than those of most of the Philippines' neighbors.

Trade liberalization was a central concern, and here the perspective of the administration was not only doctrinaire but extreme. Even in the absence of reciprocal moves by trading partners, liberalization was beneficial. Reflecting hardline free-market doctrine, one key policy paper put it this way: "the Philippines has vigorously supported global and plulilateral negotiations to reduce or eliminate barriers to trade and to foreign investment. The benefits of getting other countries to reduce barriers to trade are obvious: market access. But the Philippines has gone even further by liberalizing trade and investment of its own accord and ahead of other countries' commitments. These actions are indispensable, since they provide both home and foreign firms access to inputs… at prevailing world prices."[11]

Trade liberalization began way before Ramos came to power. Under the structural adjustment program of the World Bank and the IMF which began in the early '80s, the average tariff rate was brought down from 43 percent in 1980 to 28 percent in 1986 while quantitative restrictions were removed on more than 900 items between 1981 and 1985.[12]

After a brief interregnum, trade liberalization resumed with the issuance of Executive Order 413, when Jesus Estanislao, a prominent free marketeer, was finance secretary. This decree "rationalized" the Philippine tariff structure into four rates: 30 percent for finished products, 20 percent for intermediate inputs, 10 percent for raw materials, and 3 percent for capital equipment.[13]

But under Ramos's technocrats like Habito, unilateral liberalization took a great leap forward. Interestingly enough, the administration's economists used Chile as a model, going so far as to invite the finance minister of the Pinochet dictatorship, Rolf Luders, to speak before many Filipino audiences. In Chile, Luders and other radical free-marketeers had reduced tariffs across the board to 11 percent. Believing they could outperform the Chileans, the Filipino technocrats produced Executive Order 264, which would phase down duty rates to 3 percent for raw materials and 10 percent for finished products by 2003, and institute a uniform tariff of 5 percent on all goods, except "sensitive products," by 2004.[14]

Multilateralizing Liberalization

The administration also made sure to build external constraints that would, among other things, bind future governments to a liberal trade regime by entering a number of free-trade agreements.

The ASEAN (Association of Southeast Asian Nations) Free Trade Area (AFTA) was formed in 1992, the same year Ramos became president. Over the next few years, the administration became one of the ASEAN governments supporting speeding up liberalization commitments. The original AFTA agreement bound ASEAN members to reduce their tariffs to 0-5 percent over a fifteen-year period ending in 2008. This was accelerated to 2003, then 2002. The original six members also committed to a flat-zero tariff by 2010. Moreover, the Philippines agreed under Ramos to incorporate into the so-called Common Effective Preferential Tariff (CEPT) products such as unprocessed agricultural products.[15]

The Ramos administration took an even higher profile in promoting the Asia-Pacific Economic Cooperation (APEC). The Philippines lined up with Hong Kong and Singapore to support the US-Australia drive to create a trans-Pacific free trade area involving eighteen countries. With his slogan to make the Philippines a "NIC [newly industrializing country] by the year 2000," Ramos enthusiastically endorsed APEC's celebrated Bogor Declaration of 1994, which committed members to borderless or complete free trade by 2020. Indeed, Philippine technocrats saw themselves as playing a key role in championing free trade among neighbors that were dragging their feet when it came to opening up their economies. For instance, Estanislao, the Filipino representative to the "APEC Eminent Persons' Group," said the Philippines had to "bear the burden of APEC leadership by example."[16] Ramos himself said, "We must blaze the trail that others must follow."[17]

Pushing for a "national consensus," the administration held a number of national consultations that culminated in a National Preparatory Summit for APEC on December 10, 1995, which underlined that: "Trade and investment liberalization and facilitation must receive the highest priority. It should be the overriding concern to promote the Philippines as a location for production in the region, thus providing employment and income for our people. The APEC-wide commitment to open up regional markets in due course is an important step, but on our own and in concert with APEC partners, we must constantly find ways to improve the trade and investment regime in our country to make it comparable with the rest of the world."[18]

At the APEC Summit in Subic in November 1996 the Philippine government submitted an Individual Action Plan that rivaled, in its free-market spirit, those of Singapore and Hong Kong. In the document the Philippines promised to accelerate "its adoption and implementation of market-friendly reforms cognizant of the primacy of the private sector as the engine of growth with the government providing the proper policy environment. The deregulation of the domestic regime has been undertaken in tandem with privatization and liberalization initiatives." Then it revealed the scale of the government's ambitious free-market program:

> The Philippines has successfully privatized a number of government-owned-or-controlled corporations and returned to the private sector certain acquired assets. These include hotels, banks, an airline, a steel firm, mining companies, and a petroleum refinery. Scheduled for privatization are, among others, a fertilizer plant, a

smelting corporation, a power-generating and transmission corporation. This third wave covers social sectors such as health services and education and pension funds. Regulations governing
prices have been lifted except for petroleum products [targeted to
be eliminated soon], electricity rates, and transport fares.[19]

It was also under the Ramos administration that the Philippines
signed the General Agreement on Tariffs and Trade (GATT) Uruguay Round
Accord and entered the World Trade Organization (WTO), which came
into being in 1995. Government officials waged a dirty propaganda campaign for ratification, with anti-ratification advocates being painted as
advocating a North Korea-type isolation for the Philippines. Upon entering GATT-WTO, the Ramos administratrion immediately moved to
implement the withdrawal of quotas from key agricultural commodities,
and their replacement with tariffs, via Republic Act 8178—the Agricultural Tariffication Act—and aligned its customs valuation procedures in
accord with the WTO. It also immediately integrated 16 percent of the
total volume of the Philippines' textile and clothing imports, in accordance with the Agreement on Clothing and Textiles, despite cries of distress from local clothing and textile manufacturers. It committed itself in
the coming years to an ambitious agenda to "enact/repeal/amend legislation to align" with all the key WTO agreements, notably in the Trade-
Related Aspects of Intellectual Property Rights (TRIPS) Agreement,
wherein it promised comprehensive legislation on patents, trademarks, integrated circuits, and plant varieties, and with the Trade-Related Investment Measures (TRIMs) Agreement, wherein it promised to "phase out
local content/trade balancing requirements for soap and motor vehicle
industries."[20]

Together with financial liberalization, these measures elicited the
much-desired seal of approval from the IMF and allowed the Philippines to reenter world capital markets in the early 1990s. With the country
starved of capital in the years of draconian structural adjustment in the
1980s, the aim of the Filipino financial managers was to attract significant amounts of foreign capital to drive a high level of gross domestic
product (GDP) growth that would allow the Philippines to join the
ranks of the "tigers" and "become a NIC by the year 2000," as the
administration's slogan put it.

Attracting Foreign Capital

Attracting foreign capital was the Ramos administration's top priority. Thus, while it saw trade liberalization as important in the long run in the sense of making the Philippine economy more efficient, it saw capital account and financial liberalization as the key to growth in the short term.

To make up for the Philippines having been skirted by region-wide boom induced by Japanese capital in the late '80s and early '90s, Ramos's technocrats were on the lookout for foreign capital flows that could come in significant quantities and do for the Philippines what Japanese direct investment had done for its neighbors in the late 1980s.

As noted earlier, between 1985 and 1990, some $15 billion worth of Japanese direct investment flowed into Southeast Asia—a direct result of the landmark Plaza Accord of 1985, in which the US pressured Japan to drastically raise the value of the yen relative to the dollar in order to relieve the US trade deficit.[21] With production in Japan rendered uncompetitive by the new exchange rate, the big Japanese conglomerates or *keiretsu* relocated many of their assembly plants to China, Thailand, Malaysia, and Indonesia to take advantage of cheap labor in these areas, sparking a ten-year boom that lifted these countries from underdevelopment. Depressed by the Aquino policy of prioritizing foreign-debt service over development, the Philippines was skirted by Japanese capital.

Between 1985 and 1990, the Philippines received only $748 million in Japanese direct investment while Indonesia received $3.1 billion, Malaysia $2.2 billion, and Thailand $3.7 billion.[22] While Japanese investment was not, of course, the only factor in the dizzying growth of the Philippines' neighbors, it undeniably played a key role in explaining the difference between the Philippines' miserable 1.4 percent of GDP average growth in the period 1980-1993 and Thailand's 8.2 percent, Indonesia's 5.8 percent, and Malaysia's 6.2 percent.

By the early 1990s Japanese direct investment in Southeast Asia was tapering off, prompting Filipino technocrats to look elsewhere. Not surprisingly, officials like Gabriel Singson, Bangko Sentral ng Pilipinas (BSP) governor, and Finance Minister Roberto De Ocampo set their sights on the vast amounts of personal savings, pension funds, government funds, and corporate savings that were deposited in mutual funds, hedge funds, and other investment mechanisms that were designed to maximize their value. These funds were often placed under the management of big international banks or investment houses and they were played as portfolio investments by fund managers experienced in spotting investment opportunities that combined high yields with a quick turnaround time. In the early 1990s, an Asian Development Bank report noted that, "the declining returns in the stock markets of industrial countries and the low real interest rates compelled investors to seek higher returns on their capital elsewhere."[23]

But just like Japanese capital in the late 1980s, these funds were not simply going to walk in. They had to be invited in by creating the appropriate policy environment. To do this, the Filipinos looked at the strategies of other financial managers in Southeast Asia that had begun to successfully attract northern finance capital. And here, the Thais, who in the early 1990s were seeking alternative sources of foreign investment, seemed to provide a good role model. Ironically—and, as events would later show, tragically—the one place where the Filipinos borrowed heavily from their neighbors' experience was not in those areas where state intervention and regulation was prominent but in that area where significant liberalization had occurred: the capital account and the financial sector.

Borrowing the Thai Formula

To attract portfolio investment and massive credit flows from the international banks, the Thais had evolved a strategy with essentially three key elements: capital account and financial liberalization, maintenance of significant differentials in interest rates in Bangkok and northern money centers to suck in foreign speculative capital, and "pegging" of the local currency to the dollar at a stable rate to ensure foreign investors against foreign-exchange risk. The formula had the blessings of the IMF and the hearty endorsement of speculative investors, who were not slow to spot the fact that it essentially eliminated all risks to foreign investors.[24]

To Manila technocrats, the Thais' great success in attracting portfolio investment was the best proof of the correctness of their policies, and they proceeded to replicate the Thai experience.

In the area of financial liberalization, the government moved to create one of the most foreign capital-friendly systems in the region. The capital account was almost fully liberalized, with most foreign-exchange restrictions lifted, making the peso virtually fully convertible; it also made possible full and immediate repatriation of profits, dividends and capital, and the free utilization of foreign-currency accounts. Significant liberalization was also imposed on the financial sector. After being closed for fifty years, the insurance sector was opened up to 100 percent-foreign-owned companies in 1994. Especially critical in facilitating capital flows was the liberalization of the banking system by Republic Act 7721, which opened up the banking system to foreign banks, resulting in twelve of them setting up operations by September 1996.

Like the Bank of Thailand, the policy of the Bangko Sentral ng Pilipinas was to keep local interest rates high—some 12 percent to 15 percent—in order to suck in foreign capital. Prime lending rates in the Philippines in the early 1990s were kept about six percentage points above US rates, on average.[25] This policy transformed the view of high interest rates in financial circles; as one analyst has written, "[b]eing endowed with high interest rates turned out to be a 'virtue' that attracted external capital whereas it was once nothing but a brake upon economic activity as it served as a barrier for businesses to acquire capital."[26]

And like the Thai government, the Ramos administration pegged the peso to the dollar at a stable rate of exchange, so that in the whole of 1996, for instance, there was only a 2 percent fluctuation in the peso-dollar rate. The consequent inflow of dollars caused the peso to appreciate relative to the dollar, and the BSP intervened in the foreign exchange by buying or selling dollars to keep the peso within a certain band.

Finance Capital's Vote of Confidence

The country reentered the international bond market in 1993 and successfully floated about $1.3 billion that first year.[27] Portfolio investors were attracted to Philippine treasury bills and their relatively high yields. Foreign-exchange liberalization also drew them to the reorganized Philippine Stock Exchange (PSE), where publicly listed local firms sought to sell equities as a means of raising capital. In 1993, the first year of the Ramos presidency, the stock market price index in the PSE rose by 154 percent—the highest among all major stock exchanges in Asia and the third-best in the world.[28]

The Philippines was on the way to becoming a darling of foreign portfolio investors, a feat that was partly a function of image and contacts: Ramos projected the image of being a leader sold on foreign capital; Singson came across as a no-nonsense financial technocrat; a former high-level World Bank staff member, the cosmopolitan De Ocampo was trusted in New York and Washington.

Between 1993 and 1997, some $19.4 billion worth of net portfolio investment flowed into the country.[29] These flows dwarfed the foreign direct investment inflows, with estimates of their size ranging from 70 to 90 percent of total investment annually between 1994 and 1997.[30] US funds were a major player here, a situation indicated by the fact that while the US was the leading source of total foreign investment (33 percent), it was way behind in terms of direct investment, accounting for only 6 percent of the total.[31]

Foreign capital also flowed in in the form of dollar-denominated credits extended by local and foreign banks. A great portion of these funds were loans contracted abroad by local banks then re-lent to local firms—the so-called carry trade. Contracted at relatively low interest rates, these funds were re-lent via an innovative mechanism—the FCDU, or foreign currency deposit unit, a facility dating back to the Marcos era. The FCDU exempted its holder from government rules for domestic onshore lenders such as reserve requirements, the 5 percent gross receipts tax, and the 20 percent withholding tax on resident earnings. Not surprisingly, they became a favorite facility for relending to local borrowers. With the wide spread—some 600 basis points—between US interest rates and interest rates on peso loans in the local markets—local banks could borrow abroad and still make a clean profit relending to local customers at lower rates than those charged to peso loans. In 1996 the average interest rate for FCDU loans came to 7.41 percent compared to 12.8 percent for peso loans.[32]

Financial liberalization brought more foreign banks into the local scene by late 1993 and brought about a greater competition for customers. Attracted to the FCDU for the same reason as local banks, the newcomers also channeled much of their lending to local firms via this facility.[33] This translated into a rapid buildup in FCDU deposits and loans in the years before the crisis, with deposits amounting to $14.4 billion by the end of 1996 and loans coming to $9 billion, according to BSP data.[34] In 1996 alone, new foreign currency loans totalled $4.9 billion.[35] Other estimates showed an even sharper increase, with the investment analyst Deutsche Morgan Grenfell (DMG) asserting that dollar loans had risen to $11.6 billion as of March 1997—or almost five times the level of $2 billion in December 1993.[36]

In other words, the FCDU facility played the same role as the famous—or, in current view, notorious—Bangkok International Banking Facility: serving as an offshore platform to provide cheap dollar loans to domestic customers. As an HG Asia study put it, with the exchange rate "padlocked" for two years at Php 26.2 to Php 26.3 to the dollar, "[t]hey are not fools in Manila. They were offered US dollars at 600 basis points cheaper than the peso rates along with currency protection from the BSP. They took it."[37]

Overheating and Overbuilding

For the most part, this inflow of foreign investment and foreign capital was hailed as a vote of confidence in the management of the "new Philippine economy." By late 1996, however, fund managers began to cast worried looks as the Philippines banks' net foreign liability reached close to $14.6 billion or close to 35 percent of the Philippines' foreign debt of $42 billion. The private debt was equivalent to 13 percent of gross national product (GNP) and rising—a position which bore comparison with that of their models, the Thai banks, whose net foreign liability position at the end of 1996 was equivalent to 20 percent of GNP.[38] This picture led one investment analyst to warn:

> The Philippines has not yet had to pay its reckoning for copying Thai practices. It adopted them much later than Thailand. But its reckoning is likely to come earlier than Thailand's. The BSP does not have the resources of the Bank of Thailand and the game is heating up faster than it did in the early stages in Thailand.[39]

The volatile role of speculative capital in the Philippines mirrored its potentially destabilizing dynamics in the region as a whole. As one analyst puts it:

> The mismatch between maturity of assets and liabilities of commercial banks increased dramatically during the 1990s as banks, making use of the greater access to global financial markets, borrowed short-term capital in foreign markets and lent to long-term infrastructure projects and the real-estate sector in the domestic economy.
>
> In many cases the banks also suffered from a currency mismatch of their assets and liabilities. The assets were domestic-currency denominated while the liabilities were accumulated in foreign currency to take advantage of the lower interest rates in foreign markets with the assumption that the exchange rate would remain unchanged.
>
> In other cases, the banks tried to hedge against the exchange-rate risk by lending to borrowers in foreign currency and passing on the exchange risk to the borrower. However, when the currency depreciated sharply, these borrowers' incomes were in domestic currency and the exchange risk became a credit risk.[40]

What was clear on hindsight was not, however, evident in the glory days of the mid-1990s.

The Philippine banks had gone on a borrowing spree, but this would not have been that worrisome had the money gone to the right places. Unfortunately, much of the lending of banks went not to the really productive sectors of the economy but into the speculative areas, like the financing of consumption and property development. According to Mario Lamberte and Josef Yap, "the stock market price index of the property sector rose by 200 percent during the 1992-96 period, higher than the 150 percent increase of the overall stock market price index for the same period."[41] The banks' eagerness to lend fueled a construction boom, with construction companies undertaking countless projects in anticipation of bigger demand for both residential and office space. In 1997, the aggregate earnings of the top construction companies expanded over 46 percent to reach Php 55.8 billion, and the total money spent for all construction activities climbed up to Php 104.4 billion.[42]

But a clear indication of lending going to the wrong sectors was that while construction has been booming, industrial growth dropped from a 17 percent annual rate in mid-1996 to -2.3 percent in mid-1997.[43] Manufacturing and agriculture were not as attractive sectors to lend to because they would demand strategic commitments of large chunks of capital that would only bear fruit in terms of decent returns over the medium and long term. Moreover, their future was uncertain since the radical liberalization of trade and investment that paralleled financial liberalization was making production less and less profitable for domestic producers. Duty-free shops were flooding the country with cheap imported manufactures, and cheap rice and corn imports were coming in volumes that far outstripped the minimum access volumes committed by the country under the GATT-WTO Agreement. Indeed, with the prospects for profit making being much brighter in real estate, it is not surprising that many manufacturers were making dollar loans not for reinvestment or for research and development, but to play the stock market and the property market.

Balanced development was another victim of the process, for, as Joseph Lim, among others, has pointed out, with growth being driven "by non-tradables [real estate, megamalls] and asset bubbles," growth concentrated "in a limited number of centers at the expense of other regions, particularly the rural areas," aggravating regional disparities and not contributing to "alleviating poverty in rural areas."[44]

In any event, in the wake of the much-publicized real estate problems in Bangkok and the suspected high exposure of Philippine banks to the real-estate sector, rumors about the imminent collapse of a highly indebted developer, Megaworld early in 1997 forced people to look more closely at the Philippine real-estate sector. The result was a consensus that a glut would emerge in 1998, though analysis differed on how big it would be. All Asia, a local investment house, predicted that owing to overbuilding, by the year 2000, supply of high-rise residential units would exceed demand by 211 percent, while supply of commercial developments would outpace demand by 142 percent.[45] Fears of a coming glut were so widespread that the property index of the PSE fell by

40 percent on fears that developers would be saddled with unsold condominiums.[46]

Overbuilding was forcing developers, according to one account, to "become creative in search of new markets." More and more companies, it noted, apparently without irony, "are spending billions of pesos to develop resorts, golf courses, and other special projects."[47]

Stats Wars

To calm worries about bank exposure in the real-estate sector, the BSP, in June 1997, declared that no more than 20 percent of the total exposure of commercial banks should be in property loans. But as a DMG study found, this tightening, which paralleled similar moves by other Asian central banks, was "probably too late."[48] The BSP announced that lending to the property sector in mid-1996 amounted to only 9.2 percent of the exposure of banks, going up to about 11 percent by December.[49] BSP officials in that same survey admitted, however, that the property loan exposures of individual banks ranged from "negligible" to as high as 28.6 percent.[50]

Under pressure from a skeptical public, De Ocampo upped the figure of the banks' real estate-related exposure to 14 percent in September 1997.[51] But even this figure was considered low by foreign analysts, some of whom saw the real exposure of the banks at 15 to 25 percent.[52] These analysts felt that the higher estimate would take into account property-related loans that could be classified under other categories such as services, hotel, construction, and even manufacturing.

The huge capital inflows and the banks' real-estate exposure did begin to worry BSP officials, but this was at a rather late stage in the game. In May 1997 one BSP official warned that funds could be easily moved globally "at the tap of a finger" and the possibility of facing "abrupt reversals of capital flow."[53] And it was only in early June, shortly before the July 11 de facto devaluation of the peso, that the BSP issued "preemptive measures... aimed at curbing the growth in foreign-currency lending."[54]

Foreign investors took much earlier notice of the massive debt buildup of local banks and the crisis of the real-estate sector, and they saw these in the context of serious structural flaws that were glossed over by the growth rates of 5.7 percent GDP per annum that the Philippines registered in 1996. For them, the two most sensitive indicators became the trade deficit and the current account deficit, which, among other things, indicate if a country would have the capability in the long-term to pay for its imports and service its foreign-debt obligations. The trade deficit in 1996 stood at $12.8 billion, or a doubling in just three years!

Traditional Philippine mainstays turned in a lackluster performance, with garment exports, for instance, falling by 27 percent in 1996, contributing to foreign investors' perception that despite its 24 percent export growth rate that year (owing mainly to import-intensive electronics and machinery exports), the Philippines was facing the same difficulties of declining export capacity as Malaysia and Thailand, which registered no export growth, and Indonesia, which registered only 7 percent.

The slowdown in the growth of traditional exports was related to the very policies that had encouraged foreign capital inflows. Pegged to the dollar to assure foreign investors, the peso, like the Thai baht, became overvalued as the US Treasury went on reverse course, and allowed the value of the dollar to rise relative to the yen to stimulate the Japanese economy out of recession in the mid-1990s. This translated into decreased competitiveness for Philippine exports and increased imports of items whose prices were rendered artificially low by the peg.[55] This led to increasing conflict between two schools of free-marketeers: the BSP lobby, which favored foreign-capital inflows by keeping the peso strong, and the University of the Philippines School of Economics, which wanted a devalued peso to promote Philippine exports.[56] This conflict did not, however, preclude their broader consensus around rapid liberalization of trade and investment, accelerated deregulation, and continuing privatization of government enterprises.

In any event, to many foreign direct investors in the Philippines and other parts of the region, the export slowdown indicated not a temporary blip but the ending of the export-led "Southeast Asian Miracle," and dampened their enthusiasm to commit new funds. Many began, in fact, to consider shifting their investments to China, whose low wage-based export machine was going into high gear, displacing costlier

Southeast Asian exports in many key markets, including that of the United States.

But not to worry, said Philippine government analysts, and please do not compare us to our neighbors. For instance, they claimed that the country's current account balance, which brought to bear on the positive side of the ledger the remittances from the Philippines' vast army of overseas workers, was manageable; and the current account was, more than the trade deficit, what foreign investors, analysts, and speculators allegedly looked at in assessing the strength of the peso. But even if one were to grant this argument, things looked shaky. In 1996, according to estimates based on official figures, the current account deficit of $3.5 billion stood at 4 percent of GNP. Worrisome but not alarming, said some.

However, when one tightened up the methodology for calculating the figure to account for unexplained errors and omissions in the balance of payments (which now added up to almost 6 percent of GNP), as one prescient investment house study did, one came up with realization that the real current account deficit was around 7 percent of GNP for 1996—or uncomfortably close to the 8 percent deficit experienced by Mexico and Thailand before their economic meltdowns began. With a deficit that size, investors speculated, the pressure would increase on the Philippine financial authorities to close the deficit by devaluing the currency, a move that would allow the country's exports to remain competitive.

Uneasiness on the part of foreign investors over the possibility of a peso devaluation and the parallels between Thailand and the Philippines led them by the beginning of 1997 to significantly scale down their commitments, with foreign equity inflows to banks dropping by 97 percent in the first quarter of the year relative to the first quarter of 1996. With the jitters over property, a possible devaluation, and the massive private debt buildup, the stock market began its downward plunge—not surprising since 70 percent of the trading activity was accounted for by foreign investors.[57] Indeed, instead of being parked in peso-denominated paper, awaiting new opportunities in the domestic market, foreign investors began to demand dollars for their pesos and move out, adding pressure for the depreciation of the peso.

The Panic of 1997

It was this escalating exit of foreign investment in response to the strong possibility of a devaluation that would reduce the value of their peso holdings which attracted the attention of currency speculators looking for opportunities to cash in on large-scale foreign capital movements through the well-timed sale and purchase of dollars and pesos. In June and early July, the BSP worked mightily to contain the stampede of foreign investors to change their pesos to dollars and leave. It intervened in the foreign exchange market to maintain the peso at roughly Php 26.25 to the dollar, but, after spending almost $1.6 billion of its $11.3 billion reserves, it gave up the fight and let the peso float freely against the dollar. The unequal battle against speculative capital was underlined by the fact that accumulated non-resident portfolio investment came to over $5 billion in 1991-96 (see Table 1). When this mass began to move in panic, there was little that the government, with its relatively small $11.3 billion, could do to counteract it.

Table 3.1 Foreign Exchange flows, 1990-1997 (in US$ million)

	1990	1991	1992	1993	1994	1995	1996	1997
Trade balance	-4020	-3211	-4695	-6222	-7850	-8944	-11342	-10708
Current Account	-2567	-869	-858	-3016	-2950	-3297	-3914	-4303
Short-term capital (net)	19	349	660	-148	1002	-56	540	495
MLT loans (net)	674	835	633	2455	1313	1276	2690	4688
FDI (net)	528	529	675	864	1289	1361	1338	1117
Portfolio (net)	-56	125	62	-52	269	248	1170	-461
Nonresidents Portfolio investment (net)	-52	125	155	897	901	1485	2101	-55

Source: Mario Lamberte and Josef Yap, "Economic Policies and Measures in Response to the Asian Financial Crisis," *Economic Crisis...Once More*, ed. Mario Lamberte (Makati: Philippine Institute for Development Studies, 2001), 267.

What the authorities were up against was contagion, and in the context of a region whose governments had not put in place capital controls for fear that these would discourage capital from entering the country, the result was capital fleeing much more quickly than it came in. Since portfolio investors perceived the Philippines as part of the same region as Thailand, Indonesia, and Malaysia, they reacted to each country the same way—through panicky withdrawal. As Jeffrey Winters graphically described it:

> Suddenly, you receive disturbing news that Thailand is in serious trouble, and you must immediately decide what to do with your Malaysian investments. It is in this moment that the escape psychology and syndrome begins. First, you immediately wonder if the disturbing new information leaking out about Thailand applies to Malaysia as well. You think it does not, but you are not sure. Second, you must instantly begin to think strategically about how other EMFMs [emerging market fund managers] and independent investors are going to react, and of course they are thinking simultaneously about how you are going to react. And third, you are fully aware, as are all the other managers, that the first ones to sell as a market turns negative will be hurt the least, and the ones in the middle and at the end will end the most value for their portfolio—and likely to be fired from their position as EMFM as well. In a situation of low systemic transparency, the sensible reaction will be to sell and escape. Notice that even if you use your good connections in the Malaysian government and business community to try to receive highly reliable information the country is healthy and does not suffer from the same problems as Thailand, you will still sell and escape. Why? Because you cannot ignore the likely behavior of all the other investors. And since they do not have access to the reliable information you have, there is a high probability that their uncertainty will lead them to choose escape. If you hesitate while they rush to sell their shares, the market will drop rapidly, and the value of your portfolio will start to evaporate before your eyes.[58]

A net reversal of capital flows from the East Asian region occurred, with the commonly cited estimate of $100 billion.[59] From Southeast Asia, at the height of the crisis, some $32 billion fled, with $4.6 billion from the Philippines.[60]

To stem the outflow of dollars, the BSP, at the advice of the IMF, moved to raise local interest rates to stabilize the peso and continue to make investment in the country attractive to foreign investors. Interest rates doubled, from 15 percent to about 30 percent, but capital continued to flow out. The expected fall to Php 29:$1 was rapidly breached, and exporters, who had initially felt that devaluation would serve their interests, started to get worried as it pushed past the Php 30:$1 mark since this could significantly raise the value of their imported inputs that would more than wipe out any gains from the devaluation.

The impact on the local economy of the expected inflation owing to higher peso import prices, higher interest rates, and the sudden rise in the peso cost of servicing dollar obligations by local borrowers was expected to lead to an economic downturn and a string of bankruptcies, but Philippine officials continued to characterize the crisis as an external event, "a storm passing through," as De Ocampo put it.[61] Manila's "economic fundamentals" were sound, in contrast to Bangkok's, and investors would see that.

But the IMF was unconvinced, and in its Capital Markets Report released during the IMF-World Bank Annual Conference in Hong Kong in the third week of September 1997, IMF said that "commercial banks in the Philippines have a high exposure in the property sector."[62] The big credit-rating agencies concurred, with Standard and Poor's Corporation downgrading its outlook for the Philippine economy from "positive" to "stable" and warning that "aggressive" lending by banks "has exposed the banking system to potential asset-quality problems."[63] It estimated the total exposure of Philippine banks to the real-estate sector at 20 percent.[64] And, with the onset of the currency crisis, the "asset quality" problems of loans to this sector had most likely intensified. It seemed only a matter of time before such heavily indebted firms would surface in newspaper reports.

Rumors began to circulate in Manila that the creditworthiness of a number of banks had been damaged by loans to the real-estate sector, including Westmont Bank, Banco de Oro, Traders Royal Bank, Urban Bank, China Banking Corporation, and International Exchange Bank. To quell the rumors and avoid a bank run, the BSP director threatened to unleash the National Bureau of Investigation on people making those claims. But the threat dissipated when a member of the Monetary Board that governs BSP policies admitted that five banks had indeed overshot the government-imposed cap on real-estate loans to 20 percent of the banks' total exposure.[65] Moreover, threats could not conceal the surfacing of a succession of victims of the weaker peso and higher interest rates seeking government protection from their creditors. Among them were Vitarich, a major food processor, the big milling company Victorias Milling Company, and the EYCO Group of Companies, which had started as an appliance maker but diversified into real estate with dollar-denominated loans as well as peso loans from twenty-two banks. More key companies fell as the year wore on.

Meanwhile, the peso plunged by some 52 percent relative to the dollar in six months. By January 1998, the value of the local currency was down to Php 44:$1—a figure unimaginable just a few months earlier—prompting importers and local industrialists to call for currency controls. At this point, it could no longer be concealed that the Ramos administration had no other strategy for dealing with the crisis than to keep interest rates high to discourage an outflow of capital and stabilize the peso. These rates, which went from 15 percent prior to the crisis to as high as 30 percent by January 1998, were killing local business, while allowing the banks and whatever foreign capital remained in the country to make a killing.

More proactive measures were precluded by the Ramos administration's laissez-faire ideology, which held that the best way to manage an economy was not to try to manage it at all. What came to substitute for policy was the slogan, constantly repeated, that the Philippines was not hit as badly as its neighbors because of the "better economic fundamentals" the Ramos policies had given it. As a number of commentators rightly saw it, the administration continued in a "denial mode."

Instead of innovating on economic policy when things began to really look desperate in early 1998, the Ramos administration ran to the IMF, entering into an agreement to access a $1.37 billion standby facility as part of a "precautionary" arrangement. Not only did the move contradict the administration's much-vaunted claim that after thirty-six years, the Philippines was exiting the IMF. It also bound the administration to a regime of high interest rates, the achievement of fiscal surpluses, and continuing of the liberalization of the capital account.

This formula, however, was increasingly dubious: The liberalization of the capital account had, of course, been pinpointed as the major culprit in the Asian crisis, having facilitated the easy entry and exit of massive amounts of hot capital. And high interest rates and the prohibition against running a budget deficit—which the Ramos technocrats proceeded to implement by decreeing a cutback in nonpersonnel expenditures of government agencies by 25 percent—were guaranteed to put a damper on any recovery. Worse, it would worsen the long-term structural problems of the country, including the massive poverty which, at the end of his term, still engulfed over 32 percent of Filipinos.[66]

Indeed the IMF, in a mid-1999 paper, issued what amounted to a mea culpa, saying that in the East Asian countries it advised during the crisis, "the thrust of fiscal policy... turned out to be substantially different... because the original assumptions for economic growth, capital flows, and exchange rates... were proved drastically wrong."[67] This was, however, dubious wisdom gained from a disaster in which the institution had itself played an instrumental role in foisting on the region.

Aftermath

The Philippines never really recovered from the Asian financial crisis. GDP growth in 1998 was a -0.6, while the average for the period 1998-2000 was 2.2 percent, compared to 6.4 percent in 1995-1997.[68] Industry, which grew by an average of 6.4 percent in 1995-1997 grew on average by a lackluster 0.8 percent in 1998-2000.[69]

Though the country did not suffer the dramatic plunge of over one million Thais and 21 million Indonesians to below the poverty line,[70] the negative impact of the crisis on living standards was serious and prolonged. The United Nations Development Programme (UNDP) Human Development Report identified the East Asian financial crisis as one of the two main factors contributing to the resurgence of poverty at the beginning of the millennium, the other being the El Niño weather phenomenon.[71] The percentage of Filipinos living below the poverty line rose from 31.8 percent in 1997 to 33.7 percent in 2003, according to the National Statistical Coordination Board.[72] This translated to

26.5 million Filipinos out of 79 million, or 4.5 million families, living in poverty.[73]

For four years, the property sector, greatly dependent on bank lending, was dead in the water. Typical were the travails of Fil-Estate, perhaps the most successful property developer, whose annual revenues hit more than Php 8 billion in the precrisis period. As one account described it:

> When the bubble burst in 1997, Fil-Estate was one of the hardest hit. "Now, there are even days when we don't have a single sale," laments the marketing executive. In 2000, sales of real-estate, golf club and resort shares reached only Php 757 million, a steep 90 percent decline from their peak. A big chunk of revenues comes from golf club and resort shares, which are tied to a robust economy.
>
> The property glut also exposed the consequences of over-aggressive landbanking. At one time, the company accumulated up to 6,300 hectares for development. Funding these with debt led to its current financial woes.
>
> Fil-Estate is now in the thick of paying off its debts—estimated at Php 3 to Php 5 billion—with assets. The figure excludes payables to suppliers, contractors, and other creditors, amounting to Php 3.4 billion in 2000. With the drastic slowdown in real estate and club shares, the company has not been liquid enough to meet even its already restructured borrowings.[74]

Given the collapse of the housing market, the construction industry suffered collateral damage. Overall spending for construction, one of the most active sectors of the economy, went from Php 104.4 billion in 1997 to Php 98.8 billion in 1998 to Php 94.9 in 2000 to Php 95.3 billion in 2001.[75] At the height of the crisis, it is estimated that about 200 building projects were suspended.[76]

While real estate and construction had been the preferred recipients of cheap loans, industry and manufacturing had also borrowed heavily and thus got caught in the scissors of diminished revenues owing to recession and the skyrocketing costs of servicing dollar-denominated debts. With their profit margins already threatened or eliminated by foreign competition owing to the unilateral trade liberalization prior to the Asian financial crisis, many local industrial and manufacturing firms were pushed over the edge by the crisis. Between 1997 and mid-2000, seventy-seven companies filed for suspension of payments with the Securities and Exchange Commission. These included such key enterprises as Philippine Airlines, Victorias Milling Co. Inc., Gold-Richwell Development Corporation, Hanmen Industries Corp. Inc., Uniwide Group of Companies, ASB Group of Companies, Serg's Products Inc., Plast-Print Industries Inc., CDC Basic Packaging Industries Inc., Urbancorp Investment Inc., EYCO Group of Companies, Catmon Sales Int. Corp., Blossom Furnicraft Co., Standford Resources and Development Corporation, and National Steel Corporation.

While some managed to somehow survive, others were simply liquidated, with negative spinoffs on the rest of the economy. The country's prime steel producer, National Steel Corporation, found itself Php 16 billion in debt, forcing it to close in 1999, throwing hundreds of workers in Iligan City and nearby towns in Lanao del Norte out of work.[77]

The crisis led to the complete foreign takeover of a key sector of the construction industry—the cement industry. Caught off guard with exploding dollar-denominated debts as a result of the crisis, the industry had nowhere else to go but into partnerships with cash-rich foreign firms that had been knocking on the door for some time. As the representative of one of the firms put it, "Many of the local companies had dollar debts, contracting markets, falling prices and very big cash outflows and no apparent way to recover [from] the situation, apart from inviting some of the foreign groups to come in and become partners."[78]

The French giant Lafarge gained control of Republic Cement, Fortune Cement, Iligan Cement Corporation, Mindanao Portland Cement, Continental Operating Corporation, Rizal, and Lloyds Richfield Industrial Corporation. Swiss-based Holcim gained control of Alsons Cement Corporation and Union Cement Corporation. Mexico-based Cemex gained control of Rizal Cement Company and APO Cement Corporation in Cebu.[79]

Other capital-intensive industries may not have been taken over by foreign interests or driven out of business, but most continue to languish under conditions of high debt and postcrisis stagnation. The debt-burdened petrochemical sector, for instance, continues to operate "below capacity because the economy has not yet fully stabilized since the 1997-98 Asian crisis!"[80]

One of the high-profile casualties of the financial crisis was Maynilad, the joint venture between Benpres, the Lopez group, and the French groups Ondeo Services Limited and Lyonanaise Asia Water Ltd. The Lopez group—which won the bid to manage the western portion of the old government water service, the MWSS—had contracted billions of dollars in unhedged credit prior to 1997. Among its creditors were Credit Agricole Indosuez, which lent it $26 million; Citibank, NA; Barclays Bank PLC; Paribas; and a number of other foreign banks that provided some $100 million in bridge financing.[81] With debt-servicing costs skyrocketing after July 1997, Maynilad was practically rendered unviable. The enterprise limped on a few more years, until late 2002, when the Lopez group unilaterally terminated the contract with the government, a decision that was later ruled "baseless" by a Paris-based arbitration panel.[82]

All key dimensions of the economy suffered, including the government's fiscal capacity. Industry's lurching into a long-term recession impacted on the government's ability to raise revenue from taxes, the take from which is greatly dependent on the economy's rate of growth. The revenue to GDP ratio declined from 19 percent in 1997 to 17 percent in 1998, 16 percent in 1999, and 15 percent in 2000.[83] One can say that the record-breaking deficit in the government budget in the presidency of Gloria Macapagal Arroyo was partly a consequence of the crisis.

It was, however, the crisis of the banking sector, which in a capitalist economy intermediates between savers and investors, that had the greatest impact on the economy. In the immediate aftermath of the crisis, it was thought that the Philippine financial sector had performed relatively well compared to its neighbors. True, there were some high-profile cases involving closures, forced holidays or government intervention: Union Bank, UCPB Savings Bank, Asia Trust Development Bank, Orient Bank, Monte de Piedad, Prime Bank, and Urban Bank. Bank closures in 1997 and 1998, however, were relatively few: fourteen in 1997 (one thrift bank and thirteen rural banks) and twenty-two in 1998 (one commercial bank, six thrift banks, and fifteen rural banks).[84]

The conventional wisdom then was expressed by one economist: "[M]ost observers as well as government authorities themselves are in agreement that the Philippine banking system managed to survive the Asian financial crisis relatively unscathed and that there is no banking crisis in the Philippines."[85] While the level of nonperforming loans (NPLs) hit double digits by the end of 1997, NPLs in the Philippines came to only 4.7 percent of outstanding loans. Even in June 1998, a worsening trend in the Philippines was overshadowed by worse conditions elsewhere in the region: a Deutsche Bank estimate showed the level of NPLs at 10 percent of outstanding loans of the commercial banking sector, compared to 60 percent in Indonesia, 25 percent in Korea, 17 percent in Malaysia, and 35 percent in Thailand.[86]

By the third quarter of 1999, however, NPLs were up to 14.4 percent. By October 2001, the NPLs hit 18.8 percent. The worst was yet to come, according to a study by Salomon Barney Smith, which predicted that the NPL ratio would hit 21 percent in the third quarter of 2002.[87] In fact, the situation was worrisome. As one report in *Business World* put it: "Industry figures show that the sector's NPAs [nonperforming assets]—a combination of NPLs, restructured loans, and foreclosed assets—have reached Php 438.7 billion, or about 31 percent of its total loan portfolio. The industry's total capital base is only Php 334.64 billion by comparison."[88] Indeed, some estimates saw distressed assets as rising to almost 40 percent of the banks' loan portfolio.[89] A key factor worsening the situation—and one that, some analysts felt, underestimated the real condition of banks—was the declining value of the ROPOA ("real and other properties owned and acquired"). These were foreclosed properties previously offered as collateral but whose value continued to decline with respect to the original value of the loan.

By October 2002, while the Philippines NPL ratio was 18.1 percent, that of its neighbors had improved considerably, with Indonesia at 11.8 percent, Thailand at 10.2 percent, Malaysia at 10 percent, and Korea at 2.9 percent.[90] Nonperforming assets came to Php 600 billion, Php 275 billion of which were foreclosed assets and the rest overdue loans.[91] By the second quarter of 2003, banks' NPAs still stood at 30 percent, or almost one-third of the banking system's total portfolio. NPLs were officially recorded to have declined from 18 percent in October 2002 to 15 percent in the second quarter of 2003, but this was largely an illusion "since it did not arise from higher credit draw-downs nor the settlement of nonperforming accounts but [from] a more lenient definition of NPLs" by banking authorities.[92]

The cost to the economy was high. Total lending dropped from Php 1.4 trillion to Php 1.39 trillion from 2000 to 2001, with lending to manufacturing dropping by 1.8 percent, mining by 6.6 percent, and construction by 10.6 percent.[93] The decline continued in 2002, with total loans going down to Php 1.37 trillion in June.[94] With its NPAs rising, lending to the private sector became very unattractive, pushing banks to make their profits lending to government by purchasing rela-tively risk-free government bonds at attractive interest rates. Through-out 1998-2000, the banks were a formidable lobby keeping the ninety-one-day Treasury Bill interest rate relatively high. In 2001, however, strong political and industry pressure forced the BSP to lower its bench-mark overnight rates and the National Treasury to lower its T-bill inter-est rates. This failed, however, to get the banks to lend to industry, with high double-digit interest rates continuing to prevail in private-sector lending. BSP figures showed that from a record of 53 percent in 1997, loan growth actually reversed in 2001, registering -0.2 percent.[95] Mean-time, profitability—or return to equity—fell sharply to 3.4 percent in 2001, from a peak of 17 percent in 1995.[96]

Worry turned into alarm in 2002. It was no longer a case of the NPLs throttling economic recovery. Unless something decisive was done, the banking system could collapse. As one report underlined, "At a little less than Php 500 billion, the pool of distressed assets has even exceeded the banking sector's total capital base of Php 389 billion, putting to risk its ability to withstand further shocks to the system."[97]

As the crisis developed, financial authorities looked with envy at Thailand, Korea, and Indonesia, whose governments have set up asset-management corporations (AMCs) to buy up bad loans at a discount from the banks, enabling them to improve their financial profile. Mov-ing the economy again, said Rafael Buenaventura, BSP chief, was "why

Malaysia, Thailand, and Korea were even willing to spend their own money—government money—to clean up the banking system."[98] But with no government funds available for this, the idea was to rely on foreign firms to set up AMCs or, as they came to be known, SPAVs, or special purpose asset vehicles.

Not surprisingly, the banks were interested, with some going ahead to contact foreign financial firms like Lehman Brothers and Rabobank to set up SPAVs. The catch was that the banks wanted both to sell their bad assets at a discount and also share in the profits of the sale by becoming part owners of the AMC. For instance, Metrobank proposed to own 25 percent of the AMC it was setting up with Rabobank—creating firms that, just like the partnerships of Enron's finance officer Andrew Fastow, would merely serve as an entity in which to park the bad assets of a bank while seemingly cleaning up its books and regaining profitability. On the other hand, corporate borrowers wanted SPAVs as a mechanism to buy their foreclosed properties at a low price, and be given the opportunity to buy back these properties while their debt was wiped out. Senator Manuel Villar, a real estate kingpin, for instance, was accused of "unduly influencing the crafting of the measure for his own benefit."[99] As banks and corporations wrangled, it was unclear if indeed the SPAV would in fact stimulate lending and rekindle economic growth, or would simply be a bill that would absolve lenders and corporate debtors of the consequences of their irresponsible behavior in the years leading up to the financial crisis.

Be that as it may, the passage of a SPAV bill loaded with compromises did not result in the sale of NPAs from banks to SPAVs, except in one case.[100] The banks apparently did not want to sell their bad loans to asset management companies, which "normally ask for a discount of 80 percent."[101]

As of 2003, the banking system has remained in intensive care, unable to perform the intermediation of financial resources so important to bring about significant economic activity. The system was not cleansed of bad loans because the banks refused to clean up. As one analyst said, "The SPAV law just created an option for banks which want to reduce their bad loans through an asset management company. But if the banks aren't forced to join the bandwagon, then what is the law for?"[102]

Capital Controls—Still Missing

As in other parts of the region, the Asian financial crisis led to the discrediting of the neoliberal, free-market paradigm. Capital account liberalization—a central element in neoliberal doctrine—was universally seen as the central villain in the tragedy, though US authorities for a time tried to pin the blame on "crony capitalism." Yet, liberalization lives on, like the proverbial dead hand of the engineer on the throttle of a speeding train. While Malaysian Prime Minister Mahathir Mohammad imposed capital controls and created the conditions for his country's vigorous economic recovery, the Philippines lurched on in the years following the crisis with its external finance practices unchanged. With any sort of capital controls a no-no in the eyes of the country's technocrats, the country remained as permeable as before to the entry and exit of speculative capital. During the severe political crisis of 2000, when the country was torn by deep conflict between the supporters and foes of Ramos's successor, President Joseph Estrada, the economy was again held hostage by the moods of speculative investors. Some $2.85 billion in inflows were offset by over $3 billion in outflows,[103] resulting in a near collapse of the peso, which breached the Php 50:$1 psychological watershed. After an all too brief recovery, the peso resumed its downward trajectory in 2002 and 2003, reflecting the erosion of confidence of business in the Arroyo administration. Though inward remittances of dollars by overseas workers worked heroically to prop up the peso, the exchange rate breached the Php 55:$1 barrier in the fourth quarter.

With elite politics entering a new level of uncertainty as the campaign for the 2004 presidential elections began, speculative capital again became volatile, with some $150 million worth of speculative capital leaving the country in the first week of February. Capital controls, one of this book's authors argued in a newspaper commentary, were more urgently needed than ever. While politicians were certainly part of the problem, the country's finance technocrats must shoulder a great deal of the blame for the capital movements:

> They have had seven years since the Asian financial crisis of 1997
> to put in place a set of capital controls like mandatory deposits,
> taxes from stock-market exit transactions, and taxes on signifi-

cant foreign-exchange transactions to protect us from capital flight. We had the examples of Malaysia using capital controls to successfully control speculative capital in 1998, and yet we have done nothing. Over the last few years, more and more countries have adopted such mechanisms. Our methods of defense against speculative outflows, like using our dollar reserves to prop up the peso or increasing bank reserve requirements, remain weak. They will prove to be fragile fences in the event of a real speculative stampede—which is a very real possibility if it becomes clear that Fernando Poe Jr., will win the presidency. Then we will see not only foreign capital heading for the exit but also local capital in search of security.[104]

Capital controls were necessary to avoid a "Brazil-type scenario" that could lead to severe constraints on the country's ability to forge an independent macroeconomic policy.

The Standard Chartered Bank of London has suggested that the Philippines faces an Argentine scenario in which the fiscal situation goes out of control and the country defaults on its debt. That may well be so in the medium term. The greater worry is that in the short term, we may face a "Brazilian scenario"—one that is akin to the one in Brazil during the electoral campaign of 2002, before President Lula (Luis Inacio da Silva) came to power. There, foreign capital was leaving the country out of fear of Lula's pro-people policies, bringing down the value of the Brazilian currency, the real. To stop the bleeding, Lula promised the IMF that he would, if elected, continue the previous government's stringent contractionary program, the main element of which was a promise to achieve a budget surplus equivalent to 3.75 percent of the gross domestic product. In return, the IMF agreed to give Lula access to the remaining $24 billion of stabilization loan it had negotiated with the outgoing regime.

The consequence has been, after Lula's victory, the maintenance of austerity measures that have negatively impacted on the welfare of ordinary Brazilians and prevented the new government from innovative expansionary policies to get the economy moving. Ironically, the first year of a populist government saw hardly any rise in the gross domestic product and record unemployment of 13 percent of the workforce. Not surprisingly, this has alienated the new government from significant sectors of its popular base.[105]

The lack of capital controls, we argued, was inviting the same sort of external intervention in the Philippines,

> wherein capital flight is stanched only by external intervention by a force that requires whoever wins the elections to agree to a contractionary stabilization program that will force us to get our finances in order at the cost of economic expansion. Such an intervention could take the shape of an offer of an IMF "rescue loan." It could also take the form of the Philippines' being black-listed in international capital markets, depriving the government of access to dollars to augment its foreign-currency reserves to counteract a run on the peso.

> If this happens, if we lose a la Brazil de facto control over our economic policy, then the consequences would be disastrous. Loss of control over economic policy making is something we must avoid at all costs, for every time this has happened in the past—whether it was under Marcos (the installation of the World Bank cabinet headed by Cesar Virata) or under Cory Aquino (the adoption of the IMF policy of making payment of the foreign debt the country's top economic priority)—the cure has proved worse than the disease.

> At this point, it is probably whistling in the wind to demand that the two grossly irresponsible factions competing in the elections produce the number one need of the country today—an eco-nomic program that both addresses the fiscal crisis and generates economic expansion. This being a given, the country must pro-tect itself from a destabilizing capital flight that could lead to loss of control over economic policy making by enacting capital con-trols now. The mechanisms are there. They have proved success-ful in stemming flight in other countries—Malaysia, China, In-dia, Chile, to name a few. The Philippines would do well to install them before it is once again too late.[106]

Of course, lack of capital controls was only part of the story of the country's failure to stabilize its currency and thus its economy. The inability of successive administrations to forge a macroeconomic program designed for triggering economic recovery rather than providing a welcome mat for speculative capital was ultimately at the root of the peso collapse. In Thailand, in contrast, Thaksin Shinawatra came to power on an anti-IMF platform and proceeded to implement a Keynesian, demand-expansion economic program that restarted the Thai growth engine and drove the baht-dollar rate from Bt 44:$1 in mid-2002 to Bt 39:$1 by mid-2003.

The Ramos Legacy

What, then, can be said of the Ramos legacy? The centerpiece of the program was liberalization. As noted in the introduction, trade liberalization apparently failed to bring anything but distress to the local economy. However, capital account and financial liberalization did spark significant economic activity. It was, however, growth that was in many ways artificial, being driven by the credit-induced boom in the real estate and construction sectors, and to a lesser degree in industry. The very mechanisms promoting growth were also creating the conditions for disaster in the medium term. In exchange for a few years of 5 percent to 6 percent growth in the mid-1990s, the administration saddled the country with a neoliberal policy paradigm that eventually brought on disaster. Opportunistic protectionism was a plague on Philippine development, but the dismantling of restraints on the market, on the flow of foreign capital proved to be a panacea, a cure worse than the disease.

Ramos was a revolutionary, but his was a revolution in the wrong direction. To his successors Ramos bequeathed the worst of all worlds: an economy that combined traditional, unresolved structural problems, the overhang of opportunistic, corruption-ridden protectionism, and the tragic consequences of unthinking liberalization.

Notes

1. Noel Reyes, "Let Meralco Go Bankrupt," *Business World*, November 27, 2002.

2. Erwin Fernandez, "The Financial Executive," *Business World*, July 4, 2001, 15.

3. Ibid.

4. Quoted in Jenina Joy Chavez-Malaluan, *Shaping the Philippine Political Economy: The Role of Neoclassical Activists* (Manila: Mode, 1996), 9.

5.   Ibid.

6.   Ibid.

7.   Jesus Estanislao, interview by Marco Mezzera, Manila, November 13, 1996.

8.   Cielito Habito, "Barking Up the Wrong Tree," *Philippine Daily Inquirer*, December 8, 2003, B4, B6.

9.   Cielito Habito, "Common Economic Agenda," *Philippine Daily Inquirer*, December 29, 2003, B5.

10.   These incentives included the "take or pay provision," which required the government to purchase generated power that was not used, and the "fuel cost guarantee," which required the National Power Corporation to supply fuel to the IPPs at a determined price, with the latter absorbing fluctuations in the price of fuel; and the foreign exchange guarantee, where the IPPs were pledged payments at a fixed dollar price, with Napocor absorbing the costs of peso devaluation. Ruffy Villanueva, "Public Awaiting Efficient Service," in *Business World Anniversary Report 2002* (Manila: Business World, 2002), 64.

11.   *APEC and the Philippines: Catching the Next Wave* (Manila: Republic of the Philippines, 1996), 6.

12.   Mario Lamberte, quoted in Joy Chavez-Malaluan, "Shaping Philippine Economic Policy: The Role of Neoclassical Activists" (unpublished study, Mode, Manila, 1996).

13.   Cielito Habito, "Tariff Reversals," *Philippine Daily Inquirer*, November 24, 2003, B5.

14.   Ibid., 11.

15.   See, among other references, Myrna Austria and John Lawrence Avila, "Looking Beyond AFTA: Prospects and Challenges for Inter-Regional Trade" (Philippine Institute of Development Studies, discussion paper series no. 2001-10, April 2001), 1.

16.   Quoted in "The Philippine Blueprint for APEC," in Walden Bello and Joy Chavez Malaluan, *APEC: Four Adjectives in Search of a Noun* (Manila: Manila People's Forum on APEC, 1996), 21.

17.   Ibid.

18.   *APEC and the Philippines: Catching the Next Wave* (Manila: Republic of the Philippines, 1996), 8.

19.   Government of the Republic of the Philippines, Individual Action Plan, Manila, 1996.

20.   Ibid.

21.   Japanese Ministry of Finance figures.

22.   Ibid.

23. Min Tang and J. Villafuerte, *Capital Flows to Asian and Pacific Developing Countries: Recent Trends and Future Prospects* (Manila: Asian Development Bank, 1995), 10.

24. See, among other references, Angel Buira, "Key Financial Issues in Capital Flows to Emerging Markets," in *International Finance in a Year of Crisis* (Tokyo: United Nations University, 1998), 7; and Jeffrey Sachs, "Personal View," *Financial Times,* July 30, 1997.

25. Sheila Samonte and E. Garcia, "Risky Business," *Business World,* April 2, 1997.

26. Jude Esguerra, "Devaluation—An Accident Waiting to Happen," *IPD (Institute for Popular Democrac) Political Brief* 5, no. 4 (August 1997).

27. Tang and Villafuerte, 3.

28. Ibid.

29. Esguerra.

30. Rolando Bondoy, "Different Fundamentals," *Business World,* April 4-5, 1997; see also Edberto Villegas, *Global Finance Capital and the Philippine Financial System* (Manila: Ibon Books, 2000), 47.

31. Villegas, ibid.

32. Sheila Samonte and E. Garcia, "The Next Crisis?" *Business World,* March 31, 1997.

33. Anwar Nasution, "Recent Issues in the Management of Macroeconomic Policies in the Philippines," in *Rising to the Challenge in Asia: A Study of Financial Markets,* 10, Philippines (Manila: Asian Development Bank, 1999), 24.

34. Samonte and Garcia, "Risky Business."

35. Central Bank data cited by Solita Collas-Monsod, "Calling a Spade," *Business World,* September 30, 1997.

36. Reuters, "DMG Advises Caution on RP Banks," *Philippine Daily Inquirer,* September 13, 1997.

37. HG Asia, *Communique: Philippines,* 1997.

38. Ibid.

39. Ibid.

40. J. Lee, "The Asian Financial Crisis and Its Implications on Regional Growth and Development" (keynote address for the International Seminar to Commemorate 60th Anniversary of the Faculty of Commerce and Accountancy, Thammasat University, Bangkok, Thailand, 1998).

41. Mario Lamberte and Josef Yap, "Economic Policies and Measures in Response to the East Asian Financial Crisis," in *Economic Crisis...Once More,* ed. Mario Lamberte (Makati: Philippine Institute for Development Studies, 2001), 266.

42. Eric Boras, "Construction Industry Sees Light at Last," Special Re-

port, *Business World*, March 5, 2002, 25.

43. Calculated year-by-year on a six-month average basis. HG Asia Let. *Asia Communique*, 1997.

44. Joseph Lim, "The Philippines and the East Asian Economic Turmoil," in *Tigers in Trouble*, ed. Jomo K.S. (London: Zed Books, 1998), 220.

45. Sheila Oviedo and H.F. Oviedo, "Will Real Estate Go Bust?" *International Herald Tribune*, May 6, 1997.

46. "RP Market Faces Glut, Consultant Says," *Business World*, October 2, 1997.

47. Sheila Oviedo and H.F. Oviedo.

48. "A Costly Dream: Home Ownership," in "Fast Track 1997: Asia Business Outlook" (sponsored section), *International Herald Tribune*, September 1997.

49. "Market-determined Exchange Rate Here to Stay," *Philippine Daily Inquirer*, July 11, 1997.

50. "After Thailand, Where Next for Disaster," *Asian Wall Street Journal*, April 23, 1997.

51. "Local Banks Not Cause of Turmoil," *Business World*, September 10, 1997.

52. "After Thailand," *Asian Wall Street Journal*, April 23, 1997.

53. "Three Main Challenges for the Central Bank," *Business World*, May 9-10, 1997.

54. BSP memo, quoted in Solita Collas Monsod, "Clutching at Straws," *Business World*, September 30, 1997.

55. Probably the best exposition of the negative impact of the dollar's reverse course on the East Asian economies is Robert Brenner, *The Boom and the Bubble* (New York: Verso, 2002), 155-65.

56. The position of the University of the Philippines faction on the exchange rate is articulated in Emmanuel de Dios et al., "Exchange Policies: Recent Failures and Future Tasks," *Public Policy* 1, no. 1 (August 1997): 5-41.

57. Rosemarie Francisco, "One Feet on the Door," in *The Next Step: The Philippines into the 21st Century* (Manila: Business World, 1997).

58. Jeffrey Winters, "The Financial Crisis in Southeast Asia" (paper delivered at the Conference on the Asian Crisis, Murdoch University, Fremantle, Western Australia, August 1998).

59. Josef Yap, "Managing Capital Flows to Developing Economies: Issues and Policies" (discussion paper series no. 2001-41, Philippine Institute for Development Studies, Makati, Philippines, November 2000), 13.

60. Data from *Global Finance Data CD-ROM*, cited in Yap, table 3.

61. Statement in *Public Forum*, talk show at Channel 7, Quezon City, September 11, 1997.

62. "IMF Suspects Bank Loans to Property Sector Higher," *Business World*, September 23, 1997.

63. Quoted in *Business World*, September 29, 1997.

64. Quoted in "Rating Agency Paints Bleak Outlook on RP Banks," *Business World*, September 29, 1997, 11.

65. "BSP Approves 20% Loan-Loss Reserves," *Business World*, September 25, 1997.

66. Cited in Solita Monsod, "Para sa Mahirap," *Business World*, October 20, 1998, 5.

67. International Monetary Fund, "IMF-Supported Programs in Indonesia, Korea, and Thailand," IMF Occasional Paper No. 178, June 30, 1999, 62.

68. Figures from Asian Development Bank, *Asian Development Bank Outlook 2001* (Manila: Asian Development Bank, 2001), 208, 211.

69. Ibid.

70. See Jacques-chai Chomthongdi, "The IMF's Asian Legacy," in *Prague 2000* (Bangkok: Focus on the Global South, 2000), 18, 22.

71. United Nations Development Program, *Human Development Report 2003* (New York: Oxford University Press, 2003), 63.

72. Judy Gulane, "Poverty," *Business World*, November 7-8, 2003, 25.

73. Ibid.

74. "Deep in Debt," *Newsbreak*, February 17, 2002, 10.

75. Eric Boras, "The Construction Industry," Special Report, *Business World*, March 5, 2002, 25.

76. Ibid.

77. "NSC Rehab under Way as Creditors Ink Debt Pact Plan," *Business World*, November 14, 2002, 1, 8.

78. D'Laarni Ortiz, "Local Cement Industry Waits for '03 Recovery," Special Report, *Business World*, March 5, 2002, 28.

79. Ibid.

80. Rene Ofreneo, "How to Make the Economy Work for the People," *Business World*, December 1, 2003, 21.

81. Cecille Visto, "Lopez Water Firm Gets Debt Reprieve," *Business World*, November 18, 2003, 1.

82. Ibid.

83. "GMA Links Poor Revenues to Low Interest Rate, Prices," *Business World*, November 29-30, 2002. These were the president's figures. The figures

provided by the National Statistical Coordination Board were worse: 15.6 percent in 1998, 13.9 percent in 2000, 13.5 percent in 2001, and an estimated 12.4 percent in 2002. See Solita Collas Monsod, "Calling a Spade," *Business World*, December 5, 2002.

84. Ma. Socorro Gochoco-Bautista, "The Past Peformance of the Philippine Banking Sector and Challenges in the Postcrisis Period," in Asian Development Bank, *Rising to the Challenge in Asia: A Study of Financial Markets* (Manila: Asian Development Bank, 1999), 42.

85. Ibid.

86. Cited in Ibid., 42.

87. Felicisimo Dolor, "Major Sectors Suffer Credit Crunch," *Business World*, January 14, 2002, 15.

88. "For Imprudent Lenders: the Wages of Negligence," Fourth Quarter Banking Report, *Business World*, February 12, 2002, 23.

89. Cecile Yap, "For Banks, Slicing Expenses May Not Be Enough," 2001 Yearend Report, *Business World*, January 7, 2002, 34.

90. Norman Aquino, "Local Banking Industry Remains Robust," *Business World*, October 2002, 1. The actual improvement in the neighboring economies may be illusory, however. A bank analyst at SG Asia Credit Securities, for instance, alluded to the fact that if a bad and impaired loans set aside by Thai banks as "rehabilitated assets" were regarded as NPLs, the total bad loan figure would rise to around 25-30 percent of assets. "Thai Bank Outlook Bright Despite Rise in Bad Loans," *Business World*, February 26, 2002, 14.

91. "Senators Fail to Approve SPAV Bill," *Business World*, September 6-7, 2002.

92. Felicisimo Dolor Jr., "Bank Stocks, Interrupted," Special Report, *Business World*, August 12, 2003.

93. Felicisimo Dolor Jr., "Major Sectors Suffer Credit Crunch," *Business World*, January 14, 2002.

94. "Bank Lending Down 3%,"*Business World*, September 16, 2002, 13.

95. Ibid.

96. "Special Purpose Asset Vehicle: Tough Balancing Act," *Business World*, November 12, 2002.

97. Ibid.

98. "Government, Solons, Bankers Meet on SPAV Bill," *Business World*, September 19, 2002.

99. "Latest SPAV Version to Boost Sellable Bad Assets to Php 520 Billion," *Business World*, October 3, 2002.

100. This was the sale of Php 16.3 billion in bad assets from Metrobank

to Asia Recovery Corporation, an asset management company set up by Rabobank Nederland. See Felicisimo Dolor, "Bank Stocks, Interrupted," *Business World,* August 12, 2003, 25.

101. Norman Aquino, "Banks' Bad Loans Rise," *Business World,* December 22, 2003, 13.

102. Ehden Lllave, "Who's Setting UP Them SPV's," *Business World,* August 12, 2003, 28.

103. "Hot Money Trickled Back into RP Last Year," *Business World,* January 21, 2002.

104. Walden Bello, "Capital Controls Will Help RP Avoid 'Brazilian Scenario,'" *Business World,* February 12, 2004.

105. Ibid.

106. Ibid.

CHAPTER 4

Multilateral Punishment:
The Philippines in the WTO, 1995-2003

Storm Signals

At the October 2002 Asia-Pacific Economic Cooperation (APEC) summit, President Gloria Macapagal Arroyo proclaimed the "need to reengineer the WTO to ensure there is a level playing field" in global trade.[1] The challenge in world trade policy, she said, was to ensure that "the rules of trading are not stopped in favor of developed countries, on the one hand, but practise protectionism against developing countries, on the other."[2]

Like her recognition of the destructive consequences of "unbridled globalization," Arroyo's calling attention to the inequities fostered by what came to be known as the GATT-WTO (General Agreement on Tariffs and Trade-World Trade Organization) regime was long overdue. Back in 1994, during the great national debate on ratification of the Uruguay Round agreement establishing the WTO, she served as the point person in the Senate leading the charge of the Ramos administration to ratify the global treaty. Then, she argued the orthodox view that the agreement and the WTO made up a multilateral set of rules or institutions that would eliminate unequal power relations from global trade and provide smaller countries equal standing with the big trading powers.

But by the time she recognized that the WTO was riddled with double standards, the Philippines had been exposed to the ravages of both free trade and monopolistic competition, two contradictory principles that were nevertheless fused in the WTO. As a 2001 Department of Agriculture study admitted, despite its entry into the WTO six years earlier, the Philippines remained a "center of poverty and stagnant productivity."[3]

Yet the government could not complain that it did not have advance warning of the consequences of joining the WTO. During the debate on ratification, civil-society representatives had argued that the nineteen separate agreements that comprised the Uruguay Round were skewed against the interests of countries like the Philippines.[4]

Among other things, critics of the Uruguay Round asserted the following:

— In signing on to the GATT-WTO, the Philippines essentially gave up the ability to use trade policy as a mechanism for industrialization. This was because the Agreement banned quantitative restrictions or quotas on imports, bound or reduced existing industrial tariffs and made raising tariffs practically impossible except under import surges, and outlawed trade-related investment restrictions. Among the trade policy instruments used by earlier industrializers that were banned by the Agreement on Trade-Related Investment Measures (TRIMs) were trade-balancing mechanisms, which tied the value of a foreign investor's imports of raw materials and components to the value of his/her exports of the finished commodity, and "local content" regulations, which mandated that a certain percentage of the components that went into the making of a product be sourced locally.

— The Trade-Related Aspects of Intellectual Property Rights (TRIPS), with its rigid provisions penalizing the unauthorized use of technology, would make "industrialization by imitation" very difficult, if not impossible. A key factor in the economic takeoff of industrial latecomers like the US, Germany, Japan, and South Korea, was their relatively easy access to cutting-edge technology. But what was technological diffusion from the point of view of late industrializers was "piracy" from that of the industrial leaders. Critics claimed that not only was TRIPS anti-development but, contrary to the spirit of free trade that was supposed to animate the WTO, it actually reinforced monopoly with such draconian provisions as the generalized minimum patent protection of twenty years, the increase in the duration of protection for semiconductors or computer chips, draconian border regulations against products judged to be violating intellectual property rights, and the placing of the burden of proof on the presumed violator of process patents.

The TRIPS agreement, critics added, also opened up the way for corporations to patent life or living organisms as well as privatize knowledge developed over centuries by communities via the modification of genetic material. The gene-rich Philippines would be a big loser in this game, as would most of the rest of the South. Already, they warned, patents had been filed in the North on processes for transforming *nata de coco*, a versatile coconut byproduct, for industrial use, and extracting the medicinal elements of *lagundi,* a ubiquitous Philippine plant.

The most controversial agreement, however, was the Agreement on Agriculture (AOA). Critics charged that the AOA was the antithesis of free trade, that it simply functioned to legitimize the high levels of protection and subsidization of the agricultural markets of the European Union and the United States while opening up the markets of developing countries to monopolistic competition between the two agricultural superpowers. Death by dumping would be the fate of the Philippines under the AOA, they said, and faulted pro-AOA, pro-WTO advocates who seemed oblivious to the monopolistic structure of world agricultural trade in their quest to make Philippine agriculture more efficient via free trade.

In the wake of ratifying the WTO, the Philippines, opponents of ratification said, would have to change at least forty of its laws and regulations and promise to enact new ones. What also became clear was that at some point, it would have to amend its constitution since, in signing on to the WTO agreement, it would also have to initial the General Agreement on Trade in Services (GATS), which committed it to providing "national treatment" or nondiscriminatory treatment to foreign service providers. Section 11, Article 12 of the 1986 Constitution limits foreign ownership of key utilities (water and sewage, electricity transmission and distribution, telecommunications, and public transport) to no more than 40 percent of equity. Also, Section 11 of Article 16 limits foreign ownership of advertising agencies to 30 percent while Section 14 of Article 12 reserves the practice of licensed professions— for instance, law, medicine, nursing, accounting, engineering, customs brokerage, and architecture—to Filipino citizens. Not surprisingly, those seeking full alignment of Philippine law with the WTO have had as a key objective the elimination of the ownership provisions of the current constitution.

Hardly had the ink dried on the Philippines' signature on the WTO accord when the drive to make Philippine legislation WTO-consistent began. Pressure came from the developed countries that stood to benefit from the WTO, particularly from the United States. The dynamics of this process were illustrated in two agreements: TRIPS and TRIMs.

Making the Philippines WTO-Consistent

Restricting Technological Diffusion

By the time of its ratification of the WTO, the Philippines' intellectual property regime, based as it was on that of the United States, was relatively comprehensive, protecting as it did patents (since 1947), trademarks (since 1947), and copyrights (since 1972).[5] In addition, the government was signatory to a number of key international agreements including the Paris Convention for the Protection of Industrial Property, the Berne Convention for the Protection of Literary and Artistic Works, the Budapest Treaty on International Recognition of the Deposit of Microorganisms for the Purposes of Patent Procedure, the Rome Convention for the Protection of Performers, the Producers of Phonograms and Broadcasting Organizations, the ASEAN (Association of Southeast Asian Nations) Framework Agreement on Intellectual Property Cooperation, and the Convention Establishing the World Intellectual Property Organization.[6] Nevertheless, the Philippines was quick to promise that it would amend existing laws "to align with the WTO TRIPS agreement." Specifically, the government promised to "align existing laws on patents, trademarks, and copyrights with TRIPS," "enact new laws on the protection of plant varieties, geographical indications, layout designs of integrated circuits, and undisclosed information," and "strengthen enforcement of intellectual property rights (IPRs)."[7]

Under strong prodding from the US, the government delivered. Indeed, a US Agency for International Development (USAID) Program called AGILE (Accelerating Growth, Investment, and Liberalization with Equity) practically wrote the key TRIPS-related legislation and shepherded it through Congress. Among AGILE's accomplishments were the Intellectual Property Code (Republic Act 8293) and the Electronic Commerce Act (Republic Act 8792).[8] The Intellectual Property Code passed in 1997 made Philippine legislation WTO-consistent while the

Electronic Commerce Act (Republic Act 8792) extended IPR protection to the Internet in 2000.[9] In 2001 President Gloria Macapagal Arroyo signed into law Republic Act 9150, "An Act Providing for the Protection of Layout Designs (Topographies) of Integrated Circuits," specifying the provisions of the Intellectual Property Code to the information industry.

The US was not, however, satisfied with the WTO alignment process, with the United States Trade Representative (USTR) complaining that "legislation implementing fully the WTO TRIPS agreement commitments has been slow to develop," pointing out that the Philippines still had to enact laws "to provide IPR protection to plant varieties as required by the WTO TRIPS obligations that became mandatory for the Philippines on January 1, 2000."[10]

The USAID-funded AGILE again stepped into the breach. AGILE consultants drafted the plant-variety protection bill in 1999 for the Department of Agriculture. The bill followed the contours of the UPOV (French acronym for the Union for the Protection of New Plant Varieties) Convention, which was founded primarily to protect the intellectual property rights of Northern breeders over new plant varieties, particularly industrial crops and ornamental plants.[11] This bill eventually became the Philippine Plant Variety Protection (PVP) Act (Republic Act 9168), which was signed into law on June 7, 2002.

USAID funding for the drafting of an UPOV-type bill was not surprising since promoting adaptations of the UPOV convention was universally a way of averting the potentially dangerous implications for corporate rights of countries taking seriously Article 27.3 (b) of the TRIPS agreement, which allowed them to protect plant varieties through an "effective *sui generis* system." As one analysis notes, universalizing UPOV-type intellectual property rights systems creates "uniform market conditions for transnational corporations in developing countries," establishing "an environment that assures a return on investments through an intellectual property rights regime that privileges industrial breeders, does not recognize farmers' contributions in plant variety development, and provides equal treatment to foreign nationals—all of which are among the key features of the PVP Law."[12]

The US kept up the pressure on all fronts, including the judicial. In 2001, in what a USTR report called "a notable achievement," the Supreme Court speeded up the prosecution of intellectual piracy by establishing *ex parte* authority in civil cases involving IPR infringement, with forty-eight courts designated to handle IPR-related cases.[13]

Still unsatisfied with the pace of government movement on TRIPS, the US, citing reports from US distributors of "high levels of pirated optical discs" placed the Philippines on the dreaded Priority Watch List under Section 301 of the US Trade Law.[14] This was a move that preceded bilateral retaliatory sanctions—which were themselves illegal under the WTO.

Yet the difficulties of enforcement, even under threat of massive sanctions, stemmed from contradictions inherent in TRIPS itself. Contrary to the WTO's free trade rhetoric, TRIPS is an effort to control the market and reinforce monopoly under conditions of high market demand. As one account put it, intellectual property violators "are basically harmless… And in a developing country like the Philippines, they are welcomed by the majority of cash-strapped consumers. The most important sign of their acceptability to society: their products sell, and sell better than the original. They are in fact considered as allies of the poor—an economic leveler—because they make things affordable to all."[15]

Eliminating Trade Policy as a Mechanism for Industrialization

Prior to the WTO, developing countries routinely used trade policy, notably the use of quotas and high tariffs, as a key mechanism for industrialization. The use of trade policy for industrialization purposes in the Philippines was sketchy and incoherent, and implementation was very spotty. And yet, this already weak legislation and enforcement framework was still seen as threatening by foreign transnationals. TRIMs provided the mechanism to get rid of it, and, as in the case with TRIPS, it was the United States Trade Representative that acted as the WTO's enforcer for TRIMs.

Two industries were immediately affected by the Philippines' ratifying the WTO agreement: the auto industry and the soap and detergent industry.

Local content and trade balancing requirements had been used to build up an indigenous auto industry. Under the Motor Vehicle Development Program, participants were required to generate, through exports, a certain percentage of foreign exchange needed for import requirements as well as to source a progressively larger portion of the content of a vehicle in the Philippines. As in Malaysia, though not as successfully, TRIMs were designed to discourage transnational corporations from simply making the country an assembly point for imported components and force them to build up or stimulate the development of components and parts suppliers that would eventually become the core of an integrated industry. Naturally, as in Malaysia, too, the automobile transnational corporations (TNCs) hated local content policies as they interfered in the regional and international trade among their subsidiaries. Among other things, practices such as transfer pricing to get around taxes and other government levies were disrupted.

The Philippines notified the WTO of its TRIMs in the automobile industry in 1995, enabling it to avail of the five-year transitional period to phase out these measures, which would end on January 1, 2000. In October 1999, however, the government asked for a five-year extension for phasing out the TRIMs from the WTO. "After extensive consultations on the issue," noted a USTR report, "the United States and the Philippines agreed in November 2001 that the Philippines will discontinue all local content and exchange balancing requirements... by July 1, 2003."[16]

The US also pushed the Philippines to get rid of TRIMs in the soap and detergent industry. US transnational corporations like Procter & Gamble and Colgate Palmolive complained about Executive Order 259 (1987), which required manufacturers to use a minimum of 60 percent of raw materials that do not endanger the environment and prohibited the import of laundry soap and detergents containing less than 60 percent of such raw materials. As the USTR noted, the law had been passed to support the creation of the coconut-processing industry by promoting the use of coconut-based surface active agents of local origin. It noted approvingly that "the Philippine Department of Justice, in Opinion 88 (1999), stated that Executive Order 259 conflicts with the country's obligations under the WTO TRIMs agreement. Since then, the EO [Executive Order] has not been enforced."[17]

The USTR enumerated other TRIMs that had to be removed in order to make Philippine legislation WTO-consistent: investment incentives legislation requiring a higher export performance for foreign-owned enterprises (70 percent of production to be exported) than for Philippine-owned companies (50 percent); an executive order requiring pharmaceutical firms to purchase semi-synthetic antibiotics from a specified local company unless they could demonstrate that the landed cost of imports is at least 20 percent less than that produced by the local firm; Letter of Instruction 1387, which required mining firms to prioritize sale of copper concentrates to the Philippine Associated Smelting and Refining Company; trade-balancing requirements for firms applying for approval of projects under the ASEAN Industrial Cooperation program; and retail trade legislation passed in 2000 requiring foreign retailers, for the first ten years after the bill's enactment, to source a fixed percentage of their inventory in the Philippines.[18]

By the beginning of 2003, most of Philippine legislation had been made WTO-consistent. The process has been painful and the price high. Owing to the alignment of Philippine laws with WTO rules, which benefit mainly big northern transnationals, the broad-based diffusion of technology necessary for self-sustaining industrialization has been restricted. The TRIPS regime represents what United Nations Conference on Trade and Development (UNCTAD) describes as a "premature strengthening of the intellectual property system... that favors monopolistically controlled innovation over broad-based diffusion."[19] And its likely consequence would be to limit the possibility of an "imitative path of technological development" based on methods such as reverse engineering, the adaptation of foreign technology to local conditions, and the improvement of existing innovations."[20] This anti-industrial bias of the TRIPS regime has been supplemented by the realignment of legislation to accord with the TRIMs regime, which practically eliminates the use of trade policy for national industrial development.

Even as national industrialization is closed off by TRIPS and TRIMs, this tropical country's rich trove of genetic resources has been rendered vulnerable to biopiracy by the realignment of our patent laws as they apply to agriculture and nature. These consequences were pointed out during the ratification debate, but were ignored by legislators eager not to offend the United States.

The AOA and the Demise of Philippine Agriculture

For the Philippines, the Agreement on Agriculture was the most important agreement in the WTO. The reason was that the country's agricultural sector continued to employ nearly half of the labor force and contributed more than 20 percent of gross domestic product. However, as one paper asserts, when "all economic activities related to agro-processing and supply of non-farm agricultural inputs are included, the agricultural sector broadly defined accounts for about two-thirds of the labor force and 40 percent of GDP [gross domestic product]."[21] Agriculture thus plays "a strategic role in the country's overall economic development through its strong growth linkage effects as a source of food and raw material supply for the rest of the economy, and as a source of demand for non-agricultural inputs and consumer goods and services."[22]

During the national debate on WTO ratification, the government based its pro-WTO stance on the argument that free trade would increase the efficiency of Philippine agriculture. This was not a case of agricultural liberalization forced on reluctant technocrats as in other developing countries. The neoliberal technocrats that began to dominate state economic agencies during the Aquino and Ramos administrations wanted to liberalize agriculture. Indeed, the two administrations pushed a comprehensive liberalization program (Executive Order 470) that embraced both industry and agriculture.

Agricultural liberalization, however, lagged behind owing to resistance from farmers—big, medium, and small. Indeed, the Magna Carta for Small Farmers passed in 1991 was seen as a far-reaching attempt to consolidate protection by providing for the banning of imports of commodities that were deemed to be produced locally in sufficient quantity. In this context, subjecting the country's agricultural sector to the discipline of the WTO's AOA was seen as a key instrument to destroy agricultural protectionism.

Moreover, entry into world of the Agreement on Agriculture would make Philippine agriculture more productive by promoting the cultivation of high-value-added (HVA) agricultural commodities like broccoli and cut flowers. With HVAs regarded as the "export winners" that would increase Philippine share of world markets,[23] agricultural technocrats saw the trade liberalization that came with WTO membership as leading to the gradual phasing out of much rice and corn production which involved most of the rural workforce. The Medium-Term Agricultural Development Plan of the Ramos administration—prepared with possible entry into the WTO in mind—envisaged limiting rice and corn production to 1.9 million hectares and freeing up some 3.1 million hectares currently planted to rice and corn for raising cattle and cultivating commercial crops.[24]

To secure popular support for the ratification of GATT, the government projected that the AOA regime would, among other things:[25]

— create 500,000 new agricultural jobs annually
— increase annual agricultural export earnings by Php 3.4 billion annually, thus improving the balance of trade in agricultural products
— increase the annual gross value added of agriculture by Php 60 billion

To ease transition pains, Congress appropriated Php 128 billion, to be released at some Php 32 billion annually, to improve agricultural infrastructure and create "safety nets."

With ratification, the government moved to make Philippine legislation consistent with the WTO. The Magna Carta for Small Farmers was repealed. Comprehensive legislation, Republic Act 8178, was enacted ending quotas and transforming them to tariff rate quotas (TRQs). The TRQ system covered fifteen tariff lines of "sensitive" agricultural imports, including live animals, fresh and chilled beef, pork, poultry meat, goat meat, potatoes, coffee, corn, and sugar. For these commodities, the Philippines was required to provide "minimum access" at low tariffs to a volume equivalent to 3 percent of domestic consumption in the first year of WTO implementation rising to 5 percent on the tenth year. Beyond the quota, imports would be taxed at a much higher rate. For corn, for instance, using the agreed-upon period of 1986-88 as the basis for calculating domestic consumption, the minimum access volume (MAV) allowed to come in at a low tariff of 35 percent would be 65,000 MT in 1995, rising to 227,000 in 2004.[26] Beyond the MAV, the tariff rate rose to 65 percent.

Under Annex 5 of the AOA, countries were allowed to retain a quota on "a primary agricultural product that is the predominant staple in the traditional diet."[27] In the case of the Philippines, this was rice. The country was nevertheless required to increase the quota from one percent of domestic consumption on the first year to 4 percent on the tenth year, or from 30,000 MT in 1995 to 227,000 MT in 2004.[28]

As in the case with the other agreements comprising the WTO, the US served as the Geneva-based body's local enforcer, watching Philippine legislative and implementation processes with an eagle eye. This process could be quite intrusive and went beyond the scope of the letter of the AOA. For instance, the US intervened in the issuing of licenses to importers for pork and poultry meat, accusing the Philippine government of allocating "a vast majority of import licenses to domestic producers who had no interest in importing."[29] When the Philippines balked, the US threatened to suspend the preferential tariffs for Philippine exports covered by the Generalized System of Preferences. The Philippines gave in, and after a memorandum of understanding detailing its concessions was issued in 1998, according to a USTR report, "the review of the Philippines' eligibility to receive preferential access under the General System of Preferences... was terminated."[30]

By the end of the decade, not only had the promised benefits of AOA membership failed to materialize, but Philippine agriculture was in the throes of crisis.[31]

Contrary to the output projected by Ramon Clarete and pro-ratification technocrats that joining the AOA would spur agricultural output to grow to Php 50 billion by 2002, in fact the country's agricultural production only reached Php 12 billion.[32]

Far from increasing by 500,000 a year, employment in agriculture actually dropped from 11.29 million in 1994 to 10.85 million in 2001.[33]

Agricultural exports like coconut products were supposed to rise with WTO membership, but the value of exports registered no significant movement, rising from $1.9 billion in 1993 to $2.3 billion in 1997, then declining to $1.9 billion in 2000. On the other hand, massive importation, the big fear of GATT critics, became a reality, with the value of imports almost doubling from $1.6 billion in 1993 to $3.1 billion in 1997 and registering $2.7 billion in 2000. The status of the Philippines as a net food-importing country was consolidated, with the agricultural trade balance moving from a surplus of $292 million in 1993 to a deficit of $764 million in 1997 and 794 million in 2002.[34]

Key sectors of Philippine agriculture were in a bad state by the end of the decade.

The Crisis of Rice Production

Rice production in the country was in crisis owing to a number of factors, including failure of effective government support programs. However, the government's policy of resolving short-term "supply crises" by massive imports could not but have the effect of further discouraging increased rice production. The rice exception under Annex 5 limited the Philippines to import a volume that was only one percent of domestic consumption in 1995 rising to 4 percent by 2005. In fact, the government, citing necessity, imported amounts far beyond the quota, with imports shooting up from 263,000 MT in 1995 to 2.1 million MT in 1998, 836,999 MT in 1999, and 639,000 MT in 2000.[35]

Such massive volumes kept the price of rice low, making it unattractive for farmers to increase production. Average farm-gate prices of rice from 1997 to 2001 grew at a "measly 0.89 annually."[36] Not surprisingly, total rice production increased marginally in the late 1990s and came to an average of 1.9 per annum for the whole decade—far below the rates registered in the Philippines' two key rice suppliers: 3.0 percent per annum in the case of Thailand and 4.5 percent in the case of Vietnam.[37] In other words, massive above-quota imports were contributing to the continuing erosion of the rice sector, in turn making rice importation more and more of a permanent fixture of the agrarian economy.

Neoliberal technocrats, the Asian Development Bank, and the WTO took advantage of this situation to press for the elimination of the rice quota, which the Philippines could still take advantage of after 2005 under Annex 5 of the AOA. At a tariff rate of 100 percent, which was being considered by House Bill 3339—the so-called Rice Safety Nets

Act—the price of imported rice would be the same as that of locally produced rice. However, it would provide little protection to local rice producers since, as one study pointed out, the rate would be "insufficient to negate the potential convenience and advantage of sourcing products from one single source abroad than incurring costs attendant to consolidating and building stocks from many [local] suppliers and farmers."[38] In other words, many costs and uncertainties would be eliminated by relying on one or a few foreign suppliers than on many local suppliers.

At a tariff rate of 50 percent, which some quarters at the Department of Agriculture were considering, the tariff rate would allow imported rice, at 2002 relative prices, to be priced at Php 11 to Php 12 a kilo, which would be lower than the Php 14 per kilo that was the lowest price of domestic rice.[39]

Yet these considerations to eliminate the rice quota and move to tariffs were made with the current AOA in mind. The controversial "Harbinson Draft" (named after its author WTO Agricultural Negotiations Chairman Stuart Harbinson) that served as the negotiating paper for further agricultural liberalization under the AOA prior to the Cancun ministerial proposed to slash developing-country tariffs above 120 percent by 40 percent, and those between 20 percent and 120 percent by 33 percent. Tariffication of rice in conjunction with the WTO's adoption of the Harbinson proposal or variations of it coming from the European Union and the US would definitely lead to an even graver crisis of the country's rice sector.

With very little sympathy for their plight from a neoliberal technocracy and with tremendous pressures coming from different quarters for liberalization, the fate of the two million farmers involved in rice production—some 20 percent of the agricultural workforce—was highly uncertain.

Corn: In Terminal Condition?

The plight of the corn sector was equally grim. The main corn production area in the Philippines is Mindanao, and the cost of corn from Mindanao in Manila is less than the landed cost of foreign corn by Php 2 per kilo.[40] As with rice, the corn sector, which had long been neglected by government, has been opened up to international competition that it was ill-prepared to meet. Unlike rice, however, corn imports were not subject to quota restrictions. A minimum access volume starting from 3 percent of domestic consumption in 1995 to 5 percent in 2004 would be taxed at a low tariff of 35 percent. Beyond that, the AOA still allowed corn to come in with no volume limitation, though the tariff rate would be increased to 100 percent.

How much protection these arrangements gave was open to question. An Oxfam Great Britain study in 1996 claimed that imports from the US, the world's largest corn exporter, could be available at a price 20 percent below the current domestic price by the end of the '90s. It went on to note that by "the year 2004, the price gap may have widened to 39 percent, as tariffs are scaled down under the Uruguay Round agreement."[41]

From practically zero imports in 1993 and 1994, corn coming into the Philippines shot up to 208,000 MT in 1995 to 558,000 MT in 1996, 462,120 MT in 1998, and 446,430 MT in 2000. The government appeared to be quite liberal in managing the MAV for corn. According to one report, a significant portion of the volume of corn that came in above the MAV of 135,000 MT in 1996 appeared to have come in at the 35 percent tariff rate rather than the 100 percent rate, thanks to an administrative order allowing expansion of the MAV limit during "shortages."[42] This stemmed from the growing strength of an alliance between foreign corn exporters and local end-users, such as feedmillers and livestock raisers, that had a great deal of interest in lower-priced corn imports.

Among the factors depressing the price of corn was cheap American corn coming in under the Public Law (PL) 480 program of the United States, which sought external markets for its corn by giving foreign governments long-term low-interest export credits to import US agricultural commodities, including soybean, rice, and corn. Public Law 480 was one of several dumping devices that were legitimate under the AOA. An average of $20 million of US agricultural commodities has arrived under the program since 1997, with the figure rising to $40 million in 2001.[43] In 2002, $2 million worth of corn was brought in under the program,[44] causing local growers to protest that PL-480 yellow corn imports were particularly harmful, in terms of depressing local prices, if they arrived during the corn harvest.[45]

Not surprisingly, Mindanao was being ravaged by the new import-biased agro-trade regime. Already, the limited trade liberalization of the late '80s was plunging corn production into crisis prior to the AOA. As Kevin Watkins of Oxfam noted after a field trip to Mindanao, "increasing imports of corn have been associated with a marked decrease in domestic corn production, and in the area planted. In South Cotabato, where most of Mindanao's corn is produced, there was a 15 percent decrease in production last year."[46]

The trend appears to have accelerated after the country's adherence to the AOA. After a trip to Bukidnon in 1996, Charmaine Ramos, an analyst with the Management and Organizational Development for Empowerment (MODE), reported: "I found out that the southern part of the province is steadily being converted from corn to sugar."[47] Several years later, Aileen Kwa, an analyst for Focus on the Global South claimed that corn farmers in "Mindanao... have been wiped out. It is not an uncommon sight to see farmers there leaving their corn to rot in the fields as the domestic corn prices have dropped to levels [at which] they have not been able to compete."[48] This observation was supported by macro data. While production remained stagnant, land devoted to corn across the country contracted sharply from 3,149,300 hectares in 1993 to 2,510,300 hectares in 2000.[49]

The government admitted during the GATT-WTO ratification debate, that traditional corn and rice farmers would be among the losers under the AOA regime, with some 45,000 among them displaced annually. This would be among the 350,000 agricultural producers that were estimated to be displaced annually, according to Department of Agriculture estimates.[50] However, the growth of employment in selected export and high-value-added crops that was supposed to be a fallout of the WTO would translate into a net gain of 500,000 a year. But these estimates were highly questionable. According to the secretary of agriculture at the time of the WTO ratification debate, the 45,000 corn farmers slated for displacement would be absorbed by the silage growing industry that would service the cattle-growing industry stimulated by the WTO regime.[51] Yet, cattle raising turned out to be a very disappointing industry in the next few years, stunted by a very liberal beef and "carabeef" import regime put in place to comply with the AOA itself. Cattle production barely moved, registering 213,000 MT in 1995 and 261,000 in 2001.[52]

Charmaine Ramos underlines the depressing reality for corn farmers:"[O]nly farmers with relatively bigger farm lots are able to shift easily. Small farmers are forced to lease their lands simply because they have no means to finance the capital requirements of shifting to high value crops."[53] Kevin Watkins offered an explanation for this trend:

> [T]he argument that displaced food staple producers will simply shift to the production of commercial crops has a somewhat surreal quality. The high capital costs of entry into commercial food markets and the importance of infrastructure, which is non-existent in the more marginal areas from which people will be displaced, means most of the benefits from commercial agriculture will accrue to more prosperous producers.[54]

The "more realistic scenario" for corn producers under the AOA regime was "more intensive poverty, displacement, and migration to urban center."[55] Indeed, during the hearing on the WTO conducted by the House of Representatives' Special Committee on Globalization, the one sector that the Department of Agriculture was willing to recognize as having suffered from entry into the AOA was corn.[56]

The Assault on the Meat, Poultry, and Vegetable Industries

The negative impact of trade liberalization under the WTO regime went beyond traditional crops like rice, corn, and sugar to encompass higher value-added products like pork, poultry, and vegetables.

Massive importation of chicken parts, especially from the United States, nearly killed the industry after pressure from Washington resulted in liberal issuance of import licenses, with chicken parts imports rising by 101 percent in 1998 and 2021 percent in 1999. The import price of chicken in early 2000 came to Php 25.83 per kilo, which was 50 percent lower than the average farm-gate price of Php 53.17 per kilo price of local chicken.[57] The passage of a Safeguards Law gave chicken farmers some breathing space, but not much: chicken-leg quarters in

2003 were still being imported with a landed cost of Php 57 per kilo, below the farm-gate price of Php 64 per kilo.[58]

Compounding the woes of local industry was liberalization of the importation of frozen beef, which consumers saw as a substitute for both chicken and pork. Imports of cheap beef and "carabeef" were reported to have grown fivefold between 1993 and 1998, a trend that threatened to accelerate when an executive order withdrew beef imports from coverage under MAV.[59]

Cheap imports as well as other factors stemming from the Asian financial crisis led to the shutting down of two of the country's big poultry integrators, some 30 commercial farms, each producing 100,000 head of cattle, and five cooperatives in 1997.[60]

Poultry growers were joined in 2003 by hog producers in their threat to "mount a food blockade through their refusal to sell their poultry and livestock."[61] The hog raisers claimed that looser food imports under the AOA regime brought a yearly reduction of Php 5 to Php 10 per kilo in the farmgate price for pork, a figure which shot up to Php 14 to Php 17 in 2002. This translated to a 50 percent decline in price in just one year.[62] Data supported the claims of local producers of a sudden and massive surge in imports owing to trade liberalization. Pork imports rose from less than 1,000 MT in 1993 to 7000 MT in 1997 to 15,790 MT in 2000.[63] In 2002, imports were expected to hit almost 47 million kilos, up by 43 percent from the 2001 figure of 33 million KG.[64]

Vegetable producers were supposed to be among the gainers from AOA-led trade liberalization. Indeed, the AOA was expected to shift producers from cultivating rice and corn to producing high-value-added crops such as broccoli, lettuce, carrots, and cauliflower. Trade liberalization, in fact, hit a growing industry and hit it hard. From only 10,000 KG in 1999, the volume of imported fresh vegetables rose to 1.1 million KG in 2000 and 2 million KG in 2002.[65] Combined with smuggled fresh vegetables, the influx resulted in imported lettuce, for instance, selling at only Php 90 per kilo compared to local lettuce, which was retailing at Php 200 per kilo.[66]

Contributing to this massive differential was the application of 7 percent tariff on imported vegetables in accordance with Executive Order 470, a much lower rate than the 40 percent tariff that the Philippines committed under the WTO. Even with a 40 percent rate, however, imported produce would still enjoy a price advantage over local produce.

If Mindanao, the country's corn bowl, was threatened by maize imports, the country's salad bowl, Benguet, was endangered by the foreign vegetable invasion. According to one report,

> vegetable producers in Benguet have lost Php 2 billion in failed transactions between July and August 2002 because of the dumping of at least a million KGS of vegetables from China, Australia, New Zealand, and the Netherlands. The deluge of KGS of imported vegetables (whether smuggled or not) in the markets of Benguet, Mt. Province, the Cordilleras, Pangasinan, Central and Northern Luzon, and Metro Manila pose considerable risk and bring gross disadvantage to the nation's small vegetable growers.[67]

The report went on to warn that Php 6 billion would be lost yearly and "ten of thousands of growers will be displaced if the unabated influx of foreign vegetables continues."[68]

Keeping Out Philippine Tuna and Bananas

In becoming a member of the WTO, the Philippines entered the worst of all possible worlds: even as it opened up its agricultural markets to foreign products, key foreign markets continued to remain closed to Philippine exports.

The US, for instance, brazenly kept playing up its double-standards game. Administrative Order 25, which required meat importers to obtain additional safety certification, was put on hold in 2002, a year after it was issued, following a US threat to file a complaint with the WTO.[69] Meantime, the US itself issued a new directive requiring certification by a Philippine government agency that beef and pork exports meet some processing standards.[70]

Particularly disturbing were new market access restrictions imposed by the agricultural superpowers in defiance of WTO rules. The tuna industry was threatened with severe dislocation when the US and Europe slapped high tariffs on tuna imports. While allowing duty-free imports of tuna from the Andean countries, the US slapped tariffs ranging from 6.5 percent to 30 percent on Philippine tuna imports. The EU allowed preferential tariffs for its former colonies (the so-called ACP [African, Caribbean, and Pacific] countries) while slapping a 24 percent duty on Philippine tuna. Export earnings from canned tuna fell precipitously from $130 million in 1998 to $64 million in 2001.[71]

With the US accounting for 38 percent of its tuna exports and the EU for 15 percent, these brazen protectionist moves posed a serious threat to the viability of the Philippine tuna industry. The Department of Trade and Industry estimated possible losses from the discriminatory treatment in the US market alone could amount to $50 million a year.[72]

The government hailed an EU decision to lower the tariff on Philippine canned tuna exports, but it was hardly significant once one read the fine print. As *Business World* reported, "the 12 percent levy applies only to a specific amount of tuna imports called the tariff rate quota. This TRQ will be shared by the Philippines, Thailand, and Indonesia. Of the quota, the Philippines will get 9,000 MT while Thailand will account for 13,000 MT, and Indonesia will get 2,750 MT."[73]

Even Australia, an ally of the Philippines in the so-called Cairns Group, a grouping of developed and developing agro-exporting countries, beat up on the Philippines by invoking sanitary and phytosanitary standards, a standard Washington tactic. In mid-2002, after years of being petitioned to admit Philippine cavendish bananas, the Australian government decided against the import. The reason given was the risk of the Philippine banana carrying pests and diseases that could ruin the Australian banana industry. And yet, the Philippine bananas had been shipped since the '60s to countries with high quarantine standards, including Japan and New Zealand.

The real reason was a strong lobby from the Australian banana industry. The Australian industry produced 20 tons of bananas per hectare, compared to the Philippines, which turned out 50 tons per hectare, a difference that led to a marked disparity in price: $0.60 for each kilo of Australian bananas compared to $0.20 per kilo for Philippine bananas.[74]

The Abdication of the State

Eight years after the Philippines entered the WTO, there is now widespread acknowledgment that its agricultural sector was unprepared for adherence to the AOA. Indeed, few would now dispute the contention of critics that trade liberalization combined with government neglect of agricultural development has proved to be a deadly formula.

Neoclassical specialists in Philippine agriculture have been caught between an ideological propensity for liberalization and a recognition—though grudging—that protectionism is not the main problem of Philippine agriculture. In fact, economist Ramon Clarete, one of the prime intellectual managers of the Philippines' entry into the AOA, admitted, prior to entry into the WTO, that the agricultural sector had "the lowest effective tariff protection in the economy," with food items having an even lower effective protection than the rest of agriculture.[75] Effective protection in the 1970s and much of the '80s for agricultural products ranged from 5 to 9 percent, while effective rates of protection for the manufacturing sector ranged from 44 to 79 percent.[76] Effective rates of protection for manufacturing and agriculture tended to even out by the mid-1990s owing to tariff reforms, but this was largely due to manufacturing tariffs being brought down.

Not agricultural protectionism but problems relating to "a weak technology base, price distortions, weak property rights structure, constraints on land market operations, insufficient public support services, and poor governance," were identified by a team of neoclassical economists as the main bottlenecks to greater agricultural productivity.[77] Though they could not spell out the problem owing to the anti-state bias of their ideology, what these economists were, in effect, saying was that it was lack of effective, comprehensive, and coordinated government intervention in agriculture that lay at the root of the anemic state of Philippine agriculture.

The virtual abdication of government from agriculture is indicated by the fact that while most of the workforce was employed in agriculture and the sector contributed about 21.5 percent of gross value added, the budget allocation for agriculture in 2001 was only Php 12.8 billion or 3.4 percent of government spending.[78] Of the annual budgetary appropriations, less than 40 percent "have been historically allocated for productivity-enhancing expenditures such as irrigation, research and development, fishery extension, and other support services."[79] Research and development expenditures, at 0.27 percent of gross valued added by agriculture, was far below the one percent benchmark.[80]

Not surprisingly, only 1.34 million hectares out of 4.66 million hectares of irrigable land was actually irrigated. Only 17 percent of the Philippine road network was paved, compared to the 82 percent in Thailand and 75 percent in Malaysia. Crop yield across the board was anemic, with the average yield in rice of 2.87 MT per hectare way below average yields in China, Vietnam, and Thailand.[81]

Confronted with governments that played an aggressive, activist role in protecting and promoting their agriculture not only in the US and the EU but in the neighboring Asian countries as well, the Philippines was ill-equipped to enter the AOA.

To prevent the agricultural sector from becoming a roadblock to the ratification of the WTO agreement, the Ramos administration promised to appropriate and release funds for agricultural modernization and safety nets. The fund promised—called the Department of Agriculture Action Plan—totalled Php 128 billion, to be released at the rate of Php 32 billion annually.[82] The figure included "Php 27 billion for the improvement of irrigation facilities, Php 8 billion for the construction of farm-to-market roads, Php 762 million for the improvement of post-harvest facilities, and Php 64 million for the installation of grain centers."[83]

However, according to one agricultural expert, only 44 percent of the Php 32 billion promised for 1995 was appropriated. Of this amount, funding for new projects—i.e., projects begun after ratification of the WTO agreement—amounted to the exceedingly small sum of Php 2.8 billion. In 1996, the proposed Php 32 billion was reduced to Php 14.6 billion, of which the funding for new projects was, at Php 2.2 billion, even lower than the 1995 figure.[84] Seven years later, the Department of Agriculture admitted that only 50 percent of the proposed Department of Agriculture Action Plan had been released.[85]

The failure of the safety net program was supposed to be addressed by the Agriculture and Fisheries Modernization Act (AFMA) passed in 1998 which provided for comprehensive government assistance covering such areas as irrigation, post-harvest facilities, credit and financing, and research and development. But, as one report noted, "despite having a legislated annual budgetary allocation, AFMA was not able to take off the ground as government could not even meet the annual budgetary needs of the Department of Agriculture."[86] What limited amounts were appropriated of the original proposed Php 35 billion safety net program, some charged, were largely diverted to urban projects such as flyovers during the Ramos period.[87]

During the ratification debate, pro-WTO advocates promoted the vision that the AOA would create a situation where the Philippines would fill production niches in which it would have the "comparative advantage," such as the cultivation of high-value-added export crops such as cutflowers, asparagus, broccoli, and snow peas. These advocates, such as then-Secretary of Agriculture Roberto Sebastian, did not do their homework.

The shift to high value "non-traditional agricultural exports" (NTAEs) requires investment that is simply not within the reach of small producers. For instance, in the case of cutflowers, data from Ecuador reveals an average initial capital investment of $200,000 per hectare. Annual input costs are also high, with the costs of agrochemicals alone coming to over $18,900 per hectare.[88] In the case of snowpeas, broccoli, and cauliflower, annual production costs, according to data from Guatemala, comes to $3,145, $1,096, and $971 per hectare respectively, compared to $219 per hectare for corn.[89]

Moreover, competitive advantage in these crops can only be achieved through significant outlays in technological support and research and development. As many analysts have pointed out, NTAE cultivation is biased against small-scale producers because "many traditional crops require considerable technological sophistication, relative to traditional production, as they are either new to the region, require special care at harvest because of their perishability, or are being produced to meet the more demanding cosmetic quality standards of foreign consumers."[90]

Without massive government financial support, there was simply no way that the Philippines could manage significant increases in the production of high-value crops, much less attain comparative advantage in producing them.

Not surprisingly, Philippine agriculture entered the worst of all worlds in the mid-1990s: massive trade liberalization amidst a continuing lack of effective support from government. Despite their grudging recognition of the fact that comprehensive state support was the sine qua non of agriculture's survival, the neoclassical economists and technocrats who had gained control of the strategic heights of the economic bureaucracy in the '80s and '90s supported the WTO liberalization drive. In many cases, in fact, as in case of vegetable and meat imports, they supported deeper cuts in tariffs than was required under AOA rules. Unilateral liberalization, in their view, was still the best route to optimum welfare.

This was, however, an increasingly isolated position. Even a bastion of neoclassical economics, the International Food Policy Research Institute, admitted that "[w]ithout reform of agricultural trade barriers in industrialized countries, import liberalization in the developing world will perpetuate unfair competition."[91]

The AOA: Institutionalizing Monopolistic Competition

The prosperity for all that was promised by the GATT-WTO Accord was premised on the idea that liberalization would be universally undertaken. In the case of agriculture, however, for all intents and purposes, liberalization was unilateral—developing countries were opening up their markets while the developed countries retained their heavy structures of protection amidst superficial and cosmetic liberalization. This was the main problem with the AOA: that, contrary to its claim that it opened up global markets to free trade, in fact, it was a regime that regulated the competition among two heavily subsidized monopolistic agricultural superpowers—the European Union and the United States—for third-country markets. Perhaps convinced by neoclassical doctrine that unilateral liberalization would still result in greater welfare gains than a pragmatic trade policy based on reciprocal liberalization, the technocrats refused to acknowledge how truly dangerous for Philippine agriculture the global trading system was.

A close study of the genesis of the AOA and its provisions would probably have helped them to gain an appreciation of the hard economic realpolitik that informed the agreement.

Briefly, prior to the Uruguay Round, agriculture was de facto outside GATT discipline, mainly because the US had sought in the 1950s a waiver from Article 11 of GATT, which prohibited quantitative restrictions on imports. With the US threatening to leave the GATT unless it was allowed to maintain protective mechanisms for sugar, dairy products, and other agricultural commodities, Washington was given a "non-time-bound waiver" on other agricultural products.[92] This led to the GATT's lax enforcement on other agricultural producers for fear of being accused of having double standards.

The US and other agricultural powers not only ignored Article 11 but they also exploited Article 16, which exempted agricultural products from GATT's ban on subsidies. One effect of these moves was the transformation of the EU from being a net food importer into a net food exporter in the 1970s. By the beginning of the Uruguay Round in the mid-'80s, the EU's Common Agricultural Policy (CAP) had evolved into what was described as "a complex web of prices and sales guarantees, subsidies, and other support measures that largely insulated farmers' incomes from market forces."[93]

With domestic prices set considerably above world prices and no controls on production, European farmers expanded production. The mounting surpluses could only be disposed of through exports, sparking competition with the previously dominant subsidized US farmers for third-country markets. The competition between the agricultural superpowers turned fierce, but it was not so much their subsidized farmers that suffered. The victims were largely farmers in the South, such as the small-scale cattle growers of West Africa and South Africa, who were driven to ruin by low-priced EU exports of subsidized beef.

With state subsidies mounting to support the bitter competition for third-country markets, the EU and US gradually came to realize that continuing along the same path could only lead to a no-win situation for both. By the late '80s, for instance, close to 80 percent of the EU's budget was going to support agricultural programs, and the US had inaugurated a whole new set of expensive programs such as the

Export Enhancement Program, to win back markets, such as the North African wheat market, from the EU.[94]

This mutual realization of the need for rules in the struggle for third-country markets is what led the EU and the US to press for inclusion of agriculture in the Uruguay Round. In fact, it was just the EU and the US that negotiated the so-called Blair House Accord in 1992 and 1993. The accord then was promptly tossed to other GATT members by the two superpowers in 1994 as the proposed AOA on a take-it-or-leave-it basis. Rather than seriously promoting a mechanism to advance free trade, the two agro-superpowers resorted to the rhetoric of free trade and offered minor concessions to liberalization in order to institutionalize a system of monopolistic competition, with each seeking advantage at the margins.

How did the AOA achieve this?

First, it institutionalized the heavy subsidization of Northern agriculture, though it provided for "domestic support"—quantified into a comprehensive measure called the "aggregate measure of support"—to be reduced by 20 percent over a six-year period.

Second, it institutionalized export subsidies while making the slight concession that they would be reduced over a six-year period by 21 percent in volume terms and 36 percent in total cash value, with no commitments for further reduction at the end of the six-year period.

Third, it institutionalized and exempted from cuts direct income subsidies for farmers on the specious grounds that these had "no, or at the most minimal, trade-distorting effects on production. "[95] These included so-called Green Box or Blue Box measures such as "land set-aside" programs in the EU which entitled farmers to subsidies if they withdrew 15 percent of their land from cultivation. They also included so-called deficiency payments in the US, which was a direct income subsidy that was stable because it was the same in good or bad crop years. Deficiency payments in the US were projected to average $5.1 billion a year between 1996 and 2002.[96]

The truth of the matter is that direct income payments to European and American farmers are anything but decoupled from production, since without them agriculture would scarcely remain profitable. Deficiency payments, for instance, make up between one-fifth and one-third of US farm incomes.[97] In other words, in enshrining the notion of decoupled payments as untouchable subsidies in the Green Box, the US and the EU were, as one analyst put it, "taking away direct support of markets and replacing it with direct subsidization of [Northern] farmers."[98]

Fourth, it exempted from cuts export credit and low-interest concessional aid programs such as the US' PL-480 Title One Program and the Export Credit Guarantee Program that were mainly aimed at carving out markets abroad. The PL-480 Title One Program gives a developing country thirty years to repay a loan to buy a US commodity like rice at a one percent interest rate and a five-year grace period.[99] The Export Guarantee Program guarantees payments to US banks on loans contracted by foreign banks for the purchase of US agricultural commodities.[100]

In contrast to this massive subsidization in the OECD (Organization for Economic Cooperation and Development) countries, farmers in many developing countries have had little financial support. In the words of Philippine negotiators in Geneva, the essence of the complex section on subsidies was that "the heavily subsidizing developed countries can retain up to 80 percent of their trade-distorting subsidies while developing countries which had not applied trade-distorting support measures can subsidize no more than 10 percent of the total value of their agricultural production."[101] Certainly, in the case of the Philippines, overall subsidization was, at 4 percent, way below the 10 percent maximum, with government market price support for rice and corn coming to only 5 percent and one percent, respectively, of the total value of production in the two commodities.[102]

In fact, developing countries like the Philippines have been penalized by policies that have brought about the "negative subsidization" of their agricultural sector.[103] One study estimated that for eighteen developing countries, "taxation," or the transfer of value from agricultural production as subsidies to other sectors of the economy, amounted to an average of 30 percent of the value of production from 1960 to 1984.[104]

The institutionalization of various mechanisms of subsidization was one reason for the lack of any progress to curb the tremendous negative impact of Northern agriculture on global markets in the seven years since the AOA came into force in 1995. Another key reason was what came to be known as "dirty tariffication"—that is, converting tariffs and non-tariff barriers or quotas into high initial tariff rates.

Tariff rates were bound at their equivalents in the 1986-88 base period, which were quite high relative to levels in 1995 when the AOA took effect. In the case of the US, for instance, between 1992 and 1996, simple average tariffs rose from 5.7 percent to 8.5 percent for agriculture and livestock production, 6.6 to 10.0 percent for food products, and 14.6 to 104.4 percent for tobacco products.[105] The manipulation of tariffication to achieve the same impact as quotas was especially evident in the case of tobacco products, where the US levied an ad valorem duty of 350 percent for above minimum access imports of food products.[106] Indeed, a study conducted by the UNESCAP (United Nations Economic and Social Commission for Asia and the Pacific) of the tariffication process showed that the EU's final bindings for the year 2000 were almost two-thirds above the actual tariff equivalent for 1989-1993, while those for the US were three-quarters higher.[107]

Another mechanism used to limit actual market access to developing-country imports was selective tariff reductions, or keeping tariffs high on sensitive products and reducing tariffs on less sensitive products. This practice was possible since the 36 percent tariff reduction required by AOA was an average, unweighted reduction, with the only constraint being a 15 percent cut on each tariff line. So countries tended to reduce existing low tariffs on non-sensitive products by significant amounts while reducing only slightly the existing high tariffs if the product was of trade importance. Thus, the US reduced the existing low 6 percent tariff on common wheat by 55 percent while limiting the cut on the existing tariff of 134.7 percent on white sugar, a sensitive commodity, to 15 percent.[108]

With such a skewed agreement, it hardly came as a surprise that overall protection and subsidization of agriculture in the OECD countries increased in the first decade of the AOA. The total amount of agricultural subsidies provided by the OECD's thirty member-governments rose from $182 billion in 1995 to $280 billion in 1997, about $315 billion in 2001, and an estimated $318 billion in 2002.[109] According to Oxfam International, the EU and the US were spending $9-10 billion more on subsidies than they did a decade earlier.[110] Subsidies accounted for 40 percent of the value of agricultural production in the EU and 25 percent in the US.[111] While smallholders in the developing world had to survive on less than $400 a year, American and European farmers were receiving respectively an average of $21,000 and $16,000 a year in subsidies.[112] There was no way to describe this except as socialist agriculture!

It was, however, socialism for rich farmers. According to the OECD, two-thirds of US crop supports went to only 10 percent of cotton, grain and oilseed growers.[113] Oxfam calculated that in the US, the largest 7 percent of farms received 50 percent of government subsidies, while 60 percent of US farmers received no subsidies at all.[114]

Not surprisingly, the pressures to overproduce and thus to look for new markets likewise increased. A 1997 report to the EU farm ministers projected the surplus of wheat to rise from 2.7 million MT to 45 million MT by 2005, and total cereal surplus to shoot up to 58 million MT.[115] The solution to this condition of subsidized overproduction, said EU Agriculture Minister Franz Fischler, was intensified efforts to export grain.[116]

Continuing subsidization has also deepened US agriculture's dependence on massive exporting. Admitting that "one out of every three farm acres in America is dedicated to exports," then-US Trade Representative Charlene Barshefsky contended in 1997 that "given the limitations inherent in US demand-led growth, we must find new markets for American agriculture. We must open new markets to support the increasingly productive US agricultural sector."[117]

The Philippines' structural consolidation as a food-importing country was thus paralleled globally during the latter half of the '90s. A Food and Agricultural Organization (FAO) study of fourteen countries in Asia, Africa, and Latin America found that the levels of their food imports in 1995-98 exceeded those in 1990-94. Import surges in various sectors led to reports of "import competing industries facing consequential difficulties." Producers expressed the fear that "without adequate market protection, accompanied by development programs, many more domestic products would be displaced, or undermined sharply, leading to a transformation of domestic diets and to increased dependence on imported foods."[118] The FAO study acknowledged that while developing countries' share in world food exports increased from 30 percent in 1970 to 37 percent in 1997, their food imports increased much more, from 28 percent to 37 percent over the same period.[119] As Aileen Kwa has noted, these figures indicated that many countries "are turning from being net food exporters to net food importers."[120]

By 2003, it would be fair to say, the Philippine government, while putting a brave face and publicly hoping for fundamental change in the WTO, had become completely disillusioned with the system and especially the agricultural powers that ran the AOA. As noted above, a "rebalancing/countervailing mechanism" advanced by the Philippines that would allow developing countries to raise tariffs on crops subsidized by the rich countries by amounts calibrated to the levels of subsidization was not even mentioned in the Harbinson draft. This was not surprising given the fact that, as an exasperated Philippine negotiator noted, in earlier meetings of the WTO Committee on Agriculture, "the major blocs (US, EU, Japan, etc.) have refrained from engaging US and our developing-country allies in floor debate on the proposal."[121]

The WTO: Blind to Development and Non-transparent

The bitter reality that the whole WTO agreement and not just the AOA was an instrument that benefited the few gainers of globalization at the expense of the majority was experienced and resented all throughout the developing world. Also leading to the developing countries' disillusionment with the GATT-WTO was the fate of the measures approved during the Uruguay Round that were supposed to respond to the special conditions of developing countries. Besides the AOA, there were two key agreements which promoters of the WTO claimed were specifically designed to meet the needs of the South: the special ministerial agreement approved in Marrakech in April 1994, which decreed that special compensatory measures would be taken to counteract the negative effects of trade liberalization on the net food-importing developing countries; and the Agreement on Textiles and Clothing, which mandated that the system of quotas on developing-country exports of textiles and garments to the North would be dismantled over ten years.

The special ministerial decision taken at Marrakech to provide assistance to "net food-importing countries" to offset the reduction of subsidies that would make food imports more expensive for the "net food-importing countries" has never been implemented. Though world crude oil prices more than doubled in 1995-1996, the World Bank and the International Monetary Fund (IMF) scotched any idea of offsetting aid by arguing that "the price increase was not due to the agreement on agriculture, and besides there was never any agreement anyway on who would be responsible for providing the assistance."[122]

The Agreement on Textiles and Clothing committed the developed countries to bring under WTO discipline all textile and garment imports over four stages, ending on January 1, 2005. A key feature was supposed to be the lifting of quotas on imports restricted under the multifiber agreement (MFA) and similar schemes which had been used to contain penetration of developed-country markets by cheap clothing and textile imports from the Third World. However, developed countries retained the right to choose which product lines to liberalize and when, so that they first brought mainly unrestricted products into the WTO discipline and postponed dealing with restricted products until much later. Thus, in the first phase, all restricted products continued to be under quota, as only items where imports were not considered threatening—like felt hats or yarn of carded fine animal hair—were included in the developed countries' notifications. Indeed, the notifications for the coverage of products for liberalization on January 1, 1998, showed that "even at the second stage of implementation only a very small proportion" of restricted products would see their quotas lifted.[123] An Oxfam 2002 report claimed that the EU and the US had eliminated only a quarter of the textiles and garments quotas they were required to remove under the agreement.[124]

Given this trend, John Whalley notes that "the belief is now widely held in the developing world that in 2004, while the MFA may disappear, it may well be replaced by a series of other trade instruments, possibly substantial increases in anti-dumping duties."[125]

Non-transparency and the Seattle Collapse

The growing resentment of the developing countries extended to the processes of decision making itself, which were non-transparent, informal, and dominated by the big trading powers. Indeed, one of the key reasons for the collapse of the WTO ministerial in Seattle in December 1999 was the absence of transparent decision making. Stories abound of ministers from developing countries complaining of being lost at the Seattle Convention Center, looking for a "Green Room" where key decisions would be made, not knowing that the Green Room did not refer to a real room at the convention center but to an exclusive process of decision making.

During the WTO ratification process in 1994, partisans of the new trade organization portrayed it as a one country-one vote organization where the United States would actually have the same vote as Rwanda. In truth, the WTO is not governed democratically via a one country-one vote system like the UN General Assembly or through a grossly unequal system of weighted voting like the World Bank or the IMF. While according to its constitution it is a one country-one vote system, the process that reigns in the World Trade Organization is "consensus," one that it took over from the old GATT, where the last time a vote was taken was in 1959.

Consensus, in practice, is a process whereby the big trading countries impose their consensus on the less powerful countries. As C. Fred Bergsten, a prominent partisan of globalization who heads the Institute of International Economics, put it during US Senate hearings on the ratification of the GATT-WTO agreement in 1994, the WTO "does not work by voting. It works by a consensus arrangement which, to tell the truth, is managed by four—the Quads: the United States, Japan, European Union, and Canada...Those countries have to agree if any major steps are going to be made. But no votes."[126]

Though the Ministerial and the General Council are theoretically the highest decision-making bodies of the WTO, decisions are arrived at not in formal plenaries but in non-transparent backroom sessions known as the "Green Room," after the color of the Director General's room at the WTO headquarters in Geneva.

Non-transparency and lack of real democratic decision making was one of the reasons behind the now famous revolt of the developing countries at the Seattle Convention Center that played a central role in the collapse of the Third Ministerial in Seattle in December 2001. With surprising frankness, at a press conference in Seattle, shortly after the ministerial collapse, then-US Trade Representative Charlene Barshefsky described the dynamics and consequences of the Green Room: "The process... was a rather exclusionary one. All the meetings were held between 20 and 30 key countries... And this meant 100 countries, 100, were never in the room...[T]his led to extraordinarily bad feeling that they were left out of the process and that the results even at Singapore had been dictated to them by the 25 to 30 countries who were in the room."[127]

Barshefsky admitted that "the WTO has outgrown the processes appropriate to an earlier time. An increasing and necessary view, generally shared among the members, was that we needed a process which had a greater degree of internal transparency and inclusion to accommodate a larger and more diverse membership." This was backed up by UK Secretary of State Stephen Byers who stated that the "WTO will not be able to continue in its present form. There has to be fundamental and radical change in order for it to meet the needs and aspirations of all 134 of its members."[128]

These expressions of concern by two key officials of the trade superpowers did not, however, result in any reforms after Seattle. The Green Room process was, for instance, defended thus by a key adviser to Director General Mike Moore: "One of the myths about Seattle is that there were no Africans and hardly any developing countries in the Green Room. In fact, there were six Africans and a majority from developing countries. Moreover, any deal reached in the Green Room must still be approved by all WTO members."[129] Moore himself told developing-country delegates at the UNCTAD X meeting in Bangkok in February 2000, eight weeks after Seattle, that the Consensus/Green Room system was "non-negotiable."[130]

Doha: The Low Point

Moving into the Fourth Ministerial slated for Doha, Qatar, in late 2001, the big trade superpowers were determined to avoid a repetition of the Seattle collapse. Not surprisingly, lack of transparency marked the run-up to and the proceedings of the Fourth Ministerial in Doha, Qatar, in November 2001.

The proposed draft declaration for the ministerial meeting was a product of the sort of non-transparent tactics that the big trading powers resorted to. In the run-up to Doha, most of the developing countries were pretty much united around the position that the Ministerial would have to focus on implementation issues and on reviews of key WTO agreements, not on launching a new round of trade liberalization.

But when the draft declaration came out a few weeks before Doha, the emphasis was not on dealing with implementation issues, but on an alleged consensus on opening up negotiations on the issues of competition, investment policy, government procurement, and trade facilitation that were the priorities of the minority of rich and powerful trading countries. "Despite clearly stated positions that the developing countries are unwilling to go into a new round until past implementation and decision making are addressed," noted Kwa, who followed the process closely, "the draft declaration favorably positioned the launching of a comprehensive new round with an open agenda."[131]

The draft, which was authored by the chair of the General Council, was a product of consultations with all WTO members. In actual fact, the key consultations were conducted among an inner circle of about 20-25 participants—the so-called Green Room process that effectively excludes most of the members of the WTO. In the run-up to Qatar, this exclusive process held two "mini-ministerials," one in Mexico at the end of August and another in Singapore on October 13-14. How one got invited to these meetings was very murky. Kwa cites the case of one ambassador from a transition economy who was promised an invitation to a Green Room meeting by the WTO secretariat but never got one. Then there was the case of an African ambassador who wanted to attend the Singapore mini-ministerial: When he approached the WTO secretariat for an invitation, he was told that they were not hosting the meeting. When he tried the Singapore mission in Geneva, the response was that they were simply coordinating the meeting and were not in a position to send out invitations.[132]

The Doha ministerial from November 9-14, 2001, took place amidst conditions that were already unfavorable from the point of view of developing-country interests. The September 11 events provided a heaven-sent opportunity for US Trade Representative Robert Zoellick and European Union Trade Commissioner Pascal Lamy to step up the pressure on the developing countries to agree to the launching of a new trade round, invoking the rationale that it was necessary to counter a global downturn that had been worsened by the terrorist actions. The location was also unfavorable, Qatar being a monarchy where dissent could be easily controlled. The WTO secretariat's authority over who would be granted visas to enter Qatar for the ministerial allowed it to radically limit the number of legitimate nongovernment organizations (NGOs) that could be present to about sixty, thus preventing that explosive interaction of developing-country resentment and massive street protest that took place in Seattle.

Still, these factors would not have been sufficient to bring about an unfavorable outcome for developing countries. Tactics mattered, and here the developing countries were clearly outmaneuvered in Doha. Among these tactics the following must be highlighted:[133]

- Pushing the highly unbalanced draft declaration and presenting it to the ministerial as a "clean text" on which there allegedly was consensus, thus restricting the arena of substantive discussion and making it difficult for developing countries to register fundamental objections without seeming "obstructionist."

- Pitting officials from the capitals against their negotiators based in Geneva, with the latter being characterized as "recalcitrant" or "narrow."

- Employing direct threats, as the United States did when it warned Haiti and the Dominican Republic to cease opposition to its position on government procurement or risk cancellation of their preferential trade arrangements.

- Buying off countries with goodies, as the European Union did when, in return for their agreeing to the final declaration, it assured countries in the ACP group that the WTO would respect the so-called ACP Waiver that would allow them to export their agricultural commodities to Europe at preferential terms relative to other developing countries. Pakistan, a stalwart among developing countries in Geneva, was notably quiet at Doha. Apparently, this had something to do with the US' granting Pakistan a massive aid package of grants, loans, and debt reduction owing to its special status in the US war against terrorism. Nigeria had taken the step of issuing an official communique denouncing the draft declaration before Doha, but came out loudly supporting it on November 14—a flip-flop that is difficult to separate from the US' coming up with the promise of a big economic and military aid package in the interim.

— Reinstituting the infamous "Green Room" on November 13 and 14, when some twenty handpicked countries were isolated from the rest and "delegated" by the WTO secretariat and the big powers to come up with the final declaration. These countries were not picked by a democratic process, and efforts by some developing-country representatives to insert themselves into this select group were rebuffed, some gently, others quite explicitly, as was the case with a delegate from Uganda.

— Finally, pressuring the developing countries by telling them that they would bear the onus for causing the collapse of another ministerial, the collapse of the WTO, and the deepening of the global recession that would allegedly be the consequence of these two events.

Some accounts of the Doha process claimed that Doha represented a victory of sorts for the developing countries in that they managed to get a declaration that recognized the urgency of addressing their concerns in implementation issues and special and differential treatment as well as placed public health concerns over intellectual property rights. In fact, from the point of view of process, Doha was a low point in the GATT-WTO's history of backroom intimidation, threats, bribery, and non-transparency. There are no records of the actual decision-making process in Doha because the formal sessions of the ministerial—which is where decision making is made in a democratic system—were, as in Seattle, reserved for speeches, and the real decisions took place in informal groupings whose meeting places kept shifting and were not known to all. There being no records, there is little accountability, and the principals in any deals can deny that they engaged in questionable behavior.

This non-transparent process resulted in practically sidelining the developing countries' demand that the WTO focus on implementation issues and placing on centerstage the top agenda of the big trading powers: the eventual launching of a new set of trade negotiations that would bring into WTO jurisdiction the non-trade areas of investment, competition policy, government procurement, and trade facilitation. Bergsten, the free-trade partisan who heads the Institute of International Economics in Washington D.C., once compared the WTO and trade liberalization to a bicycle: it only stays up by moving forward. Doha set the WTO upright once more, but it was still wobbly, and this was because a great deal of resentment lingered among developing countries from the whole non-transparent process of bamboozling them into accepting a declaration running counter to their interests.

From Doha to Cancun

The centerpiece of the Doha Declaration was the decision, subject to "explicit consensus" of all WTO members, to begin negotiations on the "New Issues" of investment, government procurement, competition policy, and trade facilitation. The first three being non-trade issues, the declaration was seen by many developing countries as providing momentum for a massive expansion of the authority of the WTO.

The propaganda of Northern governments, especially of the British government, was that the Doha Round would be one that would incorporate development concerns into the trade agenda. Much of the established press—and many Northern NGOs—pointed to Article 6 of the declaration, which upheld public health concerns over intellectual property rights, as indicating that the WTO could become a development-friendly institution.

In eighteen months leading up to the Fifth Ministerial Meeting in Mexico in mid-September 2003, the agenda of the trade superpowers included concluding a new AOA initiating preliminary negotiations on the so-called new issues, launching of negotiations on industrial tariffs, and substantial progress in negotiations on services.

The hope was that at Cancun, the negotiations in the different trade and trade-related areas would come together in a new WTO agreement that would be as far-reaching as the Uruguay Round. It would be a round that would give the faltering globalization process a surge forward.

Between Doha and Cancun, however, there was barely any movement in any of the negotiating areas.

Not surprisingly, agriculture was the Gordian knot.

Even before Doha, negotiations had already begun for a new AOA. By the beginning of 2002, however, the talks were getting nowhere, with both the United States and the European Union competing to stymie the talks. Saying that "[W]e want to be selling our beef and our corn and our beans to people around the world who need to eat," President Bush signed into law on May 13, 2002, a legislation giving US farming interests $190 billion in subsidies over the next ten years. The report increased certain subsidies by 80 percent; raised price supports for wheat, cotton, soybeans, rice, and cotton; and created new subsidies for items like lentils, peanuts, and milk.[134]

Equally defiant was the European Union. In October 2002, French President Jacques Chirac and German Prime Minister Gerhard Schroeder agreed that there would be no cut in EU agricultural subsidies during their talk on EU enlargement. Indeed, the overall amount of subsidies will increase until 2006, and from 2007 to 2013, spending will be frozen at 2006 levels.[135] "The deal spells out clearly that EU dumping is going to continue till at least 2013," noted one analyst.[136]

Disagreements on agriculture between the US and the EU had been central to unraveling the Third Ministerial of the WTO in Seattle in December 1999. Some fancy rewording on the question of subsidies demanded by the EU saved the Fourth Ministerial in Doha, Qatar, from the same fate.[137] But by the beginning of 2003, so little progress had been registered that many negotiators raised the specter that the impasse would unravel concurrent negotiations in other areas like industrial tariffs, services, and the so-called new issues of investment, competition, and government procurement, leading to a Seattle-like outcome for the fifth ministerial, which was due to be held in Cancun, Mexico, in mid-September 2003.

The draft negotiating document prepared by WTO farm negotiations chairman Stuart Harbinson produced a stalemate at the so-called Tokyo Mini-ministerial on February 14-16, which was one of several restricted sessions designed to gain a rough consensus in key trade areas before Cancun.[138] Japanese Minister of Agriculture Tadamori Oshima rejected the paper's proposals for minimum cuts of between 25 and 45 percent and average reductions of 40 to 60 percent on all farm tariffs over five years.[139] The EU also attacked the Harbinson proposal as "unbalanced" for proposing that "trade-distorting" subsidies be cut by 60 percent over five years and that export subsidies be phased out entirely over nine years.[140] Both Japan and the EU denounced the paper as ensuring that the US would be the only victor in the negotiations.

In the fight between the agro-export giants, the concerns of developing countries were conveniently lost. As Kwa points out, the Harbinson text does not address their fear that EU and US subsidies will now mostly be shifted to the so-called Green Box, a listing of exempted subsidies that include the massive direct payments to farming interests that directly or indirectly distort trade. [141]

The Harbinson text also completely ignored proposals put forward by Argentina and the Philippines (both of which were not invited to the Tokyo meeting) for "rebalancing/countervailing mechanisms" that would allow developing countries to raise tariffs on crops subsidized by the developed countries by amounts proportionate to the subsidies.[142] Instead, for developing countries, tariffs greater than 120 percent were to be slashed by 40 percent, while those between 20 and 120 percent would be decreased by 33 percent, with no linkage to the subsidies maintained by the wealthy agro-exporters.

The draft also contained no meaningful recommendations that would apply the principle of "special and differential treatment" to the developing countries, giving their agricultural sectors significant protection for structural reasons—owing to their different level and conditions of agricultural development.[143] True, the Harbinson draft proposed that developing countries might classify some staple products as "strategic" and have them subjected to lower tariff cuts than other commodities. However, the proposal was vague, the number of products that could qualify as strategic was unclear, and positive impact would be limited as products would still be subject to an average tariff cut of 10 percent.[144] As Kwa noted, the strategic products proposal was "no more than wool being pulled over the eyes of trade negotiators and Ministers. It is a fictitious fig leaf offered to entice the less WTO-savvy decision makers in the developing world."[145]

In essence, the Harbinson draft proposed to change some of the terms of monopolistic competition among the EU, US, Australia, and Canada while accelerating the removal of the protective barriers of the developing country markets they are fighting over.

Agricultural negotiations remained effectively stalemated all the way up to the Cancun negotiations. The situation was much the same in other areas. One of the few positive items in the Doha Ministerial Declaration was the clear statement that "the TRIPS agreement does not and should not prevent members from taking measures to protect public health."[146] The US, however, squandered a lot of goodwill in the next few months by maintaining its position that only in the case of drugs for three epidemics—HIV-AIDS, tuberculosis, and malaria—should patent rights be loosened and that the import of cheap generic drugs by countries with no drug-manufacturing capacity should be limited to the least developed countries. With the Doha declaration on their side, the developing countries rejected the US position, leading to a stalemate until the very eve of Cancun, when a compromise agreement was forged. However, the compromise agreement was denounced by many as loaded with such restrictions as to make the import of cheap drugs a very cumbersome process and thus defeat the objective of the Doha provision. US trade policy came to be seen by developing countries as being hostage to the big pharmaceutical lobby.

On the New Issues—investment, competition policy, government procurement, and trade facilitation—the EU continued to make the commencement of negotiations a central point of its Cancun agenda. But, if anything, the developing countries were even more adamant that the Singapore issues be dropped from the negotiations. The new-issues question threatened, in fact, to derail the ministerial because there was widespread disagreement that the Doha ministerial, in fact, launched negotiations in these areas. According to the chairman's statement that accompanied the Doha Declaration, whether or not negotiations will begin in these areas would depend on the "explicit consensus" of all WTO member states at the Cancun summit.[147]

In two negotiating areas of great interest to developing countries, there was absolutely no movement. These were the issues of Special and Differential Treatment and Implementation. On the latter, it might be of interest that when Lamy, EU trade commissioner, met with NGO representatives in Bangkok in mid-March 2003, he tried to shift the blame to the developing countries, whom he accused of not being able to agree on what were the two or three top priorities regarding implementation that needed to be tackled.[148]

If Cancun was going to be salvaged, observers warned, this would have to be done by resorting to non-transparency Doha style. And indeed, there were indications that as Cancun neared, negotiations were shifting to informal mode and going "underground." In fact, in a statement that was extraordinary for its candor, New Zealand Ambassador Timothy Groser warned developing countries "not to push for greater transparency in the decision-making process." With a membership of 146, Groser warned that "if every decision-making process were to involve the entire membership, the process would go nowhere. Efforts to attain internal transparency... would be counterproductive and would push the negotiating process underground."[149] An astute observer of the Geneva process, in fact, warned, "the process already seems to have gone underground, since it is entirely in the control of the DG/Harbinson team, and the chair of the General Council, in alliance with the major players."[150] Not surprisingly, resentment mounted among the developing countries.

While the US and the EU wrangled over the issue of how much export subsidies should be reduced and over the formulas for reducing agricultural tariffs, several developing countries, led by Brazil, India, South Africa, and China, got together on August 20, 2003, to form the Group of 20 (G-20), which demanded "substantial cuts on trade-distorting domestic support, substantial increase in market access, and elimination of export subsidies."[151]

Another, larger grouping of thirty-two developing countries formed around the demand for "special products" that would be exempted from tariff reductions and "special safeguard mechanisms" against the highly subsidized agricultural exports from the developed countries.

Still another, and even larger, group of countries, which eventually came to be known as the G-90, was forming around opposition to the start of negotiations on the new issues without the explicit consensus of all WTO member countries.

Collapse in Cancun

The proposed ministerial declaration in the last week of August offered little in the way of meeting the developing countries' demands for substantial cuts in levels of government support for farming interests. Instead, it presented a detailed framework for discussion on the Singapore issues. Thus, as the Cancun Ministerial opened on September 10, a showdown was in the offing between the US-EU group that had

dominated WTO discussions and the new developing country formations. The flashpoint was an unexpected one, and that was the question
of cotton subsidies being given to European and US producers which
had contributed to a collapse of international prices. US producers were
offloading cotton on world markets at between 20 percent and 55 percent of the cost of production, leading to a severe crisis of West African
and Central African cotton farmers.[152] Four African countries—Benin,
Burkina Faso, Chad, and Mali—demanded compensation of between
$250 million and $1 billion annually and the unilateral elimination of
cotton subsidies.[153]

Roundly rejected by the developing countries, the draft declaration was revised and issued on the afternoon of September 13. Known
as the "Derbez Text"—after the Ministerial Chairman, Mexican Foreign Affairs Minister Luis Derbez—the revised declaration proposed
nothing substantive on cotton subsidies, some slight revisions in market
access, and kept two of the original new issues—government procurement and trade facilitation.

The new-market access sweeteners could have split the G-20 coalition, designed as they were to win over large agro-exporters like Brazil but were detrimental to India and others seeking protection of
their agriculture. "However," notes one account, "Brazil showed leadership and instead of settling for short-term benefits in market access
joined forces with India to keep the alliance together…."[154] But the
final Green Room meeting of some thirty countries on September 14
was not even able to get to agriculture. The discussion started on the
New Issues. Japan and South Korea declared themselves unwilling to
drop investment and competition polity from the negotiations. G-90
members from Asia and Africa fiercely rejected the inclusion of any
issue, many of them angered by the declaration's US-inspired sugges-
tion that African cotton exporters should diversify away from cotton.
At that point, Derbez brought down the gavel to end the ministerial,
declaring that the necessary consensus for the ministerial to proceed
was absent. Despite efforts by US Trade Negotiator Robert Zoellick
to pin the blame on developing countries and EU Trade Minister Lamy
to assign it to the "medieval" decision-making rules, most of the press,
including the western press, saw the EU-US inflexibility on agriculture

and the EU's unrelenting push on the New Issues as shouldering most
of the blame.[155]

The Philippines on the Road to Cancun

As the Cancun ministerial approached, there was a widespread sense
in Philippine government circles that the Philippines had lost badly
with its entry into the WTO.

Not only had nothing been gained, not only were key sectors of
the economy dislocated, but revenues had been lost—revenues which
could have gone to plug the government's worsening budget deficit.
According to the Tariff Commission, WTO-related tariff cuts lowered
tariff collections from Php 83 billion in 1997 to Php 81.2 billion in
1999 to Php 72.96 billion in 2001 and Php 59.5 billion in 2002.[156]
The difference between the collection rates in 1997 and 2002 came to
Php 23.6 billion, which came to over 10 percent of the Php 210 billion deficit for 2002.

But despite the disillusionment with the WTO, the government
was, at the beginning of 2003, ill prepared for the approaching Cancun
ministerial. Arroyo's statement at the October summit of APEC in Mexico
decrying the unfair trade rules of the WTO and her more recent rhetoric against "unbridled globalization" were long overdue. Yet, despite the
acknowledgment of the WTO's anti-development thrust, the administration appeared bereft of a strategy on how to protect the country
from its consequences.

The country badly needed a multipronged, coordinated strategy
for the negotiations in agriculture, services, and industrial tariffs, and to
meet the threat of a new round of liberalization that the trading powers threatened to launch in Cancun.

This was not for lack of activity among Philippine negotiators in
Geneva. In agriculture, Philippine negotiators worked to reject the
Harbinson draft. In a paper submitted to a special session of the WTO's
Committee on Agriculture on March 31, 2003, the Philippine delegation faulted the draft for its "fixation on market access alone," neglecting substantive reform in the areas of domestic support and export competition. "Flexibilities" or special provisions demanded by the South,
the paper said, were hardly addressed by the draft but they were more

than ever necessary. "[C]an developing countries, even with these flexibilities, ever exceed even an iota of the billions that the major contributors continue to pour into [the] cesspool of market and production distortions? What South-South trade can we talk about in the future when the North would have eaten up all of the South under these conditions?"[157]

Dissatisfaction did not, however, translate into a clear negotiating stance. On the critical question of trade in rice, rice farmers were in the dark on whether the Philippines was asking for an extension of its right to subject rice to quantitative restrictions under Annex 5 of the Agreement. With the government unable to deliver on its promise to "prepare the rice sector for global competition," and with rice farmers left with nothing else to hold on to, the extension of the country's right to subject rice to quotas was a clear demand of the sector.

Privately and sometimes publicly, officials of the Department of Agriculture said that the Philippines was pushing hard for a recognition of the principle of "special and differential treatment," the formal adoption of which would allow the government much more leeway in limiting agricultural imports than is allowed by current AOA rules under the principle that the Philippines' underdeveloped agricultural sector should not be subject to the same rules as agriculture in the developed economies. But would the Philippines be resolute in pushing for its innovative proposal of a rebalancing/countervailing mechanism—a "special safeguard mechanism," in WTO parlance—that would allow developing countries to raise tariffs proportionate to the level of subsidies maintained by the rich countries? This was unclear even to high-level officials in the bureaucracy, who worried that the secretary of agriculture, Luis Lorenzo Jr., had an inadequate grasp of the issues. The joke making the rounds among Geneva negotiators was that Lorenzo, hearing of the "Singapore issues," asked what problems Singapore had with the WTO.

More seriously, observers were worried that the Philippines might be restricted by the negotiating position of the Cairns Group, a grouping of developed and developing agro-exporting countries dominated by Australia and New Zealand. Australia and New Zealand were mainly interested in dismantling the agricultural subsidy system of the European Union while tolerating that of the United States. Pushing for protection

of the developing-country agricultural systems under the principle of special and differential treatment was not a priority for Australia and New
Zealand. In fact, Australia chose to interpret special and differential treatment mainly in terms of developing countries being able to provide their
agriculture with a minimum amount of subsidies, which they cannot afford, and not in terms of restrictions placed on access to their markets,
which Philippine farmers were demanding.

In fact, farmers groups were asking: why do we continue to voluntarily tie our hands by remaining in the rich-country-dominated Cairns
Group?

Another critical area were negotiations on services under the GATS.
In early 2003, governments had already begun the process of asking
other governments for the service sectors they want opened up, and those
requested would have to respond soon. A leaked report revealed the
breathtaking range of services that the EU wanted the Philippines to
open up completely or substantially—a long list that included legal
services, accounting and bookkeeping, telecommunications, construction
and engineering services, maritime transport, and environmental services.[158]

What was the government's response to the requests of the EU,
US, and other governments? What areas was it offering to liberalize? As
the Stop the New Round! Coalition (SNR!C) put it:

> Citizens should not be kept in the dark about these negotiations.
> They must at least be informed of what other countries are de-
> manding, what with all the service-sector employees that could be
> displaced by foreign competition in an economy already suffering
> from persistent high unemployment and underemployment."[159]

An even greater concern was that GATS was really an investment
agreement masquerading as a trade agreement, one that would override
not only existing laws governing foreign investment but the Constitution itself. In fact, current moves to amend the Constitution coincided
with this dangerous enterprise of denationalizing through GATS control of land, natural resources, and public services such as water, energy,
health, education, and other public services.

The New Issues was another source of worry. Geneva negotiators
were against incorporating them into the WTO agenda, but the Manila

leadership's position was unclear in early 2003. Next to agriculture, the EU-US push to incorporate investment, government procurement, competition policy, and trade facilitation in the WTO mandate was the galvanizing issue for Philippine civil society. Such negotiations would result in a vast expansion of the WTO's powers to non-trade areas. By extending "national treatment" to foreign investors, a new agreement, critics feared, would lead to the near-total loss of national control over investment and deprive government of its ability to conduct industrial policy and undertake strategic planning.

As the SNR!C asked:

> Will the Philippine government take a stand, draw a line on the sand, and work with other developing countries to stop this grant of vast new powers to the WTO? Will it stand by India and other developing countries that hold that, in accordance with the statement of the Chairman of the Doha Ministerial, there is as yet no agreement to launch negotiations in the "new issues"? Or will the Philippines side with the EU, the US, and other developed countries that claim that there is already consensus on launching negotiations?[160]

Trade liberalization, to use Bergsten's image, is like a bicycle: it collapses if it does not move forward. Which is why the New Issues question was seen as so critical by Philippine civil society: its resolution would mean either that the WTO, with all its institutionalized inequalities, became even more powerful by extending its jurisdiction to new areas of human endeavor, or that the WTO retreated, thus creating the space for countries to follow strategies of economic development that are congenial to their needs.

In the absence of government leadership, civil society stepped into the breach prior to Cancun. Two groupings played particularly salient roles: the Fair Trade Alliance (FTA) and the SNR!C. The latter proposed a government-civil society strategy for the Cancun meeting, the three key points of which were:

- Opposition to a new round of WTO trade negotiations
- Opposition to further WTO trade and trade-related liberalization

– Opposition to the incorporation of the New Issues" of investment, competition policy, government procurement, and trade facilitation into the WTO agenda

In addition, it advanced the following demands:

– In agriculture, unilateral extension of the quantitative restrictions on rice imports and formulation of an independent stand in the agricultural negotiations from the Cairns Group, the centerpiece of which would be the withholding of Philippine approval from any revised agreement that did not give it the right to restrict market access in key crops, the right to make food security and food self-sufficiency central principles of its agricultural trade policy, and the sovereign right to determine its agricultural and food policy.

– Opposition to the extension of WTO jurisdiction to fisheries as part of a strategy of conserving and developing fisheries primarily to meet domestic needs, and working for a fisheries policy that restricts trade and foreign investment damaging to fisherfolk livelihoods and destructive of marine ecosystems.

– Freezing negotiations in services on grounds that GATS subverts the Constitution and foreign investment laws.

– Freezing of negotiations on industrial tariffs on the grounds that this is a mechanism for dumping cheap industrial goods imports, leading to job loss and greater poverty in developing countries. This step must be taken within the broader context of an industrial and development framework to be developed after a comprehensive study carried out in collaboration with the concerned sectors. Only within a framework that provided for the necessary supporting mechanisms would trade instruments bring about comprehensive, solid, and lasting economic transformation.

– Opposition to the drive of the US and other developed countries to undermine the Doha Declaration provision allowing developing-country governments to override the TRIPS agreement in the interests of public health, stop all efforts to extend patents to life and traditional knowledge, and prevent monopoly of technological diffusion by transnational corporations.

- Working with other developing countries to prevent the launching of a new round of trade liberalization in Cancun by standing firm on the chairman's statement that there is as yet no authority to begin negotiations on the New Issues and refusing to provide the explicit consensus required to begin negotiations on investment, competition policy, and government procurement.
- Coordinating work in defending Philippine national interests in the WTO negotiations with negotiations in other multilateral areas, particularly in the AFTA (ASEAN Free Trade Area).[161]

Grassroots pressure exerted by SNR!C, FTA, and other such formations was instrumental in solidifying Philippine resistance to a ministerial dominated by a developed-country agenda. After being tight-lipped about its negotiating stance, the government announced in late August that it would "push for the scrapping of subsidies given by foreign governments to their farmers. It will also seek better Philippine access to cheap medicines from abroad, as well as exemptions to tariff cuts for essential products like rice."[162] The government also announced that it opposed the opening of its services and further liberalization of its investment policies. On the New Issues, then-Trade Secretary Manuel Roxas III said that the Philippines would resist its inclusion into the WTO agenda. "We shall continue to uphold each country's right to determine what is of interest to US and not to surrender its determination to external bodies such as the WTO."[163]

On the external front, Geneva negotiators enlisted the Philippines as a founding member of the G-20, a grouping formed to demand radical cuts in the subsidization of Northern farming interests. Philippine negotiators, along with their Indonesian counterparts, took the lead role in an alliance of fifteen—eventually thirty-two—countries to press for the exemption of "special agricultural products" (SPs) essential to food security from liberalization and for the establishment of "special safeguard mechanisms" (SSMs) such as tariff increases that would match the levels of subsidization in developed countries. Labeling the SPs and SSMs as a "defensive shield," Assistant Agriculture Secretary Segfredo Serrano, a key mover, said that they would give "developing countries more flexibility than ordinary tariff lines."[164]

While Department of Trade and Industry negotiators were confident in Roxas taking a strong stand, Department of Agriculture negotiators were not that confident in Secretary Lorenzo's holding the line. Calling on NGO representatives present in Cancun to help them, they held a special meeting with Lorenzo at his Cancun hotel late in the evening of September 11 to impress on him the necessity of supporting the Philippine position on SSMs and SPs.

The Philippines was included in the "expanded" Green Room meetings that decided the fate of the ministerial on September 13-14. By all accounts, Roxas and Lorenzo, who regarded themselves as rivals, stood by the developing-country positions. Shortly after the collapse of the ministerial, Roxas claimed that he was "elated" at the result.[165] Lorenzo, a neophyte in WTO matters just a few days before, agreed. Upon his return to the Philippines, Lorenzo said, "It was a resounding success for developing countries, especially the Philippine delegation, which was a consistent voice in all deliberations, battling for agricultural reform in WTO."[166]

Cancun was a milestone in the Philippine government's retreat from neoliberal policies, one dictated by the evident consequences they had wrought on the country and propelled by strong pressure from the grassroots. Cancun was the central event in a general reversal of policy. Executive Order 264, issued shortly after Cancun, reversed the twelve-year-old unilateral liberalization program. On the agricultural front, Executive Order 197, issued in April 2003, increased the tariffs on vegetable from 7 percent to 25 percent; Executive Order 264 froze the tariff reduction program for a number of agricultural and fishery products, and the bound tariff for sugar was raised from 65 percent to 80 percent.

But was it a retreat from neoliberal philosophy? This was much less evident, at least from Roxas's summation of the government's strategy. "My view is that a liberalized economy is a desirable end-state," he told the press. "And it is important how we get there. It is important we get there alive, robust, and healthy."[167]

Notes

1. "GMA Calls for WTO Changes, Overhaul," *Business World*, October 28, 2002.

2. Ibid.

3. "DA Notes RP Productivity Stagnant, Poverty High Despite WTO Entry," *Business World*, December 10, 2001.

4. This debate was carried widely in the Philippine media. Among the key documents from this debate are MODE (Management and Organizational Development for Empowerment Inc.), "Putting Food Security and Environmental Sustainability on the Line: The Impact of the Dunkel Act and Blair House Accord on the Philippines" (Manila: MODE, 1993), *IPR Sourcebook Philippines* (Manila: University of the Philippines Los Baños College of Agriculture and MODE, 1994); and Department of Agriculture, *Questions and Answers about GATT: The GATT and Its Implications for Philippine Agriculture* (Manila: Department of Agriculture, 1994).

5. Republic of the Philippines, "Individual Action Plan for APEC" (draft), October 31, 1996.

6. Ibid.

7. Ibid.

8. "Democracy as an Illusion? How AGILE/DAI Promotes US Interests at the Expense of Farmers' Rights," *SEARICE Notes* (June 2002).

9. A whole range of bills and laws, including the Omnibus Power Law, Anti-Dumping Act, and the Anti-Money Laundering Law, were drafted and pushed through the Philippines Congress by the AGILE group, which was supported over five years (June 1998-June 2003) by a $31.2 million appropriation from the US Congress. Ibid., 1.

10. Ibid.

11. Ibid., 4.

12. Ibid., 3.

13. United States Trade Representative, *2001 National Trade Estimates* (Washington, D.C.: USTR, 2001), 346.

14. Ibid., 345-46.

15. "Earning from Others' Intellectual Creations," *Philippine Daily Inquirer*, February 17, 2003, C7.

16. *2001 National Trade Estimates*, 350.

17. Ibid.

18. Ibid., 350-51.

19. United Nations Conference on Trade and Development (UNCTAD), *Trade and Development Report 1991* (New York: United Nations, 1991), 191.

20. Ibid.

21. V. Bruce Tolentino, Cristina David, Arsenio Balisacan, and Ponciano Intal Jr., "Strategic Actions to Rapidly Ensure Food Security and Rural Growth in the Philippines," draft for Yellow Paper 2, March 29, 2001.

22. Ibid.

23. Kevin Watkins, *Field Trip Report: The Philippines* (Manila: Oxfam UK, 1995).

24. Charmaine Ramos, "Discussion Points: Trends and Prospects in the Cereals and Grains Sector of the Philippines" (lecture delivered at the KSP Study Session on the Medium-Term Development Plan, St. Vincent Seminary, Quezon City, May 6, 1996).

25. Francisco Pascual and Arze Glipo, "WTO and Philippine Agriculture," *Development Forum*, no. 1, series 2002, 5.

26. Department of Agriculture, Rules and Regulations for the Implementation of the Agricultural Minimum Access Volume (MAV), Manila, 1996.

27. World Trade Organization, *The Results of the Uruguay Round of Multilateral Trade Negotiations: The Legal Texts* (WTO: Geneva, 1995), 66.

28. Department of Agriculture, ibid. During the Uruguay Round negotiations, the quota for rice for the first year was set at a different figure: 59,000 MT.

29. United States Trade Representative, *2000 National Trade Estimates* (Washington, DC: USTR, 2000), 330.

30. Ibid., 328.

31. Why was there such a contrast between the rosy predictions and the dismal outcomes? A story told by Riza Bernabe, a senior researcher of the Philippine Peasant Institute, is illuminating. After recounting the promises of gains in jobs, exports, and agricultural production that would come with adherence to the AOA, she was approached at a recent conference by Dr. Ramon Clarete, the DA consultant who was the source of these claims during the WTO ratification debate. Clarete expressed surprise that people still remembered his erroneous projections. This confirmed Bernabe and others' suspicions that in order to win the ratification debate, the projections were manufactured by Clarete, who went on to become the Chief of Party of USAID's Agile Program. Personal communication, June 4, 2003.

32. Riza Bernabe, senior researcher at the Philippine Peasant Institute, quoted in "Accounting of Farmers' WTO Safety Net Sought," *Business World*, September 18, 2003, 6.

33. *Selected Agricultural Statistics, 1998, 2002* (Quezon City: Department of Agriculture, 1998, 2002).

34. Ibid.

35. Ibid.

36. *Selected Agricultural Statistics, 2002*, 2.

37. *Selected Agricultural Statistics, 1998 and 2002*; Rovik Obanil, "Rice Safety Nets Act: More of a Burden Instead of a Shield," *Farm News and Views* (First Quarter 2002), 10.

38. Riza Bernabe, "Rice Trade Liberalization: Endangering Food Security," *Farm News and Views* (First Quarter 2002), 13.

39. Ibid., 13.

40. Alternative Forum for Research in Mindanao (AFRIM), "Trade Liberalization Has Meant Poverty to Mindanawans" (paper prepared for the Stop the New Round! Coalition Manila, February 20, 2003).

41. John Madeley, *Trade and Hunger: An Overview of Case Studies on the Impact of Trade Liberalization* (Stockholm: Forum Syd, 2000), 57.

42. "Fields of Woe," *Farm News and Views*, vol. 10 (January-February 1996).

43. Leilani M. Gallardo, "PL 480 Agreement Snagged by Debate on Use of Proceeds," *Business World*, May 27, 2002.

44. Ibid.

45. Cecille Yap, "Senators Say Veggie, Corn Imports Killing Local Industries," *Business World*, November 4, 2002.

46. Kevin Watkins, *Field Trip Report: The Philippines* (Manila: Oxfam UK, 1995).

47. Charmaine Ramos, "Discussion Points: Trends and Prospects in the Cereals and Grains Sector of the Philippines" (lecture delivered at the KSP Study Session on the Medium-Term Development Plan, St. Vincent Seminary, Quezon City, May 6, 1996).

48. Aileen Kwa, "A Guide to the WTO's Doha Work Programme: The 'Development' Agenda Undermines Development," Focus on the Global South, Bangkok, January 2003.

49. *Selected Agricultural Statistics, 1998, 2002.*

50. This was admitted in a series of television debates by GATT-WTO proponents during the ratification debate in 1994.

51. Comments at the television program *Firing Line*, GMA 7, Manila, December 12, 1994.

52. *Selected Agricultural Statistics, 1998, 2002.*

53. Ramos.

54. Watkins.

55. Ibid.

56. Statement of Noel Padre, officer in charge, Policy Research

Service, Department of Agriculture, at Hearing of the House Special Committee on Globalization, House of Representatives, Quezon City, June 4, 2003.

57. "Continued Regulation of Chicken Imports Sought," *Business World*, July 13, 2000.

58. Sen. Edgardo Angara, "The Empire Strikes Back : How the Developed World Always Wins against Developing Countries," *Business World*, September 11, 2003, 5.

59. "Poultry Integrators Note Shake-out, More Firms Close Shop," *Business World*, February 11, 1998.

60. Ibid.

61. *Alyansa Agrikultura*, Declaration, 2002.

62. "DA Backs Tighter Rules on Meat Imports," *Business World*, November 5, 2002.

63. *Selected Agricultural Statistics*, 1998, 2002.

64. "DA Backs Tighter Rules on Meat Imports," *Business World*, November 5, 2002.

65. "Briefer on GATT-WTO and Its Impact on the Philippine Vegetable Industry, " Manila, 2002.

66. Ibid.

67. Ibid.

68. Ibid.

69. Leilani Gallardo, "DA Meat Import Policy Enforcement Put on Hold," *Business World*, April 16, 2002.

70. Arnold Tenorio, "Food Processors Want RP to Launch Trade 'Offensive'," *Business World*, May 3-4, 2002.

71. Leilani Gallardo and Marites Villamor, "Tuna Producers to Lobby for Tariff Cut from EU States," *Business World*, August 23-24, 2002.

72. Ibid.

73. Iris Cecilia Gonzales, "EU Approves Lower Tuna for Canned Tuna Imports," *Business World*, June 10, 2003.

74. Hernani de Leon, "Banana Growers Won't Throw in Towel Just Yet," *Business World*, July 3, 2002.

75. Ramon Clarete, "Towards a Policy Environment for Agribusiness Growth in the Philippines: A Review of Policy Developments Affecting the Sector from 1985 to 1995" (paper circulated at the Dialogue with Congress [(After GATT, What?], Manila Hotel, Manila, July 28, 1995).

76. V. Bruce Tolentino et al.

77. Ibid.

78. Omi Royandoyan and the Philippine Peasant Institute Research

Staff, "The AFMA/SAFDZ: Responding to the Agricultural Crisis," *Farm News and Views* (3rd Quarter 2001), 9-10.

79. Ibid.

80. Ibid.

81. Rovik Obanil, "Rice Safety Nets Act: More of a Burden than a Shield," *Farm News and Views* (1st Quarter 2002), 10.

82. F. Gemperle, "Where are the Safety Nets?" (unpublished paper, Manila, February 6, 1997).

83. Francisco Pascual and Arze Glipo, "WTO and Philippine Agriculture: Seven Years of Unbridled Trade Liberalization and Misery for Small Farmers," *Development Forum,* no. 1 (series 2002), 5.

84. F. Gemperle, "Where are the Safety Nets?" (unpublished paper, Manila, February 6, 1997).

85. Pascual and Glipo, 5

86. Ibid.

87. "Accounting of Farmers' WTO Safety Net Sought," *Business World,* September 18, 2003.

88. L. Thrupp, *Bittersweet Harvests for the Global Supermarket: Challenges in Latin America's Agricultural Export Boom* (Washington: World Resources Institute, 1995).

89. M. Conroy, D. Murray, and P. Rosset, *A Cautionary Tale: Failed US Development Policy in Central America* (Boulder: Lynne Reiner, 1996).

90. Ibid.

91. Cited in "Trade Facts," *Business World,* September 5-6, 2003, 28.

92. Michael Trebilcock and Robert Howse, *The Regulation of International Trade* (London: Routledge, 1995), 193.

93. Ibid., 201.

94. Ibid., 202.

95. "Agreement on Agriculture," *The Results of the Uruguay Round of Multilateral Trade Negotiations* (Geneva: World Trade Organization, 1995), 38.

96. M. Zepezauer and A. Naiman, *Take the Rich off Welfare* (Tucson: Odonian Press, 1996).

97. Faeth, cited in A.P.G. Moor, *Perverse Incentives* (The Hague: Institute for Research on Public Expenditure, 1997).

98. Brian Gardner, "EU Dumping to Continue," in *The GATT Agreement on Agriculture: Will It Help Developing Countries?* (London: Catholic Institute of International Relations, 1994).

99. Embassy of the United States in Manila, "US, Philippines Sign $20-M Commodity Loan Agreement," June 28, 2002.

100. United States Department of Agriculture, "Agricultural Export

Credit Guarantee, Loan and Insurance Program Questionnaire," 2002.

101.   "Special and Differential Treatment for Developing Countries, Developed Country Reforms, and World Trade in Agriculture" (statement by the Republic of the Philippines at the Special Session of the WTO Committee on Agriculture Informal Meeting, February 4-6, 2002).

102.   Pascual and Glipo, 5.

103.   Moor.

104.   Schiff and Valdes, cited in Moor.

105.   World Trade Organization, *Trade Policy Review: United States* (Geneva: WTO, 1996), 116-17.

106.   Ibid.

107.   Cited in Aileen Kwa and Walden Bello, *Guide to the Agreement on Agriculture: Technicalities and Trade Tricks Explained* (Bangkok: Focus on the Global South, 1998), 22.

108.   Ibid.

109.   Aileen Kwa, "Comments on the Cairns Group Communique," Focus on the Global South, Bangkok, October 6, 2002; also "Wealthy Nations under Fire for Stalled Farm Reform," *Financial Times,* June 6, 2002.

110.   Oxfam International, *Rigged Rules and Double Standards* (Oxford: Oxfam International, 2002), 112.

111.   Ibid.

112.   Ibid.

113.   "The Benefits of Farming Rich," Reuters, reproduced in *Business World,* August 15-16, 2003, 30.

114.   Cited in "Trade Facts," *Business World,* September 5-6, 2003, 28.

115.   "Threats of Food Surplus for EU," *Bridges* 1, no. 13 (1997).

116.   Ibid.

117.   USTR Charlene Barshefsky, remarks prepared for delivery at the US Department of Agriculture Agricultural Outlook Forum, Washington, D.C., February 24, 1997.

118.   Food and Agricultural Organization (FAO), "Agriculture, Trade and Food Security: Issues and Options in the WTO Negotiations from the Perspective of the Developing Countries, vol . 2: Country Case Studies" (Rome, 2000), 25. Cited in Aileen Kwa, "A Guide to the WTO's Doha Work Programme: The 'Development' Agenda Undermines Development," Bangkok, Focus on the Global South, January 2003.

119.   FAO, Ibid.

120.   Kwa, "A Guide to the WTO's Doha Work Programme."

121.   Assistant Secretary of Agriculture Segfredo Serrano, "23-27 September WTO-COA Special Sessions on Agriculture Negotiations—Do-

mestic Support and Related Meetings," Department of Agriculture, Quezon City, October 1, 2002.

122. "More Power to the World Trade Organization," *Panos Briefing*, November 1999, 14.

123. South Center, *The Multilateral Trade Agenda and the South* (Geneva: South Center, 1998), 32.

124. Oxfam, *Rigged Rules and Double Standards*, 100.

125. John Whalley, "Building Poor Countries' Trading Capacity," *CSGR Working Paper Series* (Warwick: CSGR, March 1999).

126. Testimony before the US Senate Committee on Commerce, Science, and Technology, Washington, D.C., October 13, 1994.

127. Press briefing, Seattle, Washington, December 2, 1999.

128. Quoted in "Deadline Set for WTO Reforms," *Guardian News Service*, January 10, 2000.

129. Philip Legrain, "Should the WTO Be Abolished?" *Ecologist* 30, no. 9 (December 2000/January 1, 2001): 23.

130. Statement at UNCTAD X, Bangkok, February 2000.

131. Aileen Kwa, "Crisis in WTO Talks," *Focus on Trade*, no. 68 (October 2001).

132. Ibid.

133. The following account is based on discussions among participants—many of whom attended the Doha Ministerial—at the consultation held in Brussels of the "Our World Is Not for Sale Coalition" on December 9-11, 2002. See also the excellent study by Aileen Kwa, *Power Politics in the WTO* (Bangkok: Focus on the Global South, 2002).

134. Emad Mekay, "Opponents Unite to Decry US Farm Subsidies," Interpress Service, May 13, 2002.

135. Kwa, "A Guide to the WTO's Doha Work Programme."

136. Ibid.

137. Looking for escape clauses, the EU insisted on the formulation: ["W]ithout prejudging the outcome of the negotiations we commit ourselves to comprehensive negotiations aimed at: substantial improvements in market access; reductions of, with a view to phasing out, all agricultural subsidies; and substantial reductions in trade-distorting domestic support." WTO, Ministerial Declaration, Doha, November 14, 2001.

138. Stuart Harbinson, Paper on Modalities for Agricultural Negotiations, Committeeon Agriculture, World Trade Organization, February 2003.

139. "Farm Chief Nixes WTO Proposal," *Japan Times*, February 14, 2003.

140. "WTO Still Divided on Fram Trade Tariff," *Japan Times*, February 16, 2003.

141. Aileen Kwa, "WTO Agriculture Talks Set to Exacerbate World Hunger: Second-guessing Mr. Harbinson's Next Strike," Focus on the Global South, Bangkok, March 2003.

142. A paper from the Philippine delegation said that the proposal would allow developing countries to impose the tariff equivalent of export subsidies and domestic support on agricultural imports from the developed countries. This was seen as a "discipline mechanism" that would "balance and interlink reform commitments in market access, export subsidies, and production-and trade-distorting domestic support." Republic of the Philippines, "Integration of Reforms in Export Competition, Domestic Support, and Market Access in World Agricultural Trade" (statement at the Informal Special Session of the WTO Committee on Agriculture, Geneva, September 2, 2002).

143. Kwa, "WTO Agriculture Talks..."

144. Ibid.

145. Ibid.

146. World Trade Organization, "Ministerial Declaration on the TRIPS agreement and Public Health," November 14, 2001.

147. The chairman's statement reads as follows: "Let me say that with respect to the reference to an 'explicit consensus' being needed, in these paragraphs, for a decision to be taken at the Fifth Session of the Ministerial Conference, my understanding is that , at that session, a decision would indeed need to be taken by explicit consensus, before negotiations on trade and investment and trade and competition policy, transparency in government procurement, and trade facilitation could proceed... In my view, this would give each member the right to take a position on the modalities that would prevent negotiations from proceeding after the Fifth Session of the Ministerial Conference until that member is prepared to join in an explicit consensus." Chairman's Statement, November 14, 2001. Text provided by WTO Secretariat at Conference Media Center.

148. Author's notes from the meeting, mid-March 2003.

149. Ibid.

150. Ibid.

151. Group of 20, "Ministerial Communique," September 9, 2003.

152. "Trade Talks Round Going Nowhere sans Progress in Farm Reform," *Business World*, September 8, 2003, 15.

153. Robert Zoellick, "America Will Not Wait for the Won't-do Countries," *Financial Times*, September 21, 2003.

154. "South-South Cooperation in Cancun," Draft, South Centre, Geneva, December 2003.

155. See, for instance, "The Hypocrisy of Rich Countries Blocks Trade Liberalization," Editorial, *Financial Times*, September 16, 2003; "Cancun's Silver Lining," Editorial, *Wall Street Journal*, September 17, 2003; and "The WTO Under Fire," *Economist*, September 18, 2003.

156. "Tariff Commission Position Paper on House Resolution no. 482, Tariff Commission, June 4, 2003.

157. Statement of the Republic of the Philippines at the Formal Special Session of the Committee on Agriculture, March 31, 2003.

158. GATS 2000 Request from the European Community and Its Member States to the Philippines. Confidential.

159. Stop the New Round! Coalition, "A Strategy for the Cancun Ministerial," January 22, 2003.

160. Stop the New Round! Coalition.

161. Ibid.

162. "Gov't Sets Stand on Global Trade Issues," *Business World*, September 1, 2003.

163. Ibid.

164. "Philippines to Monitor Measures in Draft WTO Paper," *Business World*, August 26, 2003.

165. "The WTO under Fire," *Economist*, September 18, 2003.

166. "Iris Gonzales and Rommer Balaba, "Roxas: Industries Must Work on Competitiveness," *Business World*, September 26-27, 2003.

167. Iris Gonzales, "Gov't Sets Stand on Global Trade Issues," *Business World*, September 1, 2003.

CHAPTER 5

The Panacea of Privatization

Introduction

Privatization, or the transfer of ownership from the public sector to the private sector is currently the topic of many intense debates both in the Philippines and in the international arena.

In the Philippines, the issue of privatization has been brought to the fore because of the current debacle over water services in the Metro Manila area and the ripple effects it will have on the rest of the economy. In the international arena, the current negotiations on the General Agreement on Trade in Services (GATS) under the World Trade Organization (WTO) have put privatization of government services in the spotlight.

Privatization has also been at the core of several struggles and disputes around the globe. In Bolivia it triggered a civil uprising where many died, and the multinational corporation that had taken over water services in the city of Cochabamba was forced to leave the country. In South Africa it has become an issue of human rights. In Europe it has become a rallying point of various campaigns ranging from anti-globalization to labor rights.

In this sense, privatization in the Philippines cannot be understood without seeing the larger picture and how different factors, both external and internal, have contributed to the current situation.

This chapter will discuss privatization in the Philippines in the context of the global debates. It will begin with a discussion of the international context, followed by a brief history of privatization in the country. It will then move to a discussion of the two most controversial cases of privatization in the Philippines—water and power.

This chapter will not cover all aspects of privatization as it is too diverse a topic, and many other books and studies have already discussed theories and practices of privatization in great detail. Instead, this chapter will focus on the expectations and actual consequences of privatization in the Philippines. It will also link this paradigm to the current system of globalization and the institutions that support it, mainly the World Bank, the International Monetary Fund (IMF), and the WTO.

Privatization in the Era of Globalization

Privatization is not a new practice. It has been around since the 1940s. Many historical accounts of this era cite examples of this process of transfer of ownership or control of enterprises and services from the public sector to the private sector. It was not until the 1980s, however, that privatization as an economic tool gained people's interest and concern.

A Brief History

From the 1940s to the 1980s a distinct type of political economy was prevalent. In Japan, Europe, and the United States, state-assisted capitalism was the dominant paradigm with varying levels of state intervention in each country.

The theoretical underpinnings of state-assisted capitalism were provided by Keynesian economics, an approach developed by John Maynard Keynes in the early 1930s in response to the economic depression of the time. Keynes explained that the reason for the depression was insufficient demand. Government expenditure or intervention in the market could correct this and, therefore, avert such crisis.

In the post-World War II period, governments played an active role in the market by coordinating with the private sector, either by supporting the development of industries, regulating them, or nationalizing them. In Britain the railways, iron and steel, and other industries were nationalized. In Japan the economic bureaucracy worked closely with management to promote the development of steel, the auto industry, and electronics. In the US the state ironed out the business cycle with fiscal and monetary tools, and played a direct role in technological innovation in the military-industrial complex.

By the 1970s, however, economic stability gave way to a combination of stagnation and inflation, and a new ascendant school in economics—"neoliberalism"—saw the state as no longer the solution but the problem. State regulation stifled entrepreneurship, state ownership was inefficient, heavy taxation discouraged investment. In Britain privatization of nationalized industries became the cutting edge of the new political economy when Margaret Thatcher came to power. In the US radical deregulation became the norm when Ronald Reagan assumed the presidency in 1981.

As the First World was changing loyalties, state-assisted capitalism in the Third World was running into problems. Encouraged by US and other international banks that sought to profitably recycle the massive amounts of cash deposited by the oil-rich countries after the oil price hikes of the 1970s, many developing-country governments went on a borrowing spree to fund not only their development needs but also arms purchases and, in many cases, conspicuous consumption by corrupt elites. The result was virtual bankruptcy for many by the early '80s, the same moment that the neoliberals came to power in the US and Great Britain. Taking advantage of the Third World debt crisis, the neoliberals, working through the World Bank and the IMF, made the adoption of a comprehensive set of liberalizing measures a condition for bailing out governments in debt trouble. "Structural Adjustment," as this program was termed, had the privatization of state enterprises and services at its core, along with deregulation and trade liberalization.

The Great Coherence

By the 1990s almost all the countries in the Third World had restructured their economies to adhere to these programs. The resurgent doctrine of free trade had triumphed nearly everywhere, as Keynesianism and state-assisted capitalism ceased to be the orthodoxy.

The era of free trade reached its peak in 1995 when the Uruguay Round of the General Agreement on Tariffs and Trade (GATT) gave birth to the WTO. The WTO replaced the GATT and formed a far more comprehensive set of rules to govern world trade not only in goods but also in services.

Together with the IMF and the World Bank, the WTO issued a "coherence" document during the first WTO Ministerial Meeting in Singapore in December 1996, stating that the policies of the three institutions would be articulated closely to achieve global growth and economic stability on the basis of liberalized trade and capital flows. The unstated assumption was that this would not be a major problem since free market and free-trade principles had already been institutionalized in many countries by structural adjustment programs (SAPs).

Trade in Services

As discussed in chapter 4, the WTO encompasses all forms of trade whether in goods or in services. The rules of the WTO on trade in services impact directly on the issue of privatization. One of the agreements in the Uruguay Round was the General Agreement on Trade in Services (GATS).

The GATS agreement establishes a multilateral framework of principles and rules for all forms of trade in all services. Services under the GATS framework include 160 service sectors including health, education, water, utilities, energy, transport, and childcare.

The aim of the GATS is to promote unrestricted trade in all types of services and to remove all forms of governmental intervention that may be viewed as "trade restrictive." Article 1 of the GATS states that the agreement does not apply to services "supplied in the exercise of governmental authority." This is followed with the caveat that such services must be supplied neither on a commercial basis nor in competition with other service providers. This condition effectively puts all services under the scope of the GATS, as it is very rare that government-provided services are neither provided on a commercial basis nor in competition with other providers.

But by this time, most countries in the Third World had already liberalized their services through the structural adjustment programs. What more could the GATS ask governments to do? On closer inspection, one will see that the GATS, said to be the most far-reaching agreement under the WTO, covers much more than just liberalizing a service.

The GATS key principles are as follows:

1) National Treatment: As the name implies, host countries are to accord foreign companies the same treatment they do national companies. This means doing away with performance require-

ments usually asked of foreign companies such as establishing joint partnerships with local firms, hiring local staff, and transferring technology. Governments must also provide the same tax privileges they would grant a domestic firm.

2) Most Favored Nation Status: A core principle in the WTO, host governments must not discriminate between countries. It must grant equal privileges to all fellow WTO-member countries.

3) Least trade-restrictive business environment: Host governments must ensure a "level playing field" for foreign companies even if it means curtailing established standards for the environment, labor, and health.

And most important, the GATS is virtually irreversible. The GATS uses a "bottom-up" approach, which means that countries can choose which services they will "offer" to liberalize. However, GATS works on the principle of "progressive liberalization"—with each round of negotiation, the sectors that a government commits to liberalize must open up more than before. Liberalization may be incremental, but cannot be fully reversed. Once it is offered and implemented, it can no longer be reversed regardless of the impact of such liberalization.

This also covers services previously liberalized through SAPs. In the GATS, countries are allowed to count services they had already opened up through SAPs and add it on a score card of progressive liberalization. Doing this, however, will automatically put these services under the mandate of the GATS, including the principle of irreversibility.

What makes this liberalization under the WTO different from the IMF-World Bank is the dispute settlement body of the WTO. The WTO has legally binding rules, and if governments are proven to have disobeyed these rules they can be penalized with economic sanctions.

And this, some argue, is the main reason why corporations are keen on placing the rules of privatization under the WTO. According to Tony Clarke, director of Canada's leading policy and advocacy organization, Polaris Institute, placing agreements such as investment and trade in services under the WTO will make them enforceable because of the threat of escalating economic sanctions. "In other words, there is a whole system of economic punishment built into it."

Framed in this context, the principles of free trade, especially that of privatization, are difficult to evade, advanced as they are by loan agreements governments enter into with the World Bank and the IMF, or trade accords they sign up to in the WTO.

Services—For Profit or for People?

The critique of these policies of the IMF-World Bank and the GATS agreement of the WTO is that the eventual privatization of all state-owned assets including those of public utilities and services would exacerbate further the inequality between the haves and have-nots. The concept of government-provided services is that it will allow for the poor in the country to still avail themselves of basic services vital to decent living such as water, health, and education. This is achieved through the subsidization of services to the poor by the government while recovering costs through transfer payments from the middle class and the rich.

The sale of these services to the private sector, however, will close off this access of the poor. Under the free-market model of corporations, services will be run for profit. The privatization of the water sector has generated the most debate because according to the United Nations (UN), access to water is a human right and everyone is entitled to a basic lifeline of at least fifty liters a day.

Many argue that when corporations take over the water service and other basic services, only those who can afford will be able to avail themselves of these services. In Malaysia, for example, according to economist Charles Santiago, when the water privatization comes into full effect, people will only be able to avail themselves of water by first purchasing prepaid cards. Santiago explains that the money will have to be provided up front if one wants to receive water at home.

In Cochabamba, Bolivia, privatization raised the prices of water to an unaffordable level for the people. The prices rose to $20 a month—an unimaginable cost when compared to the minimum wage, a meager $100 a month.[1]

Corporations justify this rise in prices by citing the costs of improving infrastructure and infusing capital. Operating on a principle of cost recovery, corporations pass on these costs to the consumers, i.e., through price adjustment.

This obviously does not follow the UN-mandated basic lifeline of free fifty liters a day for the people, especially that of the poor. Under the WTO, though, water is defined as a human need and not a human right. "This," according to leading water activist, Maude Barlow, "is not a semantic thing." Barlow expounds, "If water is a human need, then anybody can deliver this water, the private sector, anybody. But if it's a human right, you can't market or trade or sell a human right."

Another issue related to this debate is the fact that most corporations which take over the government-provided services are foreign transnational corporations whose profits do not revert back to the local economy. As Patrick Bond of the University of Witterstrand of South Africa explains, "We see French and British water companies, especially German and American, coming in now, taking in the water and adding a 30-percent or more profit, and then taking that money out of the country."

This global debate on services being provided for profit instead of for the people is one of the reasons why privatization, especially that of water, in the Philippines has generated much debate and controversy. As a vice president of the World Bank, Ismail Serageldin, aptly put it, "If the wars of this century were fought over oil, the wars of the next century will be fought over water."[2]

Privatization in the Philippines

The Philippines, a recipient of nine SAPs, three standby programs, two extended fund programs, and one precautionary standby arrangement with the IMF, has undergone severe economic restructuring.

It began in 1984 when, after signing a $300-million World Bank loan, the Philippines agreed to legislate new laws for the privatization of state-owned assets.[3] President Marcos issued Presidential Decrees 2029 and 2030, paving the way for privatization. This was followed by President Aquino's Presidential Proclamation 50, which created the Committee on Privatization (COP) and the Asset Privatization Trust (APT).[4] The two programs would lead the country's privatization program. The COP identified the assets that could be sold and the APT took charge of disposing them. President Ramos would reinforce this with Executive Orders 37 and 298, Republic Acts 7661 and 7886, all of which supported the country's privatization program.

According to the Management and Organizational Development for Empowerment (MODE), privatization in the Philippines consists of three waves. The first wave was the selling off of enterprises expropriated from cronies of Ferdinand Marcos. The second wave was the selling off of profitable assets such as Petron, the Manila Hotel, Fort Bonifacio, and power and water industries. The third wave, yet to be accomplished, will be the disposal of public-service institutions like hospitals, state colleges, housing, and postal services.[5]

The disposal of these assets can take various forms. The first is the outright sale of these assets, which has been the most common mode of privatization in the country. The second is through build-operate-transfer (BOT) schemes in which corporations spend on capital and infrastructure, operate the business for an agreed period of time—recovering investment and receiving profit—and then return it to the government. The third is through joint partnerships in which the government enters into joint ventures with corporations, the rationale being that corporations would revive the industry by pumping in fresh capital.

All the administrations cited the same reasons for selling off state-owned assets. The justification used by Marcos, Aquino, Ramos, and the succeeding governments of Estrada and Arroyo fell into these general themes:
- privatization would make the industries efficient
- the profit from the sale of these assets would help augment the government's budget
- the sale of these assets would eliminate government subsidies and thereby lessen the drag on the national budget[6]

The sale of the crony assets by the Aquino administration did not meet much opposition as it was generally viewed as a taking back of assets from the crony-associates of Marcos. Most of the assets, however, were no longer profitable by the time the Aquino government auctioned them off to the private sector. In most cases, the government had to absorb the debt incurred by these corporations or infuse fresh capital to make them marketable. This meant that the government was selling at a loss of around Php 42 billion.[7]

It was also during the Aquino administration that the second wave of privatization began. The privatization of the power sector saw its early stages under Aquino's watch. It was at this time when the infamous eight-hour blackouts enveloped the country. The blackouts literally debilitated entire industries whose products or management depended on electricity. The government drew much flak as it failed to manage the crisis.

The government's response was to privatize the power sector. Through Executive Order 215, the power-generation sector was deregulated and left to the private sector. Though energy privatization began under Aquino, it was the Ramos administration that pushed it furthest, entering into deals with both local and foreign "independent power producers" (IPPs). The Ramos government also sold off profitable assets such as the oil corporation Petron and the vast real estate of Fort Bonifacio. It was also under the direction of Ramos that the two most controversial of all privatization deals were made, the selling of the water utility, the Metropolitan Waterworks and Sewerage System (MWSS), and the power sector, the National Power Corporation (Napocor or NPC).

Watery Deals

The time of the Ramos administration was the height of the climatic phenomenon known as El Niño. The unforgiving heat caused severe droughts and negatively affected both the agricultural and metropolitan sectors of the country. In response to the crisis, the government quickly enacted Republic Act 8041 or the National Water Crisis Act of 1995.

This law gave the President the power to privatize the state-owned water utility, the 119-year-old MWSS. But while the President used the water crisis as the rationale behind the new legislation, it is important to note that the privatization of the MWSS was actually listed as one of the conditionalities of the 1995-1997 SAP agreement with the IMF.[8]

The process of auctioning off the water utility began with the passage of the law but it was not until 1997 when the awarding to the winning bidders took place. The privatization of the MWSS was at the time the biggest water-sector privatization in the world.

It was, however, not an outright sale of MWSS assets. As Jude Esguerra of the Freedom from Debt Coalition (FDC), a leading expert on the issue of privatization, explains, "The physical assets are still owned by the government but the transaction gave the private sector the right to use them, and the obligation to maintain them and expand them in exchange for the private sector's right to collect a regulated fee from users."[9] Esguerra further explains that at the end of the twenty-five-year agreement, the government takes over the operation and control of the assets. The private concessionaire, on the other hand, will by then have fully recovered its investments and reaped projected profits.[10]

The privatization of the water utility, despite its massive scale, did not meet much opposition from the Congress or from the general public. This, analysts attribute to the fact that the quick resolution of the power blackouts in the '80s by the private sector gave people the impression that a similar process would resolve the water crisis.

Furthermore, whereas in the power crisis people agreed to pay higher rates for better service, the water privatization offered to bring better service for lower prices. In his study, Esguerra notes that the winning bids offered prices that were one-fourth and one-half of the existing rates of the state-run facility.[11]

This really promised to be a privatization success story. Not only did it relieve the government of the water utility, which serviced twelve million customers, it also relieved it of the crippling debt—$880 million. The privatization was hailed as a success in international circles.

A few years later, however, the success story would turn sour as water prices rose exponentially and Maynilad, one of the winning concessionaires, declared that it was walking out of its twenty-five-year contract.

To understand how the success turned into failure in barely three years, a closer inspection of the entire process is required, beginning with the bidding and ending with the current debate surrounding the controversial pullout of Maynilad.

A Tale of Two Bidders

The bidding process began on a good note as the government decided to follow the "Paris model," in which the service area was split into two and each assigned to a separate concessionaire. Experts believe that this measure would break up the monopoly and allow regulators to check the performance of one concessionaire against that of the other.[12]

The government also took steps to ensure that they got the best advice from experts before opening up the bidding process. The experts offered by "friends" came from the World Bank's private-sector lending agency, the International Finance Corporation (IFC).

The IFC consultants were tasked with, among other things, identifying the concessionaire service obligations, the tasks of the MWSS, setting up of a regulatory office and setting up of a dispute-resolution mechanism. They also gave information to prospective bidders to assist them in profit forecasts and, finally, they played the role of identifying eligible bids and winning bids.[13]

At the advice of the IFC experts, the contracts were designed to maximize the benefits for all parties—the government, the concessionaires and the consumers. The concession agreement was carefully crafted, covering all possible scenarios, from extraordinary events to requiring concessionaires to put up a performance bond of $200 million.

The contract also required concessionaires to improve the quality of service by investing in infrastructure and capital. To achieve this, it detailed a number of obligations:[14]

- increase the number of water and sewerage service connections
- gradually increase water pressure
- eliminate service interruptions
- maintain water-service quality
- implement projects for new sources of water supply
- establish a sewerage network

The contract also took into consideration the concessionaire's need to recover its capital investments and costs. While it was ideal for prices of the water service to stay low, it was acknowledged that events such as inflation and currency devaluation would need to be factored in if concessionaires wanted to keep their businesses running. To address these events, the concession agreement provided three measures by which a concessionaire could adjust their prices:

- inflation
- extraordinary price adjustment (EPA)
- rate re-basing

The first is self-explanatory. The agreement allowed for automatic price adjustments in accordance with the inflation rate of that year. The second is designed to address events such as currency devaluation. The third is a more complicated process done at the beginning of every five-year period. Esguerra explains this process as a review of tariffs to ensure that given the rates, the concessionaire is still able to recover costs and investments.[15]

When everything was set the bidding process began and by January 6, 1997, the winning bids were announced.

The two winning bids were from Manila Water, headed by the Ayala group of companies, offering only 26.39 percent of the MWSS rate, and from Maynilad, headed by the Lopez group of companies, offering 56.59 percent of the MWSS rate.[16] Manila Water was awarded the East zone while Maynilad, the second-lowest bidder, was awarded the West zone.

It is important to note that both the Ayalas and the Lopezes are key players in the Philippine business sector, owning, controlling, and managing a great number of industries from telecommunications to media to real estate. Both these families are known oligarchies that are not only well connected in business but also in politics. It is also important to know that both companies, while owning significant capital on their own, bid for the water utility together with foreign partners. Ayala bid jointly with International Water Limited, an international consortium including corporations such as Northwest Water and Bechtel. Lopez bid together with Lyonnaise des Eaux, a French transnational corporation with businesses spanning almost all continents.

The rates offered by the two concessionaires were unbelievably low and the promises were great. This caused many to suspect that the bids were in fact "dive bids" designed to win the concessions at whatever cost. In the cutthroat world of the free market, "dive bidding" is a common practice. It is therefore the responsibility of those reviewing and awarding the bids to identify these dive bids and cancel them out of the race. In this case, it was the responsibility of the IFC consultants to assist the government in identifying the unrealistic bids and rejecting them. Their main role, however, seemed to begin and end with closing a deal. And so even if they suspected the dive bids, they did nothing.

Orville Solon and Steven Pamintuan, two economists of the University of the Philippines, detail these suspicions in a report assessing the privatization of the MWSS. They list the following telltale signs of a dive bid that the IFC consultants themselves recognized:[17]

- Manila Water's consumer-demand projections were 45 percent higher than the earlier study by a French consulting firm hired by the Philippine government.
- Manila Water details a highly capital-intensive endeavor—reducing non-revenue water to half in just five years.
- Manila Water assumed it would get a yen-denominated project finance at a very low real rate of 2.79 percent—and subsequently basing its projections on this.
- Compared to other bidders, its capital spending was 25 percent less.
- Its projected internal rate of return was 3.6 percent—a very low figure compared to other bidders whose rates were set between 9 percent and 11 percent.
- If Manila Water followed all its promised performance targets, it would suffer a negative cash flow for the first ten years—a deficit to the tune of $496 million. (The IFC even notes their uncertainty on how Manila Water intended to secure debt funding with these terms.)

Maynilad's figures caused some concern. It also projected too aggressively and optimistically, casting doubt on the feasibility of such forecasts. It was also discovered later on that Maynilad's figures on the debt burden it was taking from the government was in fact Php 3.9 billion short of what bidders were instructed to assume.[18]

The bidding process, on closer inspection, reveals many flaws and signs of an impending disaster—signs that were discovered early on and yet ignored. The rush with which the bids were finalized, despite better judgment, calls suspicion to the type of advice the World Bank offers—to privatize at the soonest time possible, regardless of consequences.

This major flaw in the process formed the basis of the disaster that the water privatization became. Because the bids were not feasible, all the rest of the promises made by the concessionaires were therefore not feasible either. All the promised improved services and increase in water pressure cannot be logically achieved with unrealistic rates and forecasts. Unrealistic bidding triggered the events that came to pass: the requests of concessionaires to raise their rates, pass on foreign currency adjustments to consumers, and eventually the bailing out of one concessionaire from the twenty-five-year contract.

Spiralling into Disaster

Both Maynilad and Manila Water, after careful analysis, can be said to be guilty of dive bidding. The two, however, differed in the aftermath of the declaration of winning bids.

Maynilad

By 2000 Maynilad was clearly suffering from its own miscalculations. It won the bid by projecting rosy profits and minimal costs, but three years into the contract their skewed projections were catching up with them.

To illustrate, its figures were off the mark by more than 30 percent. First, it projected operating costs for the first three years at Php 4,369 million—a figure 43 percent off mark as their actual operating costs clocked in at Php 6,259 million.[19] Second, their projected revenues for the same period was Php 7,255 million, again a figure off target, this time by 33 percent, as their actual revenues only amounted to Php 4,729 million.[20]

Maynilad, however, attributed its poor performance to force majeure—the Asian financial crisis. Maynilad borrowed heavily using hard currency and assumed a significant amount of the debt of the MWSS, denominated in US dollars. This made it vulnerable to the crash of the Philippine peso. At the beginning of the concession the peso had relative strength to the dollar, pegging in at Php 26 to $1. After the Asian financial crisis, the peso had crashed to a low of Php 50 to $1.

But this argument is difficult to sustain. First of all, Maynilad should have hedged its borrowings or borrowed at higher interest rates that guaranteed against foreign-exchange fluctuations, a standard practice in international financial transactions. Second, it is important to note that even without the foreign-exchange losses, Maynilad's losses already amounted to a crippling Php 2.7 billion.[21]

Furthermore, as was discussed in the previous section, the concession agreement had required concessionaires to factor in currency depreciation. It had also in fact installed measures to ensure that concessionaires would be able to adjust prices accordingly.

Manila Water

The case of Manila Water differs from that of Maynilad in that, even though it had the lower bid, it was in better shape than Maynilad. This could be attributed to the fact that Manila Water, unlike Maynilad, was able to secure loans from financial institutions despite performance that deviated significantly from projections. Esguerra explains that this was due to the difference with which the two concessionaires negotiated debt financing.[22] Maynilad took the path of "limited recourse financing" or a type of borrowing that used the projected profits as the collateral. Manila Water, together with Bechtel, on the other hand, used the more traditional and secure way of borrowing, that of putting up its own assets as collateral.

Access to loans of this magnitude mattered greatly to companies in a highly capital-intensive industry. It is important to remember that these companies were committed to certain performance targets such as improvement of infrastructure and the reduction of nonrevenue water. If they were to renege on these agreed targets, the government could call on their performance bonds of $200 million.

Despite its slightly better situation, however, Manila Water was still in bad shape. It had also projected revenues too aggressively and underestimated costs too conservatively. Their tack, though, was to change the parameters of the bid.

The parameter Manila Water wanted amended was the appropriate discount rate (ADR). The ADR, as Esguerra breaks down in his study, determines the interest rate that consumers must pay for the deferred recovery by the concessionaires of costs that are approved during the EPA petitions.[23]

This translates to Manila Water wanting to change the terms it agreed to in the concession agreement. In its bid, it based its projections and rates on an ADR of 5.2 percent whereas other bids set theirs at 10 percent.[24] Manila Water wanted it raised to 18 percent. If this were approved after the awarding of the bid, this would be unfair to the losing bidders. Even without the actual figures, it would logically mean that the rate that Manila Water would operate on would in fact be a lot higher than those of the losing bids. If concession agreements could be altered after the fact then all future auctioning would see corporations offering dive bids because they would be confident that they would be able to change the terms it offered after it won the concession.

In the end, both concessionaires had one thing in mind: adjusting the prices. And in October 2001 they got what they wanted—the concession agreement was amended. Price adjustments were made and Maynilad, the more dismal of the two, was given a lifeline.

Nonexistent Regulation

Another factor in this sordid mess was the regulatory function—or rather the lack of it. According to a study done on behalf of the Friedrich Ebert Foundation, the lack of proper regulation was a key factor in explaining the failure of the privatization of the water utility. It goes on to recommend that in future cases, the regulatory agency should be established independently through a separate legislation rather than the current setup of putting up a regulatory agency on the basis of the concession agreement.[25]

In hindsight a strong regulatory agency would have been able to maximize the ideal setup of splitting the concession into two zones. It should have been able to gauge one's performance against the other and used that as a basis for granting or rejecting appeals for price adjustments. Also, a strong agency would have at the outset discouraged dive bids as corporations would not be so confident of future amendments to the agreement.

Unfortunately, the regulatory agency for the water concessionaires was established as a sort of afterthought. It only came into being after the agreement was signed, and to make matters worse, it took its funds from both concessionaires.

A Not-so-Happy Ending

In the end, the success story of the biggest water-sector privatization turned sour barely three years into the program. Water prices have risen by up to 425 percent[26] and consumers ended up with the raw end of the deal. Because of the amendment to the concession agreement, concessionaires were allowed, through a mechanism called foreign-exchange cost recovery, to pass on the foreign-exchange costs directly and immediately to the consumers.

Despite this adjustment though, Maynilad still backed out of its twenty-five-year agreement with the government. Citing the government's refusal to approve its bid for a further hike in rates, it has tried to walk out of the concession agreement. But it is not walking away scot-free. In a recently concluded arbitration case in the Paris-based International Court of Arbitration, the court ruled that Maynilad's unilateral termination of the concession agreement was "baseless" and it ordered the concessionaire to pay the MWSS Php 6.77 billion. Several advocacy groups are also demanding the return of overcharging costs to consumers.

The beginning of 2004 found the government saddled with a bankrupt concessionaire and faced with the daunting task of assuming management for Maynilad's zone of operations while waiting for a qualified bidder to take over. This means that the government would have to assume the costs and debts and at the same time run the facility to service the millions of customers in its zone. MWSS's troubles were magnified by the courts' delayed ruling on its effort to draw from a $120 million performance bond that creditors had drawn up to cover Maynilad's liabilities to the government.

As if to console itself, after all this, the government still refuses to acknowledge this as a failed case of privatization. As an official of the Arroyo government told a newspaper reporter, "This is not a failed privatization."[27]

The final arrangment worked out between the government and Maynilad were worse than expected. It was a massive sellout of the interests of the public. Maynilad's Php 8 billion debt to MWSS in unpaid concession fees was turned into equity in a new reorganized corporation, effectively cancelling it. Benpres, the controlling conglomerate of Maynilad, was also effectively released from its commitment to guarantee payment of at least $47 million of Maynilad's debts in the event of default.[28] The essence of the deal, one newspaper editorialized, was that

> ...while the Lopezes will be able to cut their losses, the Filipino cosumers and taxpayers will be left to shoulder most of the burden. All those debts, both those handed down to Maynilad by the MWSS under the original concession agreement and those incurred by the private firm, are going to be paid either by consumers through higher water rates or by taxpayers should its earnings not be enough. Thus, it is again the Filipino people who will have to pay for decisions they had no hand in making.[29]

Power Deals

On July 28, 2003, when President Arroyo declared in her State of the Nation Address that Filipinos were now enjoying lower electricity rates, the general reaction was to ask, which Filipinos?

The Crisis of Blackouts

As mentioned in earlier sections of this chapter, the early 1990s saw the country enveloped in darkness. The country was suffering from eight-hour blackouts, crippling several key industries and putting some institutions, like hospitals, in critical condition.

Againt this backdrop the Aquino government authorized the beginning of the privatization of the power sector. Private generation companies—IPPs, in the jargon of energy economics—came into the scene and basically saved the day during the Ramos administration.

The IPPs entered the power sector and, according to technical reports, yielded an additional 8,000 MW, supplying more than 50 percent of the country's energy needs. This seemed to solve the power crisis.

Buoyed by this "success" the Arroyo administration completed the privatization process in 2001 with Republic Act 9136 or the Electric Power Industry Reform Act (EPIRA). This paved the way for the full privatization of the electric-power industry in the country.

With a Little Help from My Friends

The government though did not go about this process by itself. It had a little help from its friends; in fact, more than just a little.

As a report studying the privatization process of the power sector concludes, the World Bank and the Asian Development Bank (ADB) were in this process of privatization since day one. It details how the World Bank, using its "carrot and stick" theory, bundled lending for institutional reform with lending for investments in the power sector.[30] This means that tranches would only be released on condition of targets met in the program it specifies.

The author of the study, Nepomuceno Malaluan of the Action for Economic Reform, a leading authority on the issue, further details the heavy-handed involvement of the World Bank, the IMF, and the ADB. Malaluan cites the following:

- In 1998 the ADB intensified the pressure to privatize Napocor by extending a $300 million loan for the power-sector restructuring program that culminated in the passing of the EPIRA.
- In 1998 an ADB loan was also provided in the context of a joint standby assistance program with the International Monetary Fund and the World Bank.

ADB intervention was particularly crucial. "As a condition to the government's accessing a $300-million energy sector loan from the Bank and a $400-million loan from the Miyazawa Fund from the Japanese Government, the ADB wanted the state energy enterprise privatized as quickly as possible. The ADB's Power Sector Restructuring Program document dated November 25, 1998, was blunt: release of the second tranche of the loan was contingent on the condition that the "borrower shall have enacted a law, the Omnibus Power Industry Law, to govern the power industry."[31]

What is disconcerting is that in their rush to privatize, the international financial institutions (IFIs) did not have a clear sense of the impact of the process on power rates. The 1998 ADB Power Sector Restructuring Program document admitted that "the impact of the restructuring and privatization process on electricity consumers has not yet been quantified, nor has the need to retain safety nets to protect the poor and the underprivileged."[32] As for the World Bank, Malaluan cites a 1994 World Bank

study that noted that the average price of some thirteen projects it analyzed was $0.652/kwH, which the World Bank conceded was "quite
high" compared to the $0.637/kwH bulk energy tariff of the NPC at
the time. He adds that it is important to note that the NPC rate already
covered generation, transmission, subsidies for rural and small-island consumers, peak capacity, and a provision for reserve energy.[33]

The report points out, though, that the IFIs were not the only ones
pushing for the passage of the power bill. At the time of the deliberations
in Congress, two House members went public and revealed that they were
offered a large amount of money from an unknown source in exchange for
the passage of the power bill.[34] The claims were never formally investi-
gated, despite the fact that the ADB's own Anti-Corruption Memorandum issued in June 1998 states: "Particular care must be taken in dealing
with issues of privatization. Preliminary research indicates that, when done
properly, privatization can help to lower the level of corruption." However, in many countries, the privatization process has often been fraught
with allegations of bribery, theft, and embezzlement. It continues: "To
avoid this problem, it is critical that transparent, unbiased, and fully con-
testable procedures be utilized in the sale of state assets. When the sale
involves a natural monopoly, it is also important that capable independent
regulatory agencies be established to provide adequate oversight prior to
privatization."[35] None of these safeguards were put in place prior to the
move to fast-track legislation privatizing Napocor.

Not a Hero After All

With the privatization of Napocor becoming a controversial issue
in the late 1990s, the government was forced to review the performance
and impact of the IPPs that had been contracted to generate power by
the Ramos administration during the blackouts earlier in the decade.
The main finding of a government Inter-Agency Committee investigating thirty-five IPPs was that they delivered electricity but at an exorbitant rate to both consumers and the government. After the initial eu-
phoria of having electricity again, consumers began to see the catch.
The IPPs did deliver the electricity but at an exorbitant price. Furthermore, the deals turned out to be onerous for the government and for
the consumers.

Among the findings, which were not made public,[36] were the following:

- There are some IPP contracts that are evidently more costly to the government in relation to other Philippine and international contracts in terms of "levelized" IPP-adjusted rates.
- The IPP projects that account for the biggest share in the cost of undispatched energy are those with the biggest capacities and those with high costs of fuel.
- The IPP contracts were generally entered into on the basis of lowest bid cost but subsequent adjustments over time have yielded steep increases arising from escalation clauses.
- Certain IPP contractors have exhibited high rates of return on investment and short payback period.
- There have been amendments and additions to several Power Purchase Agreements (PPAs) and Energy Conversion Agreements without passing through the same rigors as the original proposal i.e., review of the Investments Coordination Committee.

The report further details that a number of the contracts had legal and financial issues and needed renegotiation, with some requiring legal action.

Another subsidiary of the Lopez Group that figured in the Maynilad fiasco was engaged in questionable practices in the energy area. Meralco, the country's largest distributor of electricity that was also involved in setting up the IPPs, had passed the increased costs to consumers as "PPA charges" in their monthly electric bills. But public opinion had turned critical by the beginning of the century. An attempt by Meralco to raise power rates by Php 0.12 while its petition for a higher rate hike was under study by the Energy Regulatory Commission was stopped on January 14, 2004, by the Supreme Court, acting on a petition filed by the FDC and a number of progressive political parties.

The Supreme Court decision followed an earlier ruling by the body ordering Meralco to desist from including income tax payments in its operational costs and passing this on to consumers. In line with this, the court ordered the utility to return to both residential and industrial consumers Php 30 billion in overcharges between 1994 and 2003. Critics of privatization saw this as a necessary move to curb the private sector since effective regulation of the private sector by the executive had all but collapsed.

The impact of these positive measures, however, has been quite limited. As one report documents, consumers, despite energy-saving measures, still receive very high electricity bills. As one distressed consumer complained, "We don't turn on our electric fans anymore. My children have stopped watching cartoons in the afternoon... But despite all these, our monthly bill still went up above Php 3,000" (as compared to an old bill of Php 1,000+).[37]

Dismantling Napocor

The strategic aim of privatization in the Philippines was the dismantling of Napocor. According to proponents of privatization, this was urgent owing to the massive debts of Napocor, which came to Php 1.3 trillion or $23.5 billion by 2004.[38]

What proponents appear to have forgotten was that Napocor's travails were not only of its own making and that the private sector was part of the problem. As even the ADB admitted, Napocor had a good financial management record between 1992 and 1997.[39] Napocor's current crisis was a conjunctural one, brought about not by the inherent inefficiency of the public sector but by the Asian financial crisis, a crisis created by the lack of regulation of the private sector. The crisis brought about the deterioration of the agency's foreign debt-service burden and a hemorrhage of dollar-denominated payments to the IPPs that had raked off high-profit contracts to provide power during the energy crisis of the early 1980s. Failure to appreciate the conjunctural character of Napocor's crisis led government technocrats not to pay attention to an alternative route to solving the crisis, which was to renegotiate the terms of payment to foreign creditors and the IPPs to make them more favorable to the government and to the people as a whole.

Offloading Napocor from government seemed to have become, however, the one and only rationale for privatization, with little regard for its impact on consumers. As noted earlier, the move to privatize began with no study of the impact of privatization on consumers, especially the poorer sectors of the population. Privatization was expected to result in higher electric rates. Moreover, as finally provided in the EPIRA passed in 2001, consumers would have to pay for the recovery of Napocor's "stranded costs" via a universal levy or tax, meaning they would be subsidizing the sale of Napocor's assets to the private sector.[40]

Nor were the negative consequences in terms of oligopolistic control considered. The EPIRA split the generation and transmission functions of Napocor, with its transmission functions given to a private sector contractor operating on a concession basis and its power plants sold off to a few big buyers—to about seven buyers, as originally envisaged in the original government plan. Given the concurrent fiasco with price-gouging IPPs and the crisis of water provision by two giant concessionaires, this lack of attention was inexcusable.

During the heated debate over EPIRA, one of the authors of this book offered the following wager:

> Let me...put my money where my mouth is: I bet ten years of my salary at UP [University of the Philippines] (my only marketable asset) that a rush to privatization at this stage will result in the following:
>
> -The seven private "generating companies" (GENCOs) into which Napocor will be hung, drawn, and quartered will evolve into a cartel of seven sisters and not into competitive ventures.
>
> -Most of these oligopolies will eventually devolve into the control of the usual powerful groups, some of them closely allied to the administration, most of them with foreign partners (some of them now madly sniffing around Makati for "strategic alliances").
>
> -Electricity rates will escalate instead of leveling off—which is not suprising given the control of the market by profit-maximizing giants.
>
> -Millions of poor consumers will find themselves deprived of access to affordable energy.
>
> -The network of rural electric cooperatives that now distribute electricity will wither away, replaced by profit-oriented operators that will focus on serving principally the needs of *poblaciones* and industrial and commercial users rather than rural households.[41]

Nothing has changed to make the writer withdraw his offer.

The Crisis of Privatization

By 2003 privatization was in deep crisis, a fact noted even by its proponents. As Gilberto Llanto, vice president of the Philippine Institute of Development Studies, a bastion of neoclassical economic thinking, acknowledged, "There is a crisis of confidence in privatization and in public-private partnership in infrastructure provision."[42] Among the causes of the failure of privatization Llanto pointed to was the government's short-sighted perspective on privatization, which was simply to use the proceeds to improve its fiscal position.[43]

While Llanto was unwilling to clearly acknowledge the private sector's role in the matter, he indirectly attributed part of the blame to aggressive corporate actors: "The experience with IPP contracts drove home a lesson: No government guarantee should be given to shield private investors from commercial risk."[44] He also noted that "[u]nfortunately, in the rush to privatize, the government forgot to deal with the need to have an independent regulatory capacity, leaving regulatory institutions open to opportunistic political intervention."[45] What he failed to mention, however, was that the rush to privatize was instigated by the IMF, World Bank, and ADB using the power of the purse.

The Maynilad collapse, Meralco's overcharging, and Napocor's short-sighted privatization were but three of many instances that dimmed the star of privatization throughout the world at the turn of the century. The privatized railways in Britain experienced a marked deterioration, a condition brought home to the public by a succession of train derailments and collisions that took many lives. In California energy deregulation created a situation ripe for corporate abuse, the most egregious of which was Enron's effort to create an electricity shortage in order to profit from its speculative, energy-trading activities.

Meanwhile, in Asia, state-run enterprises were turning in performances that contradicted the stereotype that private is efficient and public is inefficient. Petron was one of the Philippines' most profitable enterprises—which was precisely why it was snapped up by the Saudi firm Aramco once it was put on the shopping block. Petron was not alone. In 1998 the

Pohang Iron and Steel Company (Posco) dislodged long-time industry leader Nippon Steel to become the world's number-one steel producer for the first time in history. That year, while the private sector in Korea collapsed in the aftermath of the Asian financial crisis, Posco's net profit of $946 million in 1998 was 54 percent higher than the 1997 level. In the annual list of Asia's 200 top companies, Posco is, in fact, often at the top of the list for Korea. So are other state-run enterprises: Hong Kong's Mass Transit Railway, Singapore's Mass Rapid Transit, Malaysia's Petronas, and Indonesia's Indosat.

So if the efficiency stemming from privatization is increasingly a suspect argument, why does the privatization express continue to run? Increasingly, the answer lies in the area of interests and power. Privatization is pushed because the private sector is eager to get its hold on successful public companies. In effect, these enterprises and services allow the private sector to get hold of effective public enterprises like Petron and Posco without committing the enormous investment that brought these firms into existence. Privatization, in effect, is nothing more than a seemingly neutral term for subsidizing the private sector. As for money-losing firms, they are either ignored or, as in case of Napocor's assets, the private sector is waiting for a fire sale.

Moreover, local firms are not the only interested parties. Transnational corporations have been scouring Asia for good buys, and in this they have the support of their governments. Former US Trade Representative Charlene Barshefsky revealed one of the essential reasons for Washington's aggressive support for privatization when she told the US House of Representatives a few years ago that the IMF program that Thailand was forced to adopt in the aftermath of the Asian financial crisis deserved close support from the US because the government's "commitments to restructure public enterprises and accelerate privatization of certain key sectors will enhance market-driven competition and deregulation [and] create new business opportunities for US firms."[46]

Conclusion

Initially promoted as a panacea for underdevelopment, privatization has notched up a checkered record not only in the Philippines but globally. This is not to say that it has not had successes. Yet, like all doctrinaire people, partisans of privatization have overreached, applying it to inappropriate situations. At the same time, there is now a greater appreciation of the role of the public sector and of how public services and enterprises can, in fact, be run as effectively, if not more than private firms. Because the public welfare is not something that should be subjected to doctrinal experimentation, privatization should be considered not a first but a last resort. Instead of selling off public enterprises or turning over public services to private conglomerates like Maynilad at the drop of a hat, Filipino technocrats would do well to study how Posco and other successful state-run or state-owned firms were able to create a formidable formula of effective management, high corporate autonomy, and dynamic technological innovation.

Notes

1. Vandana Shiva. *Water Wars: Privatization, Pollution and Profit* (New Delhi, India: Research Press, 2002).

2. Maude Barlow. *Blue Gold: The Global Water Crisis and the Commodification of the World's Water Supply* (San Francisco: International Forum on Globalization, 2001), 1.

3. Violeta Perez-Corral, *MWSS: Anatomy of a Privatization Deal* (Quezon City, Philippines: Freedom from Debt Coalition, May 1998), 1.

4. Management and Organizational Development for Empowerment *Fact Sheet on Philippine Water Resources* prepared for the 2nd World Water Forum, March 17-22, The Hague, Netherlands.

5. Ibid.

6. IBON, Databank and Research Center. "Privatization Corporate Takeover of Government," *IBON Issue Primer Series* (Quezon City: IBON Books, 2003), 74.

7. Ibid., 77.

8. Ibid., 78.

9. Jude Esguerra. "A Critical Assessment of the Manila Water Concession" (working paper).

10. Ibid., 1.

11. Ibid., 1

12. Jude Esguerra, "The Corporate Muddle of Manila's Water Concessions: How the World's Biggest and Most Successful Privatization Turned into a Failure" (work in progress. Writing of the paper supported by Water Aid UK. 2001-2002).

13. Ibid., 4.

14. Jude Esguerra, "A Critical Assessment of the Manila Water Concessions" (working paper). It is noted that a more detailed specification of concessionaire obligations can be found in the MWSS 1997 concession agreement, Article 5.1 to 5.4.

15. Ibid., 5.

16. Ibid., 1. Esguerra notes however that the price reductions would not have been so dramatic if compared against the August 1996 MWSS price of Php 6.43 pcm. MWSS increased its prices to Php 8.78 pcm—a 38 percent jump. Esguerra speculates that the rate was increased to "minimize" the shock of privatization.

17. Orville Solon and Steven John Pamintuan, "Opportunities and Risks in the Privatization-Regulation of the MWSS," in *The Philippine Review of Economics*, 38, no. 1, as cited in Jude Esguerra, "A Critical Assessment of the Manila Water Concession" (working paper).

18. Jude Esguerra, "A Critical Assessment of the Manila Water Concession" (working paper), 4.

19. Jude Esguerra, "The Corporate Muddle of Manila's Water Concessions: How the World's Biggest and Most Successful Privatization Turned into a Failure" (work in Progress. Writing of the paper supported by Water Aid UK, 2001-2002), 10.

20. Ibid., 10.

21. Ibid., 9.

22. Ibid., 9.

23. Ibid., 12.

24. Ibid, 14.

25. Nils Roseman, "The Human Right to Water Under the Conditions of Trade Liberalization and Privatization—A Study on the Privatization of Water Supply and Wastewater Disposal in Manila" (a study on behalf of the Friedrich Ebert Foundation), 7.

26. Ibid., 6.

27. Jose Villanueva, "MWSS to Take back Maynilad Concessions," *TODAY*, December 9, 2003.

28. "Losers All," *Philippine Daily Inquirer*, March 24, 2004; Cecille Visto, "Benpres Relieved of Debt Obligation," *Business World*, March 25, 2004.

29. "Losers All."

30. Nepomuceno Malaluan, "The Philippine Electric Power Industry

Reform: A Tragedy of ADB and World Bank Private Sector Fundamentalism and Unaccountable Government" (Action for Economic Reforms, 2003), 2.

31. Walden Bello, "ADB Hand in Power Reform Bribery Scandal?," *Business World*, April 24, 2000)

32. Ibid.

33. Ibid.

34. Ibid.

35. Ibid.

36. The report was made in July 5, 2002 and was classified as strictly confidential. The report is a review of 35 NPC-IPP contracts conducted by an inter-agency committee.

37. Felicisimo Manalansan, "Unbundling Electricity Consumers' Woes," *IBON Features* 9, no. 36, August 13, 2003.

38. Cited in Walden Bello, "Napocor Privatization: A Cure that May Prove Worse than the Disease," *Business World*, July 12, 1999.

39. "State Power Firm Lines up $400 Million Loans for Approval," *Business World*, February 26, 2004.

40. "PSALM Seeks Clarification on Napocor Rate Mechanism," *Business World*, October 16, 2003.

41. Bello, ibid.

42. Gilberto Llanto, "Private Participation in Infrastructure Provision," *Business World*, March 8, 2004.

43. Ibid.

44. Ibid.

45. Ibid.

46. Testimony of US Trade Representative Charlene Barshefsky, US House of Representatives Ways and Means Trade Subcommittee, Washington, D.C., February 24, 1998.

CHAPTER 6

Unsustainable Development

In 1987 the World Commission on Environment and Development headed by Gro Harlem Brundtland presented its famous report, "Our Common Future," to the United Nations General Assembly. The Brundtland report, as it is now known, popularized what would become the definitive definition of the concept of "sustainable development." According to the report, "[It] is development that meets the needs of present generations without compromising the ability of future generations to meet their own needs." Under this definition, development is not just limited to economic growth but is made to encompass environmental protection, and an equitable distribution of wealth and resources, with the goal of improving and raising the standards and quality of living for everyone.

With Brundtland's report, it seemed as though proponents of "sustainable development" had finally succeeded in putting the concept on the agenda after years of tireless campaigning and lobbying. The phrase would eventually become a buzzword among governments and civil societies around the world, with many environmentalists, policy makers, and even businesses all claiming to embrace the concept.

In that same period in the Philippines, the advent of a new government offered the promise of putting in place the context for a solution to the country's many problems. Among these was the worsening environmental crisis. Writing in 1993, noted American scholars Robin Broad and John Cavanagh claimed that "the plunder of resources has been taking place at a rate that is the fastest in the world. Fragile ecosystems have been pushed to the limit. As we discover firsthand, there are few places you can go to in the Philippines without meeting some sort of ecological disaster."[1]

Already bad during the Marcos period, the state of the environment at the end of the Aquino period was even worse. Particulate matter in 1993 was up by more than 60 percent from the 1984 figure, with the level in Manila almost twice the national ambient standards. Rivers in the Metro Manila area were "almost biologically dead."[2] The crisis was exemplified in many people's minds by deforestation. Forest cover in 1993 had declined by nearly half from forest cover in 1985.[3] As of 1991, forest cover was down to 17 percent, far below the 60 percent necessary for the country to maintain a stable ecosystem.[4] Natural disasters such as the massive mudslides that practically swept away the city of Ormoc in 1991, and Southern Leyte and Surigao del Norte in December 2003, exemplified the massive tragedies that could result from the systematic slashing away of Philippine forests. The emergence and the growing acceptance of the concept of "sustainable development" provided the background and the rhetoric behind the succession of attempts at achieving rapid economic growth while, at the same time, addressing the deteriorating crisis. These would, however, be critically undermined by the government's chosen economic policies.

The Promise and the Peril

Since 1986 the Philippine government has formulated and passed an impressive array of laws and regulations that appear to evince greater political sensitivity to environmental problems and to be in keeping with the spirit of the goals of "sustainable development." While arguably still inadequate, many of these policies were considered path-breaking among developing countries and were often held up as models to be emulated.

Emblematic of the newly affirmed importance of the environment during the administration of President Corazon Aquino was the creation in 1987 of the Department of Environment and Natural Resources (DENR), a cabinet-level ministry with a mandate to focus exclusively on environmental issues. Before, such concerns were the domain only of smaller agencies with limited resources and narrow directives. But with the DENR given bigger responsibilities such as the power to grant licenses for the extraction of natural resources, it was expected to be the main agency for proposing and executing environmental protection laws.

Aquino also passed the landmark legislation called the Comprehensive Agrarian Reform Program (CARP), which then created the Department of Agrarian Reform. Although its more progressive provisions had been severely watered down by the landed elite in the Congress, CARP was still seen as a significant law that promised to redistribute lands over a ten-year period. To address the apprehensions of indigenous people regarding mineral extraction, the People's Small-Scale Mining Program (Republic Act 7076) was passed. In terms of international commitments, the Aquino administration ratified the Montreal Protocol, a milestone international treaty aimed at protecting the ozone layer.

But more than any other post-1986 president, it was Fidel Ramos who cultivated the image of being the champion of "sustainable development," consistently employing the concept in promoting many of his government projects, and casting himself as the president who would turn the Philippines into an "economic tiger" without trampling on the environment as the earlier tigers did.

Right after the Earth Summit in Rio de Janeiro, Ramos created the Philippine Commission on Sustainable Development (PCSD), the first national council for sustainable development in Asia. It was, Ramos said, "a concrete gesture of our country's commitment to operationalize sustainable development."[5] The PCSD would later come up with Philippine Agenda 21 (PA 21), the country's translation of the Earth Summit's Agenda 21 to a practical local development plan. With this document, the PCSD proudly announced that it had covered everything needed for the Philippines to take the path to sustainable development. In addition, the Ramos government ratified the international Framework Convention on Climate Change and unveiled the Philippine Strategy for Biodiversity Conservation.

In terms of legislation, Ramos passed two crucial laws: the Toxic Substances, Hazardous and Nuclear Waste Act (Republic Act 6969), which regulated the use and disposal of toxic wastes, and the National Integrated Protected Areas System (Republic Act 7586), which put in place mechanisms for safeguarding habitats of endangered species and other ecologically sensitive public lands. But perhaps the most significant and most controversial of Ramos's legislative achievements was the Indigenous People's Rights Act (IPRA), which recognized and upheld indigenous people's claims to their ancestral domains. The law even called for the establishment of the National Commission on Indigenous Peoples (NCIP), an agency to be headed by indigenous people themselves.

Under President Joseph Estrada's term, the passage of the Comprehensive Air Pollution Control Policy (Republic Act 8749) was considered a breath of fresh air by its proponents. The Act banned incineration and allowed citizens and communities to file suits against corporations polluting the atmosphere.

President Gloria Macapagal Arroyo's three-year term in office saw no groundbreaking environmental policy making or legislation on the scale of Aquino or Ramos. The only bill she signed into law was the Solid Waste Management Act, a reaction to the capital's pressing garbage crisis. By Arroyo's regime, there would have been ample time for all the laws and policies to achieve their intended outcome. But by that time, it had increasingly become clear that after fifteen years, the passage of significant pieces of legislation and the establishment of key institutions had done little to mitigate the country's environmental crisis.

What the Other Hand Is Doing

From Aquino to Ramos to Estrada then Arroyo, growing environmental consciousness and the consequent promotion of the ideals of sustainable development provided the context with which government and civil society attempted to respond to the country's environmental problems. Consistently corroding these efforts, however, was the marked continuity in the overall economic policies of the post-Marcos administrations.

In the 1980s, the debt crisis in the Philippines forced the government to sign up for structural adjustment programs (SAPs) with the International Monetary Fund (IMF) and the World Bank. These loans came with the neoliberal prescriptions demanding that the government loosen its restrictions on foreign investments, open the domestic market to foreign products, sell off state-owned enterprises, and deregulate the market. While Aquino inherited two "structural adjustment" loans signed by Marcos, she also chose to follow the model-debtor strategy advocated by a faction in her government and went on to embrace policies that deregulated the domestic market, sold off government-owned corporations and liberalized foreign trade. Aquino then established the Committee on Privatization and the Assets Privatization Trust to implement the required measures of the IMF and the World Bank.

She also passed the Foreign Investment Act of 1991, which liberalized the entry of multinational investors into the country and set out to implement a tariff reduction and simplification program. By the end of her term, Aquino had managed to fully entangle the country in more loans, grants, and measures for structural adjustment, in adherence to IMF-World Bank conditionalities.

Ramos's self-avowed commitment to "sustainable development" was matched and overtaken only by the fervor with which he implemented his favored neoliberal doctrines. Ramos's vision was embodied in the Medium-Term Philippine Development Plan (MTPDP) or "Philippines 2000," a strategy plan for reducing poverty and attaining economic growth by opening up the country to foreign investment, privatizing state-owned enterprises, and removing regulations on business. As part of this strategy, Ramos—assisted by then-Senator Gloria Macapagal Arroyo in Congress— vigorously pushed for the country's ratification of the Uruguay Round of the General Agreement on Tariffs and Trade (GATT). He further relaxed rules governing the entry of foreign investors by amending the Foreign Investment Act of 1991 and allowing access to foreign banks through the Bank Liberalization Act. One by one, Ramos disposed of government holdings in key state-owned enterprises as part of his sweeping privatization program. He enacted the Downstream Oil Deregulation Act and implemented one of the biggest privatization projects in the world, the sell-off of the water utilities firm, Metropolitan Waterworks and Sewerage System (MWSS), to the private sector.

Despite his populist image, Estrada and his technocrats continued Aquino's and Ramos's neoliberal thrust. Leaving crucial policy-making decisions to his team of advisers, Estrada's macroeconomic policies followed his predecessors' steps, putting out his own medium-term development plan that basically contained the same components as the previous one and appointing officials subscribing to the same orthodoxy.

Despite the extraordinary circumstances in which Arroyo assumed office, the economic policies she set out to accomplish immediately shattered any notion of change. Under pressure from the World Bank, the IMF, and the Asian Development Bank, one of Arroyo's first important policy initiatives was the passage of the bill that would privatize the country's state-owned power-generation firm. Having been the au-

thor of key neoliberal laws passed by her predecessors, Arroyo expectably pursued as the overriding principle of development an updated but
essentially unrevised MTPDP for 2001-2004. The plan reaffirms its commitment to trade liberalization, saying that "the Philippines will continue to participate in trade and investment liberalization and facilitation initiatives under the auspices of WTO, Association of Southeast
Asian Nations (ASEAN), and the Asia-Pacific Economic Cooperation
[APEC] forum."[6] As before, the cornerstone of MTPDP was still the
belief that free markets and foreign investments should be relied on as
the engine of growth. As such, Arroyo's MTPDP is unequivocal: investment laws will be interpreted in favor of the investor.[7]

Consistent Contradictions

The economic strategy of the post-Marcos administrations directly clashed with their environmental programs, as well as with the
proposals advocated by civil society. As a result, the stated goal of achieving "sustainable development" was repeatedly eroded by the government's
consistent commitment to neoliberal economic policies through the years
and subverted by the power of narrow economic interests. On the one
hand, the government passed—but failed to meaningfully enforce—
laws to protect natural resources. On the other, it encouraged—and
strongly promoted—the exploitation of these resources by giving investors unhampered access and allowing them unfettered operations. Simply put, "sustainable development" became the new rhetoric but structural adjustment remained the practice.

The clash between protecting the environment and protecting business interests is perhaps best illustrated by the explicit contradiction between the content of the PA 21 and the MTPDP (see Table 6.1). In the
trade-off between growth and equity, the MTPDP assumes that increases
in GDP will eventually trickle down to the poor; the PA 21, on the other
hand, is committed to the redistribution of income and direct poverty
reduction. The MTPDP sees orienting production toward exports is the
way to achieve growth while PA 21 believes in harnessing the local market as an engine of growth. The MTPDP advocates the "modernization"
of the countryside while the PA 21 promotes "nurturing the inherent
strengths of local and indigenous knowledge." The PA 21 seeks to uphold

the right of the people to choose their own development strategy while the MTPDP is all for exposing them to the vagaries of corporate-driven globalization. The MTPDP is littered with rhetorical phrases such as "participatory democracy," but one will be hard pressed to find any concrete provisions for actually putting them into practice.

Table 6.1 Medium-Term Philippine Development Plan
vs. Philippine Agenda 21

Model of growth	Neoliberal framework: growth-oriented and export-oriented	Equity-oriented and local market-oriented
Agricultural strategy	Modernization of rural agriculture "We must hasten the modernization of this sector"	Cultural sensitivity "Nurturing the inherent strengths of local and indigenous knowledge, practices..."
Underlying Principles	Principle of a competitive economy "enhance competition, reduce government regulation...expose to foreign competition.."	Principle of self-determination "relying on the inherent capacity of the country & its people to decide on the course of their own development."
Stance on resource-extraction	MTPDP promoted the Mining Act of 1995	Strong positions against pollution, resource depletion and exploitation

The inconsistency is not confined to paper. While the pursuit of the MTPDP's goals was well funded, PA 21 practically got nothing.[8] The PCSD, which was supposed to be the agency for following through the PA 21, received only very limited resources and a very narrow mandate. As expected, it quickly evolved into shoptalk and has been unable to fulfill its role as an oversight body, much less ensure the implementation of the policies spelled out in the PA 21.

The contradiction between the government's lip service to "sustainable development" and its driven implementation of neoliberal policies was easily exploited by certain corporations and politicians who were profiting from exploiting the environment. The stated policy of attracting investors at all costs, the intentionally enfeebled regulatory framework, plus the state's incapacity to enforce its laws all facilitated the subversion of the goals of "sustainable development" by resource-extractive industries and politicians, resulting in the continued depletion of the country's resources.

These dynamics are illustrated in the case of the mining and logging industries.

Case Study 1: A Minefield of Disaster

In 1996 the Marcopper mine site situated atop a mountain unleashed a torrent of sulfuric mine tailings into the Boac and Makulapnit rivers in the island of Marinduque in southern Luzon. An estimated total of 1.5 to 3 million cubic meters of toxic tailings[9] inundated the whole length of the Boac River which goes through almost the entire island, thereby effectively killing the small island's ecosystems and livelihood. The biggest industrial accident in the country's history, it was also one of its worst environmental disasters.

The Marcopper spill brought into the spotlight the workings of the mining industry in a country with one of the highest mineral endowments in the world, according to several geological surveys. Since President Marcos's regime, the Philippine government has been inducing multinational mining corporations to invest in extracting the country's vast mineral resources by offering them various incentives. Dangling these enticements before investors often meant sacrificing the rights of the communities, including those of the indigenous people who live around the mine sites in order to meet the demands or preferences of the prospectors. It also meant relaxing existing regulatory mechanisms or refusing to implement necessary regulations. For many, the Marcopper accident was an unfortunate but predictable consequence of these actions.

In 1974 Marcos passed Presidential Decree 463 or the Mineral Resources Development Decree, which aimed to jumpstart the growth of the mining industry. It allowed, at least on paper, foreign investors to own up to 40 percent of the company while the Filipino partner owned the 60 percent majority. This provision was intended to open the doors to local investors but instead opened a window only to a few privileged elite. Benguet Consolidated, for example, originally a 100-percent American-owned corporation, sold its shares to businessmen like Jaime Ongpin and families like the Sorianos, well-known dominant clans both politically and economically powerful in the country. Marcopper, another originally foreign-owned company, sold a portion of its equities to the Marcoses and Marcos cronies. An important feature of Marcos's decree was the complete disregard for surface owners and present occupants of the lands to be exploited. In many cases, this meant ignoring the indigenous communities who considered the mine sites their home and source of livelihood. According to the decree, any prospector can occupy the land that it applies for and it will be protected by the government against the original occupants refusing to let it in.

In addition, Marcos threw in several more sweeteners like a lease term of twenty-five years, renewable for another twenty-five years, and the duty-free importation of any equipment. There was supposed to be a limit to the size of land a firm could own but this was rendered meaningless by another clause allowing companies to own several plots of land. Cases of pollution, such as the disposal of mine tailings, were to be sanctioned with a ridiculous fine of Php 5,000.

In other words, the government laid out a golden brick road toward an industry that raked in an average of 20 percent of the total Philippine exports[10] and contributed an average of 1.3 percent share gross value added in the country's gross national product.[11] This categorized the industry as a veritable income-generating source for the government. It paid a sizeable amount in excise taxes, reaching sums of $19 million in one year alone.[12]

By the time Aquino took over, 270 mining firms were operating in the country, most of which were partially owned by multinational mining corporations. In 1987 Aquino's Executive Order 279 gave the DENR secretary full authority to negotiate and conclude leasehold agreements with resource extracting firms in the form of Financial and Technical Assistance Agreements (FTAAs). This effectively hastened the entry of many investors. In contrast to Marcos's time, the FTAAs made the government full joint-venture partners with the private mining firms in the exploitation of the nation's minerals. Like Marcos, Aquino added some bonuses such as tax holidays and other forms of tax exemptions to encourage foreign investors to enter the industry.

When Ramos entered the picture, he cited the mining industry as an example of how the concept of "sustainable development" could be translated to action. This industry was to fuel the country's industrialization but it was also going to be a showcase of how to reconcile the needs of business with the needs of the environment. For Ramos, this meant implementing his MTPDP and kicking the industry's doors open to foreign investors. Taking the liberalization of the industry a big step further, he pushed Congress to pass the Mining Act of 1995 or Republic Act 7942, a significant piece of legislation that would have allowed foreign corporations 100-percent ownership of their investments, repatriate their profits in full, and effectively own land. (These provisions were later deemed unconstitutional by the Supreme Court.)

In this all-out effort to woo the mining companies, the Marcopper spill revealed what was often foregone in favor of investments. It turned out that Marcopper had no business permit all along and that, being one of the biggest investors in the field, it had been exempted from the requisite environmental impact assessments.[13] Moreover, subsequent inspections by engineers revealed that the spill was caused by a faulty plugging system, an obviously reckless oversight by both the company and the government regulators who, in theory, should constantly be keeping an eye on their operations. Several more covered-up errors surfaced, showing an irresponsibly run operation with government deliberately looking the other way. The DENR has a separate agency, the Mines and Geosciences Bureau, which was created to focus exclusively on monitoring and regulating the exploitation of the country's mineral resources. But as with the entire government, the bureau is wracked by conflicting goals—that of promoting industry and that of protecting the mine lands. It has no effective power to sanction firms that violate its regulations.

In the end, Marcopper's mother company, Placer Dome, one of the world's largest mining companies, got away virtually scot-free. "When we were going to file a complaint against [them], we were shocked to see that the companies no longer existed, somehow they were able to sell shares, change names, and ultimately cover their tracks,"[14] said an astonished Mitch Maling of the Marinduque Council for Environmental Concerns, of their efforts to pin down the firm. It had been easy for Placer Dome to come, it had also been easy for it to leave.

The way by which the mining companies were pampered contrasted markedly with the way by which local mining employees as well as the indigenous communities living on the mining sites were treated.

While the multinational corporations were given tax holidays and various forms of assistance to start up their operations, the plight of the workers was constantly ignored. Despite generous incentives, however, the mining industry has not lived up to its promise of delivering economic growth and has in fact been losing money. During the past twenty years, while the government was throwing incentives left and right, twenty-nine firms had declared bankruptcy because of declining world prices for minerals.[15]

The workforce consequently decreased by the thousands, with big companies like Benguet and Lepanto downsizing from a high of 15,000 to 6,000 workers.[16] Though some firms like Benguet claimed to have paid off their workers with sizeable retirement sums, most have completely relinquished their responsibilities by declaring bankruptcy, thereby escaping the legal requirements of compensating workers. And since mining is a skills-specific industry, losing a job here is not as simple as losing a job at, say, a stuffed-toy factory. Most miners enter the trade as young adults, learning and developing mining skills, and ending up spending most of their lives in the industry. Because mine sites are usually in remote areas, mining companies put up houses for their miners, as well as other basic services like hospitals or clinics, schools, and retail stores. Miners in turn end up bringing up their families with them. Unlike the mining corporations that can easily relocate to another mine site, abandoned miners often have nowhere to go and no government to turn to once a mine closes down.

In attracting the mining prospectors to mine sites in the country, the government often disregarded the fact that what it was selling off may not have been its own to sell. Some of the mine sites had actual people living on them—the indigenous communities who considered the mountains their ancestral domains. But for the government and for the mining companies these people simply did not exist. Because the indigenous people often move around the mountain from season to season, the fact that they do not have land titles and that they do not build physical infrastructure in the places where they live has been used to prove that they are not there. "Benguet has been around for ninety-eight years and we have not encountered a genuine indigenous community,"[17] said the vice president of a mining firm in Northern Luzon. For him, the indigenous people are just a figment of the imagination. Since these indigenous people are not real, mining companies—as tolerated by government—have found it all too easy to evict them from their lands. With the laws often interpreted in favor of the firms, indigenous people have been thrown out of their lands, forced to find new homes or go down to the cities where they become street urchins or part of the squatters in slum areas. Entire communities are dislocated, disrupting cultural and family ties.

All this was supposed to change in October 1997 when the IPRA, a landmark law which affirms the existence of the indigenous people, was passed. A key provision is the recognition of "ancestral domains" or lands that have belonged to these communities since time immemorial but have no regular legal documentation like land titles and are instead supported by tribal laws and practices. Tied to this recognition of "ancestral domains" is the right of the communities to explore and utilize the minerals in their lands. In other words, the mine sites were now to be owned by the indigenous people themselves and mining companies could not enter without permission. The law required a process of "informed" consultation before mining could be allowed on the community's lands. Interested mining companies now had to secure a written consent from the communities before they could begin digging. All these presented a formidable threat to the mining companies, as well as to those who wanted to attract them.

Barely three months after its enactment into law the IPRA's validity was challenged. In September 1998 former Supreme Court Justice Isagani Cruz filed a case in court, questioning the constitutionality of the IPRA. "The IPRA was a rank violation of the constitution. I have nothing against the indigenous people but their protection should be in accordance with the law," Cruz argued.[18] The basic issue raised in the petition involved the Regalian Doctrine or the law that says that the State has ownership and control over all lands and natural resources and therefore the right to sell or lease them as well. According to Cruz, the provision in the IPRA that allows the indigenous people to own and control their ancestral domains violates this doctrine. Because this provision prevents the government from inviting mining corporations, the Regalian doctrine had to be invoked and upheld.

So controversial were the provisions in question that, in a country where court cases routinely take months or even years to begin their hearings, the respondents in this case received their summons twenty-four hours after it was filed. The solicitor general abandoned it, according to Commissioner David Daoas of the NCIP.[19]

The SC eventually ruled 7-7 in favor of the law. Though it resulted in a tie, the vote effectively upheld the constitutionality of the IPRA and denied the motion to issue a temporary restraining order (TRO) that would prevent its implementation. Seven justices of the Supreme Court had rescued the IPRA from certain death. But who would deal it a fatal blow but then-DENR Secretary Antonio Cerilles himself? Despite the Supreme Court's ruling, Cerilles declared a TRO of his own and cut funding to the IPRA's main implementor, thereby effectively paralyzing the agency.[20] Cerilles justified his actions by saying that the IPRA's constitutionality had been questioned and therefore could not be implemented. But even Cruz, the original complainant, did not agree with this. "[Cerilles's action] is not constitutional because the Supreme Court itself did not issue a TRO so the IPRA should be implemented fully."[21] With the IPRA effectively nullified, the indigenous people have ceased to exist again.

The paralyzing effect of pro-environmental legislation and court rulings being contradicted by pro-business executive enforcement was again evident in the controversy over Republic Act 7942 (Philippine Mining Act of 1995). On January 27, 2004, the Supreme Court issued a ninety-five-page decision declaring a number of provisions of Republic Act 7942 as unconstitutional following a petition filed by concerned sectors questioning the constitutionality of the law and its implementing rules and regulations formulated by the DENR through Administrative Order 96-40. The petitioners pointed out that Republic Act 7942 is unconstitutional for it authorizes the execution of service contracts with foreign-owned firms for the exploration, development, exploitation, and use of country's minerals, petroleum, and other mineral oils. The SC ruled in this favor declaring Republic Act 7942 unconstitutional; it further held that even if "the statute employs the phrase 'financial and technical agreements' in accordance with the 1987 Constitution, it actually treats these agreements as service contracts that grant beneficial ownership to foreign contractors contrary to the fundamental law."[22] Likewise, all provisions of DENR Administrative Order 96-40 that do not conform to the said decision have been considered void and the FTAA between the government and Western Mining Corporation Philippines Inc. nullified.

While this should have been seen as a positive leap toward the preservation of the environment, Mines and Geo-Sciences Director Horacio Ramos contends that the SC ruling would jeopardize the revitalization program of the minerals industry, threaten existing and proposed developmental projects, and discourage foreign investments that are estimated to bring in $5 billion worth of potential investments. The government appealed.

But even before the Court could decide on the appeal, the government was already trying to devise a way out of the Court's decision that rendered illegal full foreign ownership of mining operations. The government's proposal, according to Trade and Industry Secretary Cesar Purisima, would be to outsource or contract mining to a foreign firm. This would preserve the legal fiction of ownership of the mines lying with the government, while giving actual control over investment and operations to foreign investors "for a fee."[23] It was as if the proponents of subcontracting in mining had not heard of the disaster that had overtaken the projects subcontracted to the foreign investor-linked private firms in electricity generation and water provision discussed in the previous chapter.

The court ruling should have marked an encouraging advance in battling the adverse effects of mining operations and its devastating social impact on indigenous communities. Unfortunately, the prime agency mandated to safeguard the environment spearheads the move to reverse what little victory had been won. Environmental equilibrium and economic strategy were simply in contradiction.

Case Study 2: Battles under the Foliage

As early as the American occupation of the Philippines, the forests were considered a great source of wealth because of the high demand for timber in the West at the time. As a result, the modernization of the logging industry was considered among the top priorities of the US colonial administration at the turn of the century.[24] Government worked hand in hand with large timber corporations, both foreign and domestic, to transform the Philippines from a timber importer to Southeast Asia's largest timber exporter.[25] The colonial Bureau of Forestry was only too happy to cash in on the demand, giving out promotional booklets targeting US customers saying, "When you buy Philippine lumber, you are helping not only the Filipinos, but also the American lumbermen in the Philippines and the American machine manufacturers in the United States."[26]

Though the demand from the US eventually dwindled, the lost revenues were quickly compensated for by the demand from other markets. From the 1960s to the 1990s, Japan took the lead, purchasing as much as 70 percent of timber logged in the Philippines.[27] The '60s and the '70s would be considered the golden years of the logging industry, with the Philippines ranking as the fifth-largest timber exporter in the world market. With the industry accounting for about 33 percent of total export earnings,[28] it was lavished with special treatment by the government. As a number of loggers became local and national politicians and as politicians also went into logging, they began to exercise control over the government's relation with their industry. This included the granting of concessions, grants, and exemptions. Former DENR Secretary Victor Ramos attests that most timber licensing agreements (TLAs) given out before were part of political spoils.[29]

But as the loggers rose in power, more and more trees fell. Afraid to lose their stronghold, the loggers ensured that the felling of timber would continue at an even more intense pace, peaking at an annual production average of 15,475 cubic meters for the years 1966 to 1970.[30] At this time, there were less than a hundred TLAs. This would increase significantly during the next decade, reaching a peak of 230 TLAs in 1977,[31] with each TLA covering tens of thousands of hectares.[32] Ironically, this high was reached when the government declared what was at first a total log ban but would later be downgraded to a selective log ban.

After a few years of what Secretary Ramos calls "legitimized illegal logging,"[33] the effects of irresponsible logging methods became evident. In the beginning of the '80s the government tried to curb the denudation of forests by requiring timber concession holders to reforest their areas. It was a vain attempt. Instead of replanting, companies underreported actual log production and exports[34] or, in some cases, submitted nonexistent reforestation projects.[35] Coupled with the other causes of deforestation namely slash-and-burn farmers, conversion of forest lands to croplands, migration of lowlanders to the uplands, and natural occurrences like forest fires, the outcome was a severe depletion of the forest cover.

In 1986 the DENR was established as a separate agency that would focus exclusively on the environment. A former secretary, Fulgencio Factoran, explained this decision as a tactical move to give the department more teeth in pursuing and implementing environmental protection laws. "We saw that the agencies handling the environment like the national pollution commission were small agencies with limited budgets and limited mandates."[36] The belief was that, in giving the DENR the power to grant licences for the extraction of natural resources, it would also then be in a better position to execute environmental protection laws.

With this new mandate, the DENR under Factoran dramatically reduced the number of TLAs from 137 in 1987 to 29 at the end of the term as a deliberate move to stop the rapid denuding of forests.[37] At the instance of environmental groups, the DENR also cancelled all stumpage contracts and then raised the fee for cutting a tree from a ridiculous amount of Php 5 to Php 525. Such an increase was met with resistance by the logging community but the public's growing environmental consciousness had countered the influence of the loggers and their friends in government. The abrupt change of governments from Marcos to Aquino also did not give the logging industry enough time to switch allegiances.[38] This diminished influence paved the way for the passage of a twelve-year commercial logging ban in Congress.

By the time President Fidel Ramos came to power, however, it became apparent that the loggers had found ways to circumvent the government's efforts. This was starkly evident in the statistics on forest cover. By 1993 forest cover was down to 5.8 million hectares, down by nearly half from 10.4 million figure at the end of the Marcos period.[39] The annual deforestation rate during the Aquino period was, in fact, higher than during the Marcos period, with forest cover being removed at about 5.1 percent in the former, compared to 2.5 percent in the latter.[40] By then, it became evident that the only way to save the forests was through a total log ban. Illegal loggers, however, proved adept in skirting the ban. They deliberately let the agency's officials confiscate their logs to fool them into thinking that the confiscation rate was going up. In truth, the amount confiscated was only a small percentage of their actual cut.[41] Loggers would also recycle logging permits at checkpoints, buy TLAs from legal holders for purposes of presenting to inspectors and, sometimes bribe the DENR personnel.[42]

Table 6.2 Reduction in Forest Cover
(Marcos and Aquino periods)

Year	Forest Cover (thousand ha)
1970	15,898.90
1971	15,875.01
1972	15,671.10
1973	13,893.96
1974	13,690.06
1975	13,476.04
1976	13,272.14
1977	13,068.23
1978	12,864.33
1979	12,661.00
1980	12,456.52
1981	12,252.61
1982	11,963.41
1983	11,759.50
1984	11,555.60
1985	10,368.03
1986	9,180.47
1987	6,789.64
1988	6,460.60
1989	6,307.40
1990	6,158.80
1991	6,015.40
1992	5,900.20
1996	5,590.18

Source: Ponciano Intal Jr. and Erlinda Medalla, "The East Asian Financial Crisis and Philippine Sustainable Development, in *Economic Crisis. . . Once More*, ed. Mario Lamberte (Makati: Philippine Institute for Development Studies, 2001), 97; Department of Environment and Natural Resources.

Because of the loggers' success in foiling the government's attempts at keeping logging under control, the forests continued to be denuded at an alarming rate, resulting in a dismal forest cover of six million hectares by 1991, only 700,000 hectares of which are virgin forests.[43] If anything, the failure to arrest the continued denudation of the country's forests highlighted the structural problems facing an ineffective government regulatory agency vis-à-vis a powerful industry.

First of all, the DENR does not have enough teeth to police the logging industry. It is not given enough funds and enough power to achieve its objectives. In 2004 DENR faces another budget slash, reflecting a dwindling trend in its budget. This makes life a lot easier for illegal loggers. For example, forest rangers and DENR officials use outdated means to police the forests. While loggers often have the latest technologies at their disposal, rangers do not even have the means to get to the actual logging sites except by foot. Validating reforested areas through aerial photos came as a recent development only with Secretary Ramos specifically allocating budget for the purchase of only one helicopter. Another antiquated approach at catching illegal loggers is the setting up of checkpoints at the logging roads and piers. Often, loggers transporting premium hardwood get past inspectors by simply covering the wood under bags of charcoal.[44]

The budgetary inadequacy also explains why the agency could not hire the kind of people it needs and why its employees are vulnerable to the temptation of easy money. Rey Alcances, chief of the Environmental Impact Assessment Committee, for instance, laments that he loses his best people—and their expertise—to corporations and other private firms.[45] "They come here young and idealistic and then they realize that their hands are tied because of lack of funds and the bureaucracy so they leave," Alcances relates.[46] With their low salaries, the DENR's employees are prone to accepting the wads of cash that loggers can afford to spread around.

DENR's impotence stands in stark contrast with the vast resources of the loggers, not least of which is their firepower. What, for example, can an unarmed ranger do in the face of armalites and guns? Feeling helpless, some rangers have actually requested for weapons and firearms from the department. Secretary Ramos recalls encountering several forest rangers pleading for arms. "They would tell me that they could stop the trucks and the loggers if they had the same, if not more powerful firearms," Ramos said.[47] In the lucrative business of logging, the forest ranger is not the only one used for target practice. A number of DENR provincial officials have been targeted and killed. The highest official murdered was Central Luzon Director Ric Serrano, whose pending appointment as the department's undersecretary may have been a big threat to certain quarters.

In the morning of June 24, 1998, as Serrano made his way through the usual traffic of Quezon City, armed men stopped in front of his car and blasted away. It was common knowledge that Serrano had a lot of enemies because of the way he clamped down on illegal loggers in Central Luzon. He also closed down factories he deemed environmentally harmful to nearby rainforests, rivers, and watersheds. Investigators then zeroed in on this slighted group. True enough, witnesses slowly began coming out, with one linking the murder to a powerful family that owned one of the factories that Serrano has ordered closed. But before the case could be heard, witnesses began dying or disappearing. The case remains unresolved.

The government's apparent helplessness in the face of powerful logging interests has prodded communities and NGOs to take matters into their own hands. In Palawan, for example, a noteworthy group called Environmental Legal Assistance Center (ELAC) has been doing what the DENR couldn't: apprehending illegal loggers and confiscating their chainsaws and timber. Tired of waiting for the nonexistent assistance from the government, ELAC has been assisting communities in invoking and performing "citizen's arrest." The sheer number of the community residents allows them to overpower the armed loggers and stop them from felling trees.

It's not that the communities can do without the DENR because they can't; they just want the DENR to perform its job. In one community, for example, paralegals from ELAC made it a point to stay with DENR personnel at the checkpoint to ensure that they would apprehend an oncoming truck stealthily loaded with hot lumber.[48] As ELAC's Bobby Chan explains, "We cannot keep doing their jobs! That's why whenever we can, we ask, drag or force DENR personnel to come with us during arrests and confiscation of lumber and chainsaws."[49]

But even if the government had the capacity to enforce its own laws and regulations, there is still the question of whose side it is really on. Even if the DENR had all the bright minds, the equipment, or the guns, these would still not give the assurance that the agency would be allowed to do its job properly without any interference. There have been cases, for example, of environmental offenders getting off the hook despite the valiant attempts of committed DENR officials fulfilling their roles and defying the risks. Worse, the DENR officials who went after these violations were the ones prosecuted, instead of the illegal loggers.[50]

The tug of competing interests within the DENR is played out in the agency's mandate. "The present DENR as it is presently structured is really schizophrenic," argues Von Hernandez, regional campaign director of Greenpeace.[51] On the one hand, the DENR is supposed to conserve the environment and control the extraction of natural resources. And yet, on the other, it is responsible for granting the permits to corporations from which the agency is supposed to protect the environment. Indeed, the agency's independence had been dented after certain assessments and rulings that were unfavorable to certain parties were "softened."[52] "There's a battle of interests and we are often at the losing end," laments Alcances.

Perhaps the most glaring manifestation of how the interests of the industry prevail over the interests of the environment was the installation of a known logger, Antonio Cerilles, as DENR secretary during the Estrada administration. The appointment of Cerilles, a former governor with no background in the area of natural resources, except being a former extractor, was best explained as a political favor. Cerilles, who acted as the campaign manager of Estrada's LAMMP party in the 1998 election, and a close friend of Executive Secretary Ronaldo Zamora whose family controls the nickel mining industry in the country, added to the controversy of his appointment. So notorious was Cerilles among environmental groups that he was described as being "born with a chainsaw in his hand."[53] True enough, Cerilles did not waste time appointing his fellow loggers to key positions in the department and exempting certain companies from fulfilling usual requirements including his own. His recommendation to install ex-Lapuyan, Zamboanga del

Sur Mayor Cesar Sulong, an Estrada ally with a record of graft and small-town patronage politics attached to his name,[54] as NCIP chairman, was interpreted as a clear demonstration of putting the interest of a political ally over and above the indigenous people's needs. Adding to a long string of controversy assailing the secretary was the disclosure that his very own rubber processing plant was operating without an environmental compliance certificate. A few days later, the environmental permit was quietly issued by a DENR regional director he promoted just ten days before.[55] At one point, Cerilles was even supposedly witnessed by his staff to have ordered Jimmy Pisigan, the head of an investigating team for these ocular inspections, to drop a number of names from the list of violators, explaining, "*Hindi mo pa ba kilala ang mga kaibigan natin?* [Do you still not know who our friends are?]"[56] For an agency that had often been hijacked by certain interests from the outside, DENR under Cerilles and his friends represented a takeover of the very agency that was supposed to regulate them.

At the outset, environmentalists say that Cerilles's attitude toward illegal logging was betrayed by his choice of a vacation resort. According to Chan, "[Cerilles] and his staff regularly stayed at the Dos Palmas resort... in Puerto Princesa [Palawan] for free, when it is a well-known fact that this resort is owned by apprehended illegal loggers!"[57] The very cottage where Cerilles and his staff slept in was actually made of endangered premium hardwood taken from the forests of Palawan, a no-logging zone.[58]

An Incompatible Match

As demonstrated in the cases above, it is not that the government has ignored the environmental crisis afflicting the country. It has passed a number of groundbreaking, if imperfect, pieces of legislation in an attempt to solve specific environmental concerns and has even established particular institutions entrusted to follow through these proposed solutions. For example, the DENR has been tasked to enforce log bans and to clamp down on illegal logging in the logging industry as well as to oversee the operations of the mining industry. A special council was even constituted to ensure that the country does not stray from the path of "sustainable development." But as the current state of the environment proves, all these efforts have been critically negated by the governments' consistent adherence to neoliberal orthodoxy and have been successfully sabotaged by the very resource-extractive interests that it sought to rein in.

This contradiction has subverted the work of well-meaning individuals who came to head the DENR, such as Factoran and Ramos. The latter created an activist team that incorporated key people from environmental nongovernment organizations, like Tony Lavina and Delfin Ganapin, who were appointed undersecretaries. One of the victories they notched was stopping the construction of an environmentally destabilizing cement plant in Bolinao, Pangasinan. However, their ability to go against the institutional current was limited. Vic Ramos was eventually abandoned, at the urging of the tourist industry lobby, by his namesake President Ramos, when he tried to prolong a ban on fishing and swimming at Boracay, one of the Philippines' prized beach resorts, owing to high levels of wastewater pollution.

If the DENR leadership was pro-business under Estrada and pro-environment but frustrated under Ramos, it was paralyzed by internecine conflict under Heherson Alvarez, Arroyo's first DENR secretary.

The example of the mining industry showed to what lengths the government has gone in showering potential investors with incentives and entitlements even as it sidelined the interests of indigenous communities, the workers, and the environment. Since Marcos's time, policies on mining have had the effect of privatizing what should otherwise have been the collective resources of the people. These policies have put the commons in the hands of local and multinational corporations who demanded, as a condition for their investment, that the market be liberalized and deregulated in order for them to have the widest latitude in maximizing their profits. The Marcopper tragedy politically—and literally—exposed the disastrous effects of these policies. As evidenced by the disaster, the demands of neoliberalism dictated that regulation and accountability were the first to go in the process of attracting mining companies to invest in the country. The environment and the community were the ultimate losers.

Clearly, the Marcopper disaster may not have happened had the government not relaxed its requirements—in this case, exempting Marcopper from environmental impact assessment—and if it did not weakly enforce its regulations. That Marcopper was able to leave unpunished may not have been possible had the government not surrendered its power to keep investors in check. As the fate of the IPRA showed, even efforts by civil society to subordinate mining corporations under the interests of the people and the environment would constantly be challenged for contravening the neoliberal objective of putting the interests of corporations over everything else.

The case of the logging industry, on the other hand, showed how institutional efforts to halt the continuing depletion of the forests could easily be subverted by certain interests' firm hold over the government. The ineptitude of the DENR contrasts starkly with the loggers' clout over government, as personified by the appointment of a known logger as the country's chief environmental law enforcer. Rather than just an isolated error in judgment, Cerilles's appointment should be seen as a predictable, if extreme, manifestation of the extent to which the formulation and determination of the government's environmental laws and policies have been circumvented, if not driven, by corporate interests.

That the series of legal and bureaucratic reforms undertaken by the government have not moved the country closer to sustainable development should therefore come as no surprise. Sustainable development cannot be reconciled with neoliberal policies of privatization, deregulation, and liberalization because they are ultimately about different means and aims. Sustainable development recognizes that balancing the requirements of development with the needs of the environment requires decisive state action, something anathema to a doctrine that calls for the withdrawal of the state. Sustainable development stands for equity within and among generations—something rendered impossible by a set of policies which calls for the supremacy of the market in allocating resources. Simply put, protecting the environment is fundamentally at odds with giving corporate interests free rein to exploit it. Hence, government measures to respond to environmental degradation have been and will continue to be rendered meaningless and futile for as long as the contradictory policies that undermine them as well as the interests which are capable of subverting them remain entrenched.

Notes

1. Robin Broad and John Cavanagh, *Plundering Paradise* (Berkeley: University of California Press, 1993), 31.

2. Ponciano Intal Jr. and Erlinda Medalla, "The East Asian Financial Crisis and Philippine Sustainable Development," in *Economic Crisis... Once More*, ed. Mario Lamberte (Makati: Philippine Institute for Development Studies, 2001), 96.

3. Ibid., 97.

4. Michael A. Bengwayan, "Weak Laws in Philippines Exacerbates Deforestation," in *Earth Times* (Manila, 2000).

5. Philippine Agenda 21 Document, *A National Agenda for Sustainable Development for the 21st century.*

6. Ibid., 46.

7. Medium-Term Philippine Development Plan (MTPDP), National Economic and Development Authority, November 2001, Enhancing Competitiveness of Industry and Services, 47.

8. Interview with Philippine Greens Secretary General Roberto Verzola, et al. January 27, 2002.

9. Geoffrey Plumlee et al., *An Overview of Mining-Related Environmental and Human Health Issues, Marinduque Island, Philippines: Observations from a Joint US Geological Survey—Armed Forces Institute of Pathology Reconnaissance Field Evaluation,* May 12-19, 2000. US Geological Survey Open-File report 00-397.

10. Contribution of Mining to Exports and Foreign Exchange Generation (1970-1998) Table (source: Bangko Sentral ng Pilipinas).

11. Contribution of Mining to Gross National Product 1970-1998 Table (source: National Statistical Coordination Board).

12. Contribution of Mining in the form of Excise Taxes 1980-1998 Table (source: Bureau of Internal Revenue).

13. Interview with former DENR Secretary Fulgencio Factoran Jr., BF Homes Parañaque, December 18, 2000.

14. Interview with Mitch Maling of the Marinduque Council for Environmental Concerns, Social Action Center, Boac, Marinduque, January 15, 2001.

15. CRC–IPR, 1995.

16. Corpuz, 1995.

17. Interview with Benguet Associate Vice President Roland de Jesus, February 10, 2000.

18. Interview with Justice Isagani Cruz, February 5, 2001.

19. Interview with National Commission on Indigenous Peoples Chairman David Daoas, March 14, 2001.

20. Interview with National Commission on Indigenous Peoples Chairman David Daoas, March 14, 2001.

21. Interview with Justice Isagani Cruz, February 5, 2001.

22. Joel R. San Juan, "Supreme Court Nullifies Provisions of Mining Law," *Manila Times*, January 30, 2004, b1.

23. Felipe Salvosa II, "Gov't Intends to 'Outsource' Mining to Foreign Firms," *Business World*, March 15, 2004.

24. Bello, Walden. *People and Power in the Pacific: The Struggle for the Post Cold War Order* (Foundation for Nationalist Studies, 1992), 52.

25. Ibid.

26. Ibid.

27. Ibid.

28. Interview with Victor Ramos, DENR Secretary, October 4, 2000.

29. Ibid.

30. *IBON Facts and Figures*, October 15, 1995.

31. Forest Economics Division, *Number of TLA's and Corresponding Logging Area* (table).

32. Victor Ramos. *They Fought for the Forest* (Quezon City: DENR, 2000), 16.

33. Interview with Victor Ramos, DENR Secretary, October 4, 2000.

34. Robert Repetto. *The Forest for the Trees: Government Policies and the Misuse of Forest Resources* (World Resources Institute, May 1988).

35. Eduardo Tadem et al., *Showcases of Underdevelopment in Mindanao: Fishes, Forest and Fruits* (Davao City: Alternate Resource Center, Davao City, 1984).

36. Interview with former DENR Secretary Fulgencio Factoran Jr., BF Homes Paranaque, December 18, 2000.

37. Ibid.

38. Ibid.

39. Intal and Medalla, 97.

40. Calculated from figures in Intal and Medalla, 97.

41. Ibid.

42. Ibid.

43. Victor Ramos, *They Fought for the Forest* (Quezon City: DENR, 2000), 10.

44. Robert Chan, *Swift Justice for the Last Frontier* (Puerto Princesa, Palawan: Environmental Legal Assistance Center, 2000).

45. Ibid.

46. Ibid.

47. Ibid.

48. Robert Chan, *Swift Justice for the Last Frontier* (Puerto Princesa, Palawan: Environmental Legal Assistance Center, 2000).

49. Interview with Atty. Bobby Chan, Environmental Legal Assistance Center, Puerto Princesa, Palawan, March 8, 2001.

50. Interview with Atty. Edward Lorenzo, Environmental Legal Assistance Center, Puerto Princesa, Palawan, March 8, 2001.

51. Interview with Von Hernandez, Regional Campaign Director of Greenpeace, UP Diliman, Quezon City, September 5, 2000.

52. Interview with Rey Alcances, chief of Environmental Impact Assessment Committee, DENR, Quezon City, December 20, 2000.

53. Interview with Atty. Bobby Chan, Environmental Legal Assistance Center, Puerto Princesa, Palawan, March 8, 2001.

54. Howie Severino, "Caught in Bind, Cerilles Gets 'Midnight ECC' from the DENR," *Philippine Center for Investigative Journalism*, November 23, 1998.

55. Ibid.

56. Interview with a former DENR official.

57. Interview with Atty. Edward Lorenzo, Environmental Legal Assistance Center, Puerto Princesa, Palawan, March 8, 2001.

58. Ibid.

CHAPTER 7

Corruption and Poverty:
Barking Up the Wrong Tree?

Joseph Estrada was a consummate, if clumsy, practitioner of "crony capitalism." But while corruption is to be condemned, the idea that it is to blame for the Philippines' underdevelopment is misleading. Not only does this distract us from the real reason, it is also being manipulated to underpin neoliberal policies and stabilize elite rule via liberal democracy.

In January 2001, the Philippines went through what could only have been unimaginable in 1986—another People Power. After the collapse of an impeachment trial, tens of thousands of people massed again in EDSA, the country's busiest and most famous thoroughfare, to demand the ouster of another President, Joseph Estrada. The charge: monumental corruption.

This chapter first extensively narrates the relationships that brought down the President. It examines the transactions between Estrada and four of his most notorious cronies: Lucio Tan, Mark Jimenez, Dante Tan, and Eduardo Cojuangco. The pattern is common. First, these cronies ensured Estrada's election by giving him cash, political machinery, a campaign network, political connections, and other campaign contributions without which Estrada would not have won as President. Once in office, Estrada used his vast powers to repay his friends by helping them achieve their own narrow objectives—subverting the law and further enriching him and his friends in the process.

What all the sordid details reveal, however, is that for the extraordinary brazenness, Estrada's corruption was in fact ordinary. In a political system where corruption is rampant and cronyism pervasive, the only difference that made Estrada stand out was the utter recklessness, the lack of hypocrisy, even the very honesty, by which he ironically observed the usual practice.

The chapter will attempt to puncture a very powerful discourse that has seduced the most sophisticated analysts as well as the ordinary man on the street: that the Philippines is so poor because its leaders are corrupt. It is wrong for the easily demonstrable fact that so many other countries suffering from as much or even more systemic corruption than the Philippines have succeeded in developing and reducing poverty. Even the most developed capitalism such as that of the US—as the Enron and Worldcom episodes show—is not totally immune from the grandest possible corruption imaginable.

Despite its lack of empirical basis, the discourse has proved to be very resilient not only because it is simple but also because it is very convenient and useful. Ruling elites as a whole find it extremely valuable for stabilizing their hold over power via liberal democracy; counter-elite factions in particular find it very helpful for undermining the in-cumbent elites. If for anything, the discourse highlights the absence of any real alternative and economic political program by which counter-elites seek to challenge existing power holders. Moreover, the discourse is also very useful for those who gain from the policy agenda of neoliberalism, the theoretical foundation of which will crumble with-out the threat of corruption.

While corruption definitely needs to be condemned, it is not the reason behind the country's stagnation. A more adequate explanation lies in the state being subjugated by a succession of ruling elite factions to serve narrow interests instead of the larger goals of sustainable devel-opment and social justice. In a sense then, the ties that bind Estrada with his cronies are also the ties that blind us from the reasons behind our poverty. The chapter ends by proposing an alternative to both crony capitalism and neoliberalism: a state that is free from the clutches of corrupt elite factions, free from the grip of transnational capital, and able to control both toward equity and development.

The National Hero

Television reporter Mark Cohen was on standby in Malacañang. It was New Year's eve and he was assigned to cover how the President and his official family were ushering in the last year of the millennium. Lucio Tan walks out of the presidential residence, followed by the President.

Standing nearby, Cohen hears the President assure Tan, "*Pare*, don't worry about your problems. This year will be better."

The President had Cohen and his cameraman destroy their footage.[1] When the firecrackers exploded as the clock struck twelve, Tan bid good-bye to the bad years behind.

It had not been the best of years for the billionaire businessman. During the regime of the late strongman Ferdinand Marcos, Tan's business flourished—thanks to generous concessions granted him by his man in Malacañang.[2] But after the dictator Ferdinand Marcos was ousted in 1986, former President Corazon Aquino started running after Tan's "ill-gotten wealth." Then, when Fidel Ramos succeeded Aquino in 1992, he charged Tan with what was to be biggest tax evasion case in recent Philippine history.

But in 1998, Tan began chasing the evil spirits away by betting correctly in the presidential elections. With Joseph Estrada in charge, the tax evasion case hounding him would be dismissed. His ailing Philippine Airlines (PAL) would be shielded from competition. And he would finally be able to seize ownership of his much-coveted Philippine National Bank (PNB).

The biggest tax evasion case as a favor

Eight months after Estrada promised Tan better days, the Court of Appeals upheld the ruling of a lower court dismissing the Php 25 billion tax fraud charges filed by the Ramos administration against Tan—on a technicality. For those intent on pinning the tycoon, it was the biggest setback yet in a case that had already spanned over a decade.

The arduous saga began when the Bureau of Internal Revenue (BIR) uncovered suspicious transactions by Tan's Fortune Tobacco Corporation.[3] Then-BIR Commissioner Liwayway Vinzons-Chato claimed she had truckloads of indisputable evidence proving Tan's "willful intent to evade taxes."[4] Tan had allegedly set up dummy corporations and individuals to buy Fortune products at a lower price in order to then be liable for lower taxes. The evidence was damning.[5]

The BIR then went on to file a complaint for tax evasion against Tan with the Department of Justice (DOJ). Throughout the next few years, the BIR would doggedly and relentlessly pursue the case. At the ensuing court battles, it would win some and lose some. But at some point, it seemed as though the government was for once really set to finally catch one of the biggest fish of all.

That prospect turned bleak when Estrada assumed the presidency and promised Tan a better year. Early on in his term, Estrada already declared his intention to abolish the government agency in charge of going after ill-gotten wealth and expressed his intention to settle the tax case with Tan. On top of these, he appointed people closely identified with Tan to some of the highest and most strategic posts in government.

Ronaldo Zamora, whom Tan had known quite well since the martial law years, was appointed executive secretary. Edgardo Espiritu, with whom Tan worked very closely in the campaign of a losing presidential candidate in 1992, was hailed finance secretary. He was to directly deal with Tan's pending multibillion-peso tax evasion case. Put in charge of all legal affairs—and therefore of Tan's case—at the finance department was Undersecretary Lily Gruba, who once lawyered for Tan.[6]

On his very first day in office, Espiritu announced that the tax evasion cases against Tan were "very weak" and "will likely lose."[7] In a stunning reversal of the tax agency's stance against Tan, newly appointed BIR commissioner Beethoven Rualo moved to withdraw the criminal complaints against Fortune.

With the original complainants withdrawing the case, the DOJ was stuck in a dilemma: whether to drop the case altogether or to carry on. Unlike Rualo, the new Justice Secretary Serafin Cuevas was convinced that the case stood a good chance. The DOJ eventually ignored Rualo's recommendation and went on to pursue the case. Cuevas was fired. To this day, Cuevas insists that his decision to pursue the tax evasion case against Tan was the reason why.

Under a new secretary, the DOJ filed another petition before the Court of Appeals—but it did so eleven days late. It was a tardiness that cost the department the case. The biggest tax evasion charge in recent Philippine history was dead.

How could a simple procedural rule for such a landmark case be overlooked? On September 2, 2000, the *Philippine Daily Inquirer* carried a story headlined, "Estrada caused delay in filing Tan case." A former top-ranking DOJ official quoted the President as telling the department, "*Ipahingi n'yo na sa akin iyan.*" [Give the case to me as a favor.][8]

For his "valuable support in the agency's tax collection efforts," Tan—once considered by the tax agency as the country's biggest tax evader—was awarded a plaque of appreciation by the BIR during its anniversary celebrations.[9]

The national interests of a pal

Tan was in one of those sticky situations when he was in the best position to know who his true friends were. Philippine Airlines (PAL), one of his most prized possessions, was bleeding millions of pesos a day. For the last six years, PAL had been seeing red in its books, with its debt running to as big as $2.4 billion.[10] If not for Tan's pledge to pour in Php 200 million ($4.5 million)[11] from his own pocket to rescue the ailing flag carrier, Asia's oldest airline would already have closed down in September 1998. This prompted Estrada to hail him a "national hero."

In exchange for his sacrifice, Tan was hoping some government agencies would contribute cash to keep PAL afloat. Even if the President may have wanted to help in this way, however, the government was also suffering from liquidity problems of its own. But he could not just beg off. "While Mr. Estrada proclaimed that he wouldn't use state funds to bail out distressed companies," wrote James Hookway of *The Wall Street Journal*, "his government was quietly rolling back its liberal 'open skies' aviation policy at the tycoon's request."[12]

In other words, instead of bailing out PAL outright, Estrada gave his pal a lending hand by shielding his airline from competition. Tan had been riling against the air liberalization policy, saying it is "like a big fish eating small fish." In this case, Tan—who's listed among the world's top 200 billionaires by *Forbes* magazine,[13] with a fortune of $2.1 billion in some accounts and as much as $7 billion in others[14]—was the small fry and he needed protection.

Protecting PAL entailed limiting the number of flights in and out of the country so as to assure the fledgling airline of passengers. According to a former official of the Civil Aeronautics Board (CAB), the government agency in charge of regulating air transportation, Tan was setting his sights on a monopoly of the very profitable United States route by moving for a review of air agreements with other countries.[15]

PAL accused Taiwan's China Airlines and EVA Airways of stealing its passengers from the lucrative Manila-US West Coast route by luring them to fly via Taipei at considerably lower prices. The Taiwanese airlines were allegedly violating the passenger quotas assigned them in a bilateral air-services agreement. [16]

So in October 1999, the CAB unilaterally suspended flights between the Philippines and Taiwan.[17] PAL succeeded in cornering passengers but this was to trigger a diplomatic spat that had real, damaging consequences to the economy. Between the two, the Philippines—dependent on Taiwan for jobs, trade, and tourists—was obviously not in the better position to infuriate the other.

For one, trade between the two countries was adversely affected, with Taiwan sliding from being the Philippines' third biggest export market to its fifth.[18] The Taiwanese government advised its nationals to defer their investment plans in the Philippines.[19] Some Taiwanese firms, who were among the country's biggest investors, decided to reconsider their plans of infusing capital to the economy. [20]

The aviation row also contributed to unemployment as Taiwan, one of the biggest employers of overseas Filipino workers (OFWs), imposed an indefinite ban on Filipino laborers.[21] Because of its proximity, the Philippines had been a favorite destination of Taiwanese tourists. But at the height of the air row, then-Tourism Secretary Gemma Cruz-Araneta projected a "very, very great decline" in tourist arrivals from Taiwan.[22] From the Philippine's fourth-biggest source of tourists, Taiwan slid to being its ninth.[23]

Because of all these, members of the House of Representatives accused the CAB of being captive to Tan's wishes. After a series of hearings, a congressional committee concluded that "the CAB has ceased to look after the interest of our people, and is instead more concerned with protecting one privately owned company."[24] Besides the CAB, another aviation agency, the Air Transportation Office (ATO), was also accused of acting on behalf of Tan's interests. Its chief, wrote an employee to a major daily, was "undoubtedly subservient and beholden to Lucio Tan."[25]

Needless to say, the CAB's and the ATO's actions would not have been tolerated without the passive consent or active encouragement of the Chief Executive. His intervention was evident in the manner by which the official bilateral agreement between the two countries was unceremoniously and irregularly disregarded. International procedures stipulate that any proposed revisions in an air-service treaty between two countries require at least a year's notice. This convention was all but ignored.

"We were acting on the directive of the Office of the President to save PAL, and we could not wait for a year," admitted an official from the Department of Foreign Affairs who negotiated with Taiwan.[26]

But for all the damages wrought on the economy by the air dispute, there were still those, even the usual Estrada critics, who believed that the President was correct in protecting the flag carrier. It's time, they said, that the Philippines finally stood up to Taiwan. It was supposedly the nationalistic thing to do, to protect one's own, to uphold national interests. Estrada himself justified his actions in these terms.

They could only have been right if the interests of the nation could be equated with the interests of a pal.

A "Pot of Gold"

Lucio Tan likes to think that he is rich because he is smarter than others. He believes that it was his business acumen that had enabled him to build his vast empire. True enough, how he eventually gained majority control of the Philippine National Bank certainly left financial whiz kids scratching their heads and singing paeans to the astute taipan. The MBA holders from Wharton and Harvard could not quite comprehend how and why the chemical engineering graduate from the Far Eastern University decided to and succeeded in snatching a bank that nobody else wanted.

Tan may not have been relying only on his keen business sense. "I would say that if he ever gets something," admitted Salvador Mison, a retired general who heads one of Tan's companies, "it's because of the friendships that he has cultivated for many years."[27]

In September 1999, to make its books appear financially healthier, the PNB set out to widen its capital base through a stocks-right offering. Previously its majority owner, the government, was in the process of gradually unloading its shares in the debt-laden bank. It waived its pre-emptive rights to buy the shares ahead of others not only because it had to remain faithful to its privatization program but because it did not have the money to pay for the shares.

Then-PNB President Benjamin Palma-Gil cooked up a bright idea. Instead of getting money from the deficit-ridden government, the PNB Retirement Fund Inc. (PNBRFI), a noncontributory fund owned by PNB employees, was to be used for subscribing to the shares.[28] The only condition was that the shares were to be voted with the government until June 2000.[29] In other words, the money that was used for buying the shares came from the PNBRFI but the voting rights of each share still remained with the government.

The glitch, however, was that the retirement fund was too small for such an ambitious plan. Besides that, outsiders are not allowed to join the employees-only fund.

So on top of one bright idea grew another. In order to go around the prohibitions, the PNBRFI created special purpose vehicles (SPVs) through which money can be coursed. The investors soon came but their identities remained a mystery for some time. In time, a tiny retirement fund had succeeded in securing 15 percent of the PNB on a multibillion-peso buying frenzy.

Stealthily, craftily, Lucio Tan had acquired a substantial stake in the PNB through its own employees—and not without a little help from government. Formally, the shares were PNBRFI's but ownership rights belonged to Tan. In addition to these shares, the other stocks of the government were entrusted to people appointed by the newly elected President. Coincidentally, these appointees had very deep ties with Tan and were allegedly put there on Tan's behest.[30]

In other words, with this kind of arrangement, Tan had control over the PNBRF as well as on the government shares. But he was not satisfied with this. He went on a buying spree, using other brokers to acquire even more PNB shares in the open market. By November, Tan had acquired 30 percent of the bank, with his group controlling four of the eleven seats in the board.

Still Tan could not get enough. Rumors had it that Tan was dead set on taking over PNB so that he can shed off his image as the "vice" taipan—alluding, of course, to the fact that his business empire is founded on beer and cigarettes. His reasons, however, may be more practical.

In April 2000, the government wanted to fully privatize the PNB and offered to sell its remaining 30 percent stake in the bank. If it wanted a $100-million loan from the International Monetary Fund (IMF) and the World Bank, it had to dispose of the ailing bank before the deadline lapsed.

Pundits and commentators had a field day condemning Tan's acquisition of one-third of PNB's stocks and interpreting it as a signal that cronyism was back with a vengeance. In defense, Tan was quoted in newspapers as saying he should even be acclaimed as the bank's savior.

In an effort to quell the criticism, then Finance Secretary Jose Pardo took it upon himself to convince Tan to sell his shares together with the remaining shares of the government.[31] The more pragmatic reason behind the plan was to make the combined block of shares more attractive to prospective buyers since it would give them the controlling votes in the board.

Tan was said to be hesitant at first but was eventually prevailed upon by no less than President Estrada to agree. Why Tan, after pursuing a circuitous path to accumulating his shares, easily acquiesced to the arrangement confounded observers.

The day of the bidding came. Loida Nicolas-Lewis, a rich Filipino-American who was reportedly intending to buy the bank for sentimental reasons, failed to find a local bank that would allow their group to meet the banking experience requirement of the rules. This left the Yuchengcos' Rizal Commercial Banking Corporation (RCBC) as the lone bidder.[32] But since a prerequisite for the bidding to be valid was for there to be more than one bidder, the process had to be declared as a failure.

Meanwhile, Tan had changed his mind. He no longer wanted to sell. With only the 30 percent government share for grabs, Lewis and the RCBC lost interest. Anything less than a controlling stake was not worth their while.

The IMF granted the government a reprieve, giving it another year to complete the stalled privatization. Left without a choice, the government decided to unload its remaining shares without Tan's block. It also decided to relax the rules. The bidders no longer needed to have banking experience. Also, having a single bidder could already be enough for bidding to proceed.

And so with Lewis's group and the RCBC out of the picture, Tan found himself the only one eyeing shares no one else was interested in. On the day of the bidding, the only offer came from a company called Starbuck Equities Inc. It was owned by Tan.

Tan ended up buying shares he was intending, albeit grudgingly, to sell. More accurately, he ended up buying more than he did not want to sell. In doing so, Tan became the majority owner of the PNB.

Why Tan was so hot on PNB confounded financial analysts. Everyone else, it seemed, had been cold to the offer. Others pointed out that Tan's billions could have been enough to purchase other banks with far healthier financial statements. PNB was not the sort of bank taipans with impeccable business sense would target. It did not make sense.

Although the country's fourth-largest bank in terms of assets, the PNB was saddled with problematic loans, mostly incurred by known cronies of Marcos. As of June 2000, out of every Php 3 that PNB has lent out, Php 1 would most likely not be paid back to the bank. It was also in dire need of up to Php 50 billion in fresh capital so as to stay afloat.

It begins to make sense, however, when one considers that among the PNB's largest debtors is none other than PAL, which is 70 percent owned by Tan. PAL owes PNB $117 million.[33] Also, among those who were extended behest loans by the PNB during the dictatorship was Tan's Asia Brewery.[34] By bagging PNB, Tan now owns the bank from which he owes so much. He has vowed to make it his "pot of gold."[35]

Tan has also been aiming for the National Steel Corporation (NSC), another one of PNB's biggest borrowers. If it was unable to repay its loans, the NSC would be swallowed by the PNB. Should this happen, Tan would have succeeded in indirectly taking over another one of his dream companies. Other analysts predict the inevitable merger of PNB and Tan's Allied Bank, thereby cementing Tan's image as a respectable banking taipan.

In all of these cheery scenarios, Tan could have always claimed that his keen business acumen continues to be the secret of his success. But his exploits may have required much more than razor-sharp business instincts. For if former Finance Secretary Edgardo Espiritu—who as finance secretary oversaw PNB's privatization—is to be believed, Tan's successful capture of the bank required nothing less than the direct intervention of the President.

PNB's privatization, Espiritu testified, was the biggest scam he encountered in the Estrada administration. At Estrada's impeachment trial, Espiritu narrated how he was instructed by the President to obey Tan's directives. *"Kung ano ang gusto ni Lucio, sundin mo."* [Whatever Lucio wants, you follow.] Espiritu quoted the President as telling him.

Self-reliance and Hard Work

What Lucio wanted from the President, Lucio got—mainly because the President had also gotten what he had wanted from him.

During the 1998 presidential elections, Tan was known to have contributed a hefty Php 1.5 billion (around $37 million) to Estrada's campaign chest. Besides the cash outlay, Tan's resources were also mobilized for Estrada's campaign.[36] Extending to the farthest areas in the country, the distribution network and grassroots sales organization of Tan's cigarette and liquor companies may have enabled Estrada to put up a decent fight against the political machinery of the administration party.

Aside from this, Tan was also one of those who regularly deposited millions in the multibillion-peso Jose Velarde account that was alleged in the impeachment trial to be owned by the President. The Philippine Center for Investigative Journalism (PCIJ) named Tan as among those who made sure that the Presidents' many women were taken care of by giving them or their families either businesses or jobs.[37]

Tan insists he has what he has because he worked very hard for it. "I grew up in poverty. I had no choice but to work harder than my peers, to endure more hardships and probably bigger dreams," Tan was quoted in one of the rare full-length interviews he granted to the press.[38] An apotheosis of the classic rags to riches story, Tan rose from being a janitor to become the Philippines wealthiest man.[39]

Tan maintains that through all that, he had not changed his strategy. "We can proudly say that we have never depended on dole-outs, government assistance or monopoly protection throughout our history," Tan once said. "The basic ingredients of our growth have been self-reliance and hard work."[40]

The Corporate Genius

Mark Jimenez knocked on the Archbishop's door and was answered. Two weeks after Estrada resigned from office, and Jimenez had come to seek an audience with Jaime Cardinal Sin, the powerful Archbishop of Manila. "The inner self made me realize I was on the wrong side," Jimenez said, ready to testify that Estrada had made billions in two of the largest business transactions in the economy in the past two years. [41]

"I allied myself with [Estrada] without knowing what was happening to the country. Perhaps it was also because of my stupidity,"[42] said the man whom the fallen President had once called a "corporate genius."[43] It was Jimenez who brokered the "deal of the century"—the Php 30 billion (around $733 million) takeover of the Philippine Long Distance Telephone Co. (PLDT) in November 1998 and the "largest merger in Philippine history," that of the Equitable Bank and the Philippine Commercial International (PCI) Bank in May 1999.

Just several months before coming to the Archbishop's palace, Jimenez—a billionaire who had made a fortune distributing computers in various Latin American countries—was at the pinnacle of power after returning to his homeland from the US. His Miami-based company was raking an average of $400 million annually and was ranked 327th out of the Top 500 computer businesses in the United States.

Not only was Jimenez of immense economic clout, he also had the best political connections possible . Long before he could knock at the Archbishop's door, he had already entered Malacañang's inner chambers and became as close as anybody could get to the President. Malacañang insiders considered him to be the "in of the ins."[44] For his extensive business experience in South America, Jimenez was appointed Presidential Adviser on Latin American Affairs, a position with nebulous responsibilities. In 1999, *Asiaweek* named him one of five "who have the President's ear," among "the coterie of men whom President Estrada relies on to get things done."[45]

According to the PCIJ, Jimenez was a member of the powerful "Midnight Cabinet" that hangs out at the Palace after dark—singing karaoke, playing mahjong, drinking Johnny Walker, and crafting policy with the President.[46] Jimenez had endeared himself to Estrada by "master[ing] the tricks of humoring an ill-tempered president who bawls out even members of his cabinet." He even reportedly kneels just to amuse the President.[47]

More than that, Jimenez shares with Estrada a penchant for making fun of women. Asked what among his assets he would give up if he were extradited, Jimenez replied, "My wife."[48] Estrada, who is also famous for his sexist jokes and for keeping mistresses, must have loved that one. Along with Fernando Poe Jr. (FPJ), the President's best friend, Jimenez was said to be one of the two closest people to the President.

Don't worry about the next destination

There was a pressing reason why Jimenez had to knock on the doors of Malacañang. In April 1999, Jimenez was indicted in the US on forty-seven counts of fraud, tax evasion, and illegal campaign contributions.[49] By the time of his indictment in the US, Jimenez had already been staying in the Philippines for over a year. Jimenez said he just went home to the country for a short vacation.[50] He had not left since then. But he has a history of flight.[51]

By June 1999 the US government had transmitted its formal extradition request to Philippine authorities. It was to be the first and most high-profile test case of an extradition treaty signed in 1994 after several years of long negotiations.[52]

By then, Jimenez had pushed himself closer and closer into the political center. Five days after the indictment, Jimenez entered the gates of Malacañang to seek refuge.[53] "I told the President I had a problem in the US," Jimenez recalled. "He said, 'Don't worry about it—I will take care of it.'"[54]

Although the RP-US extradition law stipulates that the request must pass through the courts first, it ultimately grants Estrada discretionary powers not to turn in Jimenez.[55] Vowing "to die with my boots on," Jimenez insisted that his cases constitute political persecution and harassment.[56] Still, Jimenez put his faith on Estrada's veto powers to elude arrest.[57]

While maintaining that he would allow the law to take its course, Estrada took the cudgels for Jimenez by repeatedly defending his friend in public. "Mr. Jimenez has no charges here in the Philippines," was Estrada's refrain. "He has done nothing illegal here, he has no criminal record in his country."

Jimenez had hired as his defense counsel Estelito Mendoza—the same lawyer who had been retained by Lucio Tan, Eduardo Cojuangco Jr., Imelda Marcos, and later, Estrada himself. Mendoza argued that the extradition proceedings violated his client's constitutional rights. Asserting the right of his client to notice, he demanded that they first be given copies of the extradition request before the extradition process could begin.[58] The DOJ, tasked to press the extradition in court, argued that Mendoza's demand would be tantamount to giving fugitives a warning to escape.

The Supreme Court sided with Jimenez at first only to eventually reverse its decision nine months later.[59] Meanwhile, President Estrada had sacked his DOJ Secretary Serafin Cuevas, allegedly for his pursuit of the extradition case against Jimenez, as well as the tax evasion case against another Presidential friend, Lucio Tan.[60]

Through all that, Jimenez had been living the life of a free man, confident in the assurance given him by the most powerful man in the land. Estrada was apparently willing to stand up to the most powerful country in the world so that his friend would not have to worry.

The US government had been explicit in the importance it placed on Jimenez's extradition. "This is a defining moment in Filipino-American relations, for the US attaches great importance to the fulfillment of our treaty commitments," a senior US diplomat said.[61] Even President Estrada's planned state visit to the US was reportedly postponed because of Jimenez's case. The *Washington Post* reported that Estrada could not be officially invited to Washington unless Jimenez is turned over to the US.[62]

By February 2001, all legal impediments to the processing in court of the US extradition request had been lifted. "The days of glory are coming to an end. Next destination is jail," read the FBI's coded memorandum on Jimenez's imminent arrest. By then, the President in Malacañang was no longer the same one who previously told Jimenez, "Don't worry about it—I will take care of it."

Keys to the White House

Jimenez was introduced to Estrada only in 1998, the very year the President took power.[63] What their friendship lacked in endurance, however, was more than made up for by other things. Estrada, at first, denied that Jimenez contributed to his campaign war chest, saying he met him after the campaign.[64] He was to be belied later, however, by no less than Zamora, who attested that the two met before the election,[65] and Jimenez himself, who confirmed giving money to Estrada.[66]

Jimenez, however, contributed something more unique to Estrada's campaign. While Lucio Tan gave Estrada billions in funds and Eduardo Cojuangco Jr. gave him party machinery. Jimenez, for his part, gave Estrada access to Washington's power corridors. In April 1998, Jimenez organized a meeting between a number of US Senators and Estrada's campaign leaders, including Zamora, Espiritu, and Orlando Mercado. He even provided the Filipino contingent a limousine and a private jet for their convenience.[67]

Jimenez had inched his way into the Capitol's and the White House's power circles by contributing heavily to the candidacies of Democratic Senators and the Clinton-Gore tandem. A frequent White House visitor, Jimenez was invited to the White House twelve times from 1994 to 1996, as proved by US Secret Service photos culled by the Associated Press. Most of the pictures show Jimenez dining with the US President and his wife Hillary.[68] With campaign donations reaching $325,000,[69] Jimenez was reportedly Florida's single largest Democratic donor.[70] In February 1996, Clinton was caught conferring with Jimenez on videotape, apparently thanking him for a donation to fund the preservation of the President's childhood home in Arkansas.[71]

Jimenez would henceforth brag about his close connections to Clinton. In 1996 the *Wall Street Journal* reported that Jimenez tipped off the Clinton administration about an impending coup in Paraguay.[72] Paraguay was one of the important markets of Jimenez's computer business in Latin America. Having entered local ruling elite circles, Jimenez had a stake in defending the Paraguay President Juan Carlos Wasmosy and his administration because its policies were conducive to his enterprise.[73] Besides Wasmosy, Jimenez also claimed to be a friend of sixteen other heads of state in South America.[74] Jimenez apparently had a habit of befriending Presidents.

After Jimenez's warning, Clinton reportedly called Wasmosy to express his support and the coup was aborted. "I saved democracy in Paraguay," Jimenez was quoted as saying by the *Wall Street Journal* a year later.

Two years later, for brokering a bank merger and a takeover of the Philippines' largest telecommunications firm, Jimenez will again be hailed as a savior—this time of the national economy—by the Philippine President.

The big time

If Jimenez's "genius" had been of any help, it was in teaching Estrada how to push the frontiers of corruption for the President. "By various accounts, it was Jimenez who first introduced Estrada to the big time," wrote Sheila Coronel of the PCIJ. "With [his] help, and the cooperation and complicity of many others, including some of the country's top banks and biggest corporations, Estrada systematically looted the country."[75]

In tandem with Jimenez, Estrada refined the plunder techniques used by former President Ferdinand Marcos. According to Coronel, Estrada combined the tried and tested methods of extending behest loans, extracting commissions from contracts, and the ownership of companies through nominees with such innovations as stock speculation and the use of government pension funds for corporate mergers and takeovers. Coronel was referring to Estrada's ownership of BW Resources and his juicy commissions from the PLDT takeover and the Equitable-PCI Bank merger.

Jimenez played a crucial part in all these transactions. It was him who brokered First Pacific's takeover of 17 percent of the shares of PLDT for close to Php 30 billion (around $750 million), as well as the sale of the controlling stake in PCI Bank to Equitable.

Jimenez's bright idea was to use state pension funds held by the Government Service Insurance System (GSIS) and the Social Security System (SSS) for his strategy. These funds were the contributions of millions of employees who relied on their pension for their future security. In the PLDT takeover, Jimenez had the SSS and the GSIS purchase PLDT shares in the open markets several months before the actual deal.

Brokerage houses observed the SSS's and the GSIS's buying spree, thereby stirring speculative interest in PLDT stocks. There must have been a good reason why SSS and GSIS were buying PLDT shares, stock-brokers thought. So they joined the bandwagon and bought too. With the increased demand, PLDT's stocks soared. Armed with its newly ac-quired shares, the pension funds were then able to get substantial voting rights to the company. Their nominees, being government appointees, could then vote according to how they would be instructed to vote by the President.

Six months later, Jimenez also practiced the same strategy of brokering for both sides. For reasons that will only be divulged later, the SSS and the GSIS bought 35 percent of the bank's shares worth Php 15 billion (around $375 million). Together with the 38 percent it previously bought, Equitable was able to take control of PCI Bank. Equitable was owned by George Go, anotherf the President's close friend. PCI Bank, on the other hand, was owned by the Lopezes and the Gokongweis, previous owners of the *Manila Times*.

Estrada described Jimenez a "corporate genius" for executing the takeovers but it was not Jimenez's brilliance that deserved the credit. Without the improper mobilization of billions of pesos of employees' contributions to the GSIS and the SSS and without the flexing of presi-dential power, the tandem's scheme would not have worked out.

"For all his audacity, Jimenez—an upstart with a sleazy past—could not have transacted with some of the country's biggest and proudest fami-lies if he did not have the President's backing," Coronel noted. A tandem had to be formed with Jimenez and the President. One had the ideas, the other had the power. Each could not have succeeded without the other.

For one, Jimenez would not have successfully inked the deals with-out the President making some crucial calls. Former PLDT chairman Antonio Cojuangco was said to have been reluctant to sell their shares. But the President reportedly called PLDT director Alfonso Yuchengco, implicitly instructing him to abandon his claim to the Cojuangco shares in favor of First Pacific.[76] The Yuchengco family said they withdrew their objections to the takeover after that call. The Cojuangcos have since been reported to have complained about how Estrada forced them to dispose of their stake. "[T]he pressure was so great, they had no choice," a source close to the family was quoted as saying.[77]

The use of the pension funds also required some action on the part of the President. Jimenez reportedly first broached using them for corporate takeovers during one of the sessions of the "Midnight Cabinet."[78] The President had appointed his childhood friend Carlos Arellano and Federico Pascual, former head of a bank owned by presidential friend Lucio Tan, to the GSIS and the SSS, respectively. It was easy marshalling them for his and Jimenez's strategy.

Arellano and Pascual, Espiritu recalled, were ordered to meet Jimenez regarding the Equitable transaction. Usually cautious in their investment decisions, the SSS and the GSIS did not even require a complete audit of PCI Bank's books.[79] According to Espiritu, Jimenez was paid up to Php 3 billion (around $75 million) in commissions for the PLDT deal and another Php 3 billion for the PCI Bank takeover. He supposedly split some of the amount with the President. It would also be revealed later that Jimenez was among the depositors in the "Jose Velarde" account, whose non-opening precipitated the collapse of the impeachment trial.

Nothing in return

Jimenez did not just "save" the Philippine economy, he also saved Estrada from the Philippine media.

In 1999, a *Manila Times* article tagging Estrada as an "unwitting *ninong*" (godfather) to an allegedly irregular deal between the National Power Corporation and an Argentine firm angered the President. IMPSA, the Argentine firm, had been stuck in a legal battle since the term of Ramos, but with Jimenez's alleged intervention, it was able to finalize its P17-billion (around $440 million) hydroelectric project.[80] The President was stung by the allegation but since he had no power to gag the press by decree, the *Manila Times* was silenced in a more insidious manner. A friend came in to save a friend.

Shortly after the story on the questionable power deal was printed, Jimenez visited the office of the owner of the paper, offered to buy it, but wanted to be a secret partner. Gokongwei refused at first but when his family's other businesses were threatened, he gave in. The identity of the buyer was initially a public mystery. It was later confirmed that Jimenez, using dummies at first, was the one who brought the paper and radically altered its politics.

Jimenez had also proved to be a generous friend. He was named by the PCIJ as among those who made sure that the President's many families are taken care of. Around the time of the *Manila Times* purchase, Jimenez reportedly bought for Estrada the penthouse of a condominium on Roxas Boulevard. Worth Php 50 million, this was reportedly where the Estrada housed Rowena Gomeri Lopez, one of his mistresses. Its listed owner's registration papers show Jimenez's family members to be its incorporators.[81]

For all that Jimenez had done for the President, he supposedly asked for nothing in return.[82] "My one and only role with regard to the President is to remain his good and honest friend," Jimenez once said.[83]

The Victim

"He's a real, true friend, and he never forgets friends," exclaimed Dante Tan to friends in his exclusive nightclub in downtown Manila. "He even returned my call at three in the morning, when I had given up and thought that he'd forgotten me after the elections."[84]

Tan was referring, of course, to President Estrada, the good friend who never forgets. A long-time resident of the town where Estrada was mayor for decades, Tan claims to have known the President for a long time. He likes to brag that he was among the first ethnic Chinese to have banked on Estrada, having had supported him since his bid for a senatorial seat in 1987. In the 1998 presidential elections, Tan was listed in documents submitted to the Commission of Elections as one of Estrada's contributors.[85]

A gambler even while he was still young, Tan went on to be one of the President's mahjong playmates during the late-night sessions of the "Midnight Cabinet" at Malacañang.[86] It is this cabinet that reportedly really called the shots in terms of many policy decisions and appointments of the President.

Tan was a little-known ethnic Chinese businessman before 1998. But with his friend's assumption of the presidency, he went on to be at the center of the stock market's attention—ready to debut as the country's new multibillionaire tycoon.

Self-made

Tan describes himself as a "self-made man."[87] In 1998, with Estrada already in Malacañang, he became president of Best World Gaming Entertainment Corp.—a company that was far from self-made. By all accounts, it was a company that would not have survived without the numerous favors bestowed on it by the President.

Shortly after its inception, the Philippine Amusement and Gaming Corporation (PAGCOR), the government gambling agency, gave Best World Gaming the license to operate a national on-line bingo game in record time.[88] The contract would make Tan's company the country's biggest non-state-owned gaming operator with a projected monthly revenue of a billion pesos (around $25 million).[89] Best World bagged the contract without competitive bidding and with a little help from the person who appointed PAGCOR's officials and board of directors, President Estrada.

Tan was adamant in saying that his friend had nothing to do with the granting of the license. Estrada, on the other hand, turned defensive. "Tan was the first to have this bright idea of an on-line lottery, and the PAGCOR is authorized by law to give such permits without bidding," said Estrada. "Is it cronyism if we give him the permit to run it? It will be unfair to him if I let another group steal his idea."

In fact, the idea of an on-line bingo was not a Tan original. An existing bingo operator was already planning to expand into on-line bingo but had to shelve its plans after learning of PAGCOR's decision. Officials of the company said they learned of Best World Gaming's existence only after they heard that it won the contract they were aiming for.

In February 1999, Best World Gaming became a fully owned subsidiary of BW Resources, a company where Tan maintained a controlling stake. Another secret partner would also be revealed much later.

Besides giving Tan's company the contract for the on-line bingo, PAGCOR gave BW Resources a concession that would ensure its continuing survival through the years. In March 1999, BW took over a hotel project being undertaken by another property firm in Manila.[90] For some reason, PAGCOR decided to move its three casinos from their current locations in three Manila hotels to BW's hotel. Without taking into consideration the rent of all other tenants, PAGCOR's lease alone, Php 3 billion ($75 million) in all, would have been enough to cover the cost of constructing the building.[91]

But perhaps the most controversial among the favors given to Tan's company was a Php 600-million loan (around $40 million) from the partly state-owned and partly Lucio Tan-owned PNB in July 1999. This, despite the fact that BW had a negative net worth when it applied for the loan. The only secondary collateral it offered was a 21-hectare Tagaytay property that had zero value because it had no right of way. Approved during the time when former Chief Justice Andres Narvasa, head of Estrada's defense team in the impeachment trial, was PNB chairman, the loan was sought when BW was experiencing a wild and seemingly inexplicable share-price upsurge.[92]

Biggest stock exchange fraud

For all its privileges, Tan's BW Resources would have been just another well-connected company had it not figured in what reporters and commentators called "one of the biggest frauds perpetrated in Philippine stock market history,"[93] an incident that sparked off a "crisis of confidence" in the Philippine capital market and brought the Philippine Stock Exchange (PSE) to "near collapse."[94]

Trading at only Php 1.98 per share at the beginning of 1999, BW stocks soared by over 5000 percent to hit Php 107 per share mark in October then descended steeply again afterward.[95] It was, in the words of one reporter, "one of the most spectacular price movements in the PSE's history."[96]

Market analysts had different explanations to offer. Some speculated that investors were simply too bullish on the gambling industry. Others said Macau gambling tycoon Stanley Ho's visit and his reported buying in on BW Resources fueled the stunning increase in share prices. There were also those who said that the phenomenon could be attributed to investors who wanted a piece of the on-line bingo action that had been awarded to BW.

An investigation by the PSE's Compliance and Surveillance Group (CSG), however, revealed a more sinister "master plan of manipulation"[97] executed by Tan and his accomplices through such anomalous schemes as wash sales, wash-through, done-through deals, and kiting—all foreign words to the lay person but all foul terms for a stock-market player. It was a plan that drove down the stock market index by as much as 40 percent to a 14-month low and that almost left stockbrokers with no more money to pay for their purchases.

It was a simple plan: Tan and his associates created the illusion that there was much buying and selling in BW shares. This, in turn, artificially increased demand for BW shares, thereby inflating its trading price.

They did this by making it appear that many different brokers were buying BW shares when in fact, it was only them, using different fronts, who were doing so. Tan allegedly made arrangements with certain brokers to make it appear that he sold them shares for Php 70 when in fact they only paid him Php 30.[98] On top of these, Tan's company also allegedly leaked misleading disclosures to the media to arouse the interest of buyers and to make it appear that BW shares were a good buy.[99]

What was perplexing about the fantastic increase of BW share prices was that BW had nothing to show for its price to reach such stratospheric heights. When BW shares peaked to Php 107 in October 1999, BW's market value reached Php 27 billion—four times that of RFM Corp., the Philippine's second-largest food and drinks manufacturer, and two-thirds that of Jollibee Foods Corp., the country's biggest food corporation. Its revenue as of June 1999 was a measly Php 3,481. This left them with a net loss of Php 4.1 million. With their only asset being a Tagaytay property worth Php 437 million but with Php 450 million outstanding shares, the book value of each share should have been around P0.80.[100]

When the quoted share prices reached record highs, Tan and his cohorts then reportedly sold their shares—which they acquired very cheaply but which they were now selling for a high price—and earned windfall profits in the process. According to the PSE, Tan earned as much as Php 820 million (around $21 million) through insider trading and price manipulation activities with BW shares.[101] The Bureau of Internal Revenue also accused Tan of owing the government P572 million in tax liabilities.[102]

The secret partner revealed

"Dante Tan is not a cheat. He is a very close friend. The truth is he only wants to help us develop the securities market," Securities and Exchange Commission (SEC) chair Perfecto Yasay Jr. quoted the President as telling him during the second of five controversial phone calls that were to be the basis of an impeachment complaint later. [103]

Tan is indeed a very close friend. Among the identified depositors in the Php 1.9 billion-"Jose Velarde" account in Equitable-PCI Bank, reportedly where the President stashed dirty billions, Tan was the biggest source with Php 300 million in deposits.[104] Tan also reportedly brought for former Philippine Airlines attendant Rowena Gomeri Lopez, one of the President's mistresses, a Php 48-million house.[105]

In October 1999, soon after he ordered the investigation of BW shares, Yasay allegedly got a call from the President reprimanding him for looking into the BW case. He called up again, this time commanding him to stop the investigation. "He told me to specifically clear individuals insofar as the investigation is concerned," Yasay told a Senate committee investigation. "He specifically gave instructions to clear Mr. Dante Tan."

On top of the phone calls, Estrada had also earlier directed Yasay to clear any statements regarding the BW investigation with his office. Moreover, the President had also chastised Yasay for the SEC's decision to narrow the trading bandwidth as a protection for investors.

Two other witnesses would corroborate Yasay's testimony during the impeachment trial: the stock exchange's former internal watchdog head Ruben Almadro and former PSE president Jose Luis Yulo. Yulo said he also received several calls from the President telling him that Tan is a good friend and a good man who became a victim. "If he is indeed at fault, we can do nothing about it. But you know, he is my friend, and he has been helping me," Yulo recalled the President as saying.[106]

Almadro, for his part, testified that the President had summoned him and Yulo to Malacañang to submit the findings of their investigation on BW. Almadro said this in itself was already irregular, the PSE being a private entity that is not answerable to the President. "The person who was responsible for the stock exchange mess is Dante Tan," Almadro quoted Yulo as telling the President. "What they did here is really blatant, that's why we should not allow it to pass."[107]

Until Espiritu spoke up, these revelations merely tended to reinforce Estrada's image as a friend who does not forget. Espiritu's testimony in the impeachment trial, however, showed that Estrada was protecting not just his friend when he interfered in the BW investigation.

In January 2001 Espiritu revealed that no less than Estrada himself was actually Tan's secret partner in BW. Espiritu, who had supervision over the securities market as finance secretary, said he was incredulous when Estrada himself privately admitted that he had made a killing from the BW shares during a one-on-one talk at the President's residence. "I have earned so much from the BW shares," Espiritu quoted the President as telling him.

Espiritu had earlier sought to discuss with the President measures to solve the stock-market problem but was disappointed when, instead of proposing anything, the President merely complained, "We also lost in that [BW]."[108]

More interestingly, Espiritu divulged that it was the President who ordered PNB to approve the Php 600-million loan to a company that—in light of the former finance secretary's disclosures—the President himself owned.[109]

The Godfather

When Marcos and his family fled to Hawaii at the height of EDSA 1 in 1986, Eduardo "Danding" Cojuangco was with them on the plane. "I knew he needed a friend. So I joined him, in what was to be his last journey. And I stayed with him to the very end," Cojuangco proudly recalled later.[110]

In 2001, another President was to be driven out of the Palace. Estrada and his family were supposed to use Cojuangco's private jet and move in to his ranch in Australia.[111] Cojuangco had no intention to join them this time. He is here to stay. With his crown jewel San Miguel Corporation (SMC) back in his possession and with his sequestration cases going favorably in the courts, Cojuangco had no more reason to leave.

Described by the *Los Angeles Times* as being "second only to Marcos in the systematic looting of the Philippines,"[112] Cojuangco had amassed $1.5 billion in corporate assets during the dictatorship—then estimated to be equal to one-fourth of the country's gross national product.[113] A journalist had christened him "Pacman"—after a character in a computer game whose objective is to gobble as much as it could—because of his propensity to create monopolies in industries where he invested.[114]

With the dictator's support, Cojuangco established an agricultural and industrial conglomerate in coconut, sugar, agribusiness, banking, and other interests. How was "Pacman" able to gorge on all these? An original member of the party that Cojuangco founded, the Nationalist People's Coalition, said "[Cojuangco] is convinced that it was through his labor that he was able to accumulate his wealth." Cojuangco would often tell her, "Do not diminish the fruits of my labor. *Hindi ko naman ninakaw ito, nagtrabaho naman ako, pinaghirapan ko ito.*" [I did not steal these, I worked hard for them.][115]

In a way, he did. Cojuangco's design required a lot of work. The Presidential Commission on Good Government (PCGG), the agency tasked with running after illegally acquired wealth during the Marcos years, contends that Cojuangco grew rich from the toil of coconut farmers. It accuses Cojuangco of acquiring corporations and properties using billions of pesos exacted from coconut farmers in the form of the infamous coco levies during the Marcos regime.

During his rule, Marcos imposed Presidential Decrees requiring coconut farmers to pay taxes to the Philippine Coconut Administration (PCA) ostensibly for the financing of development programs for the coconut industry. Cojuangco was appointed by Marcos as the director of the PCA Board, putting him in a position where he could make use of the funds as though they were his own. [116]

Using the collected money, Cojuangco bought a bank that was eventually designated by presidential fiat as the sole depository of coco levies. This bank did not even have to pay the deposits' interest. At the same time, Cojuangco was also appointed as its President and, hence, administrator of the coco levy fund. Moreover, the contract giving Cojuangco management over the bank also stipulated that he be given 10 percent of the coconut farmers' shares.

In simpler terms, Cojuangco as director collected the coco levies through the PCA. These collections were then deposited with the UCPB where Cojuangco was president. He, in turn, used the money to invest in scores of corporations, including SMC, UNICOM, Pepsi Cola, Dutch

Boy, etc. This was how public funds became private funds and this was how Cojuangco grew to become one of the country's wealthiest and most powerful men.

Until now, Cojuangco maintains that the funds are private and had come from the coconut millers; while the farmer-claimants, on the other hand, insist that the funds are public and rightfully belong to them.[117] Estrada, in what was to be his most overt way of siding with Cojuangco, would later on issue a seemingly innocuous executive order that effectively reversed Ramos's proclamation that the coco levy funds were public.

Whether public or private, the funds were with Cojuangco for the taking. With all the millions at his disposal, Cojuangco tried to create cartels in rice, sugar, flour, groceries, and soft drinks until he ran out of time.[118] Marcos suddenly had to flee to Hawaii and he had to be with him to the end.

"This could not have been smoother"

In 1989 Cojuangco sneaked back to the Philippines to reclaim all the lost time. In a speech during his birthday party in 1990, Cojuangco remarked, "I am still the same Danding that you knew from the past."[119]

Cojuangco had millions of reasons to come back, most of them in shares. Unlike most cronies who stashed their wealth abroad, Cojuangco chose to retain his assets in the country. This made him easy target for the PCGG who sequestered his shares in scores of companies during the Aquino administration.

After his return, Cojuangco spent his time trying to thwart the cases filed against him by the PCGG. The presiding justice of the graft court, Francis Garchitorena, admitted that Cojuangco's case was "unique to the point of being scandalous" because it had been the one case that had been stuck at the pre-trial stage for the longest time.

According to PCGG prosecutor Mario Ongkiko, Cojuangco's lawyers had been raising all kinds of peripheral issues to prevent the graft court from hearing the case. For Ongkiko, "The defendants are buying time in the hope that a new and favorable government will come in."[120] If Ongkiko's assertion was true, then Cojuangco's and his lawyers' prayers may have been answered with Estrada's election.

Seven days after Estrada swore, in his inaugural speech, to honor no friends, Cojuangco reclaimed his most cherished possession: the Philippines' largest corporation, San Miguel Corporation. It was one of those companies he allegedly bought using the coconut farmers' money.[121]

In a special emergency board meeting, Cojuangco was reelected chairman of its board,[122] a post he once held during the twilight of the Marcos years. The Sandiganbayan had earlier ruled that Cojuangco and his forty-three companies could vote their 20 percent shares of San Miguel, shares previously voted by the PCGG.[123]

"I was taken out unceremoniously, so it's nice to be here again and see old faces I used to work with," Cojuangco told his employees upon his return.[124] Remarked his lawyer: "This could not have been smoother."[125]

Estrada insisted he had nothing to do with Cojuangco's election, pointing the finger instead on his predecessors Fidel Ramos and Corazon Aquino.[126] It was Aquino who allowed Cojuangco to return to the country eight years back.[127] The Sandiganbayan decision that allowed Cojuangco to vote his shares was handed down during the Ramos administration, with Ramos-appointed lawyers in the PCGG and the Office of the Solicitor General (OSG) in charge of prosecuting the case.

Ramos's PCGG, as well as Aquino's, had been at the receiving end of criticism for their alleged incompetence. There were the reports, for example, that they had been losing a roomful of documents and that, at one point, they failed to show even just the minutes of the PCGG's meetings to the court. Besides this, the PCGG also suffered from constant replacement of lawyers as well as perennial bickering with the OSG.[128]

But if Aquino's and Ramos's attempts to legally pin down Cojuangco and the other cronies were beset by incompetence, the composition of Estrada's prosecution team and its efforts to actually go after the ill-gotten wealth were highly suspicious. Early on in his term, Estrada had already announced his desire to end the twelve-year-old cases that had been languishing in the courts and his willingness to enter into out-of-court settlements with the Marcoses and their cronies. He also called for the outright abolition of the PCGG, arguing that it had not achieved anything that would excuse its continued existence.

To discard the PCGG meant to close down the one government entity that had been invested the legal power to exercise provisional ownership over the sequestered companies. Without the PCGG, Cojuangco would be free to legally reclaim his stake in his 275 other corporations.

Despite declaring his intention to abolish the commission, Estrada still appointed people to the PCGG, thereby throwing the agency into an awkward position: Should it continue its prosecution and sequestration efforts even if they would all eventually be put to waste anyway? And whom did the President assign to head the PCGG and go after Cojuangco but a former subordinate of Cojuangco's lawyer: Judge Felix de Guzman who once worked as one of Mendoza's lawyers while the latter was solicitor general in Marcos's time. Besides de Guzman, Estrada also appointed to the DOJ, the department that supervises the actions of the OSG, Serafin Cuevas, a former Supreme Court justice who was previously retained by Imelda Marcos for a graft case.

De Guzman would later on announce that he would not pose any objections to Cojuangco's plan to retrieve the companies that the Supreme Court had earlier described as "repositories of the fruits of ill-gotten wealth."[129] He also defended the decision of the PCGG nominees in the SMC board to vote in favor of Cojuangco, saying they did not in any way violate the commission's mandate to prevent the dissipation of sequestered assets.

In October 1998 a Special Prosecutor working under Cuevas surprised Supreme Court justices when she said she had a weak case against Cojuangco regarding one of the suits the government filed in relation to the coco levy funds. She also announced that the government intended to withdraw a criminal complaint filed against Cojuangco.[130]

In March 2000 the PCGG and the OSG failed to submit a pre-trial brief on an ill-gotten wealth case involving SMC. Garchitorena scolded an OSG lawyer for his lack of familiarity with the case as well as the PCGG for not briefing the lawyer. This prompted former Solicitor General Francisco Chavez to accuse the two offices of conspiring to sabotage the government case. "They are now obviously leading up to a situation where the cases will be dismissed by the court for failure to prosecute and the government would then lose by default," he opined.

"Are they deliberately presenting a state of mental disarray so the case could be conveniently lost this time?"[131]

Pacman's lands

When Cojuangco turned sixty-five, Estrada dropped everything in his schedule to fly to a sprawling hacienda in Negros island. It was a hush-hush affair. The media did not even know where the President was going.[132] It was only after news of the visit was leaked that the country learned that the President had flown all the way to a distant island to greet a friend.

It is in Negros where Cojuangco holds dominion over his lands. His scion originally found its wealth in agriculture and had grown to become one of the biggest landowners in Central Luzon. In Negros, Cojuangco owns several haciendas encompassing eight municipalities that he began purchasing after 1975. His entry into the province resulted displaced thousands of workers as one of his conditions for purchase was mass eviction of laborers in the farms he was buying. According to Alfred McCoy, Cojuangco's presence in Negros was "clearly a product of State resources beyond the reach of even the wealthiest local planter."[133]

Even before he finished high school, Cojuangco was already involved in the operations of the family sugar business. In college, he studied agriculture at the University of the Philippines Los Baños. It took more than specialized education, however, for his agribusiness to really flourish. During the time of the dictatorship, Cojuangco and Marcos executed a "Deed of Exchange" that allowed the former to swap one hectare of his land for ten hectares of "undeveloped" lands.[134] Cojuangco's lands were then subject to land reform so the "Deed of Exchange" was meant to be a form of compensation for what were to be taken away from Cojuangco. This gave Cojuangco 19,884 more hectares of land in Agusan del Sur and Palawan.[135]

Because of his extensive landholdings, Cojuangco knew that he was going to be significantly affected by any effort at land reform. Department of Agrarian Reform (DAR) officials expected him to put up a difficult resistance to the land reform program legislated during the Aquino government. They were surprised, however, when Cojuangco easily and willingly gave in. Cojuangco, who only had contempt for land reform, apparently had it all figured out.

In April 1997 Cojuangco and the farmers forged an agreement putting the contested property on a voluntary land transfer, direct payment scheme. According to the arrangement, each land reform beneficiary would be allocated 2.6 hectares which they would buy from Cojuangco for Php 350,000 per hectare. Just a few months after the signing of the contracts, however, Cojuangco gathered the farmers again and discussed a different scheme. There he proposed to buy back the land from the beneficiaries for Php 50,000, payable in five years—something explicitly prohibited by the law.

His staff then asked the farmers to line up to get their first installment from Cojuangco. A precondition for getting the cash, however, was for them to sign on twenty-eight blank pages of white bond paper. Cojuangco denied this ever happened although he was recorded, while addressing the farmers in an assembly, to have admitted buying back land from the farmers. A DAR undersecretary was among those in the audience.

When Estrada became President, Cojuangco was finally given a crack at implementing the so-called corporative scheme which he had been proposing to DAR officials in the past.[136] Under the scheme Cojuangco would sell 4,361 hectares of his lands in Negros for only Php 1 per hectare to 1,750 agrarian reform beneficiaries. But these farmers will then be obliged to enter a joint venture agreement with Cojuangco requiring them to give him back the leasehold rights in exchange for 30 percent of outstanding shares of the joint-venture corporation.

According to Anna Marie Karaos of the Institute of Church and Social Services, "the proposal reveals itself to be a disguised attempt by Cojuangco to retain control over the land while ostensibly giving up his claims as a landowner."[137] This is because, first, Cojuangco would still have a controlling stake of 70 percent in the corporation. Second, members who may reject the arrangement will be shut out since the land would be under the collective ownership of all workers regardless of each individual owner's stance toward the joint venture. Third, the fifty years during which the joint venture will be implemented is too long for an agreement with onerous provisions. Finally, since the farmers' land will constitute their equity, they will be left landless in case the joint venture fails.

The Institute of Popular Democracy's Saturnino M. Borras and Jennifer C. Franco pointed out that, in the first place, since the land involved had been sequestered, it should have been distributed long ago. Cojuangco had no right dictating the terms of the distribution. Moreover, they also questioned how and why a number of farm workers were excluded from the deal. They assailed the collective ownership clause, as this would supposedly deprive the farmers of an escape route in case they decide to withdraw for whatever reason in the future.

Despite all these objections to his scheme and his record of eluding land distribution, Cojuangco's scheme was endorsed by the President as the solution to the land reform stalemate in the country. Cojuangco was even publicly extolled by Estrada as "the godfather of land reform."

The boss's gift

On hindsight, Estrada could have been the President as early as in 1992. He was convinced by Cojuangco to slide down to being his vice presidential candidate for a reason best known only to the both of them. Cojuangco's lawyer, Gabriel Villareal, was not lacking in candor when he divulged the reason behind his client's decision: "Let's not waste time with a lot of propaganda about the national interest. The bottom line is he's running for president to protect his own private interests."[138] In that election, Cojuangco placed a decent third.[139]

Estrada, Cojuangco's running mate, won convincingly. He would repeat the same feat six years later, this time as President. Although his popularity had a lot to do with it, he arguably could not have won the presidency had he failed to match the financing and machinery of his opponents—two things Cojuangco, said to be his political godfather, readily supplied. Although most of his riches were tied in sequestration cases, Cojuangco apparently still had money to spare, as he easily became one of Estrada's major financiers. More important, he had built up, through the years, what had become one of the major parties in post-Marcos political history, with grassroots networking all over the country and with members noted for their allegiance.

As President, Estrada continued to be lavished with presents from Cojuangco, better known as the "Boss" by his employees. The PCIJ reported that a company linked with him was building mansions for two of the President's mistresses in the posh South Forbes Park and Wack Wack subdivisions respectively.[140] Estimated to be worth close to half a billion pesos, the two houses were being built by Centech International, a company closely associated with Cojuangco and a certain Ramon S. Ang.[141] The PCIJ interviewed several contractors and suppliers working on the houses. They revealed that the mansion was *"regalo ni Boss"* [the Boss's gift].

Corruption's Perfect Poster Boy

Make no mistake about it then: Estrada was a corrupt President. This long and sordid tale of four cronies has reinforced and detailed what was so dramatically exposed during the historic impeachment trial that ousted him: Estrada was a crooked careless bumbling thief.

In exchange for campaign contributions and commissions, Estrada used the government to engorge himself and his friends. Lucio Tan lent Estrada his nationwide sales distribution complex for his grassroots campaign network on top of over a billion pesos in campaign financing. In return, the President protected Tan's airline, killed the tax evasion cases against him, and gave him his creditor bank on a silver platter. Danding Cojuangco backed him up with his political machinery and Estrada returned the favor by giving him back his crown jewel of a corporation and allowing him to elude land reform. Mark Jimenez not only contributed campaign funds, he also interceded for the candidate in an attempt to get the White House's blessings. Through the takeovers and mergers they engineered together, Jimenez then gave Estrada hundreds of millions of pesos in kickbacks. The President, in exchange, expressed his gratitude by making sure Jimenez did not fall into the hands of US federal agents. Dante Tan also bankrolled the President's campaign and, like the others, took care of his mistresses, deposited regularly into his "Velarde" bank account, and gifted him with mansions. In exchange, Estrada made sure that Philippine regulators understood perfectly well that Tan was a "good friend."

For many, Estrada and his relationship with these four sample cronies represent what is so wrong with the Philippines and so many other poor countries—the rampant bribery and fraud—the unbridled rent-seeking, the brazen patronage politics, the flagrant abuse of public resources for private gain, and the widespread clientelism.[142]

Estrada, a former movie actor, is a perfect contemporary poster boy for a very persistent and very powerful discourse which blames the plight of the South to its failure to curb and restrain corruption. So popular is this explanation that as many as three in every four Filipinos believe that corruption is bad because "it hurts national development."[143] Even the proliferating academic research on corruption in the country is motivated largely by the fear that corruption repels investment and retards growth through various channels.[144]

Through the years, this discourse has appeared in various formulations and in varying degrees of sophistication. But its core thesis, stripped to the bare essentials, is simple, resonant, and unyielding: A country is poor because it is corrupt. This family of ideas blames the South's stagnation to the depravity, avarice, and decadence of its corrupt politicians, bureaucrats, and businessmen.[145]

In 1997 this discourse was reincarnated in the popular "crony capitalism" thesis advanced by US Treasury Secretary Robert Rubin and his predecessor, former World Bank chief economist and subsequent Treasury Secretary Lawrence Summers, to explain the cause of the Asian financial crisis. Economies were battered, currencies plummeted, and thousands of jobs were lost because Asian governments were, well, corrupt. "The problems related to crony capitalism," Summers would repeat in speech after speech, "were at the heart of the crisis."[146] If only the Asian governments were less ravenous, so the idea goes, there would have been no Asian crisis.

Today the discourse guides the World Bank's extensive and well-funded anticorruption program all over the world. For the World Bank, corruption is "the single greatest obstacle to economic and social development."[147] In the Philippines, this is the view taken to heart by the high-profile and USAID-funded Transparent Accountable Governance (TAG) Project, which involves such organizations as the Makati Business Club, the Philippine Center for Investigative Journalism (PCIJ), the Philippine Center for Policy Studies (PCPS), and the Social Weather Stations (SWS).[148]

If only the Philippines were less corrupt, so this discourse goes, the country wouldn't be so poor. Almost half of the population wouldn't be starving and homeless. Over 10 percent of the people wouldn't be unemployed. Foreign investments should be flooding in. The country would have been the roaring tiger that its neighbors are. But Filipinos seem to be so fond of people like Marcos and Estrada they keep electing them as Presidents. No wonder then that the country is so poor, or so the accepted wisdom goes. Let's go get rid of corruption and we'll get out of this rut.

Same difference

But wait—if corruption is the reason why the Philippines is poor, why are so many rich countries also corrupt?

The South Korean political system, just to cite one example, has been as corrupt as that of the Philippines, if not more so. And yet, the average income in South Korea is now five times larger than in the Philippines even if both started at around the same level—with the average Filipino even earning slightly more fifty years ago. In the span of around fifty years, the South Korean economy has grown by over ten times while the Philippines has only doubled. In terms of the more holistic United Nations Human Development Index, which takes into account not just a country's economic wealth but also its achievement in providing education and health services to its citizens, South Korea gets a high mark of 0.88 while the Philippines only gets a 0.754, with 1 as the highest.

	Real GDP per capita 1953	Real GDP per capita 2000	Growth in Real GDP per capita (1953-2000)[149]	Human Development Index [the closer to 1, the higher]	Average Unemployment Rate (1969-2001)[150]	Income Ratio of Highest 20% to Lowest 20%[151]	Inequality Index (GINI) [the closer to 100, the more unequal] 1988[152]	National Poverty headcount as percent of population[153]
Philippines	$1,576	$3,424	117%	0.754	6.80%	5.3	46	40%
S. Korea	$1,393	$15,881	1040%	0.882	3.70%	12.6	34	7%

Not only that, South Korea is a more egalitarian society, with the richest 20 percent of the population getting only five times more yearly than the poorest 20 percent, as opposed to thirteen times for the Philippines. For the past thirty years, the unemployment rate in South Korea has averaged at no more than 4 percent while the Philippines registers at 6.8 percent. Only 7 percent of Koreans are considered poor; in contrast, two in five Filipinos are living below the officially defined poverty line.

So the Same Yet So Different

But for all these striking divergences in fortune, South Korea and the Philippines actually have very much in common. Not only have the two countries been cursed by corrupt politicians, bureaucrats, and businessmen, they also have very similar political arrangements and social structures. Both countries have arrested and sent their former heads of state behind bars for corruption charges: Estrada in 2001, on the one hand, and Chun Doo-Hwan and Roh Tae Woo in 1995 on the other.[154] Both political systems have been regularly rocked by a parade of corruption scandals. Further stressing the similarity is the fact that both societies are lorded over by a handful of powerful elite families and clans who dominate business and politics.

David Kang of Darthmouth College details all these very interesting parallels in his book *Crony Capitalism: Corruption and Development in South Korea and the Philippines* in an attempt to confront the perplexing bottom-line question: "If both Korea and the Philippines experienced extensive corruption, why did Korea grow much faster than the Philippines?"[155] If a country can be rich even if it's corrupt, could it possibly be that corruption may not be the cause of poverty after all?

And it's not just South Korea, there's Thailand too. Add in Indonesia and Malaysia, which both significantly accelerated their economic growth and reduced their poverty rates during the past decades—at exactly the same time when rampant corruption characterized their economic systems.

For that matter, add in the richest and most powerful country in the world: the United States of America—"the most legally corrupt political system in the world today."[156] For Tan's PAL, Cojuangco's San Miguel, and Tan's BW Resources, there's an equivalent Enron, Halliburton, and Bechtel. The Princeton economist and professor Paul Krugman—who was once hired as a consultant by the Philippine government and who once jokingly noted the resemblance between George W. Bush and Marcos—has written about how US President George Bush gave some "repulsively corrupt, but perfectly legal, favors" to his cronies.[157]

As corruption scholars Doig and Theobald explain, grand corruption is not as easily detected in developed countries for two reasons. First, there is a large private sector that gives better opportunities for creating wealth than the state. Second, institutions like elections and the media are relatively more highly evolved in ensuring a higher level of transparency.

And yet, Doig and Theobald assert, "There have been numerous scandals of dubious party financing and elected politicians with audacious self-enrichment through parallel company directorships, outside consultancies, the selling of information and contacts, and classic bribery."[158] Even the US, which is so used to lecturing developing countries about cleaning up their electoral systems, has not been immune from these campaign-finance scandals.[159]

But perhaps, the US invasion of Iraq in 2003 shows most forcefully—and most violently—just how legally corrupt the world's only superpower can be: The corporations that were awarded billion-dollar contracts to "reconstruct" what the US destroyed and to exploit the world's second largest oil reserves were also President Bush's biggest campaign financiers and his administration officials' former employers.[160]

What happened on the way to war, observed Columbia University economist Jeffrey Sachs, was not just "guilt by association." The White House itself trashed every rule to benefit its cronies. Says Sachs, "America has shown itself to be second to none in practicing cronyism, first with its rotten corporate scandals of recent years, and now in Iraq."[161]

But it's not just Iraq and it's not just now. The relationships and transactions within the military-industrial-corporate complex has been one big web of corruption where politically connected defense contractors get the bulk of billion-dollar contracts to build bombs and fighter planes for the US's wars and military interventions. Politicians then do their part by selling these wars to the public. In exchange, they are assured of campaign funds come election time.[162]

Besides military-industrial complex, there's also what Columbia University economics professor Jagdish Bhagwati dubbed the "Wall Street-Treasury Complex" to highlight the links between the interests of giant US financial firms and the IMF and the World Bank.[163] Since the US has majority shares in both institutions, the US Treasury Department gets to say what these multilateral institutions should or shouldn't do.

In most cases, as with the Mexican and the Asian crises, the order is to bail out the big Wall Street banks. As the conservative economist Rudiger Dornbusch once commented, "The IMF is the toy of the United States to pursue its economic policy offshore."[164] And that policy usually entails protecting Wall Street firms that, in turn, happen to be very generous donors to the occupant of the White House.[165]

Clearly, as scholar Chalmers Johnson put it, "The ultimate in crony capitalism is actually the US-dominated IMF and its bailing out of Thailand, Indonesia, and South Korea; the IMF's money does not go to the people of those countries. It goes to the foreign banks that made too many shaky and imprudent loans to Thai, Indonesian, and South Korean banks and businesses in the first place."[166]

Farther back into the past, it could be convincingly argued that the dominant history of US interventions and wars abroad—and American foreign policy in general—were pursued to protect and advance the interests of what could only be called "crony capitalists."[167]

In 1953, for example, the US overthrew the regime of a democratically elected Guatemalan government that subjected to land reform the holdings of the American corporation United Fruit Company which happened to have very intimate ties with the Truman administration.[168] Latin America would be rocked by more CIA-orchestrated interventions in the following decades, prodded by the threatened shared interests of American businesses and their government.[169]

In the Middle East, Iran's democratically elected prime minister was also overthrown in a US-engineered plot in 1953 after he nationalized the oil industry, thereby blocking access for US oil corporations. In 1964 Brazil's president was removed for putting a lid on the profits that multinationals could remit home. During the 1990s, the US gave hundreds of millions of dollars for the Mexican government to crush the Zapatistas who were causing problems for the implementation of the

North American Free Trade Agreement. During this decade also, Colombia became the third-largest recipient of foreign aid as the ill-disguised "war on drugs" sought to protect massive US interests in the country from rebels.

These are just a handful of examples among the US' 200-plus cases of overseas interventions.[170] But as Andrew Bacevich of Boston University argues in his book *American Empire: The Realities and Consequences of US Diplomacy*, the story of US foreign policy—regardless of which party dominates the government or no matter how the policy is packaged—is actually simple and continuous: it has and continues to be driven by the aim to open up markets abroad for its corporations' expansion.[171]

How different are the actions of US presidents who executed these grand foreign policy decisions from that of a petty President changing his country's policies to suit his friends? Clearly, the extent and damage of legalized corruption in the US can make saints out of Marcos and Estrada. And yet, for all its corruption, the United States is still the richest country in the world—with its GDP accounting for almost a third of the world's total GDP combined.[172]

Corruption is not seen as corruption in the US and in many developed countries only because it has been redefined and made more respectable. But corruption, of the type practiced in poor countries, is arguably as endemic there as in the South. This may not be easily verifiable though because corruption is packaged as something else. And this underscores a common criticism of how corruption is defined and analyzed: it treats as corruption only transgressions of *formal* rules. If those who are in the position decide to legalize bribery, for example, then legalized bribery would no longer be considered corruption.

What the numbers say

Even with this inconsistent definition of corruption, however, the thesis that countries are poorer the more they are corrupt remains problematic. Various econometric studies have used "illegal" corruption as it is conventionally defined to test the above assertion but yielded less than supportive results. Is it corruption of the illegal kind that consigns a country to poverty? Economists could dismiss as anecdotal the cases of South Korea, Thailand, Indonesia, Malaysia and the US but even sophisticated statistical studies seriously challenge the "crony capitalism" thesis.

Jens Chr. Andvig and Odd-Helge Fjeldstad surveyed econometric studies testing the relationship between corruption and economic growth. They conclude that the widely held assumption that corruption lowers growth is questionable because of ambiguous and contradicting results.[173] Brunetti, Kisunku, and Weder in 1997 and Paldam in 1999 found out that if at all, the impact of corruption on GDP growth and GDP levels is insignificant.[174]

The assumption that corruption repels investment and therefore lowers growth—which the World Bank believes as a matter of faith—is also "not entirely justified."[175] Mushtaq Khan contends that even if a country tried its darndest best to reduce its corruption now, it still would not be assured of upping its growth rates in the future.[176]

Paldam and Treisman argue that, based on cross-country regression analysis, the causation is not from corruption to economic development but the other way around. In fact, the most important reason why a country is formally corrupt, Paldam and Treisman found out, is precisely because it is poor.[177]

Narrowing the field to Asia to test the "crony capitalism" thesis, Mushtaq Khan and Jomo K.S. unambiguously point out that "Not only was there no simple correlation between the *extent* of rent-seeking and long-run economic performance, there was also little correlation between the intensity of rent-seeking and the country's vulnerability to the financial crisis of 1997."[178]

What all these studies are saying is simple: there are many corrupt countries that are poor and there are many corrupt countries that are rich. Too many empirical anomalies undermine the discourse. What all these studies are saying, in other words, is that the discourse on corruption, as it is currently understood and purveyed, may not provide a way out of the rut.

Corruption redefined

Over the years, researchers have long been laboring to pin down the concept and practice of "corruption" with the most adequate definition conceivable. Of the attempts, there have been many; the debates, long-running. The proposed definitions, however, are often merely more sophisticated variants of the simplest definition: corruption as the misuse of public resources by a public agent for private gains.[179]

What most studies fail to explore, however, is that the public agent under this definition could be seen in two ways: either as an individual, such as a government bureaucrat or politician, or as a class, such as a country's ruling elites who—by virtue of their control over economic and political resources—often determine who gets to sit in public offices. Hence, transactions of individuals such as Estrada and his cronies may be defined "corrupt" but so could entire groups of people or classes.

In fact, whenever the ruling class in the aggregate uses the state or public resources for private gains, then—by definition—the ruling class is being corrupt. When the ruling elite uses the powers of the state to pass or enforce laws and policies which preserve or promote their class interests, then that—if we are to follow the definition to its logical end—is also corruption.[180] Seen this way, the landed class' protection of their landholdings by state police power or the business class' control over the fiscal and monetary policy for their enterprises to flourish is no different from the use of government power and resources as practiced by Estrada and his cronies to advance their interests as individuals.

Whether the state could ever be resistant to corruption practiced by individuals or by classes then depends on one's view of the state. On one end are those who believe that the state is inherently captive to ruling elite interests and by nature incapable of exercising any kind of autonomy. Corollary to this view is the belief that ruling elite "corruption" is inherent to the state.

On the other side are those who implicitly or explicitly deny the class character of the state, seeing it instead as a neutral and level arena for resolving various competing interests.[181] This view limits corruption to individual actions and often proceeds to design rules or incentive mechanisms for countering it.

Somewhere in between are those who believe that the state is neither totally captured by the ruling class nor is it totally immune from their machinations. This view argues that while the state cannot shed its class character, it nevertheless has its own potential source of power which allows it to exercise relative autonomy from the ruling class.[182]

important in form of TN

This is the view taken by this chapter. Two of its assumptions can be easily demonstrated empirically. First, the ruling class has historically dominated the Philippine state either by directly fielding some of its own as politicians or bureaucrats or by indirectly ensuring the election or appointment of non-ruling class personnel that owe their allegiance to or share the same interests with the ruling elite. In the system of liberal democracy in the Philippines, where running for President requires Php 3 billion to Php 5 billion pesos for campaigning[183] together with the backing of the landed or business elites, no President and few legislators have ever been elected without the approval of the ruling class.

Second, while the state has often served to protect and entrench ruling elite interests, there have also been numerous instances when the state directly challenged ruling elite power, thereby putting into question the assertion that it is merely "the executive committee for managing the common affairs of the bourgeoisie." The very fact that non-state powers have been seeking to eliminate or undermine the capacity of the state through neoliberal policies of privatization, deregulation, and liberalizaton, for example, is in fact a very powerful acknowledgment that the state does matter. While economic interests constrain and circumscribe the range of actions by the state, it does not simplistically determine them.

A choked state

In conceiving of the state and its relative autonomy in this manner, however, it needs to be stressed that the ruling class is not monolithic. There are always competing factions. This then allows for two possibilities: the state is able to exercise relative autonomy over all factions or the state is successfully taken over by one faction in order to dominate the other factions. These different possible dynamics—more than just the presence or absence of corruption itself—can explain more sufficiently the reason behind the Philippines' poverty and underdevelopment relative to other equally corrupt political systems.

Seen this way, South Korea prospered while the Philippines stagnated not because it was less corrupt but because its corruption was confronted differently. In answer to his question, Kang posits that the divergence between the Philippines and Korea can be accounted for not by the extent of corruption but by the balance of power among ruling elites as well as by the balance of power between these elites and the state.

In Korea, not only was there a case in which elites were in a constant position of equilibrium, they were also constantly disciplined by the state. Not one faction enjoyed sizeable advantage over others at a any given time. In the Philippines, in contrast, the elites were locked in a permanent state of rivalry and whoever was winning at a certain moment also got to control the state.

"Corruption in Korea, although endemic, was constrained by the collusion of a powerful business class and a coherent state. Each major group was able to benefit from its close relationship with the other but neither could ever gain the upper hand. Each needed and relied upon the other," explains Kang. "In contrast, corruption in the Philippines swung like a pendulum. As one group or the other gained predominant power, it would busily set about lining its own pockets, aware that in the next round its fortunes might well be reversed."[184]

These important characteristics of the Philippine state and its ruling elites go a long way in explaining what's gone wrong for the country. "The point is that in Korea, there was a state that was relatively autonomous from private interests that not only kept private capital in check but channelled it to preferred policy paths," notes one of this book's authors in an earlier work. "In the Philippines, in contrast, the state has traditionally been hijacked at all levels by private interests, making it an ineffective instrument of national development."[185]

Dr. Joel Rocamora of the Institute for Popular Democracy seconds this, saying, "[The class factions'] competing demands on government have made it impossible to formulate and implement a coherent economic development policy or to develop political institutions capable of providing a reliable regulatory framework for the economy."[186]

In South Korea the elites could squabble all they want but they would toe the line and behave once the relatively more autonomous state begins calling the shots. In the Philippines, on the contrary, the state is but a prize for momentarily winning chronic inter-elite rivalry.[187] Paul Hutchcroft labels this condition "booty capitalism," in which rela-

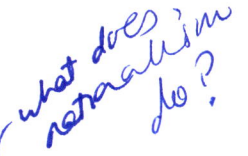
what does
neoralism
do?

tive to a strong oligarchy, "[t]he state apparatus has repeatedly been choked by an anarchy of particularistic demands from, and particularistic actions on behalf of… oligarchs and cronies."

Hutchcroft blames this on the remarkable absence of any attempt to consolidate the state throughout the country's history. First, the Spaniards failed to establish an effective bureaucracy. Then, the Americans concentrated more on introducing representative institutions than on organizing a central bureaucracy. The legacy of US colonialism, concludes Hutchcroft, was oligarchy—building, not state building.

"If in Thailand we find an elite traditionally based in the bureaucracy," Hutchcroft notes, "in the Philippines we find a bureaucracy long subordinated to particularistic elite interests." The Spanish and the American failure to strengthen the state, Alfred McCoy, for his part asserts that historically, the modern Philippine state did not evolve organically from Filipino society. Because of this it became incapable of enforcing compliance through shared myth.

While the state and its bureaucracy remained stunted, landowning families and other powerful local forces became entrenched in their localities. Because of the central government's failure to penetrate distant provinces, the local elites—organized primarily in terms of families—strengthened their economic and political foothold. Even after independence, the government could not pursue strategies that would act against these families' interests because the President and most other national politicians depended on them to deliver votes come election time.

In effect, Presidents had to use the state's licensing and regulatory powers for transacting with these local elites, in the process granting and formulating contracts and policies according to political expediency. "The Philippine bureaucracy," Hutchcroft posits, "has long been penetrated by particularistic oligarchic interests, which have a firm independent economic base…yet rely heavily upon their access to the political machinery in order to promote private accumulation." Thus, throughout its history, the Philippine state's autonomy weakened as public resources were privatized to strengthen a few families.

In sum, the Philippines' relative stagnation can be more adequately explained by the state's inability to control elite factions—dominated as it is by one of them at a given time—and to harness them and their resources for development. But if this is the case, why is corruption still always blamed for the country's plight? Why, despite its obvious analytical and empirical loopholes, does the corruption discourse continue to hold sway? Why do we still hear it so often and how can so many people adhere to its assumptions?

Part of it has to do with its utter simplicity. It's popular because it is easy to explain. Part of it has to do with its appeal to morality. But a larger part of it lies in its indispensability.

Ideas survive and flourish not necessarily because they are empirically or analytically sound but because they are useful for advancing and protecting the interests of certain people—forces who would then have the material incentive to ensure that such ideas are perpetuated and propagated. Simply put, the flawed discourse linking corruption to stagnation, crisis, and poverty thrives because it is needed by people like Arroyo and Summers—and all the interests they represent.

The Pendulum Swings

For all the promise of renewal and reform, EDSA 2 could well be but another episode in the recurring history of inter-elite rivalry in the Philippines. Fourteen years after state power was passed from one elite faction to another—with "corruption" as the battlecry again, though more so than before—the country witnessed another reshuffling of sorts.

Estrada's ouster was undeniably a triumph of a vigilant press, a mobilized middle class, independent elements in the judiciary, an empowered and aggressive civil society, and a political culture that—thanks mainly to Marcos—is slowly becoming more and more averse to official corruption.[188] But it may also be seen as yet another episode in the swinging of the pendulum. More than a struggle for the presidency, it was a power struggle in which those who had just been thrown out attempted to come back in.

Certainly, all the factors listed above were critical and EDSA 2 would not have happened without them coming together at a specific conjuncture. These factors, in other words, may be considered, in social science-speak, as the "necessary condition" for the uprising. But at the same time, the uprising would conceivably not have succeeded without the consent, encouragement, and participation of the elite factions that were alienated or threatened by Estrada's presidency.

At some point, these factions not only withdrew their tacit support or grudging toleration of Estrada's rule, they also actively began to undermine it. By November 2002, or two months before EDSA 2, key sections of the elites were having private meetings in their mansions, eventually reaching a decision to actively lead the campaign for Estrada's ouster. Members of the Makati Business Club, the very influential association of the country's top corporations, were among those who vigorously started lobbying for Estrada's resignation.[189]

Don Jaime Zobel de Ayala, of one of the country's richest families, for example, was terrified at the prospect of Estrada politically exploiting the real class cleavages in the country. Among those who vigilantly sat at the gallery of the impeachment trial were high-society matrons from the capital's most exclusive villages. Though they comprise a tiny segment of the population, as many as one in every five rallyers in EDSA came from the perfumed set.[190] Popular political analyst Amando Doronila at the time warned that, "it is elite interaction that will bring down the President."[191] It certainly did. The elite's active consent may be considered the "sufficient condition" that sealed Estrada's ouster.

For if Estrada's election, as economist Joseph Lim argues, was the "takeover of a faction of the old elite that viewed election victory as a feudal conquest that would put the state apparatus at the helm of the winning clique and friends,"[192] then surely his removal could only be seen as but the takeover of another faction. Because for all his *masa* rhetoric and his successful packaging as an outsider, Estrada was undeniably part of the ruling elite, albeit from a different faction. He was one of them.

While the contemporary Philippine political elite scene has many concentric circles, intermingling, splits, mergers, and comings and goings, it can be basically grouped into four collapsible blocs: the old elite composed of the Osmeñas, the Lopezes, the Ayalas, the Aquinos, and others who were sidelined by Marcos; the Marcos bloc composed of all those who emerged during the dictators' regime and never broke away such as Estrada, Lucio Tan, Danding Cojuangco, and many others; those who derive their legitimacy from and define their public persona by projecting themselves as anti-Marcos such as former President Ramos as well as the network that emerged during his presidency; and then there are the other upstarts that include the likes of Dante Tan and Mark Jimenez.[193]

The rehabilitation of Estrada's biggest cronies, Lucio Tan and Danding Cojuangco—as well as the introduction of new ones, Mark Jimenez and Dante Tan—not only blocked access to the state for the other elite groups. It also represented a direct attack on the very factions who derive their legitimacy or "soft power" primarily from projecting themselves as being anti-Marcos. These factions include the blocs of former Presidents Aquino and Ramos and their supporters who, in coalition with other elite factions, were at the forefront of the elite section of the anti-Estrada protests and at the lead of the undercover negotiations for the transfer of power. Gloria Macapagal Arroyo herself, who was installed to succeed Estrada, was part of Ramos's faction.[194]

Discourse as a weapon

It is here in these inter-elite dynamics that corruption discourse can prove very useful: Arroyo and her faction needed something by which to denounce Estrada without necessarily attacking the system she and her faction sought to take over.

For counter-elites out of power, the cronyism discourse has long been used as a very effective weapon for wresting legitimacy away from incumbent elite factions. It is a way for the "outs" to strike back at the "ins." Corruption charges are always a weak spot for any current power-holding faction and it comes as no surprise that most counter-factions use the discourse to delegitimize the ruling faction with the hope of taking over power.

The mere threat of corruption exposés—whether true or baseless—is sometimes enough leverage for extracting concessions from incumbents and holding them hostage. Accusations of corruption are also especially powerful in mobilizing the middle classes not only because their sensibilities are most easily outraged by official wrongdoing but also because they are often more politically active and sometimes even politically decisive. In EDSA 2, for example, they easily constituted almost 60 percent of the demonstrators.[195]

Domestically, the discourse gives local ruling elites something to blame for the country's less-than-impressive development over the past one hundred years—without having to point the finger at themselves as a whole. If they are to retain legitimacy and continue to get the consent of the people, ruling elites know that they must be able to coherently explain why, after all these years, despite an enviable headstart, and the availability of so much resources and opportunities, the Philippines continues to be a poor country. And because it is a simple historical fact that the country was indeed ravaged by Marcos's kleptocracy for over twenty years, the understandable aversion to "corruption," especially with the middle class, becomes all too easy to manipulate.

Pointing fingers

It's not that these counter-elite factions are themselves untainted, however. Previous administrations have consistently used the public power of the state for private gain, though in various degrees of brazenness.

The Estrada faction's direct predecessors, for example, were accused of concocting what one Senator labeled the "grandmother of all scams" and which investigative journalists concluded to be "the single biggest scam in memory."[196] In the sale of reclaimed public lands to a Thai company, Php 3 billion (around $100 million) in bribes were allegedly given to some of the highest-ranking men in the Ramos administration from 1995 to 1997.[197] Then in 1998, using the centennial celebrations of Philippine independence as cover, millions of pesos in public funds were reportedly diverted to the campaign chest of Ramos's party.[198]

In relation to the power scandal surrounding the contracts with Independent Power Producers (IPPs), Ramos himself was accused of pushing for speedy and onerous deals in order to benefit friends and campaign supporters. The PCIJ discovered that individuals and companies with close ties to Ramos cornered the lucrative consultancies for deals that Ramos himself railroaded.[199]

In asking people to support one ally, Ramos supposedly said, *"Kaibigan natin ito. Malaking naitulong sa atin."* [This is our friend. He has helped us a lot.][200] How different is this from Estrada's *"Ipahingi na ninyo sa akin ito"* [Give this case to me as a favor] or "[Dante Tan] is a good friend and he has been helping me"?

The faction of Aquino, Marcos's immediate successor, was itself not beyond reproach. In fact, one reason for early disillusionment with her administration was the alleged nepotism she practiced and which people branded *Kamag-Anak Inc.* or Family Incorporated. And if one sticks to the definition of corruption as the use of public power for private gain, shouldn't the exemption from land reform of Aquino's vast landholdings in the Hacienda Luisita be considered monumentally corrupt?[201]

Hence, it's not that these counter-elites factions who cloak themselves with a shroud of innocence are really against corruption or rent-seeking of any kind. They are definitely against any form of corruption—especially that which doesn't enrich them. But when they are out of power, it is usually the form that corruption takes, and hence, the form that they also rabidly denounce.

No shortage of hypocrisy

There will be no shortage of examples to prove the hypocrisy by which Filipino elites defile the rhetoric of corruption.

Take Manuel Pangilinan, president of PLDT and one of the country's most influential businessmen, who grew rich and powerful from the former Indonesian dictator Suharto's legendarily tainted money. An Indonesian professor who is considered an expert on Suharto's ill-gotten wealth says, "Manny Pangilinan is to Liem [Suharto's business operator] and Suharto what, say, Herminio Disini was to Marcos... but on a much bigger scale."[202]

Evidence now shows that the Suharto-financed Pangilinan group's takeover of PLDT, one of the country's most important corporations, was also stained with corruption. Affidavits executed for Estrada's trial indicate that the former President ordered the SSS to unload its shares in PLDT to enable Pangilinan to buy them and takeover PLDT management. Pangilinan himself admitted that he deposited a Php 20-million check in the "Velarde" account—at a time, says the PCIJ, when the President's intervention on some of PLDT's problem were direly needed by Pangilinan.[203]

And yet, in November 2000, Pangilinan was among the many elite figures who attended one of the first public rallies that eventually culminated in EDSA 2. He has also been reported as one of the biggest financiers of the January EDSA mobilizations that finally drove Estrada to resign.[204]

But perhaps there is no better example of the Philippine elites' pragmatic ambivalence toward corruption or rent-seeking than the story of the Lopez family, one of the most important and most enduring elite families in the country—and also one of the most corrupt. "More vividly than any other, the story of Eugenio Lopez illustrates the close connection between state power and private wealth in the Philippines," writes McCoy, who wrote an extensive history of the rent-seeking practices of the Lopez family. "For thirty years, Lopez had used presidential patronage to secure subsidized government financing and dominate state-regulated industries, thereby amassing the largest private fortune in the Philippines."[205]

Corruption vs corruption

Lopez's rise to power—from the time he founded a small provincial bus company to the founding of his giant corporate conglomerates—is replete with striking similarities to the actuations of Estrada's own cronies. Like Lucio Tan, Cojuangco, Jimenez, and Dante Tan, Lopez was a rent-seeker who had "mastered the logic of political investment, risking great capital in presidential elections and reaping even greater rewards."[206] During his lifetime, Lopez consistently used his capital to buy political protection by investing in candidates and reaping profits in the form of political favors once they are in office.

In the 1930s, Lopez courted President Manuel Quezon by being one of his most important sources of campaign funds and by making his newspapers the propaganda paper of Quezon's party in the Western Visayas. In the 1946 elections, the Lopez family gave the appearance that it was supporting Sergio Osmeña even as Eugenio financed his rival Manuel Roxas's candidacy. In an act that, on hindsight, smacks of Jimenez's decision to abandon Renato de Villa for Estrada, Eugenio switched sides at the last minute to support Roxas. According to McCoy, Lopez also supported and benefited from the presidency of Elpidio Quirino, Ramon Magsaysay, and Carlos Garcia.

Like Estrada's cronies Lopez often succeeded in having presidents appoint people sympathetic to his interests. In Magsaysay's time, for example, Lopez's compadre and closest political ally Oscar Ledesma was appointed secretary of commerce and industry, a ministry that Lopez had to deal with directly for his businesses. In the Ramos administration, the Lopezes managed to plant their former employee as a press secretary, a post that they always had to transact with for their media operations.

Lucio Tan's efforts to shield PAL from competition was a case of déjà vu relived by another person. As early as 1933, Eugenio Lopez also succeeded in securing monopoly rights for his airline INAEC. Likewise, in 1945, Lopez's FEATI was granted a monopoly over international routes from Manila, thanks largely to a compadre who was appointed in charge of aviation policies. In accusing his competitor airlines of poaching, Tan was echoing Lopez's charges against his rival bus company in Iloilo in the 1930s.

Lucio Tan's purchase of his creditor bank follows the precedent set by Lopez in organizing a bank that served his own interests, the Philippine Commercial and Industrial Bank (PCIBank). Lopez's takeover of the Philippines' largest sugar-milling factory is reminiscent of how Tan bought PNB as well as of how Jimenez helped take over PLDT and PCIBank. The common denominator in all takeovers was state intervention.

In taking over the *Manila Times,* Jimenez must have learned from Lopez that a newspaper makes for a very good investment. Throughout his business career, Lopez made sure that media entities were included in his portfolio. In Iloilo, Lopez put up a newspaper which he used for attacking his political and business opponents as well as for campaigning for Quezon. Later when he moved to Manila, Lopez acquired the *Manila Chronicle* and a network of radio stations.

"Throughout the next two decades of their controversy-laden climb to power," writes McCoy, "the *Chronicle* served the Lopez interests as a flexible political instrument, hammering away at the venality of their enemies and trumpeting the virtue of their allies." Jimenez must have had the same objective for buying *Manila Times,* an erstwhile critic of Estrada, but which he eventually used against his many enemies. Lopez's ABS-CBN media network has grown to become one the most important political forces in the country today.

Lopez, like the four cronies, had a talent for survival. Jimenez's apparent cooperation with the Arroyo government in helping prosecute

Estrada, on the one hand, as well as his reported funding of the pro-Estrada rebellion to oust Arroyo, on the other, is analogous to Lopez's actions during World War II. Through some unique talent, Lopez managed to get into the good graces of the anti-Japanese guerillas, while at the same time nurturing cordial social relationships with the local Japanese command. Unlike many others who tried to do the same, Lopez was never found out by both sides. Collaboration charges against him did not prosper, thanks again to his political connections.

But in a plight that was to be subsequently experienced by Lucio Tan and Cojuangco under the Aquino and Ramos administrations, Lopez was suddenly thrown to the sidelines of power during the Macapagal presidency. In order to climb back to power, Lopez was all out in his support for Marcos when he ran against Macapagal in 1965. Lopez used the family's television, radio and newspaper network to actively campaign for his candidate, besides spending up to Php 14 million, then a sizable sum, to ensure that Macapagal is defeated.

Eugenio Lopez later had a falling-out with the Marcoses when he accused them of demanding shares in their family corporations. Marcos shot back by alleging that the Lopezes were demanding government concessions to favor their companies. The President then stripped them of their prized corporations, including their TV station and their newspaper.

Here was a family that became immensely rich through rent-seeking but when it got dislodged from its position of privilege, it used charges of corruption to hit back at the dictator.

Throwing all the rascals in jails

During the snap elections in 1986, Eugenio's family threw its support behind Corazon Aquino, thereby paving the way for their restoration and the retrieval of their corporations. Not only did Aquino give back the Manila Electric Co. (Meralco) to the Lopezes, she also signed an executive order that effectively allowed the company to directly compete with the state-owned power corporation. Without this generous help, Meralco would not have prospered as it did.

In 1992 the Lopezes invested in Aquino's anointed, Fidel Ramos, and went on to expand their already vast business operations. Ramos

had barely warmed his seat when he gave the Lopezes government—
and therefore public—backing for their private loan. Meralco was asking for a million-dollar loan from the Asian Development Bank (ADB)
but the bank would only give the corporation cash if the government
promised to extend it its credit standing. Not only that, a government
corporation was also made to stand as its loan guarantor—meaning that
in case Meralco defaulted, it would have been the taxpayers that would
have paid for the Lopezes' debts.[207]

It was also in Ramos's time that some of the most onerous deals
with IPPs—some owned by the Lopezes themselves—were signed.
The Lopezes have profited from deals that allow Meralco to charge
higher prices for electricity that consumers do not even use. They are
able to do this by having Meralco, as a power distributor which controls 60 percent of the market, buy from Lopez-owned power-generating IPPs. These extra collections were then used to cover for the
other bleeding companies of the Lopezes.[208] Without this arrangement in place, it is conceivable that the Lopez business empire would
have already crumbled.

Similarly, during Macapagal-Arroyo's administration, the Lopez-
owned Maynilad Water Services Inc. was also on the verge of collapse—
threatening once again to bring with it the entire conglomerate. After
six years, the privatization of the water utility and its transfer to the
hands of the Lopezes had proved to be a massive failure. Not only were
the Lopezes unable to deliver on their promise to drastically reduce
water prices, they also failed to make water delivery more efficient.

Due to utter mismanagement, the water company was teetering on
the brink of bankruptcy and the only way it could stay afloat was to
illegally overcharge its customers as high as 40 percent of their bills.
Instead of terminating Maynilad's services for flagrant breach of contract, however, the government went on to entertain the Lopez company's
demand for Php 19 billion in undeserved compensation and more price
hikes.[209] (The Maynilad is more fully discussed in Chapter 5.)

Spanning several decades, Eugenio Lopez Sr. and his family had
used their closeness to the Presidents to build what has become one of
the largest fortunes in the country today, with stakes extending across
the economy. They now own major utilities—water, telecommunica-

tions, and electricity, besides owning the biggest and most powerful media network in the country.

And yet, for all that the Lopezes did to be where they are now, this is what Oscar Lopez, current head of the family's group of companies had to say about EDSA 2: "The lesson of EDSA 2 is that people, especially the young, are sick and tired of corruption and moral turpitude in government... President Arroyo must realize that she was put in power by the people, not to conduct government and business as usual, such as the distribution of spoils of office to political allies, but to create the conditions to make the moral revolution possible, which includes first and foremost throwing all the rascals in jail, and then recasting the bureaucracy to reflect a system based on merit rather than political patronage, and creating a much more efficient tax collection system that will at the same time go after the big tax evaders. Unless all these things and more are done, EDSA 2 may not be too far enough behind EDSA 3."[210]

True enough, Lopez's fear came to life three months after Lopez's speech. But perhaps EDSA 3, in which as many if not more people massed in EDSA in May 2002 to protest the arrest of Estrada, showed that, if anything, the masses are no longer so gullible, no longer vulnerable to the manipulations of elite factions wishing to deploy the corruption argument for their own political purposes. Ironically, of course, they were also mobilized and financed by a faction of the elite who were trying to get back at the ruling faction that threw them out a year earlier.

The people, not the structure

So Estrada may have been a crooked careless bumbling thief but this does not make him stand out in a land of saints. It only makes others, well, more careful, more skillful, luckier thieves.

As University of the Philippines economics Professor Emmanuel de Dios points out, "The more radical critique... is not that Estrada was aberrantly corrupt, but that he merely took the institutions of society at that time for what they were—namely, like himself. Estrada's gargantuan appetites were remarkable to be sure but he was also the product and the logical culmination of political and social institutions that had been long permeated by corruption and the betrayal of the public."[211]

Corruption discourse becomes very handy for elite factions wishing to discredit the ruling faction and to present themselves as the alternative. Implicit in this discourse is that all will be well if only the voters remove those who are corrupt and replace them with other elite factions. All that is needed is a replacement of personnel, not of the arrangement in place.

If anything, the prevalence of the corruption discourse, or what one author calls "scandal politics," only serves to underscore the deliberate shutting off from public discourse discussions on any other real political and economic alternatives. The ease by which politicians rattle off corruption charges against their enemies only highlights the lack of any real meaningful difference among the political and economic programs of the competing parties and personalities.

After all, accusing one's political opponents of graft or fraud can sometimes be the only way for criticizing other elite factions whose politics one generally agreed with in the first place. "In the absence of an alternative standpoint from which to criticize," notes Russell Grinker, "it is difficult to criticize at all." When one doesn't fundamentally disagree with the incumbents' policies, then one is left with nothing else to criticize but their personal integrity. Given that politicians and parties can hardly be differentiated, the only distinguishing mark becomes people's honesty. "Personal character has become the substance of modern politics," laments Grinker.[212] Without ideology, there's always morality.

The best thing about the discourse then is that the system of liberal democracy under which ruling elite factions are allowed to rotate power never comes into question. Elites from all factions understand full well that regular elections—by giving citizens the illusion of political equality within a reality of economic inequality—are still the most effective way for placating discontent and deriving continued legitimacy for their rule. They all understand that elections—as opposed to periodic coup d'etats or a revolution—still provide the cheapest and least bloody way to contest power among themselves and to ensure that it stays within them.

Elections are very effective in deflecting and defusing energy aimed at political change toward an exercise whose results are predetermined because its rules inherently favor those with existing economic and social power. As Resil Mojares puts it, "In Philippine elections, we have a case in which the elite or dominant class usually constructs reality for citizens. This process may be seen in the centrality accorded to the election itself as a field of action and a channel for effecting political change… In effect, the periodic holding of elections nourishes and renews the system. In the process, it also tends to reify the existing regime and de-emphasize other areas of political work such as mass organizing, interest-group lobbying, and 'armed struggle'."[213]

In blaming corruption for the country's woes and in packaging elections as the way to end it, ruling elites are able to project accountability and responsiveness by conceding that something's wrong and presenting themselves as the only means to solve it. Corruption gives them something believable to point at without necessarily undermining the arrangement which allows for their merry-go-round. Everyone and his or her mother will pay lip service to condemning corruption, rent-seeking will be attacked on all sides, but in the end, liberal democracy remains unscathed.

Domestically, the discourse on corruption thrives because it is a useful scapegoat and stabilizer.

The case collapses

For external actors, the discourse flourishes because it is indispensable for keeping friendly regimes in place and for pursuing a certain policy agenda. Institutions like the World Bank, together with people like Rubin and Summers, find the idea valuable because it gives them a coherent rationalization for defending and pursuing the interests of those on whose behalf they are acting.

For external players, the discourse on corruption is also extremely useful because it effectively exonerates them from whatever mess they have caused and are still causing in the South.[214] The poverty in countries like the Philippines has little to do with the "structural adjustment policies," for example, but has everything to do with local politicians' greed. Blaming the South's economic woes on the greed of a section of the domestic ruling class deflects attention from external forces' actions and policies. For if the problems are internal, the solutions must therefore be internal as well. There will be no need to question the role that external agents have on the inside.

In attempting to explain the causes of the Asian financial crisis of 1997, for example, Rubin and Summers needed to resort to "crony capitalism"—an explanation which few scholars of the crisis subscribed to[215]—in an attempt to conceal how, in this case, the dogma of financial liberalization may have been at fault.

It is easy connecting the dots. After all, the discourse on corruption is one of the lynchpins that hold the neoliberal discourse together. It could even be said that it is neoliberalism—the idea that states should keep out of the market as much as possible— which gave birth to rent-seeking analysis. "Rent-seeking theories," explain Khan and Jomo, "were initially constructed by liberal economists who wished to show that state intervention induced additional rent-seeking costs by artificially creating rents."[216] This was necessary for proving that in the ideal free market, nobody earns any rents.

No wonder then that the very first point of the World Bank's recommended *Nine-Point Approach to Fighting Corruption in the Philippines* is "reducing opportunities for corruption by policy reforms and deregulation." According to the World Bank, this recommendation entails overhauling the tax policy so that the system of preferential tariffs, exemptions, and investment incentives can be "reformed." It also requires rethinking the regulation of infrastructure services and public utilities such as power, telecommunications, water, and aviation, as well as import and trade arrangements. The fifth point of the approach, "reforming budget processes," calls for opening up public procurement to international competition, i.e., to multinational corporations, and ending the governments' preference for domestic producers.[217]

The World Bank insists that eliminating corruption requires economic reforms such as liberalization and deregulation "to move toward a smaller, more efficient government"; privatization of corporations owned in part or in whole by the state; and opening domestic markets for products from abroad.

Says the World Bank, "Simplifying rules and replacing administrative processes with market mechanisms are strong measures to reduce corruption. Trade regime reforms and licensing changes in areas such as imports and foreign exchange reduce discretionary treatment. In other cases, the appropriate privatization of state enterprises can reduce the size of the economy under bureaucratic control."[218] Incidentally, these are also the main elements of the anticorruption policy of the regional multilateral lending agency Asian Development Bank.[219] The trademark stamp of the "Washington Consensus" is everywhere to be seen.

Without the World Bank and the ADB singling out corruption as the reason behind the country's underdevelopment, they would not be able to argue for such "reforms" listed above. Indeed, as this example shows, the case for trade liberalization, privatization, and deregulation often stands on the discourse of corruption. Without it, the case falters.

Examine the two strands of arguments used for some neoliberal commandments:

- A country should privatize its public services and state corporations and desist from nationalizing resources because the state and its personnel are intrinsically corrupt and inefficient. Sure there may be some honest people here and there but on the whole, state-owned corporations are bound to be wasteful and poorly run for the simple reason that there's no profit motive guiding its managers and employees. They know that the state will never go bankrupt and that it does not face any competition so there's no incentive to be efficient and no incentive to minimize corruption. The best thing to do, therefore, is to give these services to the more efficient and less corrupt private sector where the profit motive makes sure everyone's upright and hardworking.

- A country should liberalize its trade and allow as much imports to come in for two reasons. First, a complicated tariff system will only give corrupt customs officials more opportunities for extortion. More importantly, setting tariffs, quantitative restrictions, and subsidies would only make people spend resources bribing those who are in the position to set them. Protecting domestic industries means protecting local manufacturing elites who often have corrupt ties with those who are in the position to protect them. So the best thing to do is for the government to keep out of trade altogether, swing the gates open, and keep the goods coming.

Blackmailed

Depending on how strong one's version of the neoliberal doctrine is, the theory basically implies that the public sector is bad and the private sector is good. The World Bank sees the state as just one big "opportunity" for corruption that must be rid of. The argument suggests that states and their personnel are helplessly prone to corruption and that any state intervention in the market would only provide more opportunities for corruption to thrive. Eliminating corruption, therefore, entails eliminating or disempowering the state.

Indeed, no one comes out of an undergraduate class in economics at the University of the Philippines, for example, without having taken to heart the mantra that free trade is good because the alternative— supporting local industries—will only breed rent-seeking. Hence, those who question the policy of trade liberalization and advocate industrial policy of some kind are almost always caricatured as defenders of local rent-seeking elites who, true enough, have often profited from trade restrictions and protection.

Broken down to its component parts, neoliberalism essentially says: State intervention in the market promotes rent-seeking or corruption. Rent-seeking is bad because it is inefficient and results in deadweight losses. In other words, rent-seeking is bad because it retards growth. Therefore if you want your economy to grow, goes the neoliberal advice, keep the state out of the market. Or else, if your state keeps interfering, your economy will be doomed to stagnation. Thou shall liberalize! Thou shall privatize! Repent or be cursed.

And who wanted to be doomed? Who wanted to be seen as tolerating corruption? Neoliberalism entailed some serious blackmailing in which economies were held hostage by the twin threats of rent-seeking and creeping growth. This was achieved by making the definition of "corruption" as vague and as inconsistent as possible so that hegemonically defined "corruption" or "rent-seeking" is vilified even as unofficially recognized "corruption" is legitimized and even sanctified.

This way, the IMF's and the World Bank's bailing out of Wall Street investment banks, the billion-dollar support for multinational corporations, the privileging of well-connected firms, or the use of state capacities by the ruling elites for public gains, are to be called by other names. In this manner, condemning "illegal" corruption will allow those who engage in "legal" corruption to assume a moral high ground.

Seen this way, Rubin's and Summers' lashing out at "crony capitalism" and their accompanying rescue of Wall Street creditors could be seen as an example of an attempt to curb corruption in the South even as corruption in the North—at the expense of the South—can go on unfettered. The discourse on corruption as it is currently purveyed allows those who practice corruption of the worse kind to hide their deeds even as they continue to rile against corruption.

And yet, while the threat of corruption has often been real and valid enough, the assumptions underlying the discourse—especially the jump from eliminating corruption to eliminating a strong state role in the economy—were questionable. For with corruption discourse, achieving growth, reducing poverty, and narrowing inequality are unimaginable through such other forms of social compromise such as state socialism or state-assisted capitalism. "Crony capitalism" upholds Margaret Thatcher's dictum that there is no alternative.

The specter of Enron

In their important book *Rents, Rent-Seeking and Economic Development*, Khan and Jomo contend that almost all political activity is a form of rent-seeking. For if rent-seeking is to be defined as "activities which seek to create, maintain, or change the rights and institutions on which particular rents are based" then "all institutional change involves creating or destroying rents and almost all distributive conflicts can be described as conflicts where one or both sides are seeking rents." Add Khan and Jomo: "There are no societies, developing or developed, which have resolved the rent-seeking problem by abolishing rents."[220]

They explain that, contrary to myths fostered by liberal economics to push for free markets, rent-seeking can actually promote or inhibit growth and equity depending on the circumstances. While many rents can be destructive, others could in fact be essential for growth and efficiency. Since this growth, in turn, does not automatically assure that requirements of social justice and equity are met, state intervention must also enter the picture.

Khan and Jomo therefore argue that current rent-seeking analysis could be misleading and should be augmented by insights from classical political economy as well as by advances in information economics and institutional economics. But if the mainstream analysis of rent-seeking is too narrow—and hence, invalid—then so are the prescriptions that take their life from it.[221]

First—as was already shown by the examples of South Korea and the US—as buttressed by various statistical studies, more rent-seeking does not necessarily mean lower growth. Some of the fastest growing countries of the past decades were in fact those that were inhabited by the most consummate rent-seekers. Empirically, the idea that higher tariffs mean more corruption has also been disproved. As Andvig and Fjeldstad note in their survey, "the empirical relationship between trade barriers and corruptions appears surprisingly weak."[222]

Second, the assumption that the private sector is structurally less prone to corruption and more efficient has proved to be pure fantasy. The massive failures of privatization projects around the world, as exemplified locally by the fate of the Lopezes' Maynilad, should have already been a rude awakening. Not only have privatized utilities led to skyrocketing prices, the quality of service and the efficiency of operations have also worsened—in complete breach of privatization's promises.

Moreover, the corruption scandals that have rocked corporate America in the last few years should once and for all bury the myth of the immaculate private sector. The spectacular corruption discovered in Enron is widely considered the biggest corporate scandal of the century and the amount stolen dwarfs by any measure that stolen by some of the world's most heartless plunderers combined.

After Enron came a parade of other scandals such as that which engulfed the giant accounting firm Arthur Andersen, Merrill Lynch, Worldcom, Xerox, Tyco, Adelphia, Imclone, Qwest, Global Crossing, Healthsouth, and Ahold. To think that, due to the inherent difficulty of detecting accounting fraud, these were just the tip of the iceberg. As Nobel Prize winning economist Joseph Stiglitz put it, in terms of relative corruption, "This is where the private sector has really won the race."[223] Enron and all these corruption scandals prove that, in a world of globalized capitalism, there is a very fine and permeable line separating rent seeking from profit making.

Third, the absence of state intervention does not necessarily mean the absence of rents. In fact, as de Dios points out, Estrada and his cronies profited precisely from what he calls "market-mediated corruption" such as the use of pension funds for the corporate takeovers and mergers. "The source of rents," de Dios points out, "was not the national treasury itself, but seemingly autonomous and non-manipulatable markets."[224] For, interestingly, Estrada himself was an avowed neoliberal. It was in fact him who commissioned the World Bank anti-corruption study. He ardently believed in the goals of privatization, deregulation, and liberalization. Early on, he promised to continue the neoliberal reforms of former President Ramos and invariably appointed free marketeers as his economic advisers.[225]

Still, despite these conceptual and empirical objections, neoliberal ideas live on—enshrined in the "Washington Consensus" that is pursued and imposed by the International Monetary Fund, the World Bank, and the World Trade Organization and accepted by developing country governments around the world. These three institutions have been severely delegitimized by events in the past years: the IMF by the Asian crisis and a little-heralded but extremely significant IMF publication admitting that financial liberalization does not necessarily benefit developing countries;[226] the World Bank by a US House of Representatives committee report concluding that it has been worthless in fighting poverty; and the WTO by the so-called Battle of Seattle in November 1999 and the "Second Seattle" in Cancun, Mexico, in 2003.

But these ideas, which stand on the foundation of corruption discourse, live on because the beneficiaries of doctrinal neoliberalism find them extremely profitable. Count among them all the corporations that have rushed in to the newly opened markets as well as Wall Street firms that have grown wealthy from freely moving their capital around the world. Count among them the US and other Western multinational corporations as well as domestic elites that have rushed in to fill the vacuum created by the withdrawal of the state. They have profited tremendously from providing services which the state has abandoned and from buying off the once state-owned corporations at rock-bottom prices—with debts wiped off, thanks to the use of taxpayers' money.

As eminent intellectual Susan George put it, "This is one of the greatest holdups of ours or any generation."[227] And for what they've got, they ought to at least mutter thanks to the very useful idea that corruption causes poverty and that the best way to end both is to keep the state out of the market.

Another People Power?

To summarize, the idea that we are poor because we are corrupt is conceptually and empirically flawed. It is being used as a public discourse to advance private narrow interests: to maintain and strengthen ruling elites' grip on power, and to further undermine the state's capacity to control and manage domestic and foreign capital. The idea that poverty is caused by corruption is a very seductive one that is being manipulated to stabilize liberal democracy and to advance the neoliberal agenda. It is blinding and disempowering.

The more convincing explanation for the country's poverty and underdevelopment lies more with the ruling elite factions' control over people, production, markets, and resources and the successful subordination of the state to their interests. The country has failed to develop and so many of its people are mired in poverty because the state, strangled as it is by competing factions' demands, has been rendered too powerless to even chart the country's direction, much less subordinate ruling elites under its control. Further sapping the state's potential to act according to democratic and developmental lines have been external interests constraining its range of allowable actions in the larger context of the North's persistent and often successful efforts to subordinate the South.

The state's relative autonomy, in other words, has been too successfully impaired by other power wielders in society as well as by external forces. Unlike other, more autonomous states, the Philippines has been unable to craft and pursue a coherent development and redistribution strategy, rein in the private sector, and implement progressive policy initiatives.

The answer, therefore, is to empower the state rather than to further weaken it, to fortify it rather than to roll it back. The relative autonomy of the state must be enhanced rather than diminished so that it does not just always remain a prize in the inter-elite struggle but also becomes a serious and more powerful contender in its own right. Only by unshackling it from the manipulation of entrenched interests can the state—always subject to the supervision of an empowered civil society—marshal surplus and capital toward sustainable and equitable development, redistribute income and assets to the masses and the marginalized, and harness the market's potential to society's benefit.

Indeed, corruption must be condemned and excised but it shouldn't stop there. Freeing the country from poverty and corruption will require more than designing and implementing incentive compatible anti-corruption programs and palliatives. It will entail more than convicting and jailing corrupt politicians, bureaucrats, and businessmen. It will call for more than simply periodically removing one faction of the ruling elites and replacing them with another. It will require much more than another People Power.

Notes

1. Luz Rimban, "We Love Lucio," *Philippine Center for Investigative Journalism's I Magazine* 5, no. 1 (January to March issue).

2. Fortune Tobacco, a pillar of Tan's empire, allegedly saved millions in tax obligations when cigarette tax laws then in operation were formulated by the company's own executives. Asia Brewery, another company, was not only given the permit that enabled it to challenge market leader San Miguel, it was also reportedly among the companies that were granted behest loans by the Philippine National Bank, then state-owned but now controlled by Tan himself (*Far Eastern Economic Review*, December 15, 1988, as quoted in Ricardo Manapat, *Some Are Smarter than Others* [New York: Aletheia Press, 1991], 346).

3. The following narration is based mostly on a synopsis of the case written by JTR Bentulan for *FinanceAsia* magazine.

4. Liwayway Vinzons-Chato,"The Truth about the Law and the Evidence Involved in the Tax Evasion Cases Against Fortune Tobacco, Lucio C. Tan and Their Co-accused," in www.pldt.com/luciol.html.

5. BIR examiners investigating the 1990, 1991, and 1992 tax liabilities of Fortune came across the following intriguing facts regarding the dummy wholesalers: Shortly after the implementation of the Executive Order shifting the excise tax from specific (based on volume) to ad valorem

(based on manufacturer's wholesale price), nine marketing firms were registered at the Securities and Exchange Commission within a few days of each other. They were all incorporated by former Fortune officers. A single lawyer notarized the incorporation papers of all nine companies. All nine companies had their "liaison offices" in one location: in Allied Bank Center. Fortune's external auditor is also the auditor of seven of the companies. Four of the companies have only one employee and he/she works for all four of them. All of them had no visible and tangible assets.

As regards the fictitious individual dealers, the following were established: From official certifications, all of the individual dealers were nonexistent and hence, fictitious. Each individual dealer transacted with Fortune only once but each one had enough cash to pay for Php 1 million to Php 6 million for the one-time transaction (Liwayway Vinzons-Chato, "The Truth about the Law and the Evidence Involved in the Tax Evasion Cases against Fortune Tobacco, Lucio C. Tan and Their Co-accused," www.pldt.com/lucioI.html).

6. Tan had also managed to put his former employees and relatives in posts close to Malacañang. His former secretary, Rosario Yu, was named presidential assistant. His second wife's uncle, Julio Tan, was appointed presidential consultant for Chinese affairs. Finally, his daughter's father-in-law, John Ng, was enlisted as presidential consultant on the steel industry (Sheila Coronel, "Into the Light," in *Millions, Mansions, and Mistresses: Investigating Estrada* [Quezon City: Philippine Center for Investigative Journalism, 2000], 157).

7. Ibid., 157.

8. Rocky Nazareno, "Estrada Caused Delay in Filing Tan Case," *Philippine Daily Inquirer,* September 2, 2000.

9. *Business World,* August 3, 1999.

10. "Lucio Tan Wants Out," www.orientaviation.com/pages/back_issues/00_05/oa_v7n7_tan.html.

11. All succeeding Philippine peso amounts are converted using the average exchange rate at the relevant year as recorded by the Central Bank of the Philippines in www.bsp.gov.ph/Statistics/sefi/P$MonAnn.htm.

12. "Reclusive Philippine Tycoon Becomes a More Public Figure After PAL Crisis," *The Wall Street Journal,* September 7, 1999.

13. Konrad Muller, "Ring-in at VIP Line-up Shows Rampant Cronyism," August 26, 2000, www.smh.com.au/news/0008/26/text/world8.html.

14. Hugh Williamson, "Lucio Tan, Master Dealmaker," *Financial Times,* February 28, 2001.

15. "PAL Monopoly of US Route Feared," *Philippine Daily Inquirer,* October 7, 1999.

16. "Lucio Tan: PAL's Friend," *The Economist*, February 5, 2000.

17. Deidre Sheehan and Simon Burns, "Altering Course," *Far Eastern Economic Review*, June 15, 2000.

18. Ibid.

19. Leotes Marie T. Lugo, Daxim L. Lucas, Norman P. Aquino, "Lucio Tan Puts Flag Carrier PAL on Auction Block," *Businessworld*, September 26, 2000.

20. *The Economist* noted how electronic firms such as Acer and Intel had to waste millions of dollars in additional expenses for finding slower and more expensive routes to ship their chips and circuit boards to Taiwan, the main PC maker in the region ("Lucio Tan PAL's Friend," *The Economist*, February 5, 2000). The Foreign Chambers of Commerce of the Philippines complained that the air dispute led to "unacceptably high added shipping costs and time delays" especially for high-tech electronic exporters ("Foreign Business Groups Tell Gov't to Settle Manila Air Dispute," *Philippine Daily Inquirer*, April 28, 2000).

21. Concerns were also raised about possible retaliatory actions by the Taiwanese government against the 110,000 workers based in the island who remit home $1 billion each year ("Reclusive Philippine Tycoon Becomes a More Public Figure After PAL Crisis," *The Wall Street Journal*, September 7, 1999). At one point, manpower agencies reported losing about as much as 10,000 job orders from Taiwanese employers (Eloy Calimoso, "Once Again, Lucio Tan," *Cyberdyaryo*, www.codewan.co.ph/Cyberdyaryo/commentary/c2000_0320_01.htm).

22. Travellers from Taiwan now had to go through Hong Kong or take an expensive charter flight to Subic to get to the Philippines. A return ticket that previously cost $220 began selling for $500. As a result, the country reportedly risked losing as many as 200,000 Taiwanese tourists, a considerable percentage of all tourists expected to visit that year ("Gemma Fears Loss of 200,000 Tourists," *Philippine Daily Inquirer*, March 17, 2000). If each Taiwanese tourist spends a conservative amount of $100 during his or her stay, that would have translated into $20 million in foregone tourism revenues.

23. Deidre Sheehan and Simon Burns, "Altering Course," *Far Eastern Economic Review*, June 15, 2000.

24. "House Leaders Hit CAB for Air Row with Taiwan," *Philippine Daily Inquirer*, March 8, 2000.

25. Solita Collas-Monsod, "No Cronies, Huh?" *Philippine Daily Inquirer*, May 20, 2000.

26. Pronouncements by top government officials themselves betray Tan's power over Malacañang decisions. Then Finance Secretary Jose Pardo was

quoted as saying, "Lucio Tan... is agreeable to negotiations with the new Taiwanese administration," as if the government needed Tan's consent to proceed with the talks. In another instance, Pardo said, "It appears that Mr. Tan is amenable to open [the negotiations] again," as if they would not resume talks if Tan were not amenable. Pardo even reportedly admitted that Tan sought assurances that PAL would be protected under the new air pact (Solita Collas-Monsod, "No Cronies, Huh?" *Philippine Daily Inquirer*, May 20, 2000).

27. Sheila Coronel, "Into the Light," in *Millions, Mansions, and Mistresses: Investigating Estrada* (Quezon City: Philippine Center for Investigative Journalism, 2000), 159.

28. JTR Bentulan, "The Arithmetic of Lucio Tan," *FinanceAsia.com*, www.financeasia.com/articles.

29. Solita Collas-Monsod, "Supercrony," *Philippine Daily Inquirer*, April 1, 2000.

30. Put to the board were a certain Macario Te, a businessman who is referred to in his golf club as Tan's caddy; Washington Sycip, who sits on two other Tan companies supposedly to deodorize Tan; and Feliciano Miranda, a former Central Bank official who is very close to former Central Bank Governor Gabriel Singson—a vice chair of PAL who, in turn, is very close to Tan (Solita Collas-Monsod, "Supercrony," *Philippine Daily Inquirer*, April 1, 2000).

31. Eloy Calimoso, "Once Again, Lucio Tan," *Cyberdyaryo*, www.codewan.co.ph/Cyberdyaryo/commentary/c2000_0320_01.htm.

32. Meera Tharmaratnam, "Lucio Tan Moves Closer to PNB Goal," *FinanceAsia.com*, www.financeasia.com/articles

33. Deidre Sheehan, "Win Some, Lose Some," *Far Eastern Economic Review*, August 3, 2000.

34. Eloy Calimoso, "It's Lucio Tan Once More," *Cyberdyaryo*, www.codewan.co.ph/Cyberdyaryo/commentary/c2000_0612_01.htm

35. *Associated Press*, July 25, 2001, www.bangla2000.com/News/Archive/Business/7-5-200/.

36. Sheila Coronel, "Into the Light," *Millions, Mansions, and Mistresses: Investigating Estrada* (Quezon City: Philippine Center for Investigative Journalism, 2000), 148.

37. Sheila Coronel, Yvonne T. Chua, Luz Rimban, and Vinia Datinguinoo, "The Other Women," *Businessworld*, November 30, 2000.

38. Ibid.

39. Konrad Muller, "Ring-in at VIP Line-up Shows Rampant Cronyism," August 26, 2000, www.smh.com.au/news/0008/26/text/world8.html.

40. *Far Eastern Economic Review,* December 15, 1988, as quoted in Ricardo Manapat, *Some Are Smarter than Others* (New York: Aletheia Publications, 1991), 344.

41. Norman Bordadora, Michael Lim Ubac, and Donna Pazzibugan, "Mark Jimenez Confesses Sins to Cardinal Sin," *Philippine Daily Inquirer,* February 3, 2001.

42. Ibid.

43. Juliet L. Javellana, "Estrada Calls Pal a Corporate Genius," *Philippine Daily Inquirer,* April 25, 1999.

44. "Like FPJ, Mark Jimenez Asks Nothing from President," *Philippine Daily Inquirer,* April 22, 1999.

45. Antonio Lopez and Sangwon Suh, "The Troubleshooters," *Asiaweek,* March 19, 1999.

46. Ellen Tordesillas, "The Nocturnal President," *Millions, Mansions and Mistresses: Investigating Estrada* (Quezon City: Philippine Center for Investigative Journalism, 2000), 17.

47. Ellen Tordesillas, "Mark Jimenez: Marked Man," *Millions, Mansions and Mistresses: Investigating Estrada* (Quezon City: Philippine Center for Investigative Journalism, 2000), 167.

48. Marites Vitug, "Secret Deals, Public Exploits of Mr. MJ," *Manila Times,* July 23, 1999.

49. First, for fraud, Jimenez's company, Futuretech International (FTI) had a deal with a certain Quantum Corporation for the latter to reimburse the former's advertising expenses for Quantum products. Jimenez and other FTI officials allegedly faked the expenses, attaching falsified copies of the ads to bills, and defrauding Quantum by about $600,000. Second, Jimenez allegedly had FTI transfer $5 million of its own money out of the United States for himself. On its tax returns, FTI reported the amount as advertising expense. On his own personal returns, Jimenez did not report the money as income, thereby evading up to $3.5 million in taxes. Third, Jimenez went beyond the allowable limits for illegal campaign contributions in making his donations to the campaigns of Clinton, Gore, and five Democratic senators namely, Edward M. Kennedy, Thomas Strickland, Ann Henry, Roger Bedford, and Robert Toricelli. Jimenez had allegedly used twenty-three of his FTI employees as "straw donors" by having them draw $1,000 from their personal checks and having them reimbursed using company money later. FTI then presented these costs as deductible expenses on its income tax returns. FTI's Chief Financial Officer had later pleaded guilty to these charges. ("Erap Pal Indicted in US on 47 Counts," *Philippine Daily Inquirer,* April 18, 1999; Ellen Tordesillas,

"Mark Jimenez: Marked Man," in *Millions, Mansions and Mistresses: Investigating Estrada* [Quezon City: Philippine Center for Investigative Journalism, 2000], 168; Juliet Javellana, "Estrada: US Fugitive Not Charged Here," *Philippine Daily Inquirer,* April 20, 1999; "Future Tech International and Its CFO Agree to Plead Guilty to Tax and Campaign Finance Charges," www.usdoj.gov.opa/pr/1998/December/597crm.htm.)

50. Ellen Tordesillas, "Mark Jimenez: Marked Man," *Millions, Mansions, and Mistresses: Investigating Estrada* (Quezon City: Philippine Center for Investigative Journalism, 2000), 166.

51. In the 1980s, Jimenez migrated to the United States allegedly because of a run-in with then President Ferdinand Marcos's right-hand man, Gen. Fabian Ver, chief of staff of the Armed Forces of the Philippines. He also left behind an estafa case filed against his brokerage company by the Globe-Mackay Cable and Radio Corp. It was alleged that Jimenez forged the signatures of Bureau of Customs officials to keep more than Php 1 million to himself. The case was dismissed when Jimenez was already in the US. (Marites Vitug, "Secret Deals, Public Exploits of Mr. MJ," *Manila Times,* July 23, 1999; Ellen Tordesillas, "Mark Jimenez: Marked Man," *Millions, Mansions and Mistresses: Investigating Estrada* [Quezon City: Philippine Center for Investigative Journalism, 2000], 164).

52. Raul Palabrica, "President Can Veto Extradition," *Philippine Daily Inquirer,* June 19, 1999.

53. "Mark Jimenez: Spare Estrada," *Philippine Daily Inquirer,* April 21, 1999.

54. Liu Yuan and Kristina Luz, "Another Crony Fidgets," *Asiaweek,* December 29, 2000 to January 5, 2001.

55. Raul Palabrica, "President Can Veto Extradition," *Philippine Daily Inquirer,* June 19, 1999.

56. Christine Avendaño, "I Will Die with My Boots On," *Philippine Daily Inquirer,* June 19, 1999.

57. Donna Cueto, "Jimenez Banking on Erap Help," *Philippine Daily Inquirer,* March 30, 2000.

58. Christine O. Avendaño, "Jimenez's Defense Frivolous," *Philippine Daily Inquirer,* July 7, 1999.

59. Rocky Nazareno, "Supreme Court Rules vs Mark Jimenez," *Philippine Daily Inquirer,* October 18, 2000.

60. Philip Bowring, "The Justice Secretary's Fate Bodes Ill for the Philippines," *International Herald Tribune,* February 23, 2000.

61. Donna Cueto and Christine Avendaño, "US Officials Are Very Concerned," *Philippine Daily Inquirer,* January 21, 2000.

62. Donna Pazzibugan, "Cuevas Denies Stalling Jimenez Extradition to US," *Philippine Daily Inquirer*, July 27, 1999.

63. Marites Vitug, "Secret Deals, Public Exploits of Mr. MJ," *Manila Times*, July 23, 1999.

64. Juliet L. Javellana, "Estrada Calls Pal a Corporate Genius," *Philippine Daily Inquirer*, April 25, 1999.

65. Juliet L. Javellana, "Estrada to Keep Jimenez as Adviser," *Philippine Daily Inquirer*, April 26, 1999.

66. Liu Yuan and Kristina Luz, "Another Crony Fidgets," *Asiaweek*, December 29, 2000 to January 5, 2001.

67. "Jimenez was Erap's Link to Clinton Pals," *Manila Times*, June 20, 1999.

68. Ellen Tordesillas, "Mark Jimenez: Marked Man," *Millions, Mansions and Mistresses: Investigating Estrada* (Quezon City: Philippine Center for Investigative Journalism, 2000), 166.

69. "The White House: That Invisible Mack Sure Can Leave his Mark," www.cnn.com/ALLPOLITICS/1997/08/25/time/notebook.html.

70. "Erap Pal Indicted in US on 47 Counts," *Philippine Daily Inquirer*, April 18, 1999.

71. "Videos May Force Investigation of Clinton," www.usatoday.com/news/index/finance/ncfin/125.htm.

72. *Wall Street Journal*, February 20, 1997.

73. Marites Vitug, "Secret Deals, Public Exploits of Mr. MJ," *Manila Times*, July 23, 1999.

74. Ellen Tordesillas, "Mark Jimenez: Marked Man," *Millions, Mansions and Mistresses: Investigating Estrada* (Quezon City: Philippine Center for Investigative Journalism, 2000), 166.

75. Unless otherwise stated, most of the following were based on Sheila S. Coronel, "The Multibillion-Peso President," *The Investigative Reporting Magazine*, January to March 2001.

76. Sheila Coronel, "Weather-weather," in *Millions, Mansions and Mistresses: Investigating Estrada* (Quezon City: Philippine Center for Investigative Journalism, 2000), 13.

77. Liu Yuan and Kristina Luz, "Another Crony Fidgets," *Asiaweek*, December 29, 2000 to January 5, 2001.

78. Ellen Tordesillas, "The Nocturnal President," *Millions, Mansions and Mistresses: Investigating Estrada* (Quezon City: Philippine Center for Investigative Journalism, 2000), 17.

79. Christine Avendaño, Stella O. Gonzales, and Lynda T. Jumilla, "Estrada: Jimenez No Criminal in RP," *Philippine Daily Inquirer*, June 20, 1999.

80. Marites Vitug, "Secret Deals, Public Exploits of Mr. MJ," *Manila Times*, July 23, 1999.

81. Sheila S. Coronel, Yvonne T. Chua, Luz Rimban, and Vinia Datinguinoo, "An Embarassment of Houses," *Millions, Mansions and Mistresses: Investigating Estrada* (Quezon City: Philippine Center for Investigative Journalism, 2000), 94.

82. "Like FPJ, Mark Jimenez Asks Nothing from President," *Philippine Daily Inquirer*, April 22, 1999.

83. Aries Rufo and Richel Langit, "Miriam: Jimenez's Fate Rests on Erap," *Manila Times*.

84. Rigoberto Tiglao, "Estrada and Co.," *Far Eastern Economic Review*, August 12, 1999.

85. Yvonne T. Chua, "The Company He Keeps," *Millions, Mansions and Mistresses: Investigating Estrada* (Quezon City: Philippine Center for Investigative Journalism, 2000), 140.

86. Ellen Tordesillas, "The Nocturnal President," *Millions, Mansions and Mistresses: Investigating Estrada* (Quezon City: Philippine Center for Investigative Journalism, 2000), 16.

87. Raul Dancel, "Dante Tan: Self-made Bingo King," *Philippine Daily Inquirer*, January 21, 2000.

88. Sheila Coronel, "The Multi-billion Peso President," *The Investigative Reporting Magazine*, January to March 2001.

89. Rigoberto Tiglao, "Estrada and Co.," *Far Eastern Economic Review*, August 12, 1999.

90. Zinnia dela Peña, "BW Cover-up Bid Confirmed," *Manila Times*, December 3, 1999.

91. Rigoberto Tiglao, "Estrada and Co.," *Far Eastern Economic Review*, August 12, 1999.

92. Efren Danao, "'Erap Ordered PNB to Grant Loan to BW'," *Philippine Star*, January 13, 2001.

93. Raul Dancel, "Dante Tan: Self-made Bingo King," *Philippine Daily Inquirer*, January 21, 2000.

94. Efren Danao, "Estrada Pressured PSE to Clear Dante Tan – witness," *Philippine Star*.

95. Reuters, "Stockholders Took Biggest Losses," *Philippine Daily Inquirer*, November 8, 1999.

96. Raul Dancel, "Dante Tan: Self-made Bingo King," *Philippine Daily Inquirer*, January 21, 2000.

97. "Erap Orders Review of Report on BW," *Philippine Daily Inquirer*, February 21, 2000.

98. Zinnia dela Peña, "BW Cover-up Bid Confirmed," *Manila Times*, December 3, 1999.

99. Transcript of impeachment trial, January 10, 2001.

100. Ibid.

101. Cathy Yamsuan, "'Erap Knew Dante Tan Bribed Yasay but Did Nothing," *Philippine Daily Inquirer*, January 10, 2001.

102. Katherine G. Adraneda, "BIR Says Dante Tan Owes Php 72 million in Taxes for BW Stock Transactions," *Cyberdyaryo*, January 17 2001, www.codewan.com.ph/CyberDyaryo/features/f2001_0117_05.htm.

103. Transcript of impeachment trial, January 12, 2001.

104. Sheila Coronel, "The Multibillion-Peso President," *The Investigative Reporting Magazine*, January to March 2001, 10.

105. Sheila S. Coronel, Yvonne T. Chua, Luz Rimban, and Vinia Datinguinoo, "An Embarrassment of Houses," *Millions, Mansions and Mistresses: Investigating Estrada* (Quezon City: Philippine Center for Investigative Journalism, 2000), 84 -92.

106. Gemma Bagayaua, "Estrada Intervened on Behalf of Tan," *Cyberdyaryo*, www.codewan.com.ph/CyberDyaryo/features/f2001_0111_03.htm.

107. Efren Danao, "Estrada Pressured PSE to Clear Dante Tan - witness," *Philippine Star.*

108. Efren Danao and Marichu Villanueva, "'Erap Made a Killing from BW Insider Trading," *Philippine Star*, January 12, 2001.

109. Efren Danao, "'Erap Ordered PNB to Grant Loan to BW ," *Philippine Star*, January 13, 2001.

110. Pamphlet of speech delivered on June 10, 1995, in Sison, Pangasinan.

111. www.time.com/time/pacific/magazine/20010129/cover1.htm

112. *Los Angeles Times*, December 30, 1990, as quoted in Ricardo Manapat, *Some Are Smarter than Others* (New York: Aletheia Publications, 1991), 216.

113. *Far Eastern Economic Review*, February 8, 1990, as quoted in Ricardo Manapat, *Some Are Smarter than Others* (New York: Aletheia Publications, 1991), 217.

114. Hilarion Henares, "Danding's Pearl of the Orient Seas," *Philippine Daily Inquirer*, July 5, 1986 as quoted in Ricardo Manapat, *Some Are Smarter than Others* (New York: Aletheia Publications, 1991), 218.

115. Former Deputy Speaker Daisy Avance Fuentes, quoted in Earl G. Parreño, "Back in the Game," *Institute of Popular Democracy Political Brief*, September 1999.

116. Coconut Industry Reform Movement (COIR) 1999, "Php 100

Billion Coco Levy Scam Brief Overview," in www.codewan.com.ph/anihan/campaigns/doc_coco_levy_scam_.htm.

117. For more on the coconut levy, see Joel Gaborni, "The Coconut Levy," *Institute of Popular Democracy Political Brief,* September 1999.

118. *Wall Street Journal,* April 12, 1990, as quoted in Ricardo Manapat, *Some Are Smarter than Others* (New York: Aletheia Publications, 1991), 217.

119. Pamphlet of speech delivered on June 10, 1995, in Sison, Pangasinan.

120. Joel Gaborni, "After 11 Years, 2 Presidents, Case vs Danding Unresolved," *Manila Times,* July 6, 1998.

121. In 1983, the cousins Enrique Zobel and Andres Soriano Jr. were slugging it out for the control of the corporation. With their energies and resources drained, Cojuangco entered and bought shares from Zobel using coco levy money (Raissa Espinosa-Robles, "Saga of the Shares: How San Miguel Got into Its Present Mess," *Asiaweek,* ww.pathfinder.com/Asiaweek/97/1212/biz2.html). Through a series of secret and complicated agreements, Cojuangco also succeeded in eventually acquiring the shares of the Sorianos (Ricardo Manapat, *Some Are Smarter than Others* [New York: Aletheia Publications, 1991], 236).

122. Lawrence Agcaoili and Mia Gonzales, "Danding Makes a Comeback at SMC," *Today,* July 8, 1998.

123. Cynthia Balana, "Danding Allowed to Vote SMC Shares," *Philippine Daily Inquirer,* April 21, 1998.

124. Antonio Lopez, "The Return of a Crony: Is Eduardo Cojuangco Good for San Miguel," *Asiaweek,* July 24, 1998.

125. "12 Years: Danding's Long Wait," *Today,* July 8, 1998.

126. "Erap Washes Hands of Danding Case," *Philippine Daily Inquirer* July 8, 1998.

127. There are even those who claim that Cojuangco's flight home actually had the consent of Aquino because she was also indebted to Cojuangco. Ricardo Manapat, author of *Some Are Smarter than Others,* notes that when the Aquino family was in exile in Boston, it was his first cousin Cojuangco who partially paid for their house rent. Moreover, the President's side of the Cojuangco family reportedly profited richly when Eduardo Jr. bought their First United Bank from the President's father Jose Cojuangco Sr., allegedly using proceeds from the coco levy (Ricardo Manapat, *Some are Smarter than Others* [New York: Aletheia Publications, 1991], 221).

128. Nes Barrameda, "How Government Bungled Ill-gotten Wealth Cases," *Manila Times,* July 6, 1998.

129. "PCGG Won't Stop More Takeover by Danding," *Manila Times* July 28, 1998.

130. Donna Cueto, "Government Has Weak Case vs Danding," *Philippine Daily Inquirer,* October 22, 1998.

131. Donna S. Cueto, "Ill-gotten Wealth: Ex-Solgen Accuses Gov't of Sabotage," *Philippine Daily Inquirer,* March 15, 2000.

132. "Erap Attends Danding Birthday," *Sunstar Bacolod,* June 12, 2000.

133. Alfred McCoy, "The Restoration of Planter Power in La Carlota City," *From Marcos to Aquino: Local Perspectives on Political Transition in the Philippines,* ed. Benedict J. Kerkvliet and Resil Mojares (Quezon City: Ateneo De Manila University Press, 1991).

134. Most of the following were taken from Earl G. Parreño, "The Landlord and the CARP," *Institute of Popular Democracy Political Brief,* September 1999.

135. Still, no one knows for sure the actual expanse of Cojuangco's holdings—except perhaps himself. Not the PCGG nor the Sandiganbayan which is hearing his sequestration cases. The information of the Department of Agrarian Reform, the agency tasked to distribute Cojuangco's lands, relied mainly on data provided by the landowner himself. According to DAR, Cojuangco has 2,354 hectares in Davao del Sur, 4,329 hectares in Negros Occidental, and 3,000 hectares in Agusan del Sur. What makes it difficult to ascertain how much land Cojuangco really has is that most of his properties are either still in the name of previous landowners or in the name of a corporation.

136. Most of the following were taken from Saturnino M. Borras Jr. and Jennifer C. Franco, "The World According to CARP: Agrarian Reform under Morales," *Institute of Popular Democracy Political Brief,* September 1999.

137. Anna Marie A. Karaos, "Clearing the Confusion Over 'Corporatives'," *Philippine Daily Inquirer,* July 25, 2000.

138. In the *Green Left Weekly Home Page,* jinx.sistm.usnw.edu.au.

139. Observers say Cojuangco, who garnered four million votes could have clinched the presidency had the Marcos loyalists' vote not been split between him and the strongman's widow Imelda, who had 2.3 million votes. Ramos, the winner, only had 5.3 million votes.

140. Most of the following are based on Sheila Coronel, Yvonne T. Chua, Luz Rimban, and Vinia Datinguinoo, "An Embarrassment of Houses," in *Millions, Mansions and Mistresses: Investigating Estrada* (Quezon City: Philippine Center for Investigative Journalism, 2000), 81-99.

141. Better known as Cojuangco's right-hand man, Ang was San Miguel's vice chair, chief financial officer, and treasurer. "As Cojuangco's chief po-

litical and business operator, Ang's actions were likely at the Boss's behest," the PCIJ quoted SMC insiders as saying. Centech was formed in 1988 as one of many purchasing arms for Cojuangco companies. Centech was also the company hired by the SMC and the UCPB to perform third-party reviews of purchases. Centech has not been involved in the construction of mansions until then.

142. In the following discussion, the terms "corruption," "rent-seeking," and "clientelism" will be used interchangeably. But to be very strict, they refer to different concepts and are not entirely substitutable for each other. Corruption's most simple definition is "the misuse of public resources by public officials for private gains." For an elaboration on the nuances of corruption's definitions, see Chapter 2 of Andvig and Fjeldstad's survey (Jens Chr. Andvig and Odd-Helge Fjeldstad, *Corruption: A Review of Contemporary Research* [Bergen, Norway: Chr. Michelsen Institute, 2001]) and the Introduction, *Political Corruption: A Handbook,* ed. Arnold Heidenheimer, Michael Johnston, and Victor T. Levine (New Jersey: Transaction Publishers, 1989).

For how the various terms may differ, Hutchcroft's explanation could be useful: "Rent literature focuses on what happens when state actions distort markets, corruption literature examines how public roles and private influences conflict within state agencies and clientelism encourages clearer analysis of the relationships of powers that permeate states, societies, and markets" (Paul D. Hutchcroft, "Obstructive Corruption: The Politics of Privilege in the Philippines," in Khan and Jomo, 207-47).

143. Social Weather Stations (SWS) Survey, December 2000 (Manila, Philippines: SWS, 200).

144. See, for example, Joseph Y. Lim and Clarence Pascual, "The Detrimental Role of Biased Politics: Frameworks and Case Studies" and Eric Batalla, Fernando Aldaba, Men Sta. Ana, and Nepo Malaluan, "Governance and Corruption in the Philippines," *Yellow Paper II series,* Action for Economic Reforms, April 2001. According to Batalla et al., the absence of corruption, as evidenced by "a predictable and reliable regulatory environment," is "key toward a healthy investment climate." Lim and Pascual, for their part, cite Estrada's folly as showing "the clear link between weak institutions and governance structures and the poor economic performance of the country."

145. See for example Gordon Tullock, widely considered one of the foremost theorists on rent-seeking, who said rent-seeking "is one of the basic reasons for Asia's backwardness," in *Toward a Theory of the Rent-Seeking Society,* ed. J. Buchanan, R.D. Tollison, and G. Tullock (College Station: Texas A&M University Press, 1980); A. MacIntyre, "Clientelism and Economic Growth:

The Politics of Economic Policymaking in Indonesia" (paper prepared for annual meeting of Asian Studies Association, Washington D.C., April 6-9, 1995).

146. Speech at the Annual Meeting of the Association of Government Economists, January 4, 1999; Testimony before the Senate Committee on Foreign Relations, November 5, 1999; speech before the World Economic Development Congress, October 2, 1998.

147. The World Bank Anticorruption Homepage, www1.worldbank.org/publicsector/anticorrupt/; See also the World Bank's comprehensive report and recommendations on corruption in the Philippines, "Combating Corruption in the Philippines" (Pasig City, Philippines: World Bank, May 2000) and the follow-up "Combating Corruption in the Philippines: An Update" (Pasig City: World Bank, September 2001).

148. See www.tag.org.ph. One aspect of the project is a research paper series which includes the following: Emmanuel S. de Dios and Ricardo Ferrer, "Corruption in the Philippines: Framework and Context" and Joseph Y. Lim and Clarence Pascual, "The Detrimental Role of Biased Politics: Frameworks and Case Studies."

149. Alan Heston, Robert Summers, and Bettina Apen, *Penn World Table Version 6.1*, Center for International Comparisons at the University of Pennsylvania, October 2002, http://pwt.econ.upenn.edu.

150. International Labor Statistics, http://laborsta.ilo.org.

151. Data from Korea is for 2000 while data from Philippines is for 1996; from Asian Development Bank, *Key Indicators of Developing Asian and Pacific Countries* in www.adb.org.

152. Klaus Deininger and Lyn Squire, *Measuring Income Inequality: A New Database* in www.worldbank.org/research.

153. Percentage of population living below poverty line to total population; data for Philippines is for 2000 while for Korea is for 1995; from Asian Development Bank, *Key Indicators of Developing Asian and Pacific Countries*, www.adb.org.

154. In 1996, a South Korean court convicted Chun and Roh of—apart from treason and mutiny—illegally amassing hundreds of millions of dollar. Other businessmen from South Korean giant corporations such as Daewoo and Samsung were also found guilty. Roh had earlier tearfully admitted receiving $650 million in bribes. See "Chun, Roh, Others Sentenced in South Korean 'Trial of Century'," CNN, August 26, 1996; "Time of Reckoning," *Asiaweek*, December 27, 1996.

155. David Kang, *Crony Capitalism: Corruption and Development in South Korea and the Philippines* (Cambridge, UK: Cambridge University Press, 2002), 11.

156. John Carlin, *The Independent*, May 24, 1998, as cited in Chalmers Johnson, "Economic Crisis in East Asia: The Clash of Capitalisms," *Cambridge Journal of Economics*, 22 (1998): 653-61.

157. Krugman, Paul, "Crony Capitalism, USA," *New York Times*, January 15, 2002; See also his "Cronies in Arms," *New York Times*, September 17, 2002; "Cronies reap Iraqi Contracts," *International Herald Tribune*, October 1, 2003.

158. Doig and Theobald in Andvig and Fjeldstad, 41.

159. See Dan Clawson, Alan Neustadtl, and Mark Weller, *Dollars and Votes: How Business Campaign Contributions Subvert Democracy* (Philadelphia: Temple University Press 1998) and Elizabeth Drew, *The Corruption of American Politics: What Went Wrong and Why* (Secaucus, New Jersey: Carol Publishing, 1999)

160. Vice President Richard Cheney was chairman of Halliburton, the world's largest oil services company which was granted the bulk of Iraq's reconstruction projects without any transparent and competitive bidding. Cheney himself continued to receive millions of dollars from Halliburton even while he was already vice president. Defense Secretary Donald Rumsfeld, one of the most passionate hawks in the Cabinet has ties to Bechtel Corporation, the corporation which was subsequently charged to run Iraq's lucrative utilities. National Security Adviser Condoleeza Rice was Director of Chevron Texaco while Commerce Secretary Don Evans was an oil company CEO.

161. Jeffrey Sachs, "America's Crony Capitalists Go to War," *Project Syndicate*, April 2003.

162. See John L. Boies, *Buying for Armageddon: Business, Society, and Military Spending since the Cuban Missile Crisis* (New Brunswick: Rutgers University Press, 1994), and Sanford Gottlieb, *Defense Addiction: Can America Kick the Habit?* (Boulder, CO: Westview Press, 1997).

One company which epitomizes the high-level cronyism within the intersection of politics, military, and business would be the Carlyle Group which counts among its officials some of the most powerful men in the world, including former President George H.W. Bush, former State Secretary James Baker, and a number of presidents of various countries. See Dan Briody, *The Iron Triangle: Inside the Secret World of the Carlyle Group* (John Wiley & Sons, 2003).

163. Jagdish Bhagwati, "The Capital Myth: The Difference Between Trade in Widgets and Trade in Dollars," *Foreign Affairs*, May-June 1998.

164. Cited in Doug Henwood, "Marxing up the Millenium" (paper presented at the "Marx at the Millenium" Conference, University of Florida, March 19, 1999.)

165. Goldman Sachs, the firm where US Treasury Secretary Robert Rubin came from, was one of the biggest donors to President Clinton's campaign (see Howard Fineman et al., "It's Dole Inc vs Clinton Inc.," *Newsweek*, April 8, 1996); On Rubin's influence over Clinton policies, see John B. Judis, "The Second Rubin Administration," *New Republic*, February 10, 1997.

166. Chalmers Johnson, "Economic Crisis in East Asia: The Clash of Capitalisms," *Cambridge Journal of Economics* 22 (1998): 653-61.

167. For a concise summary, see William Blum, *Rogue State* (London: Zed Books, 2002), and Nicholas Guyatt, *Another American Century?: The United States and the World After 2000* (London and New York: Zed Books, 2000).

168. Gleijeses, Piero, *Shattered Hope: The Guatemalan Revolution and the United States, 1944-1954* (Princeton: Princeton University Press, 1991).

169. Coatsworth, John H. *Central America and the United States: The Clients and the Colossus* (New York: Macmillan 1994), and Schoultz, Lars, *Beneath the United States: A History of US Policy Toward Latin America* (Cambridge MA: Harvard University Press, 1998).

170. According to the Congressional Research Service, as cited in Minxin Pei, "Lessons of the Past," *Foreign Policy*, July-August 2003.

171. Andrew Bacevich, *American Empire: The Realities and Consequences of US Diplomacy* (Cambridge MA: Harvard University Press, 2002).

172. Organization for Economic Cooperation and Development, June 2003, www.oecd.org; *The Economist*, June 29 to July 5, 2003.

173. Jens Chr. Andvig and Odd-Helge Fjeldstad, *Corruption: A Review of Contemporary Research* (Bergen, Norway: Chr. Michelsen Institute, 2001), 74.

174. A. Brunetti, G. Kisunku, and B. Weder, "Credibility of Rules and Economic Growth—Evidence from a Worldwide Private Sector Survey," background paper for the *World Development Report* 1997 (Washington, DC: World Bank, 1997), cited in Andvig and Fjeldtsad, 74; for a contrary view see P. Mauro, "Corruption and Growth," *Quarterly Journal of Economics*, 1995: 681-712.

175. Andvig and Fjeldstad, 78.

176. M.H. Khan, "The New Political Economy of Corruption," *Department of Economics Working Paper* (London: School of Oriental and African Studies, Universtity of London 1999); "New Approaches to Corruption and Governance and their Limitation," paper presented at *Rethinking the World Bank* conference, Northwestern University, US, May 14-16.

177. Andvig and Fjeldstad, 64.

178. Mushtaq H. Khan and Jomo Kwame Sundaram, eds., *Rents, Rent-Seeking and Economic Development: Theory and Evidence in Asia* (Cambridge: Cambridge University Press, 2000), 4.

179. This is also in fact the definition that the World Bank uses, see *Combating Corruption in the Philippines*, 3.

180. On how the parliamentarians legislate to advance class interests, see for example Sheila S. Coronel, "Open for Business," *The Investigative Reporting Magazine*, July to September 2003.

181. For example, see Eric Batalla, Fernando Aldaba, Men Sta. Ana, and Nepo Malaluan, "Governance and Corruption in the Philippines," *Yellow Paper II series*, Action for Economic Reforms, April 2001. According to this paper, "While a certain level of policy incoherence is intrinsic in a democracy due to pressures from competing interest groups, the state must be able to *reconcile* and *manage* [italics mine] these divergent interests." The operative assumption is that the interests of the ruling elites can always be reconciled with the interests of the ruled—as though the issues facing the state always satisfy the requirements for Pareto optimality.

182. See for example, Theda Skocpol, "The Potential Autonomy of the State"; Michael Mann, "The Autonomous Power of the State," in *Power in Modern Societies*, ed. Marvin Olsen and Martin Marger (Boulder: Westview Press, 1993).

183. World Bank, *Combating Corruption in the Philippines*, May 2001.

184. Kang, 20.

185. Walden Bello, *Dragons in Distress: Asia's Miracle Economies in Crisis* (San Francisco CA: Institute for Food and Development Policy, 1990), iii.

186. Joel Rocamora, "Formal Democracy and Its Alternatives in the Philippines: Parties, Elections, and Social Movements," paper presented at the conference "Democracy and Civil Society in Asia: The Emerging Opportunities and Challenges," Queens University, Kingston, Ontario, Canada, 19-21 August 2000.

187. Paul Hutchcroft, *Booty Capitalism: The Politics of Banking in the Philippines* (Quezon City: Ateneo de Manila University Press, 1998); Alfred McCoy, *An Anarchy of Families: State and Family in the Philippines* (Manila: Ateneo de Manila University Press, 1994).

188. For an account of how the impeachment trial proceeded, see Raul Palabrica, "The Road to Impeachment Was Short and Bumpy," and for an analysis of the social classes that animated People Power II, see Maria Cynthia Rose Banzon Bautista "People Power 2: The Revenge of the Elite on the Masses?" *Between Fires: Fifteen Perspectives on the Estrada Crisis*, ed. Amando Doronila (Pasig City and Makati City: Anvil Publishing Inc. and Philippine Daily Inquirer Inc., 2001).

189. Alejandro Reyes and Kristina Luz, "The Elites vs Estrada," *Asiaweek*, November 17, 2000.

190. Maria Cynthia Rose Banzon Bautista, "People Power 2: 'The Revenge of the Elite on the Masses'?" in Doronila, 2001, 8.

191. Cited by Alejandro Reyes and Kristina Luz, "The Elites vs Estrada."

192. Joseph Lim, "The Detrimental Role of Biased Policies: Governance Structures and Economic Development," in Doronila, ed., 126.

193. For more on Philippine elite dynamics, see Emmanuel De Dios, "A Political Economy of Philippine Policy-Making," in *Economic Policy-Making in the Asia Pacific Region*, ed. John W. Langford and K. Lorne Brownsey (Halifax: Nova Scotia: Institute for Research on Public Policy, 1990); Paul Hutchcroft, "Oligarchs and Cronies in the Philippine State: The Politics of Patrimonial Plunder," *World Politics* 43 (April 1991): 422; Alfred McCoy, ed., *An Anarchy of Families: State and Family in the Philippines* (Manila: Ateneo de Manila University Press, 1994); David Wurfel, *Filipino Politics: Development and Decay* (Ithaca, New York: Cornell University Press); David Wurfel, "Elites of Wealth and Elites of Power, the Changing Dynamics: A Philippine Case Study," *Southeast Asian Affairs* (Singapore: Institute of Southeast Asian Studies, 1979), 233-45.

194. For a glimpse into the ruling elite dynamics at play during People Power II, see Harry Tubongbanwa, "A View on the Developments and Prospects in the Philippines Today," *International Viewpoint*, February 11, 2001, www.3bh.org.uk/IV.

195. Maria Cynthia Rose Banzon Bautista, "People Power 2: 'The Revenge of the Elite on the Masses'?" in Doronila, 2001, 8.

196. Ellen Tordesillas and Sheila S. Coronel, "The Grandmother of all Scams," *Betrayals of the Public Trust: Investigative Reports on Corruption*, ed. Sheila Coronel (Quezon City: Philippine Center for Investigative Journalism, 2000), 147.

197. Ibid, 162.

198. Chay Florentino-Hofilena and Ian Sayson, "Centennial Scandal," in *Betrayals of the Public Trust: Investigative Reports on Corruption*, ed. Sheila Coronel (Quezon City: Philippine Center for Investigative Journalism, 2000), 163.

199. Luz Rimban and Sheila Samonte-Pesayco, "Ramos OK'ed Most Expensive IPPs," Philippine Center for Investigative Journalism, www.pcij/org/stories/print/ramos2.html.

200. Luz Rimban and Sheila Samonte-Pesayco, "Ramos OK'ed Most Expensive IPPs."

201. "The Philippines: Cory Coups, and Corruption," *TIME* January 15, 1990; Conrado de Quiros, *Philippine Daily Inquirer*, April 30, 2002.

202. Walden Bello's interview of Professor George Aditjondro, "Pinoys

Easy Targets of Suharto Cronyism," *Philippine Daily Inquirer,* December 6-7, 1998. Professor Aditjondro, a lecturer at the University of Newcastle in Australia is author of *From Suharto to Habibie: Corruption, Collusion, and Nepotism in the New Order.* He obtained his Ph.D. from Cornell University.

203. Malou Mangahas, "The Estrada Plunder Case, Year 1: Politics and Other Nightmares Hound Prosecution," *Philippne Center for Investigative Journalism,* www.pcij.org, January 16-18, 2002.

204. Malou Mangahas, "The Estrada Plunder Case, Year 1: Politics and Other Nightmares Hound Prosecution."

205. This portion is based on Alfred McCoy, "Rent-Seeking Families and the Philippine State: A History of the Lopez Family," in Alfred McCoy, ed., *An Anarchy of Families.*

206. Ibid., 435.

207. Sheila Samonte-Pesayco and Luz Rimban, "Ramos Friends Got Best IPP Deals," Philippine Center for Investigative Journalism, www.pcij.org.

208. Sheila Samonte-Pesayco and Luz Rimban, "Ramos Friends Got Best IPP Deals."

209. See Rep. Mario Aguja, "Privilege Speech on Maynilad Over-charging," Philippine House of Representatives, April 28, 2003; Jolette Fajardo, "The Mess that Is Maynilad: Legal Wrangling at the Expense of Consumers and Taxpayers," *Focus on the Philippines,* no. 29, July 1, 2003; Jude Esguerra, "The Corporate Muddle of Manila's Water Concessions: How the World's Biggest and Most Successful Privatization Turned into a Failure," *Institute for Popular Democracy Work in Progress;* Center for Public Integrity, International Consortium of Investigative Journalists, "Loaves, Fishes and Dirty Dishes: Manila's Privatized Water Can't Handle the Pressure," February 7, 2003.

210. Oscar Lopez, speech during his acceptance of the Management Man of the Year Award, January 29, 2001, in www.benpres-holdings.com; also published as "Built to Last: Time-tested Values Guide the Company's Existence Beyond Mere Bottomlines," *Philippine Business Magazine,* 8, no. 1, www.philippinebusiness.com.ph.

211. Emmanuel S. de Dios, "Corruption and the Fall," *Between Fires: Fifteen Perspectives on the Estrada Crisis,* ed. Amando Doronila (Makati City and Pasig City: Anvil Publishing and Philippine Daily Inquirer, 2001), 58.

212. Russell Grinker, "The Politics of Corruption," unpublished essay.

213. Mojares, 1995, 319-20, cited in Rocamora.

214. For various accessible works on how the South's poverty and underdevelopment has been caused by external actors using such institutions as the World Bank, the International Monetary Fund, and other big regional and private banks through structural adjustment programs (SAPs) and for-

eign debt, see Walden Bello, *The Development Debacle: The World Bank in the Philippines* (Food First: San Francisco, 1982); Walden Bello with Shea Cunningham, *Dark Victory: The United States, Structural Adjustment, and Global Poverty* (London: Pluto, 1994); Douglas M. Boucher, ed., *The Paradox of Plenty: Hunger in a Bountiful World* (Oakland: Food First, 1999); Robin Broad, *Unequal Alliance* (Berkeley: University of California Press,1985); Noam Chomsky, *Profit Over People: Neoliberalism and Global Order* (New York: Seven Stories Press, 1999); Susan George and Fabrizio Sabelli, *Faith and Credit* (London: New York, 1995); Nicholas Guyatt, *Another American Century?: The United States and the World After 2000* (London and New York: Zed Books, 2000); Payer, Cheryl. *The Debt Trap* (New York: Monthly Review Press, 1974); and Joseph Stiglitz, *Globalization and Its Discontents* (New York: W.W. Norton, 2002).

215. See Jomo K.S., "Lessons from the East Asian Crisis of 1997-1998" and Jomo K.S., ed., *Tigers in Trouble: Financial Governance, Liberalization, and Crises in East Asia* (Hong Kong: Hong Kong University Press; London: Zed Press, 1998).

216. See A.O. Krueger, "The Political Economy of the Rent-Seeking Society," *American Economic Review,* 1974: 64(3); R.A. Posner, "The Social Cost of Monopoly and Regulation," *Journal of Political Economy* 1975: 83; J.M. Buchanan, "Rent-Seeking and Profit Seeking," in *Toward a Theory of the Rent-Seeking Society,* ed. J. Buchanan, R.D. Tollison, and G. Tullock (College Station: Texas A&M University, 1980). Cited in Kang and Jomo 2000.

217. World Bank, *Combating Corruption in the Philippines,* viii, x; for details, see also World Bank, "Helping Countries Combat Corruption," PREM Report, Washington, 1997, and the Anticorruption Knowledge Resource Center at www.worldbank.org/publicsector/anticorruption.

218. World Bank, Combating Corruption in the Philippines, 23-24.

219. World Bank, Combating Corruption in the Philippines, 66.

220. Khan and Jomo, 18.

221. Khan and Jomo, 2-3.

222. Andvig and Fjeldstad, 76.

223. Lecture in Manila, April 8, 2003

224. De Dios in Doronila, 2001, 55.

225. David in Doronila, 2001, 151.

226. Eswar Prasad, Kenneth Rogoff, Shang-Jin Wei, and M. Ayhan Kose, "Effects of Financial Globalization on Developing Countries: Some Empirical Evidence," *International Monetary Fund,* March 17, 2003.

227. Susan George, "A Short History of Neoliberalism" in *Global Finance: New Thinking on Regulating Speculative Capital Markets* ed. Walden Bello, Nicola Bullard, and Kamal Malhotra (London and New York: Zed Books, 2000), 32.

CONCLUSION

Is There a Way Out
of the National Impasse?

In a recent article citing a study by a local university, one writer pointed to the fact that while Vietnam, which started out in 1990 with 51 percent of its people living under the UN-defined standard of $1 a day for extreme poverty, had reduced this figure to 8.4 percent in 2000, the comparable figure for the Philippines was 11 percent. He also pointed out that "government capital expenditures in the Philippines account for the lowest share of capital expenditures" among seven Northeast and Southeast Asian developing economies:

> In 2000-2002, the share averaged less than 9 percent for the Philippines, against 16.2 percent for Thailand, 36 percent for Malaysia, and 43 percent for Indonesia. The result? Inferior infrastructure facilities relative to our competitor countries nearby, which is easily evident to anyone traveling around the region.

> Social expenditures in the country likewise pale in comparison to what our neighbors invest in this crucial budget item. Thailand and Malaysia spend about two-fifths of their budget for the social sector, the Philippines only one-fourth.

> Clearly those two countries have been investing much more than the Philippines in two critical areas of productivity and competitiveness: infrastructure and human resources. Unless we are able to close this public investment gap, we are doomed to remain uncompetitive in the international economy, and condemned to lag behind indefinitely into the future.[1]

Forget the fact that the writer, Cielito Habito, head of the National Economic Development Authority under President Ramos, was one of the architects of the anti-public sector, pro-privatization, and pro-free market reforms that had gutted the government's capacity to serve as the cutting edge of capital spending in the 1980s and 1990s.

Though the responsibility of Habito and his neoclassical brethren for the current state of affairs continues to elude them, few of them could deny the grim economic realities of the Philippines circa 2004.

Economic and social development is the crying need of the Philippines today but, as the preceding chapters have demonstrated, it cannot take place without decisively abandoning the disastrous neoliberal policies of Habito and his band of doctrinaire technocrats. More controversial but equally critical is the realization that equitable, sustainable development cannot come about without dismantling the dysfunctional elite democratic regime that is the EDSA state and replacing it with a political arrangement that is more congenial to this goal.

Neoliberal polices are being reversed in practice, though much remains to be done to end its influence on key sectors. Replacing the EDSA state is equally unavoidable, though more daunting. Approaches to this challenge over the next few years will, we predict, crystallize into four, largely conflicting, strategies.

Four Scenarios of Political Change

The first would be one of reforming the system of governance, perhaps through a constitutional convention. The so-called peaceful way, it is also the route most likely to be successfully sabotaged by the elite, with the support of the United States, which has no desire to see the emergence of a structurally strong Philippine state and is satisfied with the weak, easily permeable or influenced system of governance we now have. Whatever change will be promoted by this reformed elite democracy is likely to be marginal.

The second approach would take the form of a military coup led by "Young Turks" within the Philippine military, like the junior officers that led last year's "Oakwood Mutiny." The coming together of several factions within the military could create the critical mass necessary for a successful coup. At that point, depending on the degree of independence of the *golpistas* or coup plotters, the state could move in either of two directions: 1) toward a modernizing populist but authoritarian state such as that set up by Kemal Ataturk in Turkey, or 2) toward a conservative modernizing regime such as that of the Brazilian military junta that seized power in 1964 or the Park Chung Hee dictatorship in Korea that initiated the so-called Korean economic miracle. In the latter, the military pursues rapid economic growth to gain legitimacy for its staying in power while maintaining tight political control from the top. The problem with this alternative, whether in its leftist or rightist version, is that as Filipinos learned during the Marcos period, one cannot trust the military with power, especially absolute power.

The third route would be that of a Communist Revolution a là China in the Mao period. In an age that has seen the collapse of centralized socialist regimes in the Soviet Union and Europe, the adoption of capitalist development strategies by post-Maoist China, and the discrediting of super-hierarchical communist parties as democratic agents, the appeal of such an alternative is likely to be limited. However, the Communist Party of the Philippines-New People's Army bloc, like the traditional left in Colombia, will not go away and will be able to maintain itself as a significant presence in the more geographically marginal and poorer parts of the country and play a role in parliamentary politics.

The fourth route would derive inspiration from that "other" dimension of the EDSA system—its insurrectionary side. Both EDSA 1 and EDSA 2 began as mass mobilizations that developed into insurrections. Owing to the threat that prolonged insurrection posed, however, the dominant faction of the elite quickly pushed to normalize politics by asserting the continuity of the elite democratic tradition and institutionalizing elections. In contrast, an "EDSA 4" might have two stages. First is the displacement of the old system via a mass insurrection in which the working class, urban poor, peasants, and the middle class are the central actors, the key partners of an alliance built on that potent combination of tremendous class resentments of the poor and the disgust of the middle strata with corrupt elites. In the second stage, the new configuration of social power forges a democratic state, but one that is more thoroughly democratic than the EDSA state in that it institutionalizes effective mechanisms of asset and income redistribution and the methods of participatory democracy. These institutions would serve as the pillars of a strong state that would make national development one of its priorities. This would, in short, be the "road not taken" after the EDSA uprising of 1986—a truly democratic state oriented to development.

As of early 2004, it is not clear along which road the Filipino people will eventually travel. What is clear is that the EDSA system is in a terminal state and the Philippines has entered an era marked by great conflict and struggle to bring about a new and more responsive system of governance.

Toward a Post-EDSA Development Strategy

Assuming that the Philippines does not descend into chaos (a big assumption) but moves toward the consolidation of a system of governance that is more genuinely democratic and responsive to development, what could be the elements of a post-EDSA system of social and economic transformation?

More State, Not Less

High up on the list is adopting the dictum that what is needed for development is not less, but more state. The Philippine state must be given greater relative autonomy vis-à-vis the elite. It must be able to discipline the private interests that have constantly hijacked it for particularistic ends. In this regard, the problem with protectionism as it has been practiced in the Philippines is not protectionism per se but that it has been opportunistic—one simply oriented to promoting narrow vested interests and without reference to a strategic plan to deepen the economy.

Yet this prescription must be taken in light of the experience of the newly industrializing countries (NICs) with a strong state. In Korea and Taiwan, development was accompanied by authoritarianism, by regimes whose lack of democratic accountability resulted not only in human-rights abuses but in the adoption of strategies that had the effect of degrading the environment and sacrificing agriculture. In any future arrangement, both private sector and the state must be checked by the participation of civil society in both political and economic decision making. Owing to its recent history, in particular the struggle against dictatorship, a significant organized civil society has developed in the Philippines. It is time to institutionalize its participation in any future political arrangement. Democracy does not contradict the development of an effective state. Indeed, democracy promotes an effective state by endowing it with legitimacy.

The Domestic Market as the Driver of Growth

A second element of a post-EDSA development strategy is focusing on the internal market as the driver of development. Export-oriented growth of the kind that was pursued by the NICs is no longer possible in an era of tremendous manufacturing overcapacity and the resulting protectionism in developed-country markets that this has spawned. And even if developed-country protectionism were not a problem, export-oriented manufacturing would not be an advantageous strategy today, given the tremendous advantage that China has in labor costs. Given the renewed centrality of the internal market, the imperative for massive income distribution to create consumers with purchasing power becomes very critical. Concretely, this means renewing the drive for effective land reform with effective support systems. It would also mean effective programs of taxation of the richer parts of the population, in order both to increase mass purchasing capacity through transfer payments, as well as to accumulate the capital necessary for strategic investments.

Strategic Policy

Creating a viable internal market is one priority. Protecting it from artificially cheap imports that stem from subsidization or overexploitation is another. However, protectionism can no longer remain opportunistic, an incoherent policy that is simply dictated by vested interests. Industrial policy must be strategic, one that is linked to deepening the country's industrial and manufacturing structure through selective tariffication or selective liberalization. Building up capital-intensive industries such as steel, transportation equipment, and computers will necessitate a flexible tariff policy, coupled of course with investment incentives and state-sponsored technological development.

Taking Sustainable Development Seriously

A fourth important dimension of a post-EDSA economic strategy is sustainable development. The pillage of our natural resources has proceeded to the point where the economic future of generations of Filipinos has been severely threatened. The high 6-8 percent growth rates of the NIC model is simply not possible to replicate without inviting more environmental dislocations. The key lies in opting for a strategy of lower, sustainable growth rates, which is only possible if there is much more equitable sharing of the fruits of a sustainable economy (meaning, there can be no sustainable development without radical social reform), a reinvigoration of agriculture along the lines of a smallholder system producing mainly for local and national markets with environmentally friendly agro-technology, and the greening of manufacturing technology. It will also mean reinvigorating local manufacturing and agricultural industries through flexible application of the principle of subsidiarity, i.e., whatever can be produced at the local level at the least cost should be undertaken at that level. Strong central leadership of the strategic planning process must be coupled to decentralized, sustainable production in key areas like agriculture. This is the challenge of development in a Philippine context in the twenty-first century.

Development in a Regional Context

A fifth critical element for the Philippines is coordinating its national development strategy with those of its neighbors. The reality of international economics in the twenty-first century is the existence of large economic blocs, the most important of which are the European Union, the United States, and China. It is difficult to see small and medium nation states being able to effectively develop or participate in the international economy without becoming part of a larger formation, whether this is based on common interests as developing countries—for instance, the Group of 20—or being part of a regional bloc such as ASEAN (Association of Southeast Asian Nations).

The problem with ASEAN, however, is that its most important economic project, the ASEAN Free Trade Area, or AFTA, is one that is strategically directionless. The aim of AFTA is to reduce and eliminate tariff barriers among participating economies, but whether this is for the purpose of serving as a step toward global free trade or as one toward a regional market protected by tariffs and quotas that would serve as the base for regionally coordinated import substitution has not been decided. This indeterminacy has left the regional formation unable to effectively undertake planning, technology sharing, and institutionalizing a division of labor at a regional level. Without such a program, the different national economic actors will see tariff reductions as leading to a zero-sum game in which the more advanced industrial elites will end up dominating the regional market.

An even greater concern is the democratic deficit in ASEAN. This regional formation was created by government elites with no consultation of peoples in the region. Not surprisingly, being part of an entity called ASEAN is not in the consciousness of the peoples of ASEAN. This means that projects which technocrats agree to in the name of ASEAN unity such as AFTA enjoy little legitimacy and binding power. Democratizing ASEAN is essential if it is to become an effective participant in a world marked by the dynamics of big economic blocs.

Transforming ASEAN should just be one of several cooperative initiatives the Philippines must engage in. The Philippines is already part of the Group of 20 (G-20), a larger formation that also includes India, China, Brazil, and South Africa. The potential of this group in terms of coordinating the policies of its members beyond the immediate issue that brought them together in Cancun—opposition to agricultural subsidies maintained by the developed economies—is great and can extend to technology sharing, transborder industrial policy, shared investment policies, and common environmental strategies. The organizational framework for what has been called, in the language of development economics, "South-South development cooperation" is present in the G-20. A forward-looking Philippine government can make an invaluable contribution in translating this potential into reality.

Transforming the System of Global Economic Governance

Finally, national, regional, and South-South initiatives must be coupled with Philippine leadership in restructuring the system of global economic governance, which is today dominated by the powerful developed economies. The key institutions that have institutionalized the hegemony of the North are the International Monetary Fund (IMF), the World Bank, and the World Trade Organization (WTO). Reform of these institutions has proved to be extremely difficult, while dismantling them seems to be a political impossibility. A coalition of developing countries could, however, aim at reducing the power of these institutions and work to gradually supplant the current system of global governance with a more pluralistic system of institutions and organizations interacting with one another, guided by broad and flexible agreements and understandings. In other words, this strategy would aim at turning the current multilateral giants into just another set of actors coexisting with and being checked by other international organizations, agreements, and regional groupings. It would include strengthening such diverse actors and institutions as the United Nations Conference on Trade and Development, multilateral environmental agreements, the International Labor Organization, and regional economic blocs.

The aim of such a strategy is to create space in the global economy for developing countries like the Philippines to put together unique strategies for development that respond to their values and rhythms as societies, something that is currently not possible owing to the one-size-fits-all neoliberal model promoted by the IMF-World Bank-WTO complex.

In sum, there is an alternative to the political economy of anti-development that currently reigns in the Philippines. This, however, cannot be pursued without first doing away with the anachronistic system of governance that is the EDSA state.

Notes

1. Cielito Habito, "Alarming Contrasts," *Philippine Daily Inquirer*, March 15, 2004.

Index

About the Authors

Walden Bello, Ph.D., is professor of sociology and public administration at the University of the Philippines at Diliman and executive director of Focus on the Global South. He is the author of *Deglobalization: Ideas for a New World Economy* (London: Zed Press, 2002), *The Future in the Balance: Essays on Globalization and Resistance* (Oakland: Food First Books, 2001), and 11 other books on global issues, Asian affairs, and Philippine issues. He was awarded the Right Livelihood Award ("Alternative Nobel Prize") in 2003 for "outstanding work" in educating global civil society on the impact of corporate-driven globalization. An earlier work of which he was principal author, *Development Debacle: the World Bank in the Philippines* (San Francisco: Food First, 1982), was an intellectual milestone in the struggle against the Marcos dictatorship. He is also the former chairman of *Akbayan!*, the Citizens' Action Party of the Philippines.

Herbert Docena, a graduate of the University of the Philippines (UP) School of Economics (magna cum laude, 2001), is a research associate with Focus on the Global South's peace and security program.

Marissa de Guzman, also a UP graduate (cum laude, 1999), served as a research associate in Focus and is currently completing her graduate work in International Peace Studies and Development at the University of Notre Dame in South Bend, Indiana.

Mary Lou Malig is the trade liaison for Asia of Focus on the Global South. Also a graduate of the University of the Philippines (2000), she is the author of the study *Sustaining Poverty: The National Report on Sustainable Development in the Philippines* (found in *Civic Entrepreneurship*, Volume 5, UNEP and SEI-Boston, 2002) that was presented at the World Summit on Sustainable Development in Johannesburg in September 2002.

Home birth chat: Friday 2pm May 7th.

Manos .

Aquino

Ramos 1992 – 98

Estrada

Arroyo 2001 –